More Praise for Business Continuity Management

"Can my company afford not to be prepared? Should we allow our destiny to be dependent upon luck or put in the hands of others? A company well prepared for a disaster WILL weather the storm. Mike has provided not only the substance to develop a plan that addresses *all* types of incidents, but the "ground zero" detail required to make it effective. You have everything here to design a plan that works—practice and communicate that plan across your company at all levels will prepare you for the next storm."

Glenn W. McLea
CPP, Corporate Security Director, Parsons Corporation

"Anyone operating in the international market place, either as a commercial or government organization, knows that you will face crisis incidents. How well you weather that storm is a reflection of how effective your policies, plans and training area. This book adds real value to the understanding of your vulnerabilities and the development of effective mitigation plans."

Timothy Bowen
Director of Global Investigations and Security, BearingPoint, Inc.

"*Business Continuity Management* is a rare, uniquely valuable resource, cleverly managing to be practical and comprehensive while simultaneously thought provoking and inventive. Truly terrific."

Garett Seivold
Editor, IOMA's Security Director's Report
Author, Disaster Preparedness 2008: The Guide to Building Business Resilience

"Another blockbuster by Mike Blyth and a most useful companion to his earlier work *Risk and Security Management Protecting People and Sites Worldwide*. This is an excellent book for the security practitioner and for those who have an interest in managing risk."

Tom Mulhall
Director of Security Programmes, Loughborough University, UK

"Lots of people talk about crisis management and business continuity, but Michael Blyth's book provides real, tangible details for crisis management planning. Whether you're a security professional or a senior manager, you will find his guidance practical and – particularly should you ever need to use it – incredibly valuable."

Joe Gleason
Director of Global Security and Operations, National Democratic Institute

Business Continuity Management

Building an Effective Incident Management Plan

MICHAEL BLYTH

WILEY

John Wiley & Sons, Inc.

Published by John Wiley & Sons, Inc., Hoboken, New Jersey.
Published simultaneously in Canada.

For general information on our other products and services, or technical support, please contact our Customer Care Department within the United States at 800-762-2974, outside the United States at 317-572-3993 or fax 317-572-4002.

Wiley also publishes its books in a variety of electronic formats. Some content that appears in print may not be available in electronic books.

For more information about Wiley products, visit our Web site at http://www.wiley.com.

Library of Congress Cataloging-in-Publication Data:

Blyth, Michael, 1972–
  Business continuity management : building an effective incident management plan / Michael Blyth.
       p.   cm.
  Includes index.
  ISBN 978-0-470-43034-7 (cloth : acid-free paper)   1. Crisis management.
2. Emergency management.   3. Business planning.   I. Title.
  HD49.B59 2009
  658.4'77–dc22

                                                            2008048334

10 9 8 7 6 5 4 3 2 1

Dedicated to my wife Kristen, who is the Crisis Team Leader
for our family, both at the point of every emergency event,
as well as when undertaking the post incident reviews
with the cause for most of our emergencies . . . our children
Alexander, Amber, and Christopher.

Contents

Preface

Whether an international corporation or a small business, developing and utilizing a Business Continuity Management (BCM) Plan protects companies and their personnel, facilities, materials, and activities from the broad spectrum of risks that face businesses and government agencies on a daily basis, whether at home or abroad. Although crises are unpredictable, they are not unexpected. Disasters are part of the human condition, whether they result from a tornado, an earthquake, or a pandemic; from an industrial accident or a structural failure; or from criminal activities or terrorist attacks. As the global business footprint increases, so do the risks faced by companies, whether these are threats posed to extended supply chains, result from organizational and technological dependencies, occur due to political and social instabilities, effect information technology (IT) vulnerabilities, result from maturing tactics by organized crime, insurgency and terrorist groups, intrastate conflicts, or occur due to a myriad of natural disasters. While crisises can be devastating in their effects, often companies focus more on market and credit risk rather than on those risks that directly affect people. Despite being more personal in nature, operational risk management has yet to mature sufficiently to reflect the wide spectrum of interrelated threats facing companies within today's dynamic and evolving global commercial environment. While advances in technology and management methodologies might increase an organization's capacity to forecast and plan for such catastrophic events, the ability of an individual or organization to survive a crisis event relies often on the underresourced and frequently overlooked field of operational contingency planning and crisis response—or *business continuity management*.

The impetus behind developing a sound Business Continuity Management Plan and its constituent elements (e.g., an incident management plan [IMP]) is reflected in the fact that large companies on average face a crisis every three to five years, and during the next five years it is estimated that 83 percent of companies will face a crisis that will negatively impact their profitability by 20 to 30 percent (Oxford Metrica, Aon, 2006). From personal experience, the effects of commercial globalization have been reflected in organizations becoming increasingly reliant on fragile supply chains, vulnerable communications mediums, and remote power and food sources. When supporting companies with crisis events, it has been evident on every occasion that it is the ability for people to manage a crisis—rather than infrastructures, capital, or technologies—that makes the real difference, and often response plans are absent, out of date, or do not provide effective guidance to those managing an emergency. Internally, companies also struggle to understand individual and group roles, successfully navigate in-house friction, and avoid duplication and gaps as managers start working a crisis together. Traditional risk management systems and solutions struggle to handle today's expanded and often nebulous spectrum of business risk, rarely being linked to strategic corporate planning or project operating methodologies. Often companies fall short in terms of contingency planning, as those with little or no training within the crisis management sector handle the initial response requirements and information needs, often exacerbating the emergency situation and unintentionally creating new threats through poor decision making and uncoordinated response measures. The human psychic response to a crisis situation also presents unique challenges to organizations facing a catastrophic event, as doubt, fear, and inertia frequently impede the ability of a responding group to bring swift and effective control and resolution to a situation.

Often companies fail to truly understand risk, not comprehending that emergencies may be short-lived or long-lasting, that their impacts may be focused and succinct, or may ripple outward to affect a surprising range of peripheral activities or groups. Understanding the scope of a crisis can also be challenging; a crisis might affect only an individual, or may be of catastrophic proportions and affect an entire nation. A crisis can affect every aspect of a company, group, or culture, both physically and psychologically. The term *crisis* is also subjective, having different connotations for those affected by or managing a crisis situation. The destruction and debris caused by hurricanes Andrew and Katrina; the devastation of the Chernobyl reactor accident; the attack on the World Trade Center; the reputational challenges for CACI International Inc. following the Abu Ghraib allegations; the 2008 earthquake in China; and the 1994 passenger ferry sinking of the *MV Estonia* all vividly highlight the toll, both emotional and monetary, that a crisis, whether natural or man-made, can wreak on business. Companies often underestimate their ability to forecast and prepare for a crisis; often they are caught unaware and unprepared. Enterprise resilience meets the traditional threats facing domestic and international businesses, while also monitoring and protecting earnings drivers and company values. The areas of contingency planning and crisis management have grown in prominence during recent decades as governments and businesses suffer serious losses through inadequate risk analysis and the poor management of emergency situations, necessitating the requirement for comprehensive Business Continuity Management Plans (or enterprise resilience plans).

While advising companies and groups on contingency planning and crisis management—either for new operations within remote, volatile, or challenged environments, or for business expansions within existing operating areas—it quickly became apparent to me that a considerable amount of time, resources, and capital was invested in short-term measures that met the needs of only a narrow user audience, rather than designing sustainable and transferable solutions which could be continued past the point of initial requirement and therefore better support organizations in effectively managing risk over the long term. While this seems an obvious requirement, it is one which is often poorly managed or even overlooked, and surprisingly it is common for policies and plans to become quickly redundant, or difficult to sustain. When developing my first book—*Risk and Security Management: Protecting People and Sites Worldwide* (John Wiley & Sons, 2008)—my intent was to provide companies with the tools and systems which would allow them to develop sustainable and effective risk and security management solutions most cost-effectively. Or alternatively, to enhance the ability of executive officers to better understand how to direct outsourced security and risk management expertise in developing the systems, tools, policies, and services that would effectively meet immediate, interim, and long-term risk and security management objectives. The same approach has been adopted to this book, seeking to fuse strategic concepts with practical methodologies to support effective and structured crisis management, while meeting the different layered requirements within an organization. This book is designed to provide an understanding of Business Continuity Management, as well as provide practical tools, systems, and reports to help companies create their own plans, or best manage outsourced support. The aim of this book is to provide the fundamental concepts for effective and sustainable Business Continuity and Incident Management, as well as detailed frameworks and pre-prepared materials for companies and security professionals to utilize. Such planning is fundamental to profitability, shareholder value, and market competitiveness, yet despite the clear value of developing sophisticated and convergent methodologies to plan for and manage crisis events, frequently companies fail to adequately develop effective contingency and crisis response plans, policies, and systems.

This book is focused on supporting a broad spectrum of users, including corporate boards and executive officers in terms of developing mature and comprehensive corporate governance structures and policies; chief financial officers in terms of saving costs and reducing insurance and liability premiums; legal officers in terms of reducing risk exposures to the corporation or its officers; health and safety departments in terms of defining an additional component of personnel safety policies; public relations departments in terms of supporting effective communications, both internally and externally; the corporate communications department in terms of supporting the more effective and streamlined dissemination of information; business, program, and project managers in terms of ensuring that both the planning and the delivery of services are conducted within a risk management context, increasing productivity and the bottom-line profits, as well as evidencing to conservative boards how business can operate within the group's risk tolerance parameters; and of course security professionals, both in-house and subcontracted, in terms of how well-defined structures, policies, and protocols can be developed, implemented, and sustained. This book is also designed to support freelance security professionals and security companies, who are often so engrossed in managing security and risk at the coal face that they have little time to create complex solutions and time-consuming policies and plans. As such, this book is intended to be part educational and part functional, providing the context behind the needs for business continuity planning, as well as some tear out guidelines and recommendations for the structuring and content of such policies. Holistically, the book is designed to bring confidence, structure, and concepts for the benefit of commercial and government groups and their workforces at all levels.

Within today's litigious environment, corporations and their leadership can no longer claim "we didn't know" as an excuse for risk management failures—exposing individuals and groups to increasing levels of liability risk. Business resilience is now an established need within corporations and should be an embedded institutional capability and defining ethos within the day-to-day business operations of a company—with executive officers and implementers taking ownership and accountability for the management of risk management policies and plans. Effective business continuity management provides a safe harbor for companies in terms of financial stability and legal liability assurance, demonstrating that companies are taking all necessary precautions to protect personnel, business interests, and operational delivery. It is also a moral obligation to protect people and business investments within a fluid and challenging international risk environment. The ability to establish a Business Continuity Management Plan incorporating the areas of contingency planning and crisis management (to which an incident management plan belongs) enables the company to be cognizant of the risks that its business activities and corporate interests face, as well as methods by which to reduce or manage these risks. It also ensures that some predetermined measures are in place (through such procedures as incident management plans) to allow a company to most effectively respond to a crisis situation. For example, in a crisis situation there are first-line responders who identify and begin crisis management, and defined and experienced incident response and crisis management groups who are mobilized to bring developed and mature response plans to bear in order to control the crisis event and assist the company in recovering from the resulting impacts—making companies more insulated from risk, more resilient to the spectrum of challenges they may face if risk mitigation is not successful, as well as more likely to effectively recover from the effects of a crisis event.

As a component of the overarching Business Continuity Management Plan, the incident management plan (IMP) provides the vehicle by which employees can receive both training and instruction on how to respond to a crisis, regardless of their professional backgrounds or appointments within the company—*supporting enterprise resilience from the bottom up*. The IMP provides a mechanism for bringing confidence on how to respond to, and enable control of, a crisis. Psychologically, people perform better when they believe they have control over a situation, and the incident management plan offers a method by which companies can provide such confidence, guidance, and direction to managers and employees. The incident management plan forms a pragmatic component of an overall contingency planning and crisis management approach, offering education as well as realistic and user-friendly guidelines and simple procedures by which to support inexperienced first-line responders, as well as more experienced and competent incident management and crisis response teams. The IMP typically is focused on the first steps of crisis response, bringing initial control to a situation (the first 72 hours) while more developed plans are initiated and appropriate expertise is brought to bear. The incident management plan is designed to provide a period of relative stability and focused response while companies seek to understand the nature, scope, and implications of a situation and then respond accordingly.

The concepts in this book can be applied in part or in full to both small and large businesses and organizations. Concepts offered may be too complex or detailed for the needs of some groups, while other groups may require a more comprehensive and detailed solution. A considerable amount of information should be contained within any plan—without making it confusing or impractical. The use of tables and charts is therefore a method by which to capture considerable detail within a more refined approach—although such approaches must be intuitive and explained to ensure that they are applicable and understood. The main components of consideration for incident management are captured within this book's six chapters, which form the central influences and requirements of an effective and usable incident management plan. The following is a chapter-by-chapter breakdown of the topics covered:

Chapter 1: The Business Continuity Management Plan is the focal point within a company for understanding risk and designing methods by which to mitigate the wide spectrum of threats a company may face domestically, or abroad, within its business operations. It defines the difference between a problem and a crisis, as well as the corporate ethos and management strategies for developing and sustaining the policies, plans, and protocols for effective risk management, while structuring the organization's crisis management organization to best response to an event. It defines decision making authorities and responsibilities, communication systems, alert states, and trigger response mechanisms. It supports the leveraging of internal and external resources and knowledge, and also provides business recovery protocols in order to enable crisis recovery to be effective and timely. This chapter provides a guide to readers on the aims, structures, and systems that support the design and development of a Business Continuity Management Plan, placing the IMP into an understandable context.

Chapter 2: The Incident Management Plan is a tactical component of the Business Continuity Management Plan. It provides education and instructions to a wide range of first responders, incident, and crisis managers in order to empower the company to deal with the first stages of a crisis event, when the most confusion occurs and the most damage is done. It provides a handrail of crisis-specific response measures in order to walk a company employee, manager or executive through a sensible series of predefined steps associated with a particular form of emergency, as well as structuring information capture so that accurate and timely information can flow through the company, supporting informed and effective decision making. This chapter provides guidance to the reader as to the structuring and objectives of an IMP, and the functional components which enable an IMP to operate as a practical element of the Business Continuity Management Plan, while being sufficiently robust to operate as a stand-alone policy where required.

Chapter 3: Crisis Management Structures within an organization determine how effectively companies can respond to a crisis event. Companies should take advantage of the calm preceding any emergency to appoint, educate, and practice crisis leadership teams. Companies should also seek to exploit external capabilities and weave this into their management structure, with explicit instructions and guidelines to avoid internal frictions or confusion. Sound crisis leadership brings confidence and knowledge to often dynamic and fast-moving crisis events, enabling effective and timely decision making. Organizations are also responsible for creating environments in which effective crisis leadership can operate, empowering leadership within defined parameters. Crisis management should focus at the corporate, country, program, and project levels, with defined appointments, groups, and functions for each.

Chapter 4: Scope of Risk provides both organizations, as well as the stakeholders and users of the Business Continuity Management Plan, and more specifically the IMP, a plan to place the wide range of threats their organization might face into an understandable context, whether these are common domestic issues, or more unique risks presented with foreign environments. This chapter provides a pragmatic Risk Register which captures both primary risks, whether man-made or natural, as well as significant by-product risks such as the challenges of media management and family liaison. Covering 44 risk types, from espionage, workplace violence, suspect calls, hostage taking, road traffic accidents, and terrorist attacks, to floods, hurricanes, pandemics, and landslips, it provides a framework for organizations and individuals to understand the risk landscape and so effectively design contingency plans and crisis response measures.

Chapter 5: Incident Response Guidelines supports first responders, incident managers, and experienced crisis management teams in bringing logic, structure, consistency, and focus to a crisis situation by predefining the common management steps required for different forms of crisis situations. Emergencies are often confusing, fast moving and highly stressful, as such providing a sensible handrail for incident and crisis teams will channel their efforts, ensure that major management considerations are not overlooked, and provide confidence during what might be an unnerving situation. This chapter provides sensible management considerations and steps for the 44 different forms of threat captured with Chapter 4, and are linked to the information capture reports within Chapter 6. They provide companies a readily usable management framework for the most common threats they may face domestically or abroad, protecting people and business activities, as well as providing an evidenced governance system for the company as part of corporate liability insulation.

Chapter 6: Crisis Information Capture Reports provide a mechanism by which accurate, detailed, and timely information can be shared between those dealing with the crisis event firsthand, and those supporting groups requiring accurate information needed to make informed and effective decisions. A major failing within most organizations is the effective passage of information; this chapter provides sensibly frame-worked information capture reports which can be used by companies to ensure that critical information is captured and transmitted for individual crisis events, covering the 44 risk types addressed within Chapter 4, as well as some additional threats a company might face. In addition, verbal reporting structures and formats are also included to help support crisis responders in organizing verbal briefings, as written reports are being generated. The capture reports provided will guide users through which questions will need to be addressed, and how to best present information to multiple crisis management stakeholders. The chapter provides companies a complete and detailed report section which can be adapted, or readily used within their organization's Business Continuity Management Plan.

About the Web Site

As a purchaser of this book, you have access to the supporting Web site:

www.wiley.com/go/businesscontinuity

The Web site contains Microsoft Word files of the response guidelines in Chapter 5 and the sample serious incident reports that appear in Chapter 6. These forms can be downloaded and tweaked to meet your specific needs.

The password to enter the site is: Blyth

CHAPTER 1

Business Continuity Management Plan

The incident management plan (IMP) is a detailed component of a Business Continuity Management (BCM) Plan. Also known as the enterprise resilience, emergency preparedness, or risk management plan, it forms the advance planning aspects that enable the initial crisis response activities to be conducted in a prearranged and organized fashion. The IMP is designed to support business continuity and incident recovery at the early stages, meeting immediate event response needs as resources are mobilized and more mature and comprehensive management measures are brought into play. The IMP can bridge, or be part of, more detailed crisis response plans such as evacuation management, disaster response, and reputational recovery, as well as dealing with kidnap and ransom situations and pandemics. However, these stand-alone plans are often better served as comprehensive components within the overall Business Continuity Management Plan (as they will likely be more oriented to specific divisions, fields, or regions), whereas the IMP addresses more common and generic risk types that the organization might face at the outset of a crisis event. The IMP at the basic level supports immediate tactical considerations and management functions, rather than long-term risk management and business recovery needs. Where feasible, the company should seek to transfer decision making to the lowest levels possible for the initial response requirements, as this will strengthen and empower local managers to contribute effectively to the management and early resolution of a crisis event.

Business Continuity Planning Terms

- Contingency planning and crisis management
- Enterprise resilience
- Emergency preparedness
- Enterprise risk management
- Emergency management
- Critical situations management

For the purposes of this book, incident management focuses not on the strategic, specialist, or sustained response measures, but on more granular and tactical support mechanisms that are the precursors to more complex and corporate-driven crisis management and business recovery policies and plans: *the first 24 to 72 hours of an emergency.* This book touches on the broader aspects of risk management in order to support the reader in placing the IMP within an understandable context. However, the book is principally designed to discuss the first stages of crisis response where incident management will play an active part in bringing an emergency situation under control, as well as feeding crucial information to company officers. The IMP is a tool for a wide spectrum of users, not only security professionals or corporate leadership. As such, the IMP supports local management in collating accurate information and following simple response guidelines to reduce the initial impacts of an emergency event, bringing control to a situation and further mitigating the risks that could escalate out of control from a problem, or be created as secondary or peripheral effects as a result of the initial crisis event. The IMP in these terms is also a short-term measure, allowing a degree of organized control to be implemented while the company mobilizes resources and specialists during the early stages of an emergency.

Companies should be aware that the social fabric of a culture or an area can be quickly undermined by a crisis situation, resulting in unique and challenging risks to commercial organizations, their employees (and families), facilities, and business activities. Even within Western countries, the speed at which deteriorations in governance, basic amenities, and societal rules can be surprising. The implications can be widespread and catastrophic, or localized and disruptive. Crisis events may result from a natural disaster: a flood, earthquake, hurricane, or pandemic. They may result from widespread civil disorder: a coup, political instability, insurgency, or war. Or a crisis event may be localized: a riot following a football match, aggressive measures over farming disputes, fuel shortages, a focused labor dispute issue, or directed attacks against individuals, groups, or facilities.

The following list illustrates some macro-level considerations companies should incorporate into their strategic planning for crisis management:

- **Governance.** The loss of governmental control and policing authority can be swift and widespread. Government offices may be directly affected or overwhelmed by a crisis event, and officials may not have the knowledge, capacity, or resources to quickly support the affected populace. Government offices dedicated to dealing with a crisis situation may also be undermined as personnel respond to personal emergencies or to care for families, diminishing a government's expected capacity to respond to a crisis effectively.
- **Social Fabrics.** The social norms that regulate our societies can be quickly lost or undermined as the effectiveness of governance is diminished. Rioting, thefts, looting, and other social crimes can quickly spread to otherwise law-abiding sections of the community. This is a cyclic effect and can create a further loss of governance which might exacerbate a crisis and add additional elements of risk to the original crisis event.
- **Utilities.** Common utilities and services can be disrupted, such as power, water, sewage, and communications, during a crisis. Basic amenities like food availability, financial services, and fuel provisions can also be affected. Modern cultures are not best engineered to weather a loss of power or disruptions to food, fuel supplies, or utilities, and often struggle to manage if common services are disrupted, and such losses can also result in secondary crisis events.

- **Movement.** Movement can be affected by crisis situations, whether due to man-made risks presented by hostile or disruptive groups, or due to damaged infrastructures or the unavailability of fuel or power supplies. This can affect every aspect of emergency management, from those dealing with emergencies at the point of crisis to those attempting to respond in support of the emergency or evacuate from an affected area.
- **Critical Services.** Critical services, such as fire response, medical provisions, and health care, or critical infrastructure power and utilities can be seriously undermined with the loss of basic utilities, undermining the ability for such groups to respond to or support an affected population. Infrastructure damage and affected supply chains of critical materials or resources can quickly devalue otherwise effective critical service providers.
- **Communications.** Communication mediums may be affected by a crisis event disrupting or preventing the effective passage of information and instructions which might support an understanding of the crisis event, as well as the effective response to an emergency. Communication systems may be damaged, or overwhelmed by a surge of use. Often voice mediums are lost before text and this can affect both government entities' ability to mobilize and respond to a crisis, as well as a commercial organization's respond measures.

Crisis Definitions

A crisis is (1) an unstable condition, as in political, social, or economic affairs, involving an impending abrupt or decisive change, or (2) an abnormal or unique event that threatens groups or individuals, as well as their goals and enterprises, through disruptive or harmful effects.

A crisis event can also be considered in terms of the micro- and macro-level crisis. The micro crisis is the point of the event: a collapsed building, fuel leak, or roadside fatality. The macro crisis consists of all of the risks that originate and ripple outward from that event: threats posed to surrounding buildings, recovering trapped persons, bringing control to the oil leak, dealing with the media, and reducing reputational and liability risks. In these terms, the IMP typically focuses on the micro-level crisis: the event itself. The IMP does, however, play a fundamental role in supporting the company in dealing with macro-level considerations and threats. Therefore, the IMP may be considered the first of many steps within a broader crisis response plan, acting as a precursor to the fuller crisis response measures being implemented by the company, as well as the transition point at which a company goes from managing the incident to controlling the effects of the wider crisis. This is a subjective delineation and will of course be influenced by the nature of the event, the composition of different management teams involved within the emergency, and the operating environment in which a company is performing work. An effectively designed and implemented IMP reflects the level of effort a company invests into ensuring the safety and welfare of its employees, protecting its business interests and brand value, and maximizing operational productivity through pragmatic contingency planning measures that enable effective, immediate, interim, and long-term crisis response mechanisms and methodologies to be implemented.

Given the ease at which organizational control and governmental support can be lost during a crisis, companies should seek to design and resource a degree of self-reliance within their crisis planning that takes into consideration these factors, while still leveraging and exploiting external governmental and other resources to support their response measures and capabilities.

Crisis Management

For the management of risk within a nonspecialized industry or more tangible fields such as construction, development, power and water, fuels, maritime and air, consulting, and training, the company's or its security vendor's crisis response team typically comes from a military or law enforcement background where the concept of incident management and crisis response has been an integrated aspect of their careers. In addition, subject matter experts within areas such as health and safety, engineering, administration, and legal considerations will also support critical crisis response decision making. Where risk elements are more market sector focused, such as business, financial investments, and mergers and acquisitions, more specialist risk managers may be required within defined fields such as information technology (IT), investments, and business intelligence. Typically, outside of pure investment and business risk areas, the initial point of a crisis event will be operationally oriented and occur at a point or location away from such expertise, although more nebulous risks will result from a physical event. The IMP should be designed to withstand a lack of experience or knowledge by users who operate outside of the risk and security management field. It should be a pragmatic, simple, and user-friendly tool; and the design and testing of such a plan should incorporate users as well as managers and specialists in order to ensure that plans are logical and unambiguous, reflect the operating conditions, and, most importantly, are implementable and understood.

Companies should seek to leverage the capabilities, knowledge, and resources of both in-house experience and knowledge, as well as that of their security vendors to provide, supplement, or augment their business continuity policies and plans. When operating within more challenging environments where the probability or impact of risk is higher, companies should consider the value of transferring both the risks and the resources required for establishing the Business Continuity Management Plan, as well as its various subcomponents such as the IMP and evacuation plans, to their security vendors or outsourced consultants in order to offset both risk exposure and development effort. That said, integration for any crisis planning should be established to blend outsourced and company requirements and activities at all levels. The scope of work for any security contract in such regions should include clear requirements for the vendor to provide contingency plans and crisis management protocols as part of the overall service-level agreement. While the company can never fully defer crisis management responsibility to a subcontractor, corporate and field risk managers can establish policies and procedures by which much of the burden of dealing with a crisis event can be transferred onto an appropriate vendor, while strategic decision-making authorities are retained by the company, as well as corporate risk response measures. These agreements should be understood and the plans and responses clearly articulated and practiced in order to ensure that the most effective risk management approach is in place.

The Value

The investment in terms of time, money, and resources in developing a Business Continuity Management Plan can be seen both in tangible terms of safeguarding personnel and facilities, as well as in often bringing less visible or hard values and benefits to the company, such as increased profits and productivity, market confidence, reputational protection, and employee morale. Business Continuity Management Plans can provide companies greater supply chain assurance; be a market differentiator in terms of effectiveness, agility, and the overall competitive value; and often enable the company to identify, understand, and offset risks prior to their occurrence, as well as perhaps operate within business environments in which they would be otherwise prevented from engaging. Such focus can also be migrated to vendors, ensuring that their approach to business resilience best supports the company, and can also assure investors or clients that the company can weather a crisis effectively—without unduly disrupting business services or operational delivery. A Business Continuity Management Plan can support the company in winning as well as undertaking work through the alignment of risks to business interests and activities, as well as reducing insurance premiums and liability exposure.

What Is Risk Management?

- A system that defines an organizational structure, as well as team roles and responsibilities, to enable a company to react to situations ahead of an emergency.
- A bridge between risk mitigation (business protection), risk management (business resilience), and crisis recovery (business resumption)
- A holistic solution meeting the requirements of all corporate needs and activities, whether related to brand, operations, reputation, or ethos.
- A tool that helps companies negotiate fluid and challenging risk environments, effectively dealing with unpredictable events.
- An insurance mechanism that supports business continuity and recovery when risk mitigation measures fail.

Risk management should be considered a supporting element of business development and operational conduct, regardless of the industry sector or geographic region a company might operate in. It should be considered best practice for companies, safeguarding both corporate and employee interests through well-developed policies, procedures, and plans. The following summarizes some of the benefits that the development of a Business Continuity Management Plan may bring to companies or groups:

- Establishes a corporate agenda and strategic approach.
- Brings awareness and understanding of corporate risks and liabilities.
- Establishes a culture that embodies a common vision and taxonomy for risk.

- Supports better business planning and practices.
- Enhances business discipline and internal controls.
- Protects directors and officers against liability charges and claims.
- Ensures informed decision making to strengthen strategic plans and responses.
- Aligns business with risk management to ensure effective business.
- Reduces reputational and liability risks, and protects brand and investor confidence.
- Protects business activities, resources, and personnel.
- Strengthens business continuity and recovery—improving productivity and profit levels.
- Demonstrates duty of care and sound management practices.
- Reduces insurance premiums and liability claims.
- Improves management and employee confidence and morale.
- Ensures the identification and best use of organic and external resources.
- Provides an evidence chain for investigations and audits.
- Meets industry, governmental, and other regulatory requirements.
- Defines the business strategy, including expansion, new market entry, and downsizing.

The value of developing an effective Business Continuity Management Plan, as well as an accompanying IMP, is illustrated in Exhibit 1.1. It highlights how enterprise resilience and recovery measures can:

- Map risks and guide management responses.
- Protect the company's business and corporate interests.

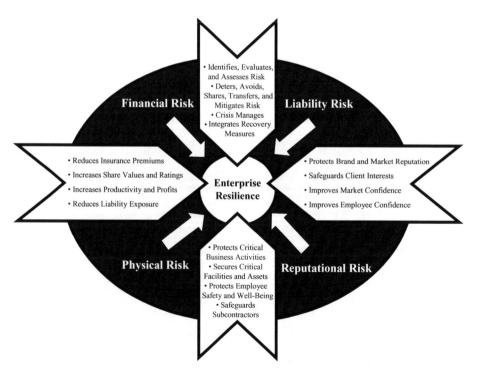

EXHIBIT 1.1 The Value of Business Continuity Management Plans

- Bring order out of chaos in order to depict a true reflection of an organization's ability to deal with a crisis.
- Provide confidence to managers, employees, clients, and investors.
- Integrate recovery measures across disparate and dispersed organizations.
- Leverage organic and external resources to manage and respond to crises.
- Increase profits and productivity, and reduce costs and liabilities.
- Protect facilities, resources, and human life.
- Meet specific regulatory and industry standards.

A well-resourced Business Continuity Management Plan will also include forms of information or advisory feeds, whether intelligence or environmental or political scanning, in order to ensure that crisis management policies and plans are triggered prior to an event occurring. Such measures will ensure that the plan, or parts of it, are set in motion before the event occurs (i.e., warning of localized flooding, notifications of civil gatherings, and so on). Contingency planning and crisis response investment in terms of money, time, and resources should be considered a fundamental aspect of sound business practice, not a cost center. While difficult to quantify in terms of cost savings, business resilience statistically increases long-term business productivity and operational recovery from crisis situations and should be considered a central aspect of corporate strategic policy and planning functions.

Common Failings

Designing and maintaining a Business Continuity Management Plan can be fraught with problems and can often result in a significant waste of time, resources, and energy in the creation of policies and plans that quickly lose their value and applicability in terms of supporting the company's strategic and tactical interests. Plans are also frequently prepared at significant cost, only to then be ignored, be poorly distributed, or be underutilized during an emergency. It is therefore useful to understand the common failure points in the development and utilization of such plans in order to design and sustain a business continuity architecture that is created—from the outset—to meet the group's long term needs, and that gains management buy-in, is kept current and applicable, and is embraced and understood by the users and stakeholders in order to be effective. The following outlines some key areas in which Business Continuity Management Plans often fall short of potential success:

- **Management Support.** A Business Continuity Management Plan that lacks high-level support is likely to fail from the outset. Corporate leadership needs to fully embrace the value of developing such policies and plans and has to ensure that different company divisions are supportive both of the strategic corporate requirements, as well as their individual areas of group interest. Support should cascade from the top downward in order for plans to be successful. Clear directives should support the plan, ensuring that each group and individual adheres to corporate policy.
- **Ownership.** Ownership of the plans should be established to ensure that participants understand and are accountable for their part within a Business Continuity Management Plan. In addition, a sensible appreciation of who should own certain aspects of the plan should be evaluated, with appropriate managers being empowered to develop, maintain, and manage elements which best

reflect their areas of expertise. Company politics should not drive ownership issues—functional capability should be the defining factor.

- **User Buy-In.** The user audience must also be supportive of the Business Continuity Management Plan. Otherwise, the value of application will be undermined, local managers will be prone to use their own approaches and methodologies, and the ability of users to apply the plan's principles and guidelines during an emergency will be hampered by a lack of awareness, understanding, and enthusiasm for the Business Continuity Management Plan. Seeking user buy-in from the outset will ensure the plan reflects the user and stakeholder needs, and so encourage their support and active participation.

- **Structure and Design.** Often plans are designed that are cumbersome, confusing, and difficult to maintain. Consistency of design and structuring is often quickly lost, and individual divisions or regions are prone to developing their own unique approaches, which can undermine the plan, create confusion, and result in redundancy—or at worst, lead to erroneous directives and guidelines that increase the potential threats. Plans should be designed to be simple, efficient, and easy to maintain or adapt. Consistency in layout, content matter, and generic directives should not prevent regional or activity-specific requirements to be met, but will ensure a clear and logical format for approach.

- **Applicability.** Plans can quickly become redundant as personnel change over, the threat environment shifts, and business activities progress. The structuring and design of plans can make sustainability of plans difficult, causing plans to rapidly become inaccurate or completely redundant—placing the company at risk, as well as incurring unnecessary costs. Plans should be designed in a manner that allows live sections to be easily updated, with static sections to remain constant where applicable. The use of supporting tables, diagrams, and other out-of-plan data feeds will help satisfy this requirement. Plans should have periodic reviews to ensure that adjustments are made and the plans are updated using internal projects, as well as corporate quality assurance mechanisms.

- **Training and Education.** The plan is only as good as the users who implement the policies and procedures within it. A failure to adequately advise, train, and rehearse personnel will significantly devalue the Business Continuity Management Plan, making its use disjointed, difficult, and confusing during an emergency. Companies must budget time, resources, and capital to ensure that managers and personnel are educated as to the plan's function, how it will be employed, as well as how to support its development and maintenance.

- **Leveraging Resources.** Business Continuity Management Plans should seek to leverage organic as well as external resources as efficiently and effectively as possible. Often plans fail to capitalize on the raft of support that is available, diminishing potential value as well as incurring unnecessary costs and risks to the company. Plans should be aligned to all possible resources available at corporate, country, and project levels.

- **Accessibility and Maintenance.** Often risk and crisis policies and plans are not accessible to the various users and stakeholders, and as such changes are difficult to undertake and track. Version control of policies and quality assurance can be problematic. Hosting policies and plans on web-based systems can support accessibility as well as the use of a central document to support version control management.

The development of a clear corporate agenda and well-structured goals prior to work commencing on the Business Continuity Management Plan will enable its design, development, and ultimately its sustainment to be achieved more effectively, and with least frustration. The plan should be considered a living and pan-organizational tool that requires group support and buy-in in order to be successful. Time spent on planning is seldom wasted, and companies should develop frameworks for their objectives and requirements fully before commencing work.

Business Continuity Goals

The veneer of safety and security, and indeed in some cases civilization, can be quickly stripped away during, or following, an emergency situation. Common social norms may be temporarily suspended, and governance and basic amenities may be disrupted—leading to unique and challenging risks for individuals and organizations. Companies should therefore have clear goals when designing a Business Continuity Management Plan, seeking to meet strategic, operational, and tactical needs. Considerable time and investment is often wasted through a poorly planned, structured, and implemented approach to designing and implementing Business Continuity Management Plans. Business continuity can be broken into three main areas:

1. **Contingency Planning.** Seeking to avoid a crisis through risk mitigation, as well as preparing for a crisis through the development of plans, agreements, and policies.
2. **Crisis Management.** Utilizing preestablished contingency plans practically in order to manage a crisis event most effectively.
3. **Recovery.** Utilizing preestablished contingency plans to quickly and effectively recover from a crisis and resume operations.

Alternatively, Business Continuity Management can be reflected in the three R's, Ready for an emergency, Response to an emergency, and Risk recovery. In order to be most effective, the Business Continuity Management Plan should address the following objectives as a guiding framework when developing such policies and plans:

- **Intelligent.** The Business Continuity Management Plan and associated policies, protocols, and plans reflect all layers and levels of need. They take into account the corporate ethos, strategic goals and agendas, shareholder interests and perceptions, marketplace and risk environment, as well as individual programmatic issues, organizational structures, cultural influences, resource limitations, and teammates' and vendor's interests.
- **Persuasive.** The Business Continuity Management Plan (where possible and appropriate) gains buy-in throughout the management and user and stakeholder population and is integrated and embraced throughout the group. Integration also occurs with supporting or leveraged agencies and organizations to make the Business Continuity Management Plan operate seamlessly with both internal and external groups.
- **Transparent.** The organizational structure, roles, and responsibilities, as well as communication and decision-making authorities and practices, should be transparent to all managers and users in order for the plan to be effective.

Elements of the plan should also be shared with external groups who might be stakeholders or who might be expected to perform specific functions during a crisis event.

The following are four recommended characteristics that form the basis for the effective development of a Business Continuity Management Plan:

1. **Comprehensive.** Establishes contingency measures that meet the holistic threats facing a company and its activities, and manages the entire life cycle of a crisis.
2. **Integrated.** Unites all appropriate organizational divisions, external agencies, vendors, teammates, and other parties into an integrated system.
3. **Flexible.** Can match the tempo and direction of a fluid business and risk environment, allowing all threats to be appropriately mitigated or managed.
4. **Benchmarked.** Is developed using mature and quantified (where possible) evaluations of the risk natures and probable impacts a company might face.

Defining a Crisis

The term *crisis* is subjective and fluid. It is important when developing a Business Continuity Management Plan, with its various components (including the IMP), to first define what is considered a commonplace problem against what might be considered significant enough to warrant the title "crisis." Each company should consider the implications of applying such terminology, as inaccuracies may result in crisis events being ignored, or conversely, common issues resulting in disproportionate levels of management attention and resource allocation. Common sense and experience will play a key role in guiding managers; however, some simple tools and definitions will support a common understanding across an organization. Such definitions might include:

- **Problem.** An everyday occurrence that does not affect an individual's safety, the integrity of critical infrastructure, or the protection of sensitive materials or information, and does not undermine significantly the operational productivity of a project, nor devalue the business interests or reputation of the company.
- **Crisis.** A singular event that places employees at personal risk (whether physical or psychological), threatens the integrity of critical infrastructure, may lead to the loss of sensitive materials or information, hinders the operational productivity of a project, and presents a threat to the business interests and reputation of the company.

Many large corporations have grown through mergers with or acquisitions of other organizations, or operate within the market space through joint ventures and teaming agreements. In these cases, there is a rapid assimilation of multiple organizations' approaches to risk management, which adds a significant degree of complexity to definition and subsequent management of risk. Aligning different approaches, requirements, and expectations is critical to ensuring that complex and integrated organizations can best manage a crisis event.

Mapping Risks

Mapping risks should occur as a layered approach to enterprise resilience. It should be a top-down driven approach, meeting strategic, operational, and tactical risks in a logical and pragmatic manner. Enterprise resilience should consider the following key questions when designing the strategy:

- What is the company's risk tolerance? How can perceptions be formalized?
- How can risks be measured, tracked, and monitored? Who is responsible and how do they do this?
- What are the company's key earnings? What market and financial risks are there?
- Where does the company operate? What environmental risks are there?
- What is the company's cultural approach to risk? What are the ethos drivers?
- What liability and reputational risks are there? What impacts could result?
- Are there pan-corporate risks? What are the pockets of singular risks?
- How effectively are traditional and strategic risks being managed? Is there any supporting information?
- What knowledge, experience, and capability does the company have? Where are the gaps?

Companies can then develop a framework for designing a risk management architecture in order to manage both the tangible and nebulous risks facing their corporation and business activities. During the design of the Business Continuity Management Plan, companies should consider:

- What capabilities are available in-house, and which must be outsourced?
- What information does the board require to manage risks, and what can be delegated?
- How are risk management groups to be structured, and what interfaces are required?
- How can threats be mitigated? What impacts could result if a risk event occurs?
- How will communications be channeled? What authorities and permissions will be sanctioned?
- How will policies, plans, and systems be managed? Who takes the lead?
- How will quality assurance and monitoring be conducted? What are the metrics?
- How are supporting agencies managed? What agreements are in place?

During the implementation of a resulting risk management system, companies should ensure that the approach is supported at all levels and keep current with the fluid risk environment. Implementers of corporate risk management should consider:

- How does the corporate board ensure that it has the information it needs? How does it monitor the group's performance?
- What sensing mechanisms are in place? How are risks identified and forecast?
- How are risks measured and tracked? What metrics trigger a response?
- How can policies, plans, and systems be kept current? What investments or resources are required?

- How does the corporate culture support and sustain the risk management approach?
- How are policies shared and empowered? What training is required?
- How does information technology and other resources support implementation? What infrastructures are required?
- What are the cost benefits to risk management? How much capital investment and indirect costs should be apportioned?

The development of a strategic risk management approach will support individual business efforts across widespread operating theaters. By establishing a strategic appreciation for risk, companies can then better support singular project activities through a unified and mature and appropriately organized approach.

Critical Dependencies

The Business Continuity Management Plan should map out the critical dependencies that will affect the company's ability to operate under crisis conditions. Critical dependencies may also affect the safety and security of personnel—and might include the supply chain assurance of critical materials or services; the ability of the company, its vendors, partners, and clients to undertake or receive services; or any effects an emergency might have on the company's personnel.

The following areas of critical dependency are offered as sample considerations when designing a Business Continuity Management Plan:

- **Power and Utilities.** The reliance and risk exposures that might result from the disruption to power and other utilities on which the company, its activities, or personnel might be dependent.
- **Supply Chain Assurance.** The risk exposure and business disruptions that might occur if critical materials and supplies are delayed, damaged, or stolen—in terms of safety and security as well as business performance.
- **Critical Materials or Structures.** The risks that might be present if critical structures, facilities, or materials are lost, damaged, or stolen—in terms of performance, liability, and physical risk natures.
- **Employee Confidence.** The implications of a loss in employee or workforce confidence should they be exposed to risks that undermine their ability or willingness to work.
- **Vendor or Teammate Performance.** The degree of dependence a company has upon vendors or teammates should they be affected by risks or disruptions that might not directly affect the company.
- **Governance.** The importance of governance and social stabilities within an operating region as a holistic component of operational success and risk and security management.
- **Technology and Information.** The risk implications and impacts should technologies be damaged, corrupted, lost, or stolen either from the company or from its clients or vendors.

The examples provided are in no means exhaustive and demonstrate only some of the generic dependencies that can curb, disrupt, or stop safe and effective business operations—either directly or as a secondary effect resulting from a crisis.

Tactical Risk Evaluations

The Business Continuity Management Plan should also seek to map the common traditional risks faced by the company within different operating environments. Risks are fluid and can change rapidly due to unforeseen circumstances. However, by structuring a risk evaluation framework, the company can better place its business interests and operations into an understandable context. Risk evaluations are complex and subjective assessments, and clear and consistent matrixes for evaluating impact and probabilities are required.

By conducting such evaluations, companies can more clearly identify where their greatest risks may lie, as well as where finite resources should be focused in order to mitigate postulated threats to personnel, facilities, operations, and business interests. Risk evaluations can be conducted at a strategic level to gain a macro perspective of where challenges may lie, but should also be conducted at a local perspective, as the risk landscape within a country may differ significantly from region to region, from city to city, and in some instances from neighborhood to neighborhood. The company may also wish to consider the following points when mapping and assessing risks:

- **Hard and Soft Targets.** Is the company an easy target compared to similar businesses or operations within the region, or are hostile groups more likely to achieve success focusing on less protected companies?
- **Common or Unique.** Are certain risks common within a particular environment, or would they be considered unique or unusual if they were to occur?
- **Incentives and Objectives.** What are the incentives and objectives of hostile individuals or groups? What are they trying to achieve, and how might they best achieve their goals?
- **Capabilities and Trends.** What are the realistic capabilities of hostile groups—do they have the knowledge, technology, and funding to be successful, or are they unable to launch sophisticated attacks? Do any trends support this analysis, or suggest future risks?
- **Mitigation Reliability.** What mitigation measures have been created to deal with risks against the company or its personnel? What gaps remain, and how effective are the measures? Should gaps then be addressed, or only acknowledged?
- **Impact Evaluations.** What impacts will be associated with an incident, both to the company and its personnel, as well as to surrounding areas and populace? Consider the holistic impacts and ramifications of each risk type. Also, how does this impact teammates and subcontractors?
- **Tolerances.** What tolerances does the company have, as well as the pertinent government, population, and legal systems? How much risk will be accepted by each group, and where do tolerance-level risks get breached?
- **Response Capacity.** What response measures and capabilities are available to deal with a crisis? Do government or supporting bodies have the knowledge, resources and interest in assisting the company, or will they part of the problem? What outsourced and in-house capacities are available and might be brought to bear?

Exhibit 1.2, Strategic and Regional Risk Mapping, illustrates a simple method by which to gain a strategic picture of risk probabilities for a range of countries in

	Albania	Algeria	Afghanistan	Bulgaria	Belarus	Chili	Egypt	Iraq	Kuwait	Libya	Pakistan	Thailand
Strategic Risks												
• Opportunistic Crime	5	4	3	2	1	3	4	3	2	2	3	4
• Organized Crime	5	4	3	3	1	2	3	3	1	1	3	3
• Insurgency and Terrorism	2	3	5	1	1	3	2	5	1	2	3	1
• Social Infrastructures	3	3	3	3	2	2	2	3	1	3	2	2
• Political Stability	3	3	3	1	1	2	2	3	1	2	2	3
Specific Man-Made Risk Types												
• Kidnap and Ransom	3	4	3	1	1	2	2	3	1	1	3	1
• Domestic Terrorism (Special Interest Groups)	1	1	1	1	1	1	1	1	1	1	1	2
• Blackouts	4	3	4	2	1	1	2	3	1	1	4	1
• Road Traffic Accidents	4	4	3	2	2	1	4	3	2	3	4	2
• Mugging and Robbery	4	3	2	2	1	1	4	3	1	2	3	2
• Arrest and Detention	3	2	1	1	1	1	2	1	1	2	2	1
• Unexploded Ordnance and Mines	3	3	4	1	1	2	1	2	1	1	2	1
• Indirect Fire Attacks and Small Arms Fire	1	1	3	1	1	1	2	3	1	1	2	1
• Threats, Coercion, and Intimidation	5	4	3	2	1	2	3	2	1	2	3	1
• Nuclear, Biological, Chemical Attacks	3	2	1	1	1	1	2	3	1	1	3	1
• Complex Attacks	1	1	4	1	1	1	2	4	1	2	4	1
• Explosive Attacks and Sabotage	2	3	4	1	1	1	2	5	1	1	3	1
• Fraud and Corruption	5	4	5	3	2	1	4	4	1	2	3	1
• Espionage and Counterfeiting	5	3	2	2	1	2	3	2	2	3	4	2
• Demonstrations or Civil Disturbances	1	2	3	1	1	2	3	4	1	1	4	1
Specific Natural Risk Types												
• Floods	2	1	2	1	1	2	1	1	1	2	3	3
• Earthquakes	2	1	1	1	1	2	2	1	1	2	4	3
• Pandemics	2	3	4	2	1	2	4	3	2	2	3	4
• Tidal Waves	1	1	1	1	1	2	2	1	1	3	1	4
• Hurricanes and Tornadoes	1	1	1	1	1	2	1	1	1	1	2	3
• Volcanoes	1	1	1	1	1	1	1	1	1	1	2	1
• Sandstorms	1	3	1	1	1	1	3	4	4	3	1	1
• Landslides	3	3	3	2	3	3	3	2	2	2	2	2
• Forest Fires	2	3	3	2	2	2	1	1	1	2	2	3
Risk Grading Table	H	M	L	H	H	L	M	N	H	L	M	N

Risk Grading Table	Company Footprint
1 Negligible Level of Risk—Highly Unlikely to Occur	
2 Low Level of Risk—Remote Chance of Occurrence	H High—50-plus full-time expatriates and 100 locals
3 Medium Level of Risk—Some Chance of Occurrence	M Medium—30–49 full-time expatriates and 50–99 locals
4 High Level of Risk—Likely to Occur	L Low—10–29 full-time expatriates and 20–49 locals
5 Extreme Level of Risk—Expected to Occur	N Negligible—1–9 full-time expatriates and 1–19 locals

EXHIBIT 1.2 Strategic and Regional Risk Mapping

which the company may be operating (note that the numbers are not evidenced evaluations, and changing conditions will alter such gradings). Such simple tools, however, are relatively easy to maintain and provide a mechanism for guiding management decision making and resource allocation as they can represent risks within a visual or comparative manner. Risk mapping systems also allow for a consistent approach to be replicated throughout an organization so that a consistent evaluating tool is available to all levels of managers.

Risk evaluations should be supported by current intelligence and threat evaluations and should be kept live. Local assessments should feed into a strategic risk evaluation table to ensure consistency of risk calculations. Such tables should guide managers in terms of devoting time, resources, and effort to developing specific components of the Business Continuity Management Plan such as pandemic response policies, evacuation plans, contracting response agencies, and security professionals. In addition, such grading also illustrates where finite resources and investment should be focused, rather than waste time and effort on areas that might have less risk than others.

Determining Risk Tolerances

Defining risk tolerances within a company can be problematic, as perceptions and opinions vary significantly. There may also be a reluctance to document certain policies due to liability concerns. That said, where possible the company should attempt to define clinically what constitutes a low, medium, high, and extreme risk or threat level in order to avoid ambiguity. Exhibit 1.3 is an example of a simple risk tolerance table that illustrates how a company might capture tolerance levels for the group or for an individual project.

This simplified approach also ensures a consistent approach within a company, although regional and project differences should be applied since what constitutes a low threat for one region or activity may be considered a high threat for another. Risk tolerance tables should also be connected to alert states and trigger response plans (where appropriate) to ensure that response measures reflect risk tolerance levels.

Incident Response versus Crisis Management

The effective management of a crisis situation will be conducted by a number of response groups, each undertaking unique tasks, but with many overlapping functions. Some of the response groups may have no training or experience in dealing with a crisis situation. Others may have considerable experience and knowledge, supported by well-established policies and procedures, with well-resourced and practiced support structures. Typically for most companies, the first line of defense against an emergency situation consists of nonsecurity specialists: the receptionist, office supervisor, or work site manager. In addition, response groups are often built around need, with the mobilization of both internal and external resources to meet new and unique challenges as they occur. For the purposes of simplicity, three groups are typically required within a crisis management situation:

1. **Immediate Response Group.** The nonspecialists who by chance happen to be the first persons at the center or point of the problem and who initiate the predefined incident and crisis response groups while feeding information upward to support decision making. These individuals may also start dealing with the crisis requirements. Often the immediate response group will be subject to, or be victims of, the emergency situation itself.
2. **Incident Response Team.** A predefined or event-mobilized team whose responsibilities are to deal solely with the specific event in hand—the micro crisis—focusing mainly on the security and safety aspects associated with the

EXHIBIT 1.3   Simple Risk Tolerance Table

Risk Nature	Low Threat	Medium Threat	High Threat	Extreme Threat
• **Civil Unrest**	Nonviolent group of 5–15 persons	Semiaggressive group of 5–15 persons	Aggressive group of 3–15 persons	Aggressive group of more than 16 persons
• **Missing Person**	Has not been sighted for more than 6 hours	Has not been sighted for more than 12 hours	Has not been sighted for more than 24 hours	Has not been sighted for more than 72 hours
• **Fatality**	A single natural death over the course of one year	More than three natural deaths over the course of one year	A single death due to hostile actions over one year	More than two deaths due to hostile actions over one year
• **Theft**	The theft of nonvaluable items from a project	The theft of semivaluable items from a project	The theft of valuable items from a project	The theft of critical items from a project
• **Vehicle-Borne IED**	An explosion within another city in-country	An explosion within a remote part of the city	An explosion within an adjoining neighborhood	An explosion in the immediate vicinity
• **Hurricane**	A hurricane within the country or state	A hurricane within the state or county	A hurricane within the county or area	A hurricane within the immediate vicinity
• **Flood**	Minor flooding within the state or region	Major flooding within the state or region	Major flooding within the immediate area	Flooding that directly affects the project
• **Complex Attack**	Complex attacks conducted in-country	Complex attacks conducted in the region	Complex attacks against a similar organization	Complex attacks targeting the project or company
• **Evacuation**	Risk environment requires an evacuation alert	Risk environment requires no essential work to stop	Nonessential project personnel evacuated	Essential project personnel evacuated
Caveat	*Common sense applies when assessing the risks posed to personnel, operations, facilities, and materials. These are provided as guidelines only to remove unnecessary ambiguity and provide managers a framework from which to operate.*			

event. They will have tactical decision-making authority to manage the actual event and will take strategic direction from the crisis management team.

3. **Crisis Management Team.** A predefined team whose responsibility is to co-ordinate the activities of the incident response team in alignment with external agencies and groups, as well as managing the macro-level impacts and effects beyond the actual incident itself. Often this team is specialist in nature and re-mains on task after event closure, as well as after the incident response team has stood down, to conduct postincident reviews and evaluations.

Where possible and appropriate, management responsibilities should be delegated to the lowest levels, as these are the points at which most crisis or incident management occurs. The coordinated and combined activities of all three groups are designed to ensure that a company is in a position to effectively respond to postulated or occurring threats in a timely, coordinated, and effective manner. Top-level management commitment and sensible and usable policies and plans are critical for the success of the crisis response policies and procedures.

Stages of Incident Management and Crisis Response

There may be numerous steps within a crisis event sequence (see Chapter 2), and the Business Continuity Management Plan should take these into consideration, determining what policies and plans are required for each stage, as well as how best to transition between different management stages. The IMP could be considered the method by which to deal with the immediate response stage, allowing for the effective transition to the interim and follow-on response stages. The immediate response stage should be focused on preventing the threat from growing, saving lives and property, and feeding information to defined incident management and crisis response teams, as illustrated in Exhibit 1.4.

Understanding Risk

The concept of risk is complex, subjective, and often fluid. Often a threat will be perceived differently by various individuals, organizations, and groups. Company and individual tolerance levels also play a part in the assessment of risk, as some companies have low tolerance levels, while others are more robust in their acceptance—and this also frequently shifts over time, or is driven by events. Risk

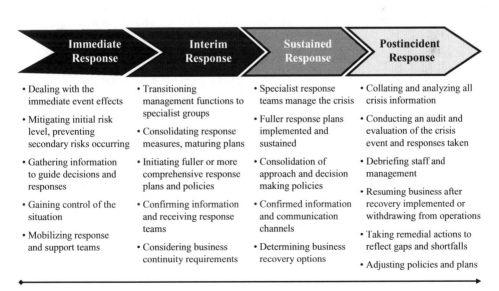

Incident Response and Crisis Management

EXHIBIT 1.4 Stages of Incident Management and Crisis Response

is effectively a phenomenon that either directly or indirectly affects businesses and employees in terms of productivity and safety. For practical purposes, risks can effectively be categorized into:

- **Personnel Risk.** It is important that companies apply due diligence to the screening and selection of their employees through reliable background investigations. This is especially important for management roles or those positions with access to sensitive information.
- **Competitive Risk.** Business activities are at risk if companies are not cognizant of how competition is strategizing commercial activities, placing them at a commercial disadvantage. Investigative services and analysis can provide companies with advice and guidance on how to compete in their markets.
- **Due Diligence Risk.** A company must be confident that its client, partner, or subcontractor is appropriate in terms of closing deals involving legal, liability, or capital investments. Investigative services can ensure that companies are reputable and appropriate to engage with.
- **Reputation Risk.** Brands and reputations underpin the status and reliability image of a business; therefore, damage to either brands or a company's reputation can undermine its commercial productivity.
- **Information Risk.** Information technology (IT) enhances commercial productivity; however, it also leaves companies vulnerable to data theft or loss. Industrial, criminal, government, or terrorist espionage has serious implications for businesses, and IT must be physically and technologically protected.
- **Intellectual Property Risk.** Commercial espionage or organized crime poses a serious threat to established products as well as emerging markets. Intellectual property is subject to theft or replication, which would undermine the value of the producer's performance.
- **Physical Risk.** Crime, insurgency, terrorism, civil unrest, and natural disasters are unpredictable and have significant impacts on companies and individuals. Risk mitigation, contingency planning, and crisis planning can be used to offset the spectrum of risks facing a company.
- **Political Risk.** Political instabilities have considerable impacts on global companies, as well as those operating within their parent country. The analysis and assessment of opaque and uncertain political environments will aid clients in complex political environments.

Risks can also be considered in terms of *internal risks* (those risks resulting from employees or company activities directly); *supported internal risks* (those risks resulting from external groups, supported by employees); or *external risks* (those risks that are a result of purely external action or attention). The concept of a risk, or indeed a crisis, is also influenced by varied and complex factors that will shape how an organization plans for and manages a wide spectrum of threats to its operations, including:

- **Subjectivity.** Risk is open to different interpretations, which themselves often change.
- **Perceptions.** Risks are influenced by human experience and opinion.
- **Tolerances.** Risks are determined by personal or group risk appetites.

- **Understanding.** Knowing what risks are and their impacts defines how organizations approach risks.
- **Fluidity.** Risks often change quickly and with little warning, rarely remaining constant.
- **Mapping.** Mapping risks presents challenges, as risks can cause unpredictable effects.
- **Quantification.** Risks are often difficult to clinically prove or gauge until after the event.
- **Measurability.** No infallible methods by which to measure risk impacts or probabilities.
- **Unpredictability.** Risks are unpredictable and may cause varied effects and follow unpredictable paths.
- **Diversity.** Risks are often numerous in number and nature.
- **Complexity.** Risk are often interrelated and with multifaceted considerations.

TIME, SPACE, AND IMPACT Risk can also be considered in terms of *time*, *space*, and *impact*. Some risk events are shortlived, while some are prolonged. Risks may be defined within a specific geographic or corporate interest area or space, whereas others may span a wide geographical and corporate interest area. The impact of a risk may be either minimal or far-reaching, as illustrated in Exhibit 1.5, Risk: Time, Space, and Impact, which demonstrates how a risk might have a medium impact and life span but impact a large area of interest or space. The Business Continuity Management Plan and its various components should include these three aspects of risk when considering appropriate contingency planning and crisis response measures. While a conceptual rather than a practical tool, such concepts help focus those developing or implementing contingency planning or crisis response measures in defining the nature, scope, and life span of possible risk events, and thus assist them in placing those events into some form of context to aid planning and impact visualization. Companies may choose to use such models for each risk type within a corporate context, or as a risk relates to a specific project or business activity.

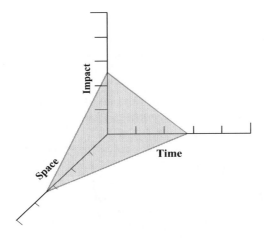

EXHIBIT 1.5 Risk: Time, Space, and Impact

PROBABILITY   Risks also come in varied levels of probability, ranging from low, where the probability of a risk occurring is highly unlikely, to extreme, where the company should expect a risk to occur at some stage. By clearly defining category levels, the company will quickly come to understand the evaluated probability of risks occurring to its business activity. The IMP should also be attuned to these risk and probability levels, as the operational decisions made by company management utilizing the incident response guides will be aligned by risk perception and the associated impact and probability levels. Some examples of how a company may attach risk management activities against risk levels are provided as a basic guideline:

- **Low Risk.** The probability of a risk occurring is unlikely, and no special or costly measures should be implemented other than standard company policies and procedures—unless the risk nature has a significant impact on the company. A detailed Business Continuity Management Plan may not be necessary, and risk awareness training may be useful only on an annual basis. The use of only a simple IMP may be appropriate.
- **Medium Risk.** The probability of a risk occurring is possible, and risk mitigation measures should be reflective of the costs and impacts of the risk on the company and the business activities, captured within a basic Business Continuity Management Plan. Low-level management training will be beneficial to the company and project groups on an annual or semiannual basis. A more focused IMP should be developed.
- **High Risk.** The probability of a risk occurring is likely; therefore, the company is advised to establish an appropriate budget to set up policies and procedures to counteract the probability of the risk occurring, as well as the subsequent impacts within a detailed Business Continuity Management Plan. Thorough management training on a semiannual or regular basis will support the organization in responding to any crisis event more effectively. A mature IMP should be in place and tested periodically.
- **Extreme Risk.** The risk is certain to occur at some stage of the project activity's life span. Therefore, the company should be advised to consider whether to continue with its activity, or acknowledge the impacts and responses within a detailed and tailored Business Continuity Management Plan, with frequent and detailed desktop exercises for varied levels of the management structure. The IMP should be connected to external organizations and agencies, and be tested and evaluated on a scheduled basis.

Often company risk tolerances are fluid and levels of risk acceptance will adjust to changing business needs or leadership perspectives. Companies also become desensitized to a risk over time, and what might have been considered a significant issue gradually becomes the norm over time or repeated exposure to a particular crisis event. Conversely, a catastrophic event outside of a specific project location might sensitize a company to risks faced in other activities, regardless of proximity or project similarity. Corporate and local risk appreciation and tolerances also frequently differ. Those project managers living the risk might disagree with their corporate counterparts on how serious a risk might be, and how best to mitigate the threats. Often this will lead to a conflict into which a vendor company or middle managers within a company might be drawn. Also, this will affect how field and corporate officers approach risks. Those responsible for risk and security management must be aware of these dynamics and should seek to represent risks using factual and clinical information where possible, with an appreciation of the dynamic tolerance and perception influences at play within the organization. The IMP is a tool used to address a risk when warning indicators are triggered or when an emergency is occurring, and as such must at all times reflect the company's official perceptions and policies.

Immediate Response and Impact Levels

The nature of the crisis event will determine the intensity, tempo, and range of effects that occur in the immediate term, near term, and long term. Some crisis events will see peaks and troughs of business or operational impacts over a protracted period. Others will see a surge of risk at the front of the event, with declining effects over time. What is true of many crisis events, however, is that the greatest degree of impact occurs at the beginning of a crisis event. This is also the period that provides the most potential for a well-prepared company to gain control over a situation, or indeed the period at which the worst effects are felt as the greatest confusion and most errors occur within an organization.

Exhibit 1.6, Immediate Response to Impact Levels, illustrates that as a general rule the greatest impact of a crisis occurs at the outset of an event, whether this is

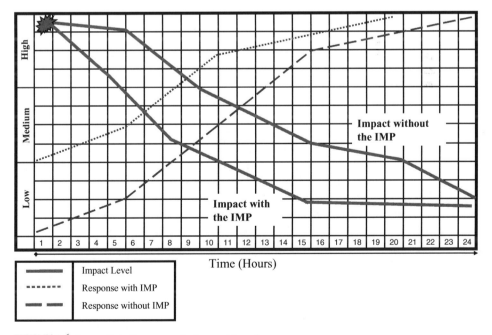

EXHIBIT 1.6 Immediate Response to Impact Levels

a forest fire, an earthquake, a hostage situation, an aircraft crash, or an industrial accident. Typically, over time the effects of the event decline as either the cause diminishes in intensity or is no longer present, the situation stabilizes itself, the initial confusion and panic decline, government or company resources are committed to respond to the problem, or appropriate company managers assume responsibility and address the threat. As shown on the graph, the level of preparedness defines how quickly control is brought to a situation, as well as the possible impact levels associated with a crisis event. The graph illustrates a subjective representation of how impact levels correspond to the ability for an organization to bring swift and effective control to a crisis; the impacts being brought under swift control with effective response measures in place, while impact levels continue at higher levels if response measures are not in place.

As the greatest level of confusion and impact generally occurs within the initial minutes or hours of a crisis event, it makes sense that an appropriate amount of focus be applied to supporting expedient and effective management responses for this stage within the crisis. A company that provides pragmatic guidance and tools to the first responders or local incident managers will generally gain better control over the event, more accurately grasp the scope and nature of the situation, and as a result develop better management approaches and decisions at the outset of a crisis in order to exert the most effective controls. In addition, supporting the local incident managers assists more experienced crisis managers in understanding the problem and responding through knowledge driven responses. Invaluable time is frequently lost during the most critical stages of a crisis situation as managers attempt, often with little success, to understand what is happening, make appropriate decisions, and mobilize essential resources to deal with the issue.

Risk Management

It is important both within the company, but especially within supporting vendors and agencies, that the different levels of focus and need within a crisis event are understood in order to develop and implement an effective Business Continuity Management Plan and associated elements such as the IMP. Corporate officers will require support in terms of strategic planning and business resilience and recovery requirements, while project managers will be dealing with more front-end-related operational issues such as resolving immediate and granular level threats to their personnel, materials, or project activities. Many focuses and needs will overlap, where both groups will be striving to reach the same overall goals; however, the particular focus areas associated with each group will determine what information or participation is needed, what parameters of authority and decision making are permitted, as well as what systems and tools will be most required. It will also shape how an organization might reach outside of its own capabilities and knowledge to tap into government or commercial groups for support. It is especially important that security and other supporting vendors understand the different needs and expectations of the different layers and groups within a company in order to provide more effective support. The Chief Security Officer of a company should also be thinking along this lines of requirement in order to direct internal and external resources. The security vendor should think in terms of corporate, country, and project issues, with the field security managers dealing with the immediate tactical requirements of incident management as part of the larger crisis approach. The country and corporate security vendor managers assist with providing strategic guidance and support, as well as assisting with the transition from immediate incident management to interim and sustainable crisis management and recovery measures.

Contingency planning presents an opportunity for the company to reduce the level of risk to its corporate structure and business activities, as well as establish a plan by which to deal with problems, while not under the pressures of the crisis event itself. It is often a failing of organizations not to develop an appropriate risk management approach, paying lip service to the creation of a pragmatic and current Business Continuity Management Plan (in which the IMP belongs), which often results in serious mismanagement and confusion during an emergency. Those organizations that engage effectively in contingency planning can significantly reduce the problems resulting from a crisis by responding in a more organized and focused manner, considerably reducing both the initial and long-term effects and impacts of a crisis, while concurrently supporting overall business continuity and recovery.

Incident management is the first step of a broader crisis management approach, often involving local project managers who will play instrumental roles in collecting vital information relating to the event, which then determines both decision making and response actions. Often incident management is the response to a problem while it is occurring, or immediately following an incident. Crisis management itself may continue long past the event and involves the broader (rather than tactical) considerations associated with an emergency, as the lingering effects of the incident persist. Incident management planning addresses the threats posed should risk mitigation measures (risk mitigation and security response plans) not be successful or should the security or risk management measures be breached. These management plans are methods by which to reduce potential business impacts or losses, and they should be readied for the company's incident response and crisis management teams to implement. There are effectively three forms of crisis that leadership might face within a company:

1. **Strategic Crisis.** A change in the business environment might call the viability of the company or activity into question (e.g., loss of productivity, hindrances to operations, serious equipment losses, or injuries or deaths that undermine commercial ventures).
2. **Public Relations Crisis.** This is more commonly called *crisis communications* (e.g., negative publicity that could adversely affect the success of the company, media coverage of liability claims, reputational damage, employee morale issues, and publicized government and legal investigations that can affect stock shares and company confidence).
3. **Financial Crisis.** These crises are typically short-term liquidity or cash flow problems and long-term bankruptcy problems. Financial crises can often result from strategic and public relations crises.

Typically, the IMP focuses on the strategic crisis, although it touches upon and influences public relations and financial crisis factors as risk events are often

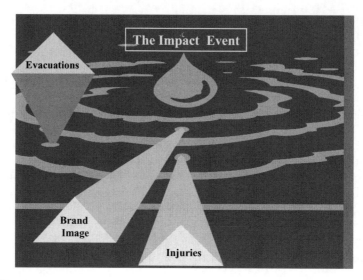

EXHIBIT 1.7 Risk Ripple Effects

interrelated and result in ripple effects that move through different areas of risk (as illustrated in Exhibit 1.7), where a singular event can create secondary hazards to a company.

The IMP addresses the immediate and tactical aspects of the crisis prior to more comprehensive and sustainable crisis responses being implemented. Established management structures, communication plans, decision matrixes, and trigger response plans should be designed to ensure that responsibilities are attributed and communication channels understood to support the overall Business Continuity Management Plan (see Chapter 2).

Response Trigger Points

Defining when a problem becomes a crisis is important, as perspective may play an important part in defining when a crisis is actually occurring. The IMP may be used both to avoid a problem developing into a crisis and in dealing with the first stages of a crisis event itself. For example, the need to evacuate a nuclear reactor facility may occur when several risk levels have been breached: Insufficient electricity is being provided to power a water pump, the reactor water-cooling system fails, the redundancy systems fail, and a reactor reaches a critical temperature. The Business Continuity Management Plan should define *trigger points* that identify when a problem has become a crisis, and at what level the crisis situation is rated. Trigger points can also be used to avoid a crisis by identifying an approaching problem so that measures can be implemented by which to avoid the effects; for example, elections are imminent in a volatile region—evacuation plans are reviewed; public disturbances start occurring—nonessential staff withdraw; government forces use unnecessary force—remaining personnel move to a safe location; mass riots occur—the company has already withdrawn from the risk area.

Companies should establish defined events or factors that require a predetermined action or activity—the trigger. Trigger points are connected to the decision matrix and will be the catalyst for decisions; for example, increased local tensions may result in a scaled response from the project leading to only critical external work being conducted and subsequently to the measured evacuation of the site itself. Trigger points may be aimed at various levels; the injury of a project employee by hostile action may require the executive board to review whether it wishes to remain on task and whether increased security measures are required. Rising community tensions may cause a local manager to stop operations and send staff home. Thus trigger points and decision matrixes may be engineered at three levels: corporate, country, and project. However, all levels should overlap, because a corporate decision or trigger will have repercussions on country and program activities and policies, and local decisions or triggers may result in corporate concerns and activities.

The grading of trigger points is subjective, driven by project staff and company tolerance perspectives. However, where possible a definitive statement should be attached to a risk-level description as well as the nature of the threat. Thus a low threat might be graded as a 2, and the definition might include: *The probability of likelihood is considered low to remote, with resulting impacts also rated low.* Some risk factors might have a low probability, but a high impact (a shooting, bomb, or tsunami) and so a definition might include: *The probability of likelihood is considered low to remote; however, the resulting impacts are rated as catastrophic.* The grading on a trigger response table may need to be more fully explained than purely attributing a numerical value.

Often companies that define triggers do not enact them, having a tendency to delay a decision in order to see how an event may unfold as a decision might affect operations, reduce performance, or call into question the decision maker's judgment. Delaying the implementation of a trigger response can devalue the Business Continuity Management Plan and prevent effective crisis avoidance and management from occurring. Exhibit 1.8 shows where managers may delay a trigger, and the possible resulting implications.

EXHIBIT 1.8   Failure to Follow Trigger Points

Trigger	Action	Delayed	Impacts
Flood Warnings	Evacuate area and sandbag facilities.	Managers wait for floods to actually start occurring.	Personnel are stranded as roads are closed, and property is damaged as not protected.
Hurricane Warnings	Move to alternative work areas and batten down facilities.	Managers wait for hurricane's direction to be confirmed.	Personnel are exposed to avoidable risks and property is damaged as not protected.
Bomb Threat	Evacuate buildings and search for suspicious items.	Managers wait until law enforcement advice or support arrives.	Explosion occurs, injuring occupants and exposing company to liability claims.

Managers should be advised it is better to "pull the trigger" than delay making decisions or alerting crisis managers. As such it is often better to pull the trigger (as defined in advance through contingency planning) as a safety measure, rather than resorting to a decision delay approach, and thus move past a predefined response protocol. Although a measured, mature, and well-informed decision is always preferable, inaction due to uncertainty or a lack of management confidence exposes the company and its personnel to avoidable risk.

Exhibit 1.9 illustrates a simple trigger response matrix that allows various elements of a crisis response organization to understand at what point a certain trigger response is required. As much subjectivity as possible should be removed from such a grading approach; there should be a focused and unambiguous description of what each crisis event and response means and entails.

Crisis Event	Threats, Coercion, and Intimidation of Local Nationals	Rising Incidents of Violence toward Local Employees	Rising Levels of Violence toward Expatriates	Reduced Rule of Law and Increasing Public Tensions	Increasing Civil Gatherings and Disturbances	Widespread Riots and Loss of Rule of Law	Possible Intelligence—Targeting of the Company	Possible Targeting of Co-Located or Adjacent Groups	Specific Intelligence—Targeting of the Company	Specific Targeting of Co-Located or Adjacent Groups	Increased Levels of Road Blocks or Illegal Vehicle Stops	Aggressive Tactics by Police and Host Nation Military	Arrests and Detentions by Local Government Forces	Arrests and Detentions by Local Militia	Western Embassy Threat Warnings and Alert States	Increasing Number of Unarmed Attacks on Personnel	Increasing Number of Armed Attacks on Personnel	Increasing Number of Unarmed Attacks on Facilities	Increasing Number of Armed Attacks on Facilities	Specific Targeting of Supply Chain	Targeting of Project Staff Moving to Project Locations	Targeting of Western Companies within Operating Area	Targeting of Local Subcontractor Companies
Increase Alert Status	2	2	2	1	1	1	2	3	1	2	2	2	1	1	2	3	2	3	2	3	2	2	3
Increase Risk Posture	2	3	2	3	2	3	2	3	2	3	3	3	3	2	3	3	3	3	3	4	3	3	4
Noncritical Travel Stops	3	3	4	4	3	3	3	4	3	4	3	4	4	3	4	3	4	4	4	5	4	4	5
Critical Travel Stops	5	4	5	5	3	4	5	5	4	5	5	5	4	4	5	5	4	4	4	5	4	5	5
Facility Security Posture Increases	4	4	4	3	3	3	3	4	3	4	5	4	4	4	4	5	4	4	3	5	5	4	4
External Project Operations Stopped	4	5	4	4	3	3	4	5	4	5	4	4	5	4	5	5	4	5	4	5	4	5	4
Project Facility Closed Down	5	4	4	4	3	3	5	5	5	5	5	5	5	5	5	5	4	5	4	5	5	4	5
Local Employees Stood Down	4	3	5	4	3	3	5	5	5	5	4	4	4	3	5	4	3	5	4	5	5	4	4
Stage 1 Evacuation	4	4	4	4	4	3	5	5	4	5	5	5	5	5	5	5	4	5	4	5	5	5	5
Stage 2 Evacuation	5	5	5	5	5	4	5	5	5	5	5	5	5	5	5	5	5	5	5	5	5	5	5

Level	Trigger Response Guide
1	Negligible levels of risk with low-impact threats to the project, personnel, or resources
2	Limited levels of risk with low to some impact threats to the project, personnel, and resources
3	Medium levels of risk with noticeable impact threats to the project, personnel, and resources
4	High levels of risk with significant impact threats to the project, personnel, and resources
5	Extreme levels of risk with unacceptable levels of impact threats to the project, personnel, and resources

EXHIBIT 1.9 Crisis Management: Trigger Response Matrix

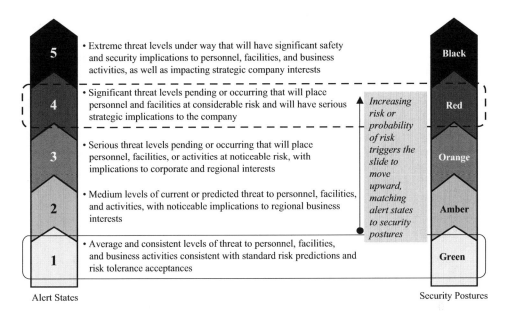

Alert States   Security Postures

EXHIBIT 1.10 Crisis Management: Simple Trigger Response Tools

Companies can also utilize more simplistic and targeted trigger tools in order to allow managers to move through response levels in a systematic and logical manner. This may be related to a specific activity or function, such as facility security responses to triggers, movement configurations and profiles, international travel permissions, or any other aspect of the company's business that might change to reflect shifting risk levels. Exhibit 1.10, Crisis Management: Simple Trigger Response Tools, illustrates how certain risk levels, or the probability of risk increases, might be used as a sliding scale to prompt changes within an emergency alert state. These alert states in turn may be connected with movement security levels, with tier 1 personal security details at alert state 1 being amalgamated or augmented to provide increasingly more robust security configurations to reflect the threats posed to traveling project staff as the threats move upwards to alert state 4. Such sliding scales can be used for facility security postures or other simple response levels, removing much of the ambiguity of decision making, while also evidencing for postincident reviews and other audit requirements the rationale and processes used to safeguard personnel and other company interests. The company security plan for a facility can be linked to such tools, connecting alert states to ranging security postures and protocols.

Such tools can be used to define numerous security management procedures and responses which are triggered by intelligence or certain risk tolerances being breached.

Decision and Authority Matrixes

Every element of the Business Continuity Management Plan, whether it is the corporate policies and management systems or individual crisis and management policies and plans such as the IMP, should be developed in alignment with defined decision matrixes and management authorities to ensure that action responses and information chains are best managed within an organization or group. Decision matrixes enable effective decision making by those best placed to determine and implement the required courses of action to bring control to a crisis event (see Chapter 2). Company management should not be debating which employee has decision-making authority, or the parameters of their permissions, while an emergency is under way, as this impedes clear and effective management at the most critical stages of an event and distracts an organization from effectively responding to an emergency. As a crisis escalates, the decision-making authorities may ascend upward to the executive board, and the point where the impacts breach certain authorities should also be clearly defined. Therefore, the Business Continuity Management Plan should clearly define authorities for decisions associated with postulated activities or responses in order to reduce as much organizational confusion as possible during a crisis event. By having decision areas and authorities defined prior to an event occurring, management can also be provided training and guidance on their lines and areas of authority, as well as be empowered to take decisive action where necessary and appropriate. Gaps and shortfalls within risk management policies and plans can also be better identified, as ownership of response and accountability of action are more clearly defined within the company. Exhibit 1.11 illustrates a simple decision and authority matrix that defines which management groups are sanctioned to implement specific policies and plans.

Each area should have a subset of instructions that unambiguously define what each response means. The instructions may be complex and detailed, such as evacuation plans, or simple and succinct, such as the destruction of sensitive materials. In addition, decision making authorities should also be tied to role descriptions for crisis managers.

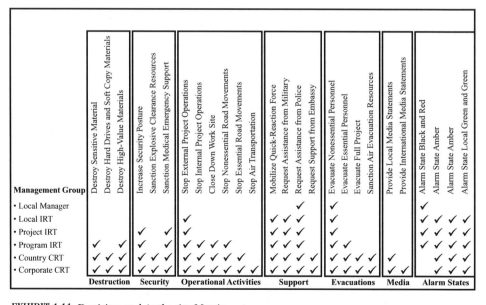

EXHIBIT 1.11 Decision and Authority Matrix

Structuring Business Continuity Management Plans

In order to understand how the IMP should be structured and where it fits within both the corporate and field risk management and crisis response policies and plans, it is important to understand that the IMP forms one of many components of the company's Business Continuity Management Plan—effectively supporting the first response steps of the plan. More comprehensive policies and plans designed to manage the subsequent stages of a crisis will invariably be undertaken by experts within appropriate fields, typically involving more complex and event tailored approaches. The Business Continuity Management Plan itself should be a logically structured policy and procedural document designed to assess and address risks in a systematic and pragmatic manner, dealing with both theoretical and tangible requirements.

Companies might wish to consider the development of their Business Continuity Management Plans with two key aspects in mind—layers and levels:

1. **Layers.** Layers might be considered in terms of organizational or management bands within a group, from corporate to country to program to project. Understanding how a company is layered in both management and operating terms will enable the plan to reflect the organizational structure and the unique and common requirements within each management or user category.
2. **Levels.** Levels might be considered in terms of management applicability, whether strategic, operational, or tactical. Strategic interests might encompass market value, reputation, and image as well as the holistic issues a company might face. Operational issues might relate to how a company conducts business or undertakes work functions. Tactical considerations might be the granular-level aspects of how specific work packages or crisis management functions are done.

Companies will structure and layer their plans according to the nature of their industry, the complexity of their organization, and the manner in which they conduct business. However, companies may find value in structuring their plans in a consistent manner, changing only the level of detail as the plan is designed for different levels of management, or for different groups within a wider organization. Consistency ensures that a standard approach to risk and response management is achieved, and that managers moving between different parts of the company understand where information is contained, and how general practices are undertaken. This should not detract from the requirement to tailor plans to suit unique operating conditions or local requirements, but should provide a common framework for sound management application, as would be found within health and safety management approaches. Different layers will also overlap as the Business Continuity Management Plan acts to fuse the complex policies, protocols, and plans found within an organization into a unified management system. Where possible the company should seek to avoid duplication and redundancies by creating umbrella information that might apply to all aspects of the organization, while creating pillars of similarly structured, yet tailored plans for different divisions or geographic regions, as illustrated in Exhibit 1.12, Layering of Business Continuity Management Plans.

All layers of the plan should be engineered to fit in at critical junctures, especially between corporate, country, and project levels, so that the Business Continuity

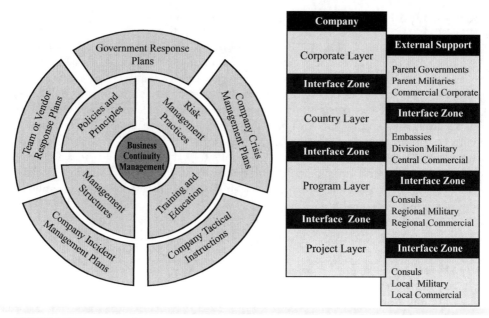

EXHIBIT 1.12 Layering of Business Continuity Management Plans

Management Plan has complementary and supporting components or layers, as illustrated in Exhibit 1.13, Convergence within the Business Continuity Management Plan.

Typically the company (or subcontracted) risk and security manager will work with the multiple stakeholders within the organization to provide a Business Continuity Management Plan that ensures that a business activity (or indeed overall

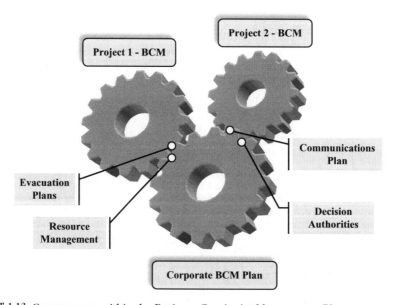

EXHIBIT 1.13 Convergence within the Business Continuity Management Plan

corporate operations) is planned within the context of risk, can operate most effectively, and exposes the company to lowest levels of threat possible. Typically, a Business Continuity Management Plan is designed to work in a logical and often chronological sequence, identifying dangers through risk assessments and deciding whether to countermand the risks with personnel or resource allocation (or whether to adopt a risk avoidance policy), before implementing the delivery of security and response measures, in all their forms, to ensure that the probability of the risk occurring is reduced to acceptable levels or dealt with most effectively. Alternatively the first stages of risk evaluation may deter a company from entering into new businesses if tolerances are breached. No organization can prevent all crises, but every organization can lower the odds of their occurrence, lower their costs, and lower potential crisis-related condemnation.

The Business Continuity Management Plan should be aligned with three basic areas of consideration, as illustrated in Exhibit 1.14. The company or contracted vendor risk manager should consider what range of risks face the company and how the company wishes to manage these risks. Risk managers should only then write policies and plans that are aligned with the considerations of contingency planning and crisis response, which include the IMP. It is important that such evaluations are not written in isolation, or from the perspective of a single risk manager, but brings together multiple stakeholders and expertise. This forms the preparedness or contingency planning aspect of risk management: where a company can reduce risks before they occur, with preemptive planning to allow the company to best manage risks prior to an event—into which the IMP will fit as a practical response component. The Business Continuity Management Plan should then consider how to address the immediate crisis requirements that typically affect the people, resources, and business goals of an affected activity, as well as how the risks pose an *impact ripple effect* on other aspects of the company's operations and business interests. It is at the immediate point of crisis that well-planned policies and procedures reduce the impacts of the risk event by managing the risks through well-defined response methodologies and training—again in which the IMP plays a key role. Finally, the Business Continuity Management Plan activities continue until all aspects of the risk event have been completed, and where both project and corporate managers have had the opportunity to review which areas within the plan were effective, and which need to be improved, modified, or augmented, allowing a company to recover effectively from a crisis. Business Continuity Management Plans should be

Contingency Planning	**Crisis Response**	**Consolidation**
Stage 1	**Stage 2**	**Stage 3**
Preparedness Planning	Incident Management	Postincident Management
• What are the risks?	• Resolve immediate problem.	• Close off issues and document.
• How will they be managed?	• Manage wider implications.	• What went right or wrong?
• Develop policies and plans.	• Implement policies and plans.	• Adjust policies and plans.

EXHIBIT 1.14 Business Continuity Management Plan Considerations

considered live documents and should be continually adjusted and validated to suit changing influences and operating practices, as well as when improved or new concepts and efficiencies are identified.

In terms of providing a framework for the risk management process, risk managers should have the three principle areas of consideration in mind when developing the four elements that comprise the Business Continuity Management Plan: the risk assessment, the contingency plans (including the IMP), crisis management, and the postincident review, as outlined in Exhibit 1.15, The Risk Management Process.

The IMP falls within both the contingency planning and the crisis response components of the Business Continuity Management Plan—designing policies, plans, and guidelines in order to prepare an organization for a crisis event, as well as then using such policies and procedures to manage the crisis response itself, especially during the early response stages of an emergency.

The Business Continuity Management Plan and its constituent components may involve the development of new corporate policies to meet strategic and complex issues, as well as bring convergence to often amorphous, dispersed, and disjointed organizations. The Business Continuity Management Plan may also address project planning procedures and tools, as well as employee education, and may require specialist support for conceptual development and plan structuring. Plans will also include executive officers, project teams, security or risk elements, legal and public relations input, monitoring groups, and administrative resources. In many cases,

EXHIBIT 1.15   The Risk Management Process

Area	Explanation
Risk Assessment	*Warning signs and analysis prior to a crisis event.* The value of a risk assessment as a diagnostic tool is measured in terms of accurate intelligence, specialist knowledge, and an achievable and pragmatic set of procedures to reduce the probability of a risk occurring.
Contingency Planning	*Preparation and prevention phase.* Contingency planning refers to measures implemented to prevent recognized or speculated serious events or emergencies. These possible activities should be identified during the risk assessment.
Crisis Management	*Incident response, damage containment, and recovery period.* Crisis management is the response to a problem while it is occurring or after an incident, utilizing the contingency planning measures, as well as the organization being able to respond quickly and effectively to unique requirements.
Postincident Review	*Review and modification of the risk management plan.* The documentation of all incident information should be conducted to support adjustments to existing policies and plans, as well as to identify shortfall within crisis management policies and management teams, in order to mitigate future crisis impact levels.

Source: Michael Blyth, *Risk and Security Management: Protecting People and Sites Worldwide.* Copyright © 2008 John Wiley & Sons. Reprinted with permission of John Wiley & Sons.

external agencies may also be involved, requiring security clearance, access to sensitive information, the formalization of contractual agreements, and the monitoring of the contract's standards. At the lower levels, basic instruction on how to use the IMP is required to ensure that it operates within the framework of the Business Continuity Management Plan—and is effectively implemented during times of need.

When the company has contracted other groups to support its business activities, whether within the project activity or as a security component, the company should consider providing, and receiving agreement on, policies and plans to enable all groups to act in unity to best respond to risk events. Without a degree of uniformity, the response will typically be disjointed and confusing, increasing the risk impacts. The IMP should be designed in such a manner to complement and support the Business Continuity Management Plan as a whole, providing information to enable sound decision making, as well as bringing initial crisis situations under control to reduce the initial and longer-term risk impacts, as well as support better business recovery. The IMP should be linked at certain points to other elements of the Business Continuity Management Plan, but might also be engineered to be able to operate as a stand-alone document where necessary. The IMP in this sense enables the transition of crisis management from nonspecialists to risk and security professionals more effectively, as well as bridging the gap between incident management protocols and crisis management plans.

Resourcing

Resourcing of Business Continuity Management Plans must occur at different levels, from strategic support from stakeholders and key decision makers to ensuring that the correct management and technological infrastructures are in place to enable the plans to be operationally effective. The design and development of Business Continuity Management Plan will be labor intensive, and consideration to contracting external consulting support should be given in order not to distract security directors or busy managers from their primary tasks. Training and practice should also be a component of resourcing, as without education and awareness of how the plan operates and interrelates with internal and external groups it will be limited in its value. The implementation of the plan should also be measured and validated at strategic design points, ensuring that it is aligned with the company ethos and operational needs. Resourcing can also be in terms of:

- **Management Capabilities.** Ensuring that the correct management expertise is applied to the plans, both for design and for implementation.
- **Specialist Support.** Ensuring that the correct expertise is applied, rather than attempting to use inappropriate and inexperienced management as a cost-false saving measure.
- **Retained Specialist Response Teams.** Establishing retainer-based expertise to deploy immediately to affected regions as the link between corporate and field management.
- **Technology and Communications.** Ensuring that effective technology supports the management expertise in the execution of their duties.

- **Risk Management Assets.** Ensuring that the correct resources are available to support risk management teams, especially special response teams.
- **Security Structures and Assets.** Ensuring that an appropriate level of security structures, as well as manpower, is in place as a mitigation measure.
- **Redundancy Measures.** Ensuring that communications, information technology (IT), and operational redundancies are in place should primary measures or facilities be affected by the crisis event.
- **Translations.** Where necessary, materials should be translated into the different user languages to ensure that incident and crisis managers can fully understand instructions and guidance offered. Documents should be translated in dual nature in order to ensure consistency and document control.

Resourcing can be considered as a range of components meeting conceptual, operational, and tactical needs. The following provides some examples of resource principles a company might wish to consider when evaluating the resources required to support their Business Continuity Management Plan:

- **Strategic Resources.** Ensuring that management support is provided to enable plans and managers to be effective.
- **Design and Development Resources.** Allocating sufficient budgets and focus to ensure that plans are designed to be reflective of the company's requirements.
- **Operational Resources.** Ensuring that the correct level of expertise is provided to enable plans to be implemented to standard.
- **Technology Resources.** Ensuring the correct technologies are provided to enable command and control of a crisis situation, as well as information flow.
- **Tactical Resources.** Ensuring that the correct equipment and training are in place to support the Business Continuity Management Plan.
- **Quality Assurance Resources.** Ensuring that adequate auditing and validation budgets and focus have been applied to ensure plans and training are kept current.

Companies will develop a Business Continuity Management Plan that meets the particular needs of their organization, or that reflects senior management or outsourced consultant design preferences. The time, money, and resources invested into the Business Continuity Management Plan will also define its structure and complexity. The Business Continuity Management Plan will typically include the elements illustrated in Exhibit 1.16, and may be considered in terms of strategic policies, plans, and considerations—the higher-level and corporate umbrella aspects of the plan, as well as the functional or response aspects. The structure of the plan will also be derived from the nature of the risks and their impacts upon the organization in order to ensure that the plan is meaningful and correctly focused on the company's unique requirements, as well as common operating considerations.

Companies should also consider methods by which to improve the sustainability of a Business Continuity Management Plan and its components with the greatest amount of ease. Often such plans quickly become redundant as the risk environment changes, personnel move, and business or project operations progress. Companies

I. Policies and Principles

- Corporate Ethos and Guiding Principles
- Corporate Operating Practices
- Corporate Communications Policies
- Corporate Procurement Policies
- Corporate Public Relations Policies
- Corporate Information Security Policies
- Special Relationships and Agreements
- Corporate Insurance and Liability Policies
- Organizational Minimal Security Standards Policy
- Corporate Due Diligence and Duty of Care Policies
- Supporting Practices and Policies
- Transfer of Critical Operations
- Contracting Supporting Agency Policies
- IT and Critical Records Management

II. Risk Management

- Corporate Risk Tolerances
- Strategic Overview of Risk Natures and Types (Risk Log)
- Strategic Corporate Risk and Impact Mapping
- Strategic and Regional Risk Evaluations
- Program Risk and Impact Mapping
- Strategic and Tactical Risk Mitigation Policies
- Strategic Risk Management Plans and Systems
- Organic Resource Management Plans
- External Resource Management Leveraging Plans
- Intelligence and Threat Analysis Reviews
- Security Surveys, Plans, and Audits
- Resource Management Planning Systems
- Training and Educational Programs
- Strategic Business Recovery Planning Measures
- Risk Tracking and Alert Systems
- Business Solution Architecture and Concept of Operations

III. Management Structures and Policies

- Corporate Organizational Structure
- Crisis and Incident Management Structure and Appointments
- Decision-Making Permissions and Matrixes
- Alert States and Trigger Response Plans
- Communications Plans and Systems
- Procurement Management and Systems
- Public Relations Management and Procedures
- Strategic Resource Management Plans
- Security and Intelligence Management Structures
- Organizational Interface Plans and Systems
- Special Agreement Management Plans
- Quality Assurance Policies and Plans
- Contracts and Relationships
- Critical Materials Management Instructions
- Contracted or Retained Specialist Support
- Response Capabilities and Times
- Business and Project Initiation Policies and Plans
- Facility and Approach Hardening Policies and Plans

IV. Tactical Instructions and Plans

- Standard Operating Procedures
- Travel Policies and Systems
- Tactics, Techniques, and Procedures
- Security Orders and Instructions
- Training and Educational Measures
- Facility Security Plans
- Procurement and Resource Management Instructions
- Reporting and Record Keeping
- Postincident Reviews
- Mapping and Schematics
- Medical Policies and Instructions
- Critical Materials Handling Instructions

V. Incident Management Plans

- Corporate Policy Flow-Downs
- Incident Management Plan Objectives
- Crisis Management Structures
- Crisis Management Roles and Responsibilities
- Decision Matrixes and Authorities
- Organizational Interface Plans
- Communications Instructions and Verbal Reporting
- Organic Resource and Leveraged Resource Instructions
- Alert States and Trigger Response Plans
- Threat Types and Overviews
- Response Information Collection Templates
- Incident Management Plan Risk Assessment Reports
- Destruction Plans

VI. Crisis Management Plans

- Evacuation Plans
- Business Recovery Plans
- Disaster Response Plans
- Kidnap and Ransom Response Plans
- IT Crisis Management
- Medical Response Plans
- Repatriation Plans
- Public Relations Crisis Plans
- Pandemic Management Plans
- Industrial Accident Management Plans
- Fraud or Corruption Management Directives
- Threats and Extortion Crises

EXHIBIT 1.16 The Business Continuity Management Plan

should attempt to broadly define which elements of the plan are static, semistatic, and fluid:

- **Static.** Information that rarely changes and is commonly centered on policy, education, or advisory information.
- **Semistatic.** Information that changes only periodically and may include significant resources, agreements, or project locations.
- **Fluid.** Information that may change on a frequent basis, including personalities, short-cycle work packages, and transition factors.

Where possible, semistatic and fluid information should be captured within tables and other informational inserts that can be replaced with ease. Placing semistatic or fluid information into the verbiage of the document can make revisions difficult, costly, and time consuming.

Where a Business Continuity Management Plan addresses various levels of a company's activities (corporate, country, and program), materials should be structured in a consistent manner, removing elements that might be redundant or not applicable. By designing a framework that can be used for each layer of need, organizations can better manage and utilize such plans. In addition, components of the plan can then be migrated to new business activities with significantly less effort than is required to repeatedly create new plans or policies.

The company should ensure that strategic and tactical elements are fused and coordinated where appropriate, and that regional tailoring occurs to reflect the nuances of a particular operating environment—without changing the structure or themes of the original plan. In addition, the company should determine where outside support plugs into the Business Continuity Management Plan, again coordinating integration to avoid friction or confusion when the policies and plans are implemented.

Design and Development

The development and design of a corporate Business Continuity Management Plan is an important aspect of how a company prepares for and responds to a crisis event. While a risk or security manager may write a Business Continuity Management Plan for a specific individual or business group, often this plan will be shared among multiple divisions and parties, spanning various levels and areas of an organization. At times the plan may also be used by supporting agencies outside of the company. Therefore, the plan should be developed to meet the needs of a wide and multi-talented user audience. Often some policies and procedures already exist, and plan development should seek to incorporate these and mature or augment them, rather than reinvent the wheel and fail to exploit existing materials.

The Business Continuity Management Plan is also a living document that will grow and adapt to suit the changes in the company's approach, methodologies, and objectives, as well as the risk environment in which the plan operates. Additional contributions may be made to enhance components of the plan at various stages of its life. The plan should be configured to readily accept and incorporate additional elements; this is often achieved by compartmentalizing the plan, where appropriate, so that components can be changed, rather than requiring an entire plan update.

Identifying *data migration points* is a useful exercise, as it allows materials to be migrated from one document or policy into another, significantly reducing effort as well as ensuring consistency within supporting policies or plans. This is especially relevant if the same forms of information are found within a series of documents and might be shared through effective information management practices. Policies should also be developed with the concept of *live* and *static data* points:

- **Live Data Points.** The unique and particular details that represent the specifics of an operating area, task, or function and are relevant to a unique product. Also, information which may change on a frequent basis.
- **Static Data Points.** Common features and generic concepts or instructions that remain true across the spectrum of the business regardless of region or activity. Also, information which will rarely change within the plan.

By developing frameworks based on a foundation of static data points, and placing live data points into tables, graphs, maps, and other capture points where possible, significant time and resources can be saved in providing consistent and detailed frameworks to which live data points can be inserted. Where sanctioned and appropriate, it is also useful to provide generic templates for local project adaptation, saving the company (and field management in particular) considerable time and effort in re-creating response plans, which will be better spent on generating revenue.

When developing such plans, it is also important to understand that executive members of a busy commercial organization likely will not review a comprehensive plan in full; thus the manager should establish the core elements and responses within an executive summary at the front of the document to capture the pertinent points and recommendations, with detailed responses captured within successive annexes that can be accessed individually when required. Cheat sheets are also useful so that managers can quickly refer to a specific area of requirement, rather than have to sift through a volume of data. Supporting materials should also be captured in annexes or attachments to enable everyone, from executive officers to the field users, to choose which components they read, according to their areas of interest. Protecting the document from alteration is also useful should elements within the company be inclined to modify or edit sections to meet their local requirements. PDFs or Word-protecting documents ensure that the original version is more easily defined. A custodian should be appointed to ensure that the document remains consistent with the corporate directives and that those improvements and augmentations are incorporated and dispersed throughout the company.

Reporting of information is also a critical element of crisis management. Often information provided from the crisis point is inaccurate, disjointed, or poorly presented. The company should develop pragmatic and user-friendly report templates in order to ensure that the right information is captured, that it is presented in a consistent manner, and that the correct people receive the reports (see the section "The Communications Plan" in this chapter, and Chapter 6). Data call reports can capture immediate information in terms of what occurred and the immediate impacts, enabling various layers of managers to better understand, throughout the crisis event, what is occurring and so allow them to make the right decisions and to mobilize the correct resources to control the event. Predefined formats remove the requirement to identify information needs or presentational formats while managers are dealing with a problem. Examples of such reports are illustrated in Chapter 6.

Corporate leaders will invariably require another layer of information (outside of the succinct data capture reports) in order to determine strategic or macro-level operational requirements that will influence corporate decision making during and following an event. Company management, as well as supporting vendors, should seek to proactively identify business continuity considerations as well as how the company may wish to proceed in terms of risk assessment validations and postincident audits. The template in Exhibit 1.17, Information Management: Strategic Planning, indicates some areas the company's field and security vendors should be considering during or immediately after a crisis event. Such strategic considerations are typically fed from the initial incident management reports; however, they reflect the transition from incident to crisis management levels and focus areas.

Companies may build business continuity management plans either from scratch or by leveraging existing policies and plans. They should seek to mature plans where possible, exploiting in-house and publicly available materials to ensure that plans are more comprehensive, to avoid duplication, and to reduce the time and effort required for design and development. In addition, maturing plans also enables more receptive implementation from users as existing policies and protocols are rationalized and put to use.

At every point within an emergency event, it is essential that information provided is as accurate and detailed as possible; assumptions should be avoided and educated assessments should be quantified to avoid inaccurate details being reported as facts. Reports should be adapted and augmented to reflect unique factors, and flexibility and innovation should be key aspects during any crisis.

EXHIBIT 1.17   Information Management: Strategic Planning

Executive Summary:
Incident Facts:

- Immediate Threat Picture
- Immediate Threats to Personnel/Business
- Immediate Response Requirements
- Sustained Response Requirements
- Highest-Risk Activities
- Low-Risk Activities
- Risk Review Requirements
- Recommendations

- Interim Threat Picture
- Interim Threats to Personnel/Business
- Interim Response Requirements
- Long-Term Needs
- Medium-Risk Activities

- Postincident Review Requirements
- Supporting Groups and Activities

Appendixes:

• Serious Incident Reports	• Intelligence Reviews	• Casuality Reports
• Communications Log	• Crisis Team Assessments	• External Agency Reports
• Actions Taken	• Policies Invoked	• Resources Engaged

Reported by	Title	Phone/E-mail

Source: Michael Blyth, *Risk and Security Management: Protecting People and Sites Worldwide.* Copyright © 2008 John Wiley & Sons. Reprinted with permission of John Wiley & Sons.

Integrated and Compartmentalized Policies

During the design and development phase of creating a Business Continuity Management Plan and associated components, it should be determined whether as a result of company ethos or corporate or operational circumstance the policies and plans being developed will be part of a broader and integrated management system, or whether they may need to operate independently and autonomously from each other. While ideally all policies and plans should be supported and work as part of an integrated system, at times an organization may allocate responsibilities for various elements of the management of risk to different divisions, and under those circumstances it may be challenging to align some of the higher-level strategies, systems, and policies across a complex and geographically and organizationally disjointed corporation. Under these circumstances, managers should develop policies and plans that are largely complete within themselves, rather than having core components for the effective operation of a particular plan be held within another document, which they may have no input into or control over.

Integrated policies and plans will typically have decision matrixes, alert states and trigger response plans, and other such elements within overarching policy documents, rather than run the risk of repetition and error within individual risk management policies and plans. From the overarching policies such elements may be migrated downward so that consistency of approach is reflected across different levels of the Business Continuity Management Plan. When organizations choose to have individual groups or divisions defining their own strategic, operational, and tactical approaches, there may be no option but for individual managers to define their own core approaches in order to ensure that their part of the contingency planning and crisis response organization is complete and effective. Ideally the fusion of multiple requirements is captured within a single corporate officer (typically the chief security officer) so that repetition is avoided, consistency is adopted, and synergies and efficiencies are identified and implemented.

Reporting and Record Keeping

Writing up the details of a crisis incident is essential to ensure that accurate facts are recorded and maintained, and that information for any subsequent internal review as well as possible government or civil audits or insurance and liability claims are presented in a fashion reflecting the company's policies, ethos, standards, and objectives. Any documentation provided to external persons or groups should also be reviewed by the country crisis response manager (at a minimum) prior to being released, as poorly worded reporting can cause a wide spectrum of issues for the company and its employees. Accurate and correctly worded reporting is also critical to ensuring that insurance for any injured person is awarded. Information should be held by an appointed custodian so that materials can be easily and accurately retrieved when required, often months or years after an event.

Implementing the Business Continuity Management Plan

The Business Continuity Management Plan must be supported at every level in order to be successful. At the corporate level, a risk policy strategy needs to be agreed on and distributed to appropriate key decision makers and groups, providing a framework for systematically developing risk assessments that corporate and program management can use to guide their activities and focuses. These in turn contribute to the focus and subsequent development of the IMP, should they not already be in place. At the program level, the plans must be usable and reflective of realistic conditions and responses. Synergies and interfaces between corporate and program-level plans and responses should also be identified and integrated to ensure that corporate and project teams do not work independently of or in isolation from each other, but undertake concurrent and complementary activities. Some of the following principal values should be considered when developing the Business Continuity Management Plan:

- Provide a convenient framework for developing a quantitative risk assessment that prioritizes both the goals and the objectives of the company in the context of the associated risks or threats.
- Provide a systematic and repeatable method for evaluating an organization's risks using the best threat information available. Seek efficiencies by drawing on existing templates and formats.
- Permit program, project, and other key managers the opportunity to identify their departmental and organizational risks.
- Identify information gaps in order to establish a better risk picture.
- Allow risk and security managers to express their expectations about the consequences of the postulated incident types, and elicit their observations and recommendations on how to mitigate or respond to these risks.
- Allow business leaders and project managers to review the risks and comment on how risk management policies, approaches, and plans might affect program design, objectives, and goals.
- Provide insights into how the uncertainty of managers' expectations affects the prioritization of risk or security requirements. Allow risk models to be easily updated with new input data.
- Develop a spectrum of policies and plans in order to reduce the likelihood of the risks occurring, as well as to effectively manage an event should it occur.
- Permit stakeholders to review and comment on the policies, plans, and procedures and adjust and improve where necessary, thereby gaining greater group buy-in.
- Train and test both the plans and managers in their use and applicability.
- Support market entry design with risk, business, and project managers working in collaboration with each other.

Risk management should be cyclic in nature, with continuity between the users (projects) and managers (corporate). In addition, the process is also cyclic in terms that the business need prompts the risk assessment, which feeds business decision making and associated policies and plans, with events driving modifications, which then influence business needs and decision making, as illustrated in Exhibit 1.18, Risk Management Cycle.

Risk information needs to be shared with appropriate groups and individuals in order to ensure that a rounded understanding of the risks is gained, and that mitigation measures (including the IMP) are most effective. Information sharing can

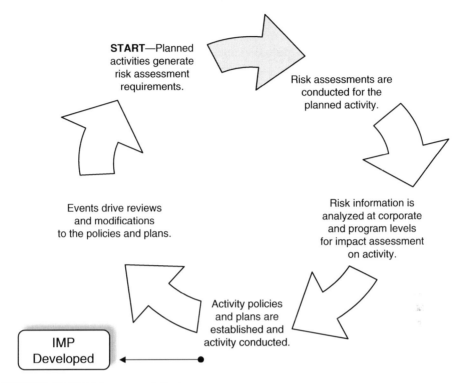

EXHIBIT 1.18 Risk Management Cycle

Source: Michael Blyth, *Risk and Security Management: Protecting People and Sites Worldwide.* Copyright © 2008 John Wiley & Sons. Reprinted with permission of John Wiley & Sons.

be through training, warning posters, leaflets, or daily intelligence briefings, which highlight specific risks or risk environments. The policies and procedures used to mitigate risk are a reflection of the requirements identified within the Business Continuity Management Plan. Dependent on the size, nature, and diversity of the organization, the procedures can vary from simple and pragmatic brochures to volumes of complicated manuals and training exercises covering a multitude of subjects. Some of the generic procedures that should be included within any organization are the establishment of a company mission statement, general policy documents, personnel training requirements, and monitoring and validation techniques (internal and external). The identification of resource requirements (supported by appropriate budgets) is also essential to ensure that a Business Continuity Management Plan can be established, and effectively implemented and sustained.

The following sections describe the elements of the Business Continuity Management Plan.

POLICY DOCUMENTS All risk management policies should be periodically updated to reflect the current intelligence-driven threats, as well as the influences that any particular operating environment or activity may have upon the company and its procedures. All personnel should be informed of the current sources of risk, with appropriate details pertaining to how the risks might impact the organization, as well as the measures taken to address them. In order to ensure that all implemented measures are effective, an established Security Management System, or set of standard operating procedures (SOPs) can be used to guide daily activities in mitigating risk. The incident management plan (IMP) then supports managers in bringing any resulting emergency situation under control. These policy documents can be engineered at both the corporate and field levels and should also provide general guidelines on how to activate the incident management and crisis response teams, how individuals are expected to respond to an incident, who they should inform, and what other assets are available to support them. It is often useful for policy documents to be accompanied by relevant training and exercises to ensure that the policies are clearly understood and thoroughly rehearsed.

REPRESENTING INFORMATION   The ability of managers to understand the information being represented is defined by the manner in which data is structured, delivered, and presented. This is as important for both those attempting to understand and use the Business Continuity Management Plan and those attempting to gain support and buy-in from corporate and project leadership when developing the plans. Often information that is unstructured and poorly presented devalues critical information contained within the text. Simple techniques and systems of representation can make information easier to digest, as well as provide concise and logical frameworks for more effective delivery.

Companies should seek logical and succinct methods by which to capture and present information to the stakeholders and users of Business Continuity Management Plans so that well-structured and logically presented documents can be developed and consistently used. Consideration should be given to design a consistent framework for such policies and plans, enabling repeated use and reducing repetition and redundancies where possible. Professionally and logically presented materials also inspire greater confidence within a group and increase the likelihood that managers will read, understand, and use the guidance provided.

TRAINING   Training and rehearsals provide the most effective method by which to instill confidence in first responders and crisis managers, as well as create the crucial instinctive responses required of personnel when facing the common threats posed to people, an activity, or organization. Corporate and project management education and training are useful tools to run the crisis response plan through its paces. This is usually done through short seminars, training sessions, or desktop exercises, which require little resource support and focus on key decision makers and how they undertake their individual roles, as well as how they fit within the wider organizational structure. Technical and practical training may also be required in order to use the wide variety of equipment and personal skills necessary to meet the measures identified in the risk assessment, sanctioned in the Business Continuity Management Plan, and implemented in the risk management procedures and incident management plan. Training agencies should be selected according to their expertise and experience, with continued training requirements identified to prevent *skill fade*. Training should also include relevant outside agencies and independent monitoring assessors to ensure that the measures used are current and effective, and regionally oriented. The use of desktop exercises and practical training can also help focus management teams at different levels, at relatively low cost to the company.

The company should also not lose sight of the need to ensure that vendors, subcontractors, or teammates, whom the company may be responsible for or reliant on, are also appropriately educated and trained. Companies may opt to include such training as an element of a security vendor's contract—incorporating training or education of company staff as part of a preselection or predeployment requirement. This is particularly relevant in remote or challenged environments where a security management element can concurrently bring training value to the company.

Training plays a crucial part in ensuring that the crisis response plans can be effectively utilized during an event, and educational packages can include management and personnel crisis response training, tactical procedures and emergency response drills, first aid, hostile environment training, and situational awareness training. The company should consider whether a vendor might also bring other skills to supplement its own training regimes and incorporate these into any training cycles. This additional element of service can be especially relevant where certain skill sets, such as first aid in Africa or cross-decking (i.e., moving from one vehicle to another during an incident) in Iraq, might be useful for company personnel to receive instruction on. Either the vendor or the company should document training program attendance and adjust other service area expectations to account for time expended on developing and imparting vendor-to-company training packages. Training records also evidence the company's efforts to minimize risk following an incident, or during an investigation or audit.

Often training is set within unrealistic conditions, without the chaos, confusion, erroneous reporting, and unpredictable responses that typically accompany a crisis situation. Training and evaluating managers should insert errors, confusion, and other debilitating factors within training exercises to create a realistic atmosphere for crisis management response. Should these problems not occur during actual crisis events, the crisis management team will typically respond better, having undergone more challenging training and exercise scenarios. The adage "plan for the best, train for the worst" will best support preparation of responding managers. Training should however always be positive in nature.

The company should also seek to capitalize on staff expertise to strengthen all professional categories within a contract. Training regimes should be in place not only to meet stipulated needs but also to expand or strengthen professional competence into supporting areas, where appropriate. Companies should seek areas in which vendors can, over time, further enhance service delivery through an expansion of staff skills sets, whether they are management capabilities or more practical skills. Training can also play a part in a socioeconomic plan whereby local employees receive sustainable employment training to better their economic situation as well as their community. For sustained operations, a "train the trainer" scheme is also highly beneficial in building up a broad base of capabilities within a project team or local workforce in order to reduce the effects of a crisis event.

COST JUSTIFICATION It is often difficult to gain support for the allocation of budgets to risk management, as costs may be spread across multiple business units with no clear delineation or evidencing of value. Often companies will seek to place risk management and security within a commercial context, aiming to minimize cost while increasing service delivery as a result. Risk management is commonly viewed as a cost center, with no identifiable or tangible benefits to the business unit, but a clear cost to the project's bottom-line profits. Justifying the investment of fiscal resources to developing a Business Continuity Management Plan and associated sub-plans such as the IMP can be a difficult part of the risk manager's function, especially when risk is based largely on professional judgment, rather than evidenced fact.

A historical cost analysis of known crisis events can illustrate risk impacts to business or project management, as well as provide a basis for cost analysis. In addition, if operations have been ongoing within a region by the company, or similar companies, a historical trend analysis of risks as well as security costs can be developed. Corporate risk tolerances and the experiences and expertise of corporate leaders will also define the approach and cost acceptance for effective risk management. To support the justification for investment in plan design and the engagement of risk policy consultancy, or the internal focus needed to create policies, plans, and procedures, companies should seek to develop systems that can be quickly and effectively realigned to meet new business or project requirements, demonstrating their versatility in terms of being used repeatedly to support company diverse needs. The development of one-time use policies, procedures, and plans might be required for unique projects; however, more frequently retailoring can be undertaken using (initially) well-developed materials—demonstrating utility and an increased value of such plans.

CRISIS MANAGEMENT TOOLS   Contingency planning should include developing tools and mechanisms that enable the flow of accurate information as well as authorized decision making and resource allocation to support the management of a crisis event. Communications plans, decision matrixes, procurement and resource plans, and other tools and policies will support a crisis team to bring control to an event quickly and effectively. Thought should be given to designing effective tools by which to meet as many concurrent and pan-dimensional aspects of the Business Continuity Management Plan as possible.

Reference Mapping   One aspect of representing information is through reference mapping. The management of a crisis at a single site is difficult under the best of circumstances, but crisis management becomes significantly more challenging when there are numerous sites involved, or when a crisis management team is seeking to control an incident response of a remote or unfamiliar location. An effective way to annotate critical locations and routes, as well as specific areas of interest, quickly and efficiently is to create project site or work area grid overlays. Such overlays allow for the immediate identification of a problem area or control point during emergencies, whether the threat comes from industrial, criminal, or natural sources. Such tools also facilitate process interfaces between the project and the executive crisis teams, as well as with supporting military, law enforcement, or civil agencies. The overlays for a specific project should all use the same scales, symbols, and numbering systems to ensure consistency. Exhibit 1.19, Project Site McKinsey Area Grid Overlay, provides an example of a simple project grid overlay. Integration with supporting groups, both in-house and external, needs to be done as early as possible in the planning process and should include the locations and routes for external groups to meet with project site groups (especially incident control points), or by

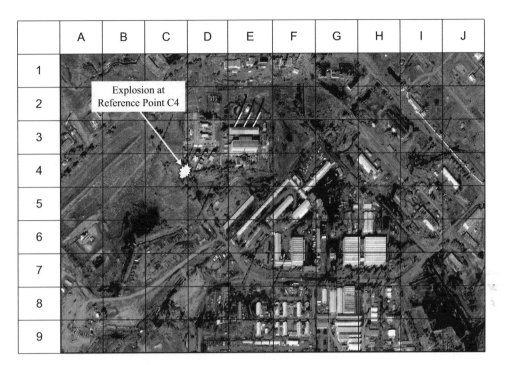

Explosion at
Reference Point C4

EXHIBIT 1.19 Project Site McKinsey Area Grid Overlay

which groups can safely enter the site. This form of visual representation is also useful to illustrate existing labor requirements by denoting staffing numbers by post or activity. Such tools should be used as part of the IMP reporting system.

Developing Schematics The company project or security managers (or a good security provider's management team) will be able to develop detailed and professional project site and building schematic plans and diagrams without the use of graphic artists or complex IT programs. Such diagrams can be overlays of satellite imagery or be drawn independently of such technological resources, bringing the same value as a project grid overlay to represent information more clearly to the company's executive and project teams. Such visuals provide an invaluable tool for crisis response management, as illustrated in Exhibit 1.20. Schematics and diagrams will be especially important if mapping or floor plans are unavailable or out of date. Schematics and diagrams form an important part of security documentation and should be as simple and clear as possible.

Facility structures should also be captured by the use of floor plans, as illustrated in Exhibit 1.21 using PowerPoint and Exhibit 1.22 using Visio. This is especially useful if personnel have not visited the site themselves, as it allows management to visualize the layout of the local areas and project facilities as well as attribute activities to space in advance of a visit for planning purposes. That said, often floor plans are restricted or not available. The company or a security vendor's security

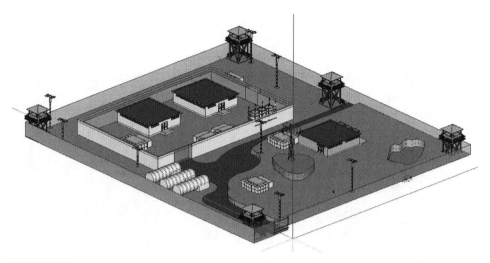

EXHIBIT 1.20 Site Schematics

manager may be required to map out building structures or layouts quickly for
reports, security plans, and response protocols.

Such schematics and floor plans should be included within the IMP or associated
security plans in order to provide a simple and clear method of reporting the location
of a crisis event. Whether building schematics and floor designs are available or must
be locally produced by managers, these tools can also be forwarded with written
reports to better illustrate the location of a crisis point. Simple IT programs such
as PowerPoint and Visio can enable consultants and managers to professionally
and accurately present information. This will be of significant value to those crisis
managers who may be remote from or unfamiliar with the layout of the affected
area, allowing them to visualize the issue and place it within a geographic context.

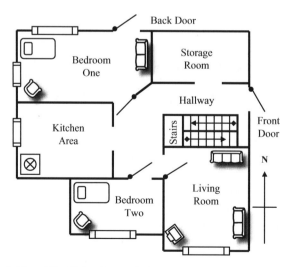

EXHIBIT 1.21 Simple Floor Plan Using PowerPoint

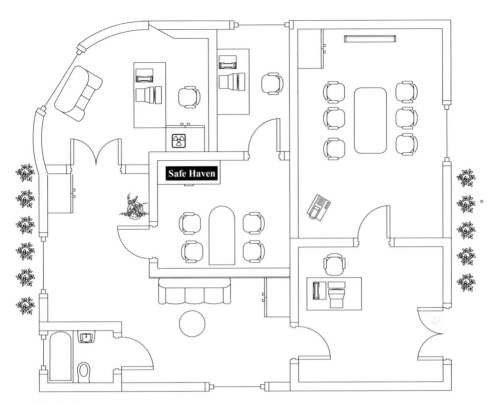

Safe Haven

EXHIBIT 1.22 Simple Floor Plan Using Visio

SUSTAINING THE BUSINESS CONTINUITY MANAGEMENT PLAN   Enterprise resilience should be a factor of the company's corporate culture. It should be used as part of general business, both in terms of market entry or business and project development planning, as well as when undertaking work. The Business Continuity Management Plan should be sustained through scheduled and event-driven audits, reviews, and amendments—without which plans will quickly become redundant and ineffective. The Business Continuity Management Plan should grow and adjust with company focuses and operations, through a cyclically driven process of understanding the organization and its goals in order to fulfill the strategic and tactical requirements of the plan—in alignment with corporate and business drivers. This will allow the focused development and implementation of the Business Continuity Management Plan measures and responses, with exercising and validating the plans on a scheduled or event-driven basis, as illustrated by Exhibit 1.23.

The Communications Plan

The *communications plan* provides the medium by which information and decisions can flow most effectively from the point or origination of the crisis event cascading or flowing to specific points throughout incident and crisis management organizations within a company. Information flow under the best of circumstances is often poor within large, complex, or geographically separated groups or organizations.

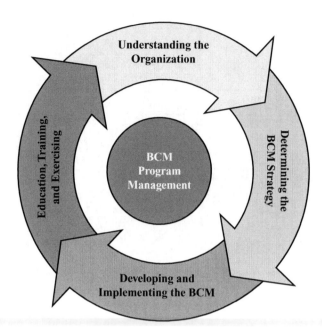

EXHIBIT 1.23 Business Continuity Management Program Management

Under crisis situations, the flow of information becomes even more disjointed and inaccurate as the event will inherently create confusion, and management is often absorbed in dealing with the issues, rather than in channeling accurate information to supporting or corporate offices. Information managers are typically those managing the incident at the field level, or the risk or security managers and directors within a company. Where multiple management elements are involved, it can be useful to designate key information managers within a crisis management organization who are responsible for collating and analyzing multiple sources of information in order to streamline information flow to appropriate decision makers and supporting groups. Where possible, multiple parties should funnel information into capture points, which then feed condensed and accurate data onward to decision makers and resource managers, as illustrated in Exhibit 1.24, Information Management Flows.

Exhibit 1.25 illustrates a simplified communications plan that can be used to support both the IMP and the broader Business Continuity Management Plan requirements. Company telephone directories are useful for capturing considerable

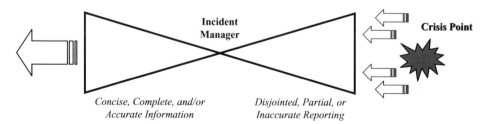

EXHIBIT 1.24 Information Management Flows

Organization	Appointment	Name	Title	Group Code	Location	Mobile No.	Office No.	E-mail	Deputy
Corporate CRT									
Company CRT	Crisis Commander	John Hopkins	CEO	A	Pasadena	011 - 223322	011 - 232221	Jhopkins@hillens.com	Les Dennis
Company CRT	Legal Counsel	Sid Arthan	Legal VP	A	Chicago	011 - 334433	011 - 192929	sartha@hillens.com	Claire Smith
Company CRT	Finance Director	Alex Rose	Finance VP	B	Pasadena	011 - 998877	011 - 819272	a.rose@hillens.com	Jim Donals
Company CRT	Physical Risk/Security	Craig Russel	Security Director	A	Pasadena	011 - 617171	011 - 929281	Crussel@hillens.com	Frank Janes
Country CRT									
Country CRT	Crisis Commander	Sal McDonal	Chief of Party	B	Khartoum	011 - 273828	123 - 818181	cop.power@hillens.com	Jane Mansfield
Country CRT	Logistics Manager	Jonny Watkins	Operations Maneger	B	Khartoum	011 - 929299	123 - 992929	opsmngr.power@hillens.com	Jack Hill
Country CRT	Physical Risk/Security	Fred Crano	Security Manager	B	Khartoum	011 - 929292	123 - 898282	sudansy@hillens.com	Mike Power
Program IRT									
Program—Power	Program Manager	Andrew Riley	Program Manager	B	Khartoum	123 - 4568987	123 - 589706	ariley@hillens.com	Sal McDonald
Program—Power	Logistics Manager	Brian Mavis	Operations Manager	C	Khartoum	123 - 002020	123 - 939292	bmavis@hillens.com	Jonny Watkins
Program—Power	Physical Risk/Security	Mick Fillis	Security Director	C	Khartoum	123 - 929281	123 - 887766	mfillis@hillens.com	Sid Andrews
Project IRT									
Juba Power Station	Crisis Commander	John McDonald	Project Manager	C	Juba City	123 - 445554	123 - 465758	Jmcdonal@hillens.com	Kevin Pillar
Juba Power Station	Logistics Manager	Sid Andrews	Security Manager	D	Juba City	123 - 446565	123 - 778888	Security@hillens.com	Fred Carney
Juba Power Station	Physical Risk/Security	Fred Carmey	Guard Commander	D	Juba City	123 - 777676	123 - 444554	Guard_cdr@hillens.com	None

Organization		Name	Title	Group Code	Location	Mobile No.	Office No.	E-mail	Deputy
Government Agencies									
Law Enforcement		Jim Harrington	Chief of Police	E	Juba City	123 - 4568987	123 - 589706	Jharrington@jubapolice.com	Inspector Davis
Military Forces		David Green	Colonel	B	Juba Camp	123 - 4567888	123 - 777668	Dgreen@sudan_mil.com	Major Smith
Embassy		Paul Simons	RSO	B	Khartoum	123 - 9909000	123 - 776545	rso@usembassy_sudan.com	Clare Williams
Commercial Support									
Medical Clinic	Medical Support	St. Francis	Emergency Room Operations	F	Juba City	123 - 999299	123 - 999929	francis@emergency.com	NA
Aviation Support	Movement	FlyGreen	Operations	F	Khartoum	123 - 002020	123 - 939292	operations@glvgreen.com	NA
Security Response	Additional Security	Shield	Tactical Operations	D	Juba City	123 - 929281	123 - 887766	TOC@shield.com	NA
Local Law Firm	Legal Support	McKinney	Legal Officer	TBD	Lagos	124 - 929292	124 - 929291	Legal.officer@mckinney.com	NA

Information Group Codes

- **Group Code A** Personnel have access to all information relating to the incident, including corporate strategic and tactical responses, as well as liability, legal, and public relations risks. Also, all secret or sensitive information from external sources, including embassies, consuls, military agencies, federal law enforcement, intelligence services, and host nation groups.

- **Group Code B** Personnel have access to all information relating to the incident, including corporate strategic and tactical responses, as well as liability, legal, and public relations risks. Also, all unrestricted or nonsensitive information from external sources, including embassies, consuls, military agencies, federal law enforcement, and other such groups.

- **Group Code C** Personnel have access to all information relating to the incident and corporate tactical responses. Also, all unrestricted or nonsensitive information from external sources, including embassies, consuls, military agencies, federal law enforcement, intelligence services, and host nation groups.

- **Group Code D** Personnel have access to all information relating to the incident and program-level tactical responses. Also, all unrestricted or nonsensitive information from external sources, including embassies, consuls, military agencies, federal law enforcement, intelligence services, and host nation groups.

- **Group Code E** Personnel have access to all information relating to the incident and program-level tactical responses, as well as selected information provided from multi-agency-agency unrestricted sources, as it relates specifically to their area of responsibility.

- **Group Code F** Personnel will have access to selected information relating to project-level tactical responses, as well as threat alerts related to their specific appointment or function within the project.

EXHIBIT 1.25 Crisis Communications Plan

amounts of personnel and organizational contact details. However, during a crisis event a narrowed selection of contact names and details should be on hand to ensure that managers can quickly place persons against functions, and so better initiate response plans and reach out to those with the knowledge and authority to offer advice, make decisions, and mobilize support. It is important to keep such communication plans current, as a typical failing of many organizations is not to update the names and numbers listed there; frequently the majority are incorrect when the time comes to use the plan. More strategic communications plans might also be developed to apportion groups or organizations to responsibilities and functions, rather than to individuals. A communications plan may be layered and involve multiple matrixes to capture both internal and external decision makers, resources, and support. Communication plans may also be linked to decision making, interface, and resource management plans, either as separate documents or as a combined matrix.

Each crisis event will be unique and will involve changing interactions with external groups, whether they are government support organizations or other commercial enterprises. Where a company has high-profile activities, or where a crisis event is significant, the media may seek information from both the incident site and the corporate offices. Typically, program management should seek to avoid contact with the press, deferring to a nominated public relations representative. In addition, care should be taken in communicating directly with families; such activities are best conducted at a personal level rather than by indirect means, and they usually are undertaken by a corporately appointed spokesperson trained in managing sensitive situations. Companies may also seek local law enforcement support when imparting bad news to families or when seeking to prevent press access to affected families. A communications plan should seek to allocate the correct responsibilities for functions within the Business Continuity Management Plan in order to avoid well-intentioned but inappropriate communications both within and external to the company. The communications plan should also focus on how information is shared, as well as permissions and authorities for information release. Some suggested recommendations that might be part of a communications plan's information and communications guidance section follow:

- Always gather accurate facts—never pass on assumptions or speculations as facts.
- Provide an incident data call report at the earliest opportunity, and update information regularly.
- Do not liaise with the press. Direct them to the appropriate spokesperson within the company.
- Do not pass casualty details outside of incident response team(s) until approval is given by authorized management. Information on fatalities should be passed only to the corporate crisis response team.
- Close communication mediums outside of the crisis management team if required (and appropriate) to control information flow and avoid rumors or erroneous information.
- Injury and casualty facts must be accurate—names, details, extent, location, and so forth.
- Warn government agencies for possible support requirements early.

- Confirm facts again. Do this on a regular basis so that information is current and accurate.
- Alert supporting agencies as to what you are doing, when it will be done, and what you need for support.
- Conduct a local group briefing at the first appropriate opportunity in order to pass on accurate information to the appropriate contractors. Conduct regular updates.
- Write all documents and reports in a manner usable for internal and external audits.
- Collate and deliver all materials to corporate offices for review and archiving.
- Ensure that information is up to date within any plans, and test them periodically.
- Make plans simple and logical to use; avoid redundancy where possible.
- Ensure that those leaving the organization are taken out of communication plans and distribution lists.

Defining information *group codes* also may be useful, or at times necessary, to ensure that only appropriate personnel receive sensitive information. Information may need to be filtered for certain management levels, or be restricted to only those who need, or are cleared to receive, that information. There is an inherent desire for managers to have access to all information—and often understanding peripheral activities and influences does support better decision making. However, the company should ask itself:

- Is real value gained from sharing a sensitive component of information—does it really support the crisis response performance for that person to know these facts?
- What risks are associated with sharing information—does sharing this information compromise the company, information provider, or employees?
- Will the group or individual be capable of protecting that information—will they then be able to filter subsequent information sharing themselves?

Exhibit 1.25 indicates a simple table that can be used to capture the different layers of internal and external crisis management functions that might be required in order to mobilize the correct resources needed to bring knowledge, expertise, and guidance to the crisis event. Such tables also ensure that the correct personnel are advised as to the situation, supporting the channeling and flow of information to multiple groups and individuals. E-mail distribution lists and text alerts can also be developed so that primary and secondary personnel are always included in correspondence.

INFORMATION CASCADE SYSTEMS   The communications plan should contain a documented information or reporting cascade system (or phone tree) to establish at the outset of a project or business activity responsibilities and communication channels for alerting management and assisting the effective flow of accurate information. Such systems can also apply to companywide response requirements. Cascade systems may involve the delivery of predetermined reports to alert company managers through e-mails and phone calls, or to mobilize internal and external resources to respond along predefined planning measures. The communications plan should be readily accessible to those implementing the IMP so that they are able to flow information horizontally and vertically within the company, as well as draw upon the right help and resources in order to best manage their part of the crisis response measures.

Cascade systems or phone trees provide an effective medium where information flows to focal or nodal points, who then have defined persons or groups to contact. This way a clean and accurate delivery of information is achieved quickly, as illustrated in Exhibit 1.26, Information Cascade System. In addition, all contact details should be listed within an easy-to-use document to avoid confusion and make the reporting system as simple and efficient as possible. This document should also provide some basic guidelines so that simple but fundamental errors are not made by the incident response and crisis response teams during times of high stress.

Such plans should be reviewed by all managers so that they are familiar with the requirements. These documents should be placed in operations or response centers or other appropriate locations as a matter of protocol. Web-based systems can also be highly effective, unless the internet or power provisions fail. Contact details and responsibilities should be double-checked and updated where necessary, as when needed the most they are often found to be inaccurate. Senior management staff should confirm that all submanagers are aware of the requirements and guidelines and that they display these documents in the required locations. However, materials should also be protected so that unauthorized persons do not have access to contact details, names, or other sensitive details.

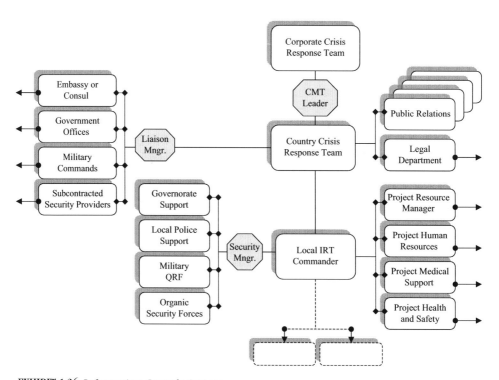

EXHIBIT 1.26 Information Cascade System

It can also be useful to annotate any particular roles or responsibilities associated with each appointment if the Business Continuity Management Plan has elements that could be considered. Companies may also wish to develop an automated messaging plan in order to text or e-mail predefined information to a wide audience, ensuring that a one-time message is delivered to a mass audience. In addition, defining an organized manner by which to impart information should support an organization's ability to cascade information quickly and accurately.

Organizational Interface Plans

Within any project environment, but especially within challenging, new or remote operating environments, it is useful for the company or its vendors to establish a network of external relationships or contacts who might be positioned to support the company in the event of an emergency. Companies should develop an *emergency management information system* (EMIS) to enable continuity and interoperability between emergency and management stakeholders. The EMIS provides the structure by which emergency plans and policies can be integrated between organic and external groups and agencies. The company (during the solicitation for subcontractors) should evaluate a security vendor's ability to draw on the strengths and capabilities of external agencies to support the company's business activities, as well as crisis response needs. The company should also seek to establish its own network of relationships in order to better position itself to operate more efficiently and respond more effectively—punching above its weight in terms of organic resources to actual capabilities.

While leveraging external resources and capabilities (either directly or via a third party) exponentially increases the company's crisis resources, it is important that the project staff and supporting vendor companies understand the parameters and limitations in which they are permitted to operate when engaging external resources to support the company. Reputational issues, corporate policies, and political sensitivities are but a few considerations that field staff may not fully take into account when attempting to find pragmatic solutions to their risk issues.

Establishing a formal integration plan (at various levels) also reduces duplication of effort between the vendor and the company, as well as limiting any other conflicts of interest when considering which agencies to approach for collaborative support agreements or memorandums of understanding (MOUs). Such elements should be included within the response guidelines of the IMP in a simplified format to guide managers to supporting groups as part of the incident management response. When using a subcontractor to support such a plan, the company should develop a policy to articulate how external agencies might be used to augment the company's business activity, and any limitations or restrictions which might apply. The following sample issues for integration consideration might be included:

- Confirm that liaison has been sanctioned by the company (and parent company).
- Confirm who is authorized to negotiate and sanction agreements, as well as the nature and scope of such agreements.
- Confirm the language to be used and the limitations imposed.
- Articulate how such integration affects the business activities, as well as any teammates or subcontractors.

- Confirm the extent of communications networking and emergency communications plans.
- Confirm the geographical proximity of support agencies, as well as the means by which to initiate support.
- Discuss the level of support available or desired—as well as what it will cost.
- Confirm whether nonreciprocal or reciprocal agreements (or mutual aid agreements) are preferred, or memorandums of understanding (MOUs) and reciprocal agreements.
- Identify where IMP responses can be augmented or enhanced by the integration of external supporting agencies.
- Identify where security plans can be integrated to further enhance project security.

THE VALUE In foreign, remote, or challenging environments, it is rare that any business operates in complete isolation, whether it is a gold mining operation in Kazakhstan, an oil refinery in Indonesia, a hotel chain in Nigeria, or a textiles plant in India. Establishing good rapport with external agencies can provide some degree of sharing or transfer of risk responsibility. External agencies can give invaluable support in identifying threats through the use of good intelligence as well as providing risk reduction measures. They may also be useful in assisting with incidents and contributing to the positive resolution and closure of incidents. A good example is the link between the civilian police and the military for the security of sensitive locations, with the provision of accurate intelligence, interception of known individuals, area cordoning support, handling of individuals, and any crime scene investigations that may result. Federal agencies can also support efforts against counterfeiting and cyber crimes, coercion and intimidation rackets, and insurgent or terrorist targeting of company interests. Comprehensive joint exercises with agencies that might provide assistance to large, complex or high profile organizations should be included in the risk management program. If necessary, external support representatives should be included on the crisis management team.

In some circumstances company project sites might have an outer security ring of collocated military forces, such as coalition or United Nations military groups or host nation government or tribal security forces. In some areas, there may be no such forces, or they might not be positioned to support project operations and security. At worst, local security may be unreliable or, in extreme cases, complicit in disrupting the project or business venture. Even in the worst cases, however, it is still useful to consider liaison with local security forces for their inclusion into the outer security ring so as to avoid unnecessary polarization of the project. Engagement plans often support an intangible but highly valuable layer of risk management for business activities. The establishment of project operations in the most extreme of environments should consider the incorporation of external support such as military organizations and local security into the project security team, ensuring a layered security footprint with overlapping security arrangements to significantly strengthen project operations, as well as allow the company to more effectively respond to crisis incidents. In these circumstances a clear understandings of the cost against benefits should be established as well as how such integration might bring additional risks to the company. Exhibit 1.27, Crisis Response: Interface Plan, illustrates how the

	Agreement	Armored Vehicle Evacuation	Soft Skin Vehicle Evacuation	Air Evacuation (Regional)	Air Evacuation (National)	Provision of a Safe Haven	Casualty—First-Line Medical Support	Surgery—Medical Support	Armed Quick Reaction Force	Emergency Armed Facility Guards	Explosive Ordnance Clearance Support	Intelligence and Threat Warnings	Legal Support	Mutual Mass Evacuation Plan	Kidnapping and Ransom Advisory Services	Emergency Water Provision	Emergency Food Provision	Emergency Generator Provision	Arrest and Detention Support
Company Y	Written MOU	✓	✓				✓		✓	✓		✓		✓					
Local Militia	Written MOU		✓	✓	✓	✓	✓	✓	✓	✓	✓	✓	✓	✓		✓	✓	✓	✓
U.S. Embassy	Verbal MOU			✓	✓	✓	✓						✓	✓	✓				✓
Coalition Forces	Written MOU	✓		✓		✓	✓	✓	✓			✓	✓		✓				✓
Company X	Verbal MOU		✓				✓					✓		✓					
Security Company Z	Contracted	✓	✓				✓			✓	✓	✓				✓	✓	✓	

EXHIBIT 1.27 Crisis Response: Interface Plan

company can display in a simple way the range of crisis response support it may have available from external groups.

Interface plans in terms of support and resource provisions will be influenced by any difficulties that the groups offering collaborative support to the company might also be experiencing. Occasionally a risk event will affect all parties, at which time those resources offered will be tied to meeting the needs of the owners. Therefore, the interface plan should not be considered the single answer to dealing with crisis events, but rather a multiplier of capability. Interface plans also are designed to indicate what support or agreements are in place, rather than the more granular level of resources actually provided in terms of quantity or frequency—this is an aspect of the *resource management plan*. The two plans should be linked where appropriate as complementary elements of the Business Continuity Management Plan.

LOCAL GOVERNMENT INTERFACE   In both passive and hostile environments, it can be useful to liaise with host nation government offices and agencies, in terms of both coordinating security plans and securing emergency support in case of a hostile incident or medical evacuation. In addition, liaison with local law enforcement and military agencies can be useful in the event of an arrest or a detention. Local government and security forces can also offer information on the risk environment and possible calendar events that might affect the company, as well as physical support to the company that might reduce risk. In addition, local government relationships can be leveraged to provide insights into how to work more effectively within a local community, although at times local government groups may be complicit within any threats faced to the company. In many countries, both national and local government officials may be corrupt; in such cases, ways to avoid supporting corrupt or illegal activities while still supporting and engaging leadership, communities, and nationals through employment should be considered as part of an overall business and security approach. The delineation between corruption and local business customs and practices should also be considered as part of the strategic approach, as these may not always be clear-cut.

LOCAL COMMUNITY INTERFACE   The success of projects often depends on local community support, and companies should leverage their own as well as any contracted vendor's local experience, relationships, and knowledge to establish a community liaison and development plan to support their business goals. This is especially relevant in challenging environments where a local community can actively oppose business operations or, conversely, reduce threats through resistance to or the reporting of hostile activities. Community opposition (or support) is frequently found in third-world or postwar environments, such as some African states, where major oil companies encounter significant issues due to poor local relationships, despite considerable local development efforts and social programs. Dealing with the local community requires an understanding of the culture, power brokers, and local influences. A significant degree of sensitivity often is required to avoid misunderstanding or offense, both by the company and by the subcontracted vendors. Successful relations and communication with the local community can be the critical aspect of risk mitigation and incident management for project operations, and corporate and program managers must establish the level of interaction that might be required to support their business needs.

Where possible, local communities and leadership should be included in both the planning and the implementation of all appropriate project activities. During the assessment phase of project planning, various community representatives—ministries, governors, local police forces, elders, religious leaders, and representatives of various associations at provincial, district, and village levels—might be included in planning conferences. It might be useful to interview these stakeholders to identify their thoughts regarding security and project impacts as well as their own community needs and possible socioeconomic or engagement plans. These same individuals and groups should be consulted during the implementation phase of the activity, and regular meetings should be held to sustain strong local relationships. By involving the local community from the outset of a project, a company can gain a level of acceptance, reducing risk and ensuring that external resources can be called upon to support incident management. The following guidelines might be useful in creating a successful relationship with a local community:

- Confirm the company's policy and intention of engagement with the local community.
- Establish an understanding of the local culture, especially sensitivities.
- Identify the *real* power brokers and leaders.
- Establish the best way in which to engage and communicate with local leaders.
- Conduct an intelligence review of local community involvement in possible hostile activities.
- Review possible methods by which to gain trust and support from the local community—investment in schools, medical support, and so forth.
- Consider local leadership meetings to discuss the impact of operations on the local community.
- Involve the community in decision making where possible to gain buy-in.
- Discuss methods by which hostile activities can be reported.

- Consider methods by which to employ the local community, where appropriate.
- Engage local businesses and ventures in partnering or subcontractor arrangements.

EXPATRIATE GOVERNMENT AND DIPLOMATIC INTERFACES   Whether a company is operating in Africa or Afghanistan, it is always useful to establish liaison with embassies and foreign forces in order to seek additional support for a business activity's crisis management and incident response requirements. This might be direct relationship development between the company with an embassy, or through working groups organized or supported by governments. At times these external groups will offer little or no support; on other occasions their support may be critical to the success and safety of the project during a crisis event. Any level of international cooperation outside of organic company-contracted resources brings additional knowledge, expertise, and capabilities that would otherwise be absent. An appreciation of the external group's strengths and weaknesses is required in order to ensure that the business activity does not become reliant on inconsistent levels of support. Where possible, memorandums of understanding (MOUs) between the company and government or military forces should be established to define what will, might, and will not be provided to the company.

Also, if the company's activities bring a benefit to a country—whether providing economic development, agricultural programs, or education and employment—embassies may consider a commercial project to be an indirect element of their own programs and goals, and may be persuaded to offer support that otherwise might not be expected. Both the company and the vendor should seek synergies with foreign government interests in order to identify and leverage any value their business may bring to that government. Companies should also research government support agencies and resources in order to ensure that they understand what is available to them—what capabilities and resources they can leverage and where they can draw upon proven experience and materials to design or enhance existing policies, plans, and approaches.

Some government agencies will support businesses operating both domestically and abroad, offering advice and practical support to enable better business preparedness and recovery. Exhibit 1.28 provides examples of such organizations.

OTHER COMPANY INTERFACES   Companies should consider establishing reciprocal or mutual aid agreements with other commercial organizations to establish and leverage a consortium of support. Such organizations as the Overseas Security Advisory Council (OSAC) and Security Information Service for Business Overseas (SISBO) set up forums to centralize issues and solutions for U.S. and UK businesses and organizations abroad, and the company may wish to exploit this concept by drawing strength from other commercial groups. It might be possible and appropriate (with permissions from the company and the vendor) for the company to develop reciprocal arrangements with other commercial organizations to augment security policies, procedures, and responses. Mindful of commercial and liability risks, companies can mitigate threats with measured integration of specified fields and areas with external organizations, through either loose or formal agreements. In addition, and perhaps more importantly, responses can be greatly enhanced if companies provide mutual

EXHIBIT 1.28   Supporting Organizations for Business Continuity Management Interface Plans

Organization	Web Site	Remarks
Overseas Security Advisory Council (OSAC)	www.osac.gov	U.S. government–based organization designed to support U.S. businesses overseas in terms of advisory councils and security education
London Resilience Forum	www.londonprepared. gov.uk	UK government–based organization focused on business risk management for companies operating within the London area (United Kingdom)
Security Information Service for Business Overseas (SISBO)	www.fco.gov.uk/en/ business-trade/sisbo/	UK foreign and Commonwealth office designed to advise British businesses overseas on security and risk management issues
Federal Emergency Management Agency (FEMA)	www.fema.gov.com	U.S. federal disaster and emergency response organization
National Response Framework (NRF)	www.fema.gov/ emergency/nrf/	Division of FEMA responsible for supporting unified responses to crisis events, as well as for organizations preparing business continuity, management protocols and plans
Department of Homeland Security	www.dhs.gov	U.S. government agency providing advice to individuals and businesses on security related issues, as well as crisis response
Locating an Emergency Agency	www.rateitall.com	Provides guidance on different emergency and disaster response organizations
Washington Military Department: Emergency Management Division	www.emd.wa.gov	State government organization focused on military cooperation for crisis response in the state of Washington
Northeast Document Conservation Center (NEDCC)	www.dplan.org/	Provides a free disaster planning tool to help organizations evaluate and manage risk

cooperative agreements where other company facilities and resources can be used by a threatened group during time of need.

Medical Response and Repatriation Plan

Often local managers will be required to deal with a range of medical emergencies—from heatstroke for site workers to falls, breaks, heart attacks, and general illnesses. A medical emergency within a domestic setting where emergency services can respond quickly and administer medical stabilization en route to more comprehensive facilities can test an organization and first responders; add to this a remote site, hostile environment, or third-world transportation mediums and medical facilities, and the crisis can become even more pronounced. At worst, companies may have to deal with a life-threatening condition that requires immediate stabilization and evacuation to distant medical facilities, or in some instances the repatriation of a fatality to the home country from a foreign work area.

Companies should develop a medical response and repatriation plan in order to manage various situations, from the common daily and mundane problems to the unique and significant medical emergencies that would face any workforce, and place this plan in the context of the operating environment in which personnel are working. For medical emergencies, companies should consider the basic elements of:

- Stabilization and initial treatment of casualties.
- Movement in-country to secondary care facilities (multiple movement mediums).
- Comprehensive (surgical and specialist) treatment facilities.
- Movement from country to Western clinics and hospitals out of country.
- Insurance coverage and payment plans.
- Safe and secure treatment considerations.

For repatriations of remains, companies should consider the following basic elements for the effective movement of a deceased employee from the country:

- Cold storage and container resources for cold storage.
- Movement in-country and transfer points for cadaver storage.
- Documentation requirements and insurance stipulations.
- Autopsy and embalming requirements and providers.
- Air freight and escort resources and policy guidelines.
- Family liaison and support services.
- Reporting and documentation needs.
- Morale and welfare implications for staff.

Companies should have clear and well-planned measures in place to deal with medical emergencies, as well as the first stages of a repatriation task. The IMP will play a key role in the initial response to both requirements, ensuring that resources are mobilized to quickly move a casualty through a medical evacuation process, or ensure that a fatality is properly administered from the outset. The medical response and repatriation plan may be linked to a section within the interface and resource management plans in terms of drawing upon or leveraging organic and external support, as well as defining which resources will support medical and repatriation tasks.

Public Relations Plan

Crisis events will invariably affect the image and reputation of a company, at times attracting hostile attention from the media or special interest groups. The company's reputation is an intangible commodity whose value has serious and at times devastating consequences to a company if undermined. The ease of broadcasting information or images worldwide and through multiple mediums can create an immediate and catastrophic crisis for companies as they struggle to establish facts and control over an event themselves, often resulting in companies lagging behind the media in terms of understanding and responding to a crisis situation. The value of the IMP in terms of separating facts from rumor or speculation, as well as exerting control over the event, is an important contributing element of a public relations plan.

Corporate or crisis communications through a public relations medium is designed to safeguard the value and confidence of a company's brand, as well as the image and reputation of a company, group, or business activity. Reputation might be defined as the social or commercial evaluation toward a person, group, or organization. It is especially important to businesses whose stock values and market productivity are directly connected to their status within a commercial sector and dependent on investor and client confidence. Mature public relations plans can also offset the effects of liability claims and publicly demonstrate the company's efforts to mitigate risk and protect employees, investments, or activities. Public relations might be focused outward, meeting external risks to the corporate interests, as well as inward, protecting the morale and productivity of the employees.

Reputation acts on different levels of agency—individual and supra-individual. At the supra-individual level, reputation concerns groups, communities, collectives, and social entities such as firms, corporations, organizations, countries, and cultures. It affects phenomena of different scale, from everyday life to relationships between nations. The impact of reputation is often ignored, with no clear or tangible connection toward associated *real* impacts upon business success and operations. Reputation includes *image*, a global or averaged evaluation of a company—its activities, productivity, capabilities, and executive management competence. Reputation often aligns with the perceived image or branding of a business. Image is a dynamic element and subject to immediate change, either through actual events or through speculation and rumor. Misinformation or erroneous reporting can severally damage a company's image and thus reputation, and reputation recovery is often difficult, problematic, slow, and highly costly. Therefore, a defining value of the IMP is supporting accurate reporting from the outset of a crisis.

Companies such as Johnson & Johnson, as well as more recently CACI International Inc., have invested millions of dollars in protecting their brands and corporate interests resulting from such incidents as the Tylenol poisonings and the Abu Ghraib prison scandal. Companies should understand their strengths as well as limitations and seek outside support where necessary to ensure they have a robust public relations plan. Developing a plan that is aligned to strategic and granular risks can better position the company to manage reputational and liability risks resulting from a crisis situation.

PUBLIC RELATIONS DEPARTMENTS   Establishing a well-trained public relations department to deal with media and general public inquiries is necessary to ensure that an organization reduces potentially harmful press coverage during normal operations, but especially in the event of an emergency situation. The establishment of an effective communications plan, media management measures, and accurate reporting measures, or a crisis communications system, ensures that the collation of information is swift and accurate, with an efficient and sanctioned means of delivery to the relevant elements of a crisis management team, employees, their families, often antagonistic news media, and other relevant agencies in a timely and accurate manner. The IMP plays a key part in developing early information reporting flows and supporting the public relations department in defining the company's stance and approach to an event—as well as the facts of the situation. Some corporate and public image aspects to contingency planning include:

- Providing only proven facts—avoid speculation or assumption.
- Understand the situation as quickly as possible—investigate immediately.
- Demonstrate that focus is being applied and resources mobilized.
- Be honest and up-front—admit blame but challenge erroneous reporting.
- Respond to inquiries and robustly question errors.
- Consider multiple communications mediums to get the message across—interviews, conferences, web sites, publications, announcements, television, and radio.
- Vet information and sanction release.
- Have a well-trained and experienced spokesperson—ensure that the spokesperson has all the facts.

Companies should establish an effective intermediate body between the management executive and external agencies (media, families, government) to ensure that the corporate image is promoted and maintained, while avoiding unnecessary speculation and inaccurate allocation of blame by the media or general public. Erroneous speculation often leads to a loss of confidence within an organization and undermines the aims and values of the group. A company may wish to provide training as well as preprepared public announcements to respond to likely threats, thus ensuring that staff are readied, with supporting materials, to deal with an incident quickly and effectively.

ESTABLISHING THE FACTS The IMP will play a critical part in allowing corporate leadership to implement an effective public relations plan during the early stages of a crisis event. Accurate and timely reporting of information allows the public relations officer to determine the company risks, their impacts, and the appropriate stance the company should take to best manage the situation. The data call reports within the IMP, sent typically from the point of crisis, will guide decision making as more senior and experienced resources are mobilized to manage the issue and consolidate the flow of information within the group. The public relations plan might therefore have stages—the immediate responses to meet initial questions from media groups, as well as more mature and measured response stages to manage longer-term issues.

Information should always be accurate and factual; speculation should be avoided. Information should be verified to ensure accuracy, and where possible transparency should be adopted as a guiding principle, as this often meets the longer-term interests of a company. Companies should avoid rushing to judgment until all the facts are known and verified.

PRESENTING INFORMATION Only trained and experienced spokespeople should interact with the media and other groups in order to protect the company's interests. Information should be vetted through corporate officers, as well as legal resources if appropriate, prior to release. Often prepreparing press releases to meet postulated public relations crisis events can support the company in delivering information in a more measured and professional manner, rather than wasting valuable time

EXHIBIT 1.29   Sample Preprepared Press Release

An industrial accident occurred at _____ resulting in ____ fatalities and ____ injuries. The cause of the accident resulted from _____. The situation at the site is now under control and we have activated our crisis response measures in partnership with the emergency response services in order to ensure the safety of the workers who have remained on-site. There is no danger to residents within the area; however, we would ask you to stay away from the site so that access routes are not blocked and the emergency services can do their work. As you can appreciate, we are working hard to gather all the facts while we manage this crisis situation, so that families can be contacted as quickly as possible and advised of the situation and the welfare of their loved ones. We would ask the media to respect and be sensitive to the losses and concerns of the workers' families at this time, avoiding speculation and rumor. We have established an emergency hotline, and families can speak to our crisis management team on _____. We will also be providing regular verbal updates at our crisis center located at _____. We will hold briefings every ____ hours, starting from _____. We will ensure that accurate information is passed on to families and the media as quickly as possible. Please be patient at this time. We will provide the next update at _____. We will also post information on _____.

during high-stress and fast-tempo crisis management situations. Such preprepared press releases might follow the simple format in Exhibit 1.29.

Such preprepared press releases can cover a broad spectrum of likely events and support timely and well-crafted public information releases to demonstrate that the company has some degree of control over the situation and is attempting to meet the needs of both families and the press concurrently. Such releases may reduce the level of speculation and might be fed from IMP data call report information.

Resource and Procurement Management Plans

The Business Continuity Management Plan will function well only if properly re-sourced. In terms of contingency planning, resource scheduling and cross-utilizations should be components of the overall service delivery goals of both the company and any subcontractors. In terms of implementing both the IMP and more comprehensive and subsequent crisis plans, resource management can be a critical component in effectively managing a catastrophic situation. Many aspects of crisis response will be dependent upon the availability of resources, whether they are buses to move evacuees to an extraction point, food and water to sustain those caught within a disaster area, or fiscal provisions to mobilize external support agencies. Resourcing can be considered in terms of:

- Corporate buy-in and senior-level support for the concept.
- Understanding and acceptance at all levels across the organization.
- Clear and known permissions, decision authorities, and operating parameters.
- Design and development of policies and procedures.
- Training and education to support policies and procedures.
- Technological infrastructure and materials to utilize plans.
- Communications infrastructure to enable information flow.
- Physical structures, materials, and resources to support the plans.

- Appropriate managers and personnel to implement policies and responses.
- Predeployment materials and resources to support responses.
- Contracted support for external advisers or specialists.
- Leveraged government or other group plans and agreements.
- Scheduling and cross-utilization policies and systems.

RESOURCE MANAGEMENT PLAN The Business Continuity Management Plan should contain crisis resource and procurement management plans in order to identify what resources might be required, where gaps may lie, and how organic and outsourced resources can be utilized, in strategic or conceptual terms, as well as practically. Exhibit 1.30, Crisis Response: Resource Management Plan, illustrates some tactical-level resource plan components.

The resource management plan might contain owned company resources spread across multiple project sites, as well as those resources that might be leveraged, either through collaborative agreements with other organizations or procured from commercial sources as required. At the corporate level, the resource management plan might contain teams within the company crisis response team, as well as outsourced support, including aviation companies, stress trauma adviser, legal support, medical services and public relations consultants.

There is also value in determining what the resources mean in terms of implementing the crisis response measures. For example, if the project site has 32 staff members and only three armored vehicles capable of transporting five people each, a maximum of 15 personnel may be moved in each motorcade lift. Only materials crucial for the crisis response plans should be included—for example, water resources in arid climates, weapons in hostile environments, or vehicles and fuel storage in remote project sites. Resource plans may also contain sections covering services in terms of medical support, transportation resources, and repatriation assistance. The resource plan should lay out materials, services, and advisory or

Organic Resources	Armored Vehicles	Soft Skin Vehicles	Passenger Buses	Safe Haven Capacity	Medical Packs	Assault Rifles	Pistols	Night Vision Goggles	External Resources	Armored Vehicles	Soft Skin Vehicles	Passenger Buses	Safe Haven Capacity	Medical Packs	Assault Rifles	Pistols	Night Vision Goggles
- Project Alfa	3	4	1	43	2	12	2	1	- 12th Battalion—ISAF	34	4	2	320	0	0	0	0
- Project Bravo	6	5	3	22	4	8	6	1	- Company Y	2	12	0	34	2	0	0	0
- Project Charlie	9	8	2	12	8	8	3	2	- Company X	4	1	1	23	0	0	0	0
- Project Delta	2	7	4	56	2	8	2	0	- Company C	0	12	0	45	2	0	0	0
- Country Center	4	7	1	98	6	22	12	2									
Total Resources	**24**	**31**	**11**	**231**	**22**	**58**	**25**	**6**	**Total Resources**	**40**	**29**	**3**	**422**	**4**	**0**	**0**	**0**
- Required Resource Level	32	12	13	332	4	65	22	3	- Required Resource Level	32	12	13	332	4	65	22	3
- Combined Resources	64	60	14	653	26	58	25	6									
- Organic Capability Variables	8	–19	2	101	–18	7	–3	–3	- External Support Variables	8	17	–10	90	0	–65	–22	–3
- Final Variable Evaluation	32	48	1	321	22	–7	3	3									

EXHIBIT 1.30 Crisis Response: Resource Management Plan

facilitatory arrangements both in-house and through leveraged or contracted agencies. This may also be linked to the procurement plan if monies need to be expended to mobilize external support for crisis response needs.

The resource management plan should consider compatibility for interfaced resources to ensure that resources can work to support each other; this is especially relevant if the IMP relies on specified support agencies that might use different consumable materials or technological features for the same resource item, whether it is short ammunition for long ammunition rifles, gasoline compared to diesel fuels for vehicles, or frequencies for radios. Exhibit 1.31 illustrates a simple resource integration chart that might be useful for companies when leveraging external group capabilities and materials. This can be used to indicate where support may be leveraged, as well as shortfalls in quantity and quality, in addition to other problems or compatibility failure points. Resource plans should generally be held within the Business Continuity Management Plan, unless specific elements relate directly to IMP activities or responsibilities. Resourcing should also be considered in terms of prepositioning equipment or resources that response teams might require. These might include food and water, tools, medical supplies, transportation and fuels, ammunition, communications technology, and temporary shelter.

CRITICAL MATERIALS REGISTER   The company should develop a critical materials register to ensure that all high-value, sensitive, or strategic materials and information are identified as part of the risk evaluation and preparedness planning aspect of the Business Continuity Management Plan. The register might include:

- Materials, equipment, and information that are critical for operational success.
- Materials that are irreplaceable or of significant monetary or reputational value.
- Materials that if lost will place the company at liability or legal risk.
- Materials that could present harm if acquired by unauthorized persons or groups.

The Business Continuity Management Plan should identify those items that are deemed critical to the company and evaluate the probability of a risk occurring, as well as the implications should the threat materialize, as illustrated in Exhibit 1.32, Critical Materials Risk Evaluation Matrix.

The company will be best placed to determine which materials will be considered part of a critical materials register from a corporate perspective; however, it should also ensure that materials that would be included as part of external value considerations—governments, industry counterparts, and so on—are listed as well where appropriate. Such materials might include:

- Radioactive materials or toxic chemicals.
- Weapons, explosives, and ammunition.
- Critical machinery, technology, or materials.
- Government-restricted items: encrypted radios, night vision technology, information technology (IT).

Relevant components of the Business Continuity Management Plan, as well as its constituent elements, should be aligned to managing the risks presented by the loss or damage to such materials. Specific response plans may also be developed to

Company Agency	Required Resource Type	Quantity	Amount	Frequency	Compatible	Quantity	Available Resource Type	Support Agency
Project Delta	Diesel Fuels	500ltrs	Neg100ltrs	Monthly	No	400ltrs	Petrol Fuels	3rd Armor Bde
Project Delta	7.62mm Ammo (long)	36,000rds	Neg10,000rds	Semiannually	No	26,000rds	7.62mm Ammo (short)	4th Armor Bde
Project Delta	Handheld Radio Type	Motorola	NA	1284.8686	No	Military	Handheld Radio Type	5th Armor Bde
Project Delta	CCTV Systems	Delta	14	768696.0	Yes	Military	CCTV Systems	6th Armor Bde
Project Delta	VHF - Freq. 1.26363	NA	NA	NA	Yes	NA	VHF - Freq. 1.26363	Company X
Project Delta	Diesel Fuels	10,000ltrs	✓	Weekly	Yes	10,000ltrs	Diesel Fuels	4th Armor Bde
Project Delta	24-Man Tentage	4	✓	Once	Yes	4	24-Man Tentage	4th Armor Bde
Project Kilo	Diesel Fuels	20,000ltrs	Neg2,000ltrs	Weekly	No	18,000ltrs	Petrol Fuels	3rd Infantry Bde
Project Kilo	7.62mm Ammo (long)	24,000rds	Plus4,000rds	Semiannually	No	28,000rds	7.62mm Ammo (short)	Company A
Project Kilo	VHF - Freq. 2.26363	NA	NA	NA	No	NA	VHF - Freq. 1.26363	Company C
Project Kilo	Handheld Radio Type	Motorola	NA	1284.8686	No	Military	Handheld Radio Type	4th Armor Bde
Project Kilo	Diesel Fuels	3,000ltrs	✓	Monthly	Yes	3,000ltrs	Diesel Fuels	5th Armor Bde
Project Kilo	24-Man Tentage	17	Neg1	Once	Yes	16	24-Man Tentage	Company A
Project Kilo	Portable Water	2,000gals	Neg500gals	Daily	No	1,500gals	Gray Water	Company A
Project Xray	5.56mm Ammo (NATO)	15,000rds	NA	Semiannually	Risk	15,000rds	5.56mm Ammo (Russian)	Group C
Project Xray	VHF - Freq. 2.26363	NA	NA	NA	No	NA	VHF - Freq. 1.26363	3rd Infantry Bde
Project Xray	Diesel Fuels	9,000ltrs	Plus1,000ltrs	Weekly	Yes	10,000ltrs	Diesel Fuels	Company A
Project Xray	24-Man Tentage	6	Plus2	Semiannually	Problem	8	16-Man Tentage	Embassy C
Project Xray	Portable Water	10,000gals	Neg1,000gals	Daily	Yes	9,000gals	Portable Water	Company D

EXHIBIT 1.31   Resource Compatibility Table

Critical Material

Critical Material	Probability of Loss	Impact Level	Project 1	Project 2	Project 3	Project 4	Project 5	Project 6
IT Server ■	3	E	✓	✓	✓			
Well Rig Unit ■	3	E	✓	✓				
Minatron Source ■	1	E	✓	✓	✓	✓	✓	✓
Industrial Explosives ■	1	M	✓					✓
Encrypted Radios ■	3	H	✓	✓	✓	✓		
Coiled Tubing Unit Rig ■	3	H		✓	✓	✓		
Night Vision Technology ■	3	M	✓		✓			
Weapons ■	1	H	✓		✓	✓	✓	
Ammunition ■	2	M				✓		✓
Toxic Chemicals ■	1	H	✓	✓		✓	✓	✓

Probability Levels	Impact Level
1 - Highly Unlikely to Occur	Negligible
2 - Unlikely to Occur	Low
3 - Possibility of Occurrence	Medium
4 - Likely to Occur	High
5 - Expected to Occur	Extreme

EXHIBIT 1.32 Critical Materials Risk Evaluation Matrix

manage both immediate response actions (the IMP) and more comprehensive and complex response measures.

PROCUREMENT PLAN Resource management policies and procedures should be components of crisis resource and procurement management plans, where management teams can most effectively understand what organic capacity the company has, both on-site and in terms of emergency resource reallocations, as well as where external agencies and vendors can be leveraged or contracted to meet resource or capability gaps.

The company will have a finite amount of in-house resources and capabilities, which is typically aligned to meet normal operating requirements. A margin may have also been factored into the project in order to meet surge requirements, or certain emergency situations—although often this additional cost is unacceptable for most groups and the "buy as you need" approach is adopted. Even when other project or supporting agencies' resources are fully brought to bear, resource gaps may still remain that must be met through commercial vendors or other supporting groups—typically at a significant cost. A useful aspect of the contingency component of the Business Continuity Management Plan is a procurement plan, providing permissions and parameters for staged procurement activities to meet immediate, interim, and long-term resource procurement needs. In order to streamline procurements, it is useful to limit the number of managers who are authorized to sanction procurements. This avoids duplication and better defines responsibilities.

It is also useful to have established some form of price estimate or basic ordering agreement with service providers prior to a crisis event in order to define

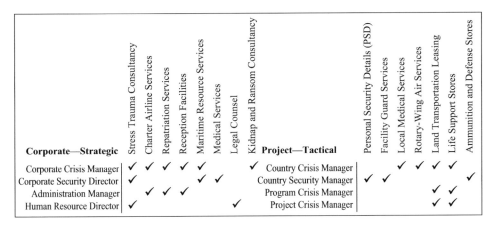

EXHIBIT 1.33 Crisis Response: Procurement Plan

the operational constraints of a service, as well as the cost implications. This can be problematic and is hard to justify if a cost is attached; however, this approach will enable outsourced services to be mobilized more quickly without placing the company at financial or operational risk. Exhibit 1.33 illustrates a simple layered procurement plan, ranging from corporately driven strategic and high-value leases and purchases to more tactical field-level procurements.

Project Initiation Plans

Integral to the Business Continuity Management Plan should be procedures, protocols, and policies for starting (or expanding) business activities within new regions. It is typically when entering a new market or geographic area with which the company is not familiar that the greatest risk exposures may occur. Managers at both corporate and program levels will be seeking to understand the new and unfamiliar operating environment, and new policies and plans will need to be created, or existing ones modified, to reflect nuances connected to cultural, geographic, or climatic influences. Establishing a comprehensive framework document, which follows a systematic and logical approach to ensuring that project requirements are planned within a risk and security context, is critical for companies seeking to operate in new, remote, or challenging environments. By adopting a system such as the one illustrated in Exhibit 1.34, companies are better positioned to ensure that strategic as well as operational and tactical requirements are met in full. This approach should be adopted throughout the business and project planning cycle—addressing each planning and management stage of business justification, proposal development, project design and planning, project initiation, and work package delivery and sustainment—until closure of each work package, as well as the overall program.

Exhibit 1.35 details how each component will support the development of comprehensive and pragmatic policies and plans for companies seeking to operate within new operating areas.

A systematic and logical approach to planning should be employed so that strategic, operational, and tactical requirements are met in full, avoiding errors or

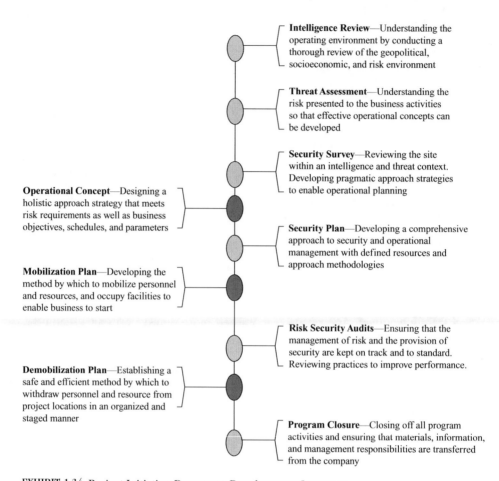

Intelligence Review—Understanding the operating environment by conducting a thorough review of the geopolitical, socioeconomic, and risk environment

Threat Assessment—Understanding the risk presented to the business activities so that effective operational concepts can be developed

Security Survey—Reviewing the site within an intelligence and threat context. Developing pragmatic approach strategies to enable operational planning

Operational Concept—Designing a holistic approach strategy that meets risk requirements as well as business objectives, schedules, and parameters

Security Plan—Developing a comprehensive approach to security and operational management with defined resources and approach methodologies

Mobilization Plan—Developing the method by which to mobilize personnel and resources, and occupy facilities to enable business to start

Risk Security Audits—Ensuring that the management of risk and the provision of security are kept on track and to standard. Reviewing practices to improve performance.

Demobilization Plan—Establishing a safe and efficient method by which to withdraw personnel and resource from project locations in an organized and staged manner

Program Closure—Closing off all program activities and ensuring that materials, information, and management responsibilities are transferred from the company

EXHIBIT 1.34 Project Initiation Document Development Sequence

gaps within the planning process that could undermine business goals, productivity, and bottom-line profits, as well as expose personnel, materials, or the company to unnecessary risks.

Business Recovery Plans

Effective business resilience measures will enable companies to better weather a crisis and continue to be productive during an event. However, in some instances business will be forced to stop and personnel and resources may go through a period of stasis, or may even be withdrawn from task until the situation stabilizes. It is in the interests of the company to determine when work can begin again, within permissible risk tolerance parameters, through a staged and predefined business recovery plan. Business recovery planning may involve corporate decision making in terms of the business risks of continuing operations, or the long-term political or liability risks associated with an event that may have initially disrupted operations. The damage to infrastructures and utilities resulting from a natural disaster may also

EXHIBIT 1.35   A Logical Sequence for Designing Policies and Plans

Strategic Stage	Description	Strategic Process	Outputs
• **Intelligence Review(s)**	Understanding the operating environment by conducting a thorough review of the geopolitical, socioeconomic, and risk environment.	Conduct intelligence reviews through open and closed sources to deliver specific information reports—enabling intelligence led management planning processes.	▪ Populace Intelligence Reports ▪ Threat Assessment Intelligence ▪ Strategic Political Reviews ▪ Key Groups and Leadership Reports ▪ Risk Register
• **Threat Assessment(s)**	Understand the risk presented to the business activities so that effective operational concepts can be developed in alignment with corporate needs.	Place the intelligence information and business requirements into a detailed threat context, mapping risks and impacts through each stage of the program.	▪ Risk and Impact Mapping ▪ Threat and Impact Matrices ▪ Strategic Mitigation Strategies ▪ Detailed Security Assessments
• **Security Survey(s)**	Review the site within an intelligence and threat context—developing pragmatic approach strategies to enable operational planning.	Undertake remote and field security surveys of operating areas and project sites in order to scope the practical requirements and define risk in practical terms.	▪ Policy and Plan Data Collection ▪ Answers to Corporate/Program Questions ▪ Formulation of Practical Approach Needs ▪ Overarching Policies and Procedures ▪ Defined Resource Requirement Plan ▪ Defined Action Plan, with Costs
• **Operational Concept**	Design a holistic approach strategy that meets risk requirements as well as business objectives, schedules, and parameters.	Design an overall operational approach to delivering services through various work stages within the program, bringing together risk and security management issues and program goals, schedules, and objectives.	▪ Aligned Risk and Project Gantt Charts ▪ Interface, Leveraging, and Outreach Plans ▪ Facility Security Policies and Plans ▪ Associated Evacuation Plans ▪ Associated Incident Management Plans ▪ Associated Interface and Leveraging
• **Security Plan(s)**	Develop a comprehensive approach to security and operational management—with defined resources and approach methodologies.	Build the operational policies and plans for specific static and mobile operations, defining methods of operation, risk mitigations, and resource development and usage approaches.	Plans, as Well as SOPs and TTPs ▪ Developing an Operations Order ▪ Designing a Resource Leveraging Plan ▪ Identifying an Advance Team ▪ Identifying Long Lead Procurements ▪ Hardening Facilities and Structures

(continued)

EXHIBIT 1.35   A Logical Sequence for Designing Policies and Plans (*Continued*)

Strategic Stage	Description	Strategic Process	Outputs
• **Mobilization Plan(s)**	Develop the method by which to safely and effectively mobilize personnel and resources, and occupy facilities to enable business to start.	Build a Project Initiation Document in order to define resource procurement, development, and deployment in alignment with program schedules and goals.	■ Risk and Security Policy Audits ■ Risk and Security Operational Audits ■ Training and Development Audits ■ Asset Management Audits ■ Financial Management Audits
• **Risk and Security Audit(s)**	Ensure that the management of risk and the provision of security are kept on track and to standard. Review practices to improve performance.	Conduct clinical and impartial reviews of performance and management in order to manage quality, and evidence corporate governance throughout the life span of the program.	
• **Demobilization Plan(s)**	Establish a safe and efficient method by which to withdraw personnel and resources from project locations in an organized and staged manner.	Develop a safe and effective policy and plan to withdraw personnel and materials from project sites, or to close down the program.	
• **Program Closure**	Close off all program activities and ensure that materials, information, and management responsibilities are transferred from the company.	Collect and collate information, materials, reports, documents, and materials for storage within effective files, documents, and reports.	■ End of Project Reports ■ End of Program Reports ■ Transition or Relief in Place Plans ■ Administrative Closure Reports

70

undermine the business rationale to continue operations. On an operational level, business recovery may be focused on two main areas:

1. **Reoccupation Recovery.** The point at which offices, work sites, accommodations, or facilities are reoccupied following an evacuation by some or all of the project staff.
2. **Business Recovery.** The point at which workers return, movement starts, meetings occur, facilities open, and operations resume, enabling staged business to restart.

REOCCUPATION RECOVERY   The evacuation of a site, facility, office, or in some cases country may be only temporary, leading to the staged return of people and materials to the project site, a situation that enables business to recover and continue after a delay. Companies should consider recovery or reoccupation plans that will enable business activities to start again in a preplanned, logical, systematic, and safe manner. The evacuation may have resulted from man-made problems or a natural disaster, and the implications of the cause of the evacuation should be carefully considered in each instance. Reoccupation of project sites and a restart of operations should be seen almost as a limited version of a mobilization plan, and there are additional factors to consider in terms of heightened security measures, as well as the likely implications of damage and looting that might have resulted following the withdrawal.

Heightened local tensions and government responses may have also changed the threat picture, and floods or other natural disasters may have undermined the rule of law and created additional security instabilities or health hazards that compound the effects of the initial crisis event. The circumstances that led to the evacuation may have made the region temporarily more volatile or, conversely, safer due to the increased presence of security forces. A simple reoccupation planning process is illustrated in Exhibit 1.36, which demonstrates a simple decision and activity path to enable the safe and productive return to work.

When the risk environment has stabilized following the evacuation of a remote site or a region as a whole, a detailed intelligence and risk assessment should be conducted to determine the known and possible new threats facing a possible reoccupation. These threat considerations should not only focus on physical threats, hostile groups, and criminal elements but should also consider disease, logistics resupply, and other more mundane factors. Contingency plans should be reviewed and modified to reflect the changes to the operating environment as part of a return planning process. The company should have already identified an advance team whose responsibilities are to liaise with local leaders or embassy officials in order to gauge the viability of return and to deploy with appropriate security support to review the associated needs for reoccupation, including reviewing the project site itself. The advance team should draft or consolidate an existing reoccupation schedule and plan, as well as project work plans so that a measured return with appropriate lead groups is achieved. This should be a collaborative effort between risk managers and business or project managers. The reoccupation goals are for a safe and productive return of project staff, and it is important that productive business activities can start as soon as personnel and resources arrive on-site. Resources sitting idle at the project site cause the company to incur unnecessary costs and expose

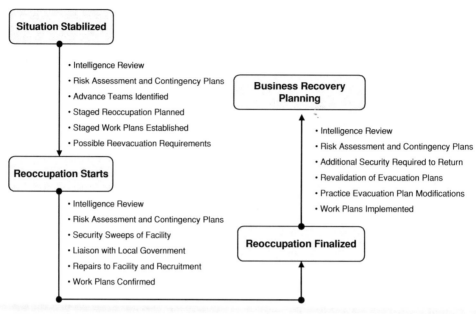

EXHIBIT 1.36 Reoccupation Planning Process

personnel to unnecessary risks. Personnel should deploy only when they can do so safely and when they can operate. The company may wish to define occupation safety levels, such as:

- **Level 1:** Only security personnel are permitted at the location; no company staff members are permitted on-site.
- **Level 2:** Only security personnel and critical project managers are permitted at the location.
- **Level 3:** Security personnel, critical managers, and key project staff are permitted at the location.
- **Level 4:** Security personnel, critical managers, key staff, and normal workforces are permitted at the location.
- **Level 5:** All personnel, including corporate leadership, are permitted at the location.

During the entire planning process, reevacuation considerations should be at the forefront of planning. When reoccupation begins, a continued process of intelligence and risk reviews should be conducted. The facility should be swept for any harmful materials that may have been planted by hostile groups or left by natural hazards. A registry of damages and materials thefts should also be established to ascertain information or material loss that might affect the business goals or the security or safety of the site and activity. Ideally a destruction plan will have been implemented as part of the IMP, meaning that little valuable information or equipment was left behind. Liaison with external groups should be conducted as part of the overall reoccupation process. Needed repairs to the facility and material requirements should be identified and the supply chain system mobilized. Recruitment of local labor forces, including security personnel, may be problematic following an evacuation, as locals may have been involved in or affected by the cause of the withdrawal. Time may have to be spent reestablishing communications and reenlisting local labor forces.

Project work plans should also be considered to determine which project staff should return and in what order, to avoid unnecessary exposure to risk and to ensure productive business activities. The staged return of project personnel is likely to require additional security resources, in terms of movement and possibly heightened security at the facility while reoccupation occurs. All plans should be revalidated to ensure they are consistent with any changes to the risk environment following the evacuation, and continued liaison and threat reviews should be conducted. The security posture should be more robust immediately following a return, as tensions or problems in the area will likely remain. In many cases the reoccupation presents more challenges and risks than the initial occupation of the site.

BUSINESS RECOVERY   Business recovery planning usually presents fewer challenges than a reoccupation recovery, as typically it will form an aspect of such a plan. Business recovery typically occurs when business operations have been forced to be reduced, or stopped, due to natural hazards or due to heightened man-made risks—whether the arrest and detention of personnel, increases in crime, increases in insurgency or terrorist activities, or specific targeting or attacks—causing work-forces to be absent, movement to stop, and facilities to close. Business recovery is the staged and logical evaluation of what activities can restart and in what sequence. Exhibit 1.37 illustrates a simple process of returning the company to work, following

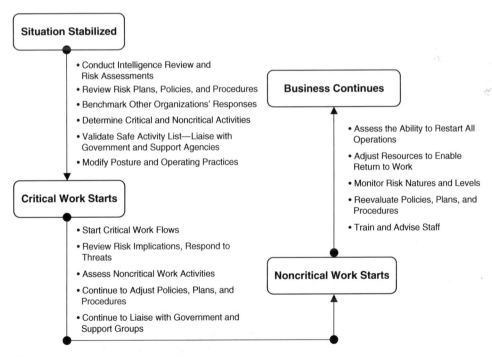

EXHIBIT 1.37 Business Recovery Planning Process

a logical and staged approach. The goal is to evaluate what activities can be conducted safely and in accordance to their order of priority to the company.

Companies should also consider the following key factors as part of their business recovery plans:

- When can local workforces safely return to facilities?
- When can foreign workers safely travel, or return to work sites?
- When can facilities reopen for business?
- What adjustments should be made to operational and risk management approaches?
- What policy changes are required to reflect changes to the risk environment?
- What are the most critical requirements—can they be started first?

Companies should evaluate all factors pertaining to the return to work, whether they be the risk implications of a route traveled by expatriate workers, threats posed to a village from which local workers are sourced, possible profile risks presented by starting business before other similar companies, and the emergency response needs should threats return at any stage of the recovery process.

Postincident Reviews

Following any crisis, the company's management elements should conduct a detailed debriefing at all levels to ensure that all mitigating measures were fully implemented and that any follow-on requirements are actioned. The postincident review should define what went right and what went wrong in terms of the contingency plan, crisis response protocols (including the IMP), and how management structures and decision makers performed. The aim of the postincident review is to address gaps or shortfalls in order that future crisis situations may be better managed. Any supporting security studies, reviews, surveys, threat assessments, or other materials should be clearly stored for internal review as well as external audit. Management should be aware that audits can occur several months or years after the incident. Typically the following auditing activities will occur following an incident:

- **Review the risk assessment.** Did it identify the risks and grade them appropriately?
- **Review mitigation measures.** Did they adequately offset the risks?
- **Review policies and procedures.** Were they detailed enough—did they meet the need?
- **Review management.** Were managers properly prepared—did they apply the contingency plans?
- **Review the vendor.** Did the vendor provide the correct services—did it support crisis management?
- **Review intelligence and risk data.** Are the risks still present—is the crisis over?
- **Strategic planning.** What needs to be done in the immediate, interim, and long term?
- **Deescalating posture.** Can security postures be reduced—if so, when and where?

- **Reviews and audits.** What further reviews and audits are required—when, and from whom?
- **Adjustment.** What approaches, training, policies, and plans need to be adjusted?

The postincident review for significant incidents should be managed by those not directly involved in the event in order to establish an impartial review, although input and participation from the various groups that managed the crisis is, of course, required. Often, utilizing external auditing groups enables corporations to demonstrate, both internally and externally, that they reviewed the incident in a nonsubjective manner.

Summary

The contingency planning measures within the Business Continuity Management Plan should reflect the threats presented within any risk assessments conducted by the company, matching each risk against an avoidance or mitigation approach, including the responses provided with the IMP. Contingency planning measures may be engineered to meet requirements at different levels, meeting corporate, country, program, and project needs. The structuring of the plan should be done in a manner that ensures that tiered policies and responses are met, and that any interaction between different levels of management within the company is understood, as well as with external groups. Contingency measures must reflect dynamic risk environments and should be modified to suit shifting circumstances and needs. The needs and operating methodologies of the business activity will also influence contingency measures, and documents should be written in such a manner as to permit efficient changes without undue effort. The use of tables and stand-alone guidance and policies sections for each risk area will facilitate this, although integration points should be identified so that the final policies and procedures demonstrate an integrated approach. Some data will also be migrated around the plan, and these should be identified and managed to ensure consistency and reduce effort and duplications. Some examples of successful utilization of the Business Continuity Management Plan include:

- **Strategic.** Johnson & Johnson recovered its brand image following the 1982 Tylenol poisonings through effective business recovery measures.
- **Operational.** Using a strategy of supply chain resilience, Wal-Mart was able to bring 70 percent of its stores in the Katrina-affected area back into operation within 48 hours of the disaster.
- **Tactical.** A major (unnamed) oil services company conducted an immediate evacuation of over 120 civilian engineers and workers from one of the most hostile project environments (northern Iraq) due to an industrial hazard.

Where considerable amounts of risk management and response material are required, risk managers may seek to create an IMP as a supplement to the overall contingency planning document, forming the granular or tactical level requirements or responses that will direct crisis management activities, typically at the start of an event. The IMP should not be confused with the corporate- or program-level contingency plans, as it is designed to assist with organizing immediate response protocols to practically support the often physical response to a crisis, rather than directly manage strategic-level or sustainable and complex response protocols. The IMP should provide outlines as to the nature of risks to place these into a context, and may have reduced or simplified components of the Business Continuity Management Plan as they relate specifically to the IMP. In essence, the goals of the IMP are to provide a series of succinct response sheets and questionnaires, enabling management to fall back on established protocols and procedures during the initial stages of a crisis event to allow them more time to focus on the unique requirements of a situation, rather than those that can be predicted ahead of an event. The contingency planning measure of the Business Continuity Management Plan is more of a corporate policy document, providing overarching rather than granular-level details. Contingency planning measures should be reviewed and appropriately modified throughout the life span of the activity, seeking to deter, detect, delay, and respond to the range of threats the company faces.

CHAPTER 2

Incident Management Plan

The incident management plan (IMP) is a generic and tactical component of the Business Continuity Management (BCM) Plan, offering pragmatic guidelines and responses to support immediate crisis events across a wide spectrum of risk issues as more mature and comprehensive measures are brought into play—typically meeting the needs of the first 24 to 72 hours of a crisis event. The IMP might cover a broad array of subjects—for example, registering information from a threatening phone call, dealing with a road traffic accident, or responding to an explosion or natural disaster. The IMP is effectively the first line of defense for companies managing a crisis situation, while concurrently seeking accurate and timely information to support both strategic and longer term tactical decision-making requirements. The IMP works to support the risk management policies, procedures, and plans, taking guidance from such elements as the organizational interface, resource management, and communication plans, while operating under the principles of corporate policies and any security instructions, such as guard orders, travel management policies, and standard operating procedures (SOPs). Therefore, the IMP should be considered another cog within the machinery of a broader Business Continuity Management Plan.

The IMP should be integrated within the Business Continuity Management Plan, while being sufficiently detailed to provide an autonomous set of instructions to first line responders who will neither have the time, nor possibly the access, to the entire Business Continuity Management Plan. In order to provide a stand-alone policy and guidelines document that can act independently of the Business Continuity Management Plan (while still being integrated where desired or appropriate), a company should consider dividing its IMP into a series of components:

- **Instructions.** Providing corporate policies and instructions as an overall guideline on how the IMP should be managed and conducted, as well as pertinent reference documents and policies within the Business Continuity Management Plan.
- **Management Tools.** Providing integration and instructional components linking the IMP to the Business Continuity Management Plan, as well as providing higher-level management tools. Placing response guidelines into a management framework such as decision making authorities and communication plans.
- **Education.** Introducing managers to the nature of the risks they might have to deal with, providing sufficient knowledge and understanding to set the scene

for implementing response plans within a context understandable to a wide user audience. Effectively providing a risk register.

- **Response Guidelines.** Comprising the actual response instructions and guidelines—walking managers through a series of simple and pragmatic steps to enable local and incident managers to bring control to a crisis as more mature plans and expertise are brought into play.
- **Data Collection.** Comprising data calls, indicating and structuring the critical information local managers will need to collate, consolidate, and distribute within the crisis management plan to ensure effective organizational decision making and resource management.

The IMP should be designed to be user-friendly, supporting managers who might not be versed in crisis management or security services to effectively bring the initial event under control—as more experienced risk and security professionals are mobilized to form a qualified and experienced crisis response team (CRT). The plan should therefore be written with a broad user audience in mind, rather than engineered to suit a particular division or industry sector.

While many aspects of an IMP will be generic and will suit a range of operating environments based on the typical risk natures and impact effects a company may face, the IMP should (where appropriate) be tailored locally to reflect any unique risks and challenges that a specific operating environment may present. Considerations to local laws, customs, risk natures, and social factors should be considered and incorporated within the IMP to ensure that responses reflect those factors that will affect them—without disrupting the structure or format of the plan. These unique influences—whether local laws, social infrastructures, political and religious considerations, or topographical and climatic conditions—should be addressed within both the management guidelines section of the IMP and the individual data call and response guidelines. The composition of both the incident management team and the crisis management team should also reflect these influences so that the IMP can be most effectively implemented and sustained.

The IMP should be considered a tactical element of the contingency planning process, as well as a functional aspect of a crisis response, providing sensible and practical considerations, guidelines, and response measures for both corporate and project management and allowing first responders, incident managers, and crisis response teams to respond quickly and effectively to a range of problems—in synchronization with each other. An effective IMP reflects the level of effort a company invests in the safety and welfare of its employees, its protection of investment capital and interests, its brand image, as well as its desire to maximize the profitability of business operations. An IMP should not be viewed in isolation, but will be supported with a range of complementary products, policies, procedures, and activities.

Incident Management versus Crisis Response

While a subjective definition, it is useful for companies to develop a concept of what they consider incident management versus crisis management. Typically, the crisis management teams have primary responsibility for strategic and complex risk issues, such as political, business, and wide ranging security risks, which can include actual or threats of kidnapping, extortion, bombing or other sabotage, illegal detention, and any conflict with the host government or authorities. The corporate team will also be primarily responsible for implementing complex or significant crisis response plans, such as major evacuations, disaster response measures, or repatriations of fatalities. Corporate management will be focused on considering events, risk levels, and operating constraints that might affect the overall company's ability to engage in or continue with operations in a country, or impact the company's reputation and brand image. Crisis management is therefore more strategic, holistic, and far-reaching, supporting the response to the actual event, but also dealing with resulting and peripheral risks and requirements outside of the crisis event.

Incident management teams generally have primary responsibility for responding to security risks involving normal operational activities dealing with industrial accidents, organized and opportunistic crime, insurgency and terrorism, as well as natural disasters and other hazards. Incident management teams may take primacy of control for immediate crisis response (typically directed through such tools as the IMP) or urgent crisis response requirements, such as short-notice evacuations. Incident management is therefore more tactical and granular, dealing with the immediate crisis event in order to bring about control and resolution—as well as supporting the broader crisis response requirements.

Often aspects of the two areas overlap or converge, and components of different incident and crisis teams may find themselves duplicating functions or transitioning responsibilities between the two levels as the event matures. It is useful for companies to organize their crisis response measures so that one group is focused on dealing with the actual event, and a second group is focused on supporting the first while also dealing with issues that would otherwise distract, or occupy the time of, those dealing with the actual emergency situation.

Principles of Incident Management

The IMP should be designed to follow some simple principles in order to be most effective. The plan should reflect the nature of the business in which the company operates and the risks associated with those activities. The plan should also reflect the challenges and nuances different socioeconomic, climatic, and topographical operating environments may bring, as well as the nature, composition, and spectrum of the user audience and supporting groups—meeting the needs of different levels of management and expertise. The plan should be generic enough to ensure consistency of application, but be tailored sufficiently to meet local needs. It should be designed and developed with as much input and buy-in from stakeholders as possible and appropriate, and tested and proven through training and exercises. The IMP is a guideline, and flexibility should be built in and acknowledged to meet unique or new challenges. The IMP should also be correctly resourced and kept live and applicable through scheduled and event-driven reviews and training exercises. In tactical terms, the following principles should be adopted by IMP users:

- Always gather accurate facts; never pass on rumor or speculation.
- Send information quickly and accurately, with regular updates.
- Use the templates provided; however, adapt and enhance as required.

- Taking decisive action is often better than delaying a response.
- Supporting organizations should be notified early to ensure support.
- Only appropriate persons should represent the company.
- Information chains and authority parameters should be clear and understood.
- Sensitive information should flow only to appropriate managers.
- Primary as well as peripheral or secondary risks and impacts should be identified.
- Gaps should be identified quickly for resolution.
- Training and education are important to enable effective implementation.

Incident Management Plan Risk or Threat Overview

It is useful to provide, either within the IMP or as part of a separate threat section (or Risk Registry) within a Business Continuity Management Plan, an introduction to the nature and implications of the threats the IMP has been designed to manage. This section places the response plan in context and should be developed to meet a wide audience's level of expertise. Simple, clear, and focused language should be used to bring an appropriate level of understanding to the threat nature so that the first responder or incident manager understands what questions to ask, how best to utilize the response guidelines, and what impacts may result from a possible threat. This element can be considered an educational or advisory aspect of the IMP; however, it is not intended as a complete review of each risk nature but purely as a usable insight to provide a foundation of understanding. As a risk or threat overview, it provides direction to the design and development of the IMP, as well as educating users in the nature of the problems they may face, and thus places their responses into an understandable context.

Objectives of the Incident Management Plan

The IMP is intended to meet immediate response needs, often undertaken by managers or personnel who may have little or no training within the field of security or crisis response. The IMP will typically go through a transition of management during the course of a crisis event, as more experienced expertise is mobilized to deal with the immediate, interim, and long-term requirements of an event. The IMP provides definition to an organization through guidelines and templates for the successful management of incidents, helping companies respond in a more organized and professional manner to manage the *tactical* aspects of the crisis event more effectively. Simplistically, crisis management meets the *strategic* aspects of managing a crisis event and the two areas should be self supporting and operate in unison.

The IMP can be designed to meet both domestic and foreign activities, supporting responses to both mundane and unique crisis events. The mandate of the IMP should include all incidents that constitute a significant threat to the life, health, or liberty of employees of the company, or those situations that might damage or undermine the image or reputation of the company, its physical assets, or its operations. The IMP might be developed for companies that are exposed to risks such as:

- Medical risks in regions where medical infrastructures are poor or remote.
- Areas subject to natural disasters such as floods, fires, earthquakes, or disease.

- Political risks in areas subject to unstable rule of law and political tensions.
- Regions with especially high levels of organized or opportunistic crime.
- Countries that have active insurgent, activist, and terrorist groups in operation.
- Companies whose activities might be subject to unwanted media attention.
- Industries that might be exposed to high-profile or spectacular risk impacts.
- Companies that might be subject to extortion, threats, sabotage, or kidnappings.
- Companies with high-value materials, technologies, brands, or assets.
- Companies whose operations might be vulnerable to industrial or environmental accident risks.
- Companies whose operations are in remote and inaccessible regions with poor transportation networks.

The IMP defines appropriate and sanctioned response guidelines and information requirements to guide personnel through the first stages of a crisis. Some of the following objectives should be considered central to the design of an IMP:

- Mobilizing the right organic and external resources quickly and effectively.
- Collating and gathering accurate and detailed information.
- Ensuring accurate information flow occurs in a timely and focused manner.
- Coordinating response activities during the first stages of a crisis.
- Preventing the crisis from expanding or reoccurring.
- Representing the company and its interests professionally.
- Reducing the likelihood of physical and psychological harm to personnel.
- Reducing the likelihood of damage to facilities, assets, or materials.
- Supporting the restoration of business activities as quickly as possible.

Incident management plans can be considered one element of a company's risk insulation policy. If risk management is considered in terms of the insulating layers surrounding a live wire (the program or business activity), each layer of mitigation or management affords an additional level of protection against disruptive or harmful influences—thus making a risk pass through several layers of protection or defense prior to being able to cause harm, as illustrated in Exhibit 2.1.

Using the IMP is a prudent manner by which a company can demonstrate they have taken all necessary measures to protect the lives and safety of their employees, as well as their business investments and activities.

Incident Management Sequence

Crisis events may be short-lived or may occur over a protracted period of time, although for both, the effects may linger for significant periods and have far-reaching consequences to the company and its employees and investors. For short-lived crises, the event itself might occur over a very brief time frame—a shooting, an explosion, a suspect package, a flood, an earthquake, or a road traffic accident—with the crisis response needs being completed quickly. For an extended or high-impact crisis, the event or its resulting effects may occur over weeks, months, or even years—a major evacuation, an oil spill, an oil field fire, or a kidnap and ransom case—and the crisis management phase may develop into an entirely separate entity in itself, with its own uniquely tailored response and recovery plan. In addition, within prolonged or

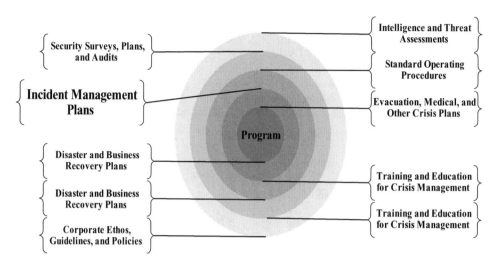

EXHIBIT 2.1 Insulating Companies Against Risk

complex crisis events a series of micro crisis events may occur within the overall crisis environment: a series of fatalities spread across a two-week evacuation, secondary explosions at an oil terminal, health issues or pandemics resulting from a flood, or continued oil leaks following a tanker collision. In addition, peripheral crisis events might also follow on once the physical effects of a crisis are complete (i.e., liability claims, reputational damages, or branding issues).

Crisis Management Flow

The company crisis response and management tempo will reflect the life span and number of micro crisis situations within the crisis event, as well as the implications of the postincident management requirements. Security and other vendors supporting the company should seek to match the pace and requirements of the company, being agile and proactive for a short-duration crisis or being measured and responsive for more extended crisis events. Typically, a crisis will be defined in terms of immediate, interim, and long-term needs, with the activities within each stage of the crisis flow being compressed or extended by the immediacy of the event requirements, or driven by business needs, as illustrated in Exhibit 2.2.

Establishing immediate actions that bring the greatest level of control over a situation will also support the initial stages of the crisis management flow and is typically where the IMP comes into play, such as stopping all personnel movement, evacuating nonessential personnel, or locking down a facility to prevent an escalation or continuance of risk.

Incident Management Sequencing

Exhibit 2.3 illustrates a possible sequence of crisis events that will be migrated from the responsibility of local staff and office management dealing with the initial data gathering and response requirements to a series of more experienced and senior

Immediate Management	Interim Management	Sustained Management	Recovery Management
0–24 Hours	**24–48 Hours**	**48–72 Hours**	**72+ Hours**
• Lock Down Facilities	• Review Facility Security	• Audit Facility Security	• Facility Security Improvements
• Stop All Movement	• Mission-Essential Moves Start	• Vital Movements Start	• Normal Movements Start
• Business Activities Stop	• Noncritical Business Stops	• Selected Business Starts	• Normal Business Restarts
• Workers Stand Down	• Review Workers Return	• Critical Workers Return	• All Workers Return
• Robust Security Posture	• Robust Security Posture	• Staged Security Posture Decrease	• Security Posture Stabilized
• Immediate Risk Analysis	• Activity Risk Analysis	• Detailed Activity Analysis	• Mitigation Measures Enforced
• Implement Emergency Plans	• Review Emergency Plans	• Modify Emergency Plans	• Emergency Plans Modified
• Send Initial Reports	• Send Interim Reports	• Consolidate Reports	• Evaluate Reports
• Mobilize External Groups	• Consult External Groups	• Consult External Groups	• Implement Consulting Advice
• Deploy Crisis Resources	• Deploy Resources	• Management Visits	• Local Management Control
• Manage Casualities	• Receive Casualities	• Manage Casuality Issues	• HR Manages Personnel

EXHIBIT 2.2 Crisis Management Flow

crisis managers. The development of both incident and more complex management responses may follow a series of steps, or the initial event may be catastrophic with little to no warning or time for more experienced managers to mobilize and support the incident management process. Transition points during crisis management should see a handover of knowledge and control, rather than a premature and poorly managed assumption of control by mobilized response teams. Often local managers will have more information and local knowledge than they are given credit for, and responding incident and crisis teams should draw on this firsthand knowledge and capability to ensure that no critical information is lost during transitions of responsibility, and that knowledge and experience are capitalized upon fully. Exhibit 2.3 illustrates a possible sequence of an incident, showing how an emergency may be broken into understandable sections, and where transfer points between management teams may occur.

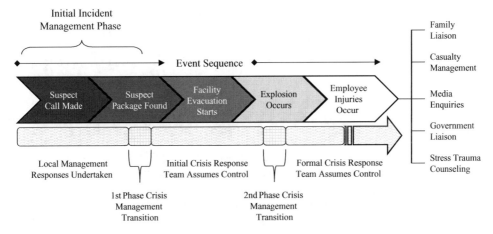

EXHIBIT 2.3 Incident Management Event Sequence

Incident Management Stages

Typically, in management and response terms, the crisis event will include a series of stages. The duration of each stage may be protracted if the company has only a limited Business Continuity Management Plan and is unfamiliar with dealing with crisis events, or where the project may be remote and have unusual environmental challenges. Alternatively, the stages may be compressed where effective response plans, leadership, and support mechanisms are in place. Exhibit 2.4 illustrates some simple stages of a crisis, taking a managing group from the initial period of confusion where few facts may be known and effective decision making is problematic, through to a point where control is exerted, management can consolidate and stabilize the situation, and business recovery measures can be implemented.

- **Confusion.** Often a period of confusion will occur at the outset of a crisis event where information is limited or erroneous, there is a lack of local expertise that can control the situation most effectively, coordination with internal and external resources is limited as understanding and control is brought to bear, and supporting resources have yet to be either identified or mobilized. It is at this stage that the highest risks and impacts might occur, as the organization may not be best placed to bring control to the situation and manage the initial and subsequent risk factors. It is at this stage that the IMP plays a significant part in defining the problem, evaluating the threats, identifying the resources required, sharing critical information with the wider crisis organization, and managing the situation tactically.
- **Control.** If a mature crisis management and incident management plan is in place, the control stage may follow quickly after the initial period of confusion, and accurate information is quickly gathered and shared within the organization, enabling effective decision making. The crisis management structure will have been mobilized with expertise being provided either directly or indirectly to assist in guiding response groups through the crisis, and coordination between groups is established, allowing for good information sharing and decision making. Supporting resources such as special response teams, quick reaction forces, and other organic and external agencies will mobilize to support the response based on several stages of evaluations of requirements. Control will be brought to bear on the problem, managing the initial risks and reducing an escalation or subsequent threats resulting from the emergency.
- **Consolidation.** The consolidation period typically sees the implementation of more matured and focused response plans, which requires a transition from

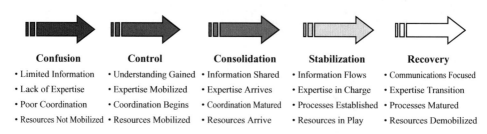

Confusion	Control	Consolidation	Stabilization	Recovery
• Limited Information	• Understanding Gained	• Information Shared	• Information Flows	• Communications Focused
• Lack of Expertise	• Expertise Mobilized	• Expertise Arrives	• Expertise in Charge	• Expertise Transition
• Poor Coordination	• Coordination Begins	• Coordination Matured	• Processes Established	• Processes Matured
• Resources Not Mobilized	• Resources Mobilized	• Resources Arrive	• Resources in Play	• Resources Demobilized

EXHIBIT 2.4 Management Stages of a Crisis

incident management to crisis response. Information-sharing procedures are defined, agreed on, and implemented—allowing for more mature communication flows and management decision making. Expertise will have arrived to start taking control of the situation or begin providing advisory services to the local response teams, either directly or remotely. Coordination requirements will have been consolidated and supporting group participation will have been agreed on to allow for full incorporation into the response activities and plans.

■ **Stabilization.** Stabilization sees the response measures running at optimal efficiency. The incorporation of organic and supporting organizations, activities, and policies is fully implemented and more matured and focused plans are in effect. It is at this stage that recovery planning is conducted. Information policies and procedures are in effect, specialist expertise may have taken over management responsibilities, and interorganizational processes and coordination are operating with full participation of supporting resources and external agencies.

■ **Recovery.** Typically recovery is when the crisis event is over or the effects are significantly diminished, communication flows are narrowed to a focused group so that business activities may occur, and management control may be migrated back to project control. Any crisis management processes and policies may be modified to reflect lessons learned from the emergency event and the effectiveness of response, and supporting resources may be demobilized as no longer required.

The value of the IMP within a Business Continuity Management Plan is seen predominantly within the *confusion* and *control* stages, where immediate actions are taken to gather and share accurate information to support better decision making, while concurrently seeking to bring control to the situation—preventing the situation from becoming worse or having more significant impacts. The other elements within the Business Continuity Management Plan then guide the company through the process to the recovery stage.

Macro and Micro Crises

A crisis situation may be initiated by a single major event (e.g., an earthquake affecting a disaster-struck region, a major flood engulfing a farming community, or the loss of governance resulting in violent civil disturbances). Within each major event there will be a series of associated risks or crisis events that form components of the larger issue (e.g., an injury resulting from the earthquake, a local evacuation resulting from a flood, or a criminal attack on company personnel following a riot). The IMP must deal with a ranging scale or problems, as well as both predictable and unpredictable micro crisis events that might result and ripple outward from the initial issue. At times, resulting crisis events may eclipse the initial crisis in terms of impact or severity and company focus and managers should seek to predict how crisis events may quickly escalate and evolve into larger and more complex crisis situations. The aim of the IMP is to prevent this from happening where possible, quickly bringing control to the initial crisis and reducing the number of micro crises that result from the macro crisis situation.

Exhibit 2.5 illustrates how during a major evacuation a series of smaller crisis events may occur. These might drive up the level of severity of the overall crisis

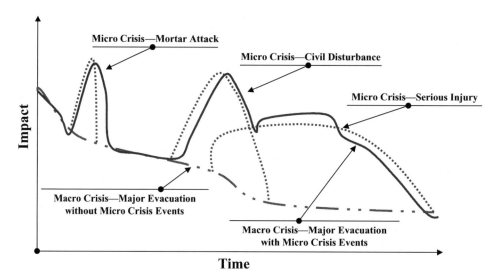

EXHIBIT 2.5 Macro and Micro Crises

situation, as well as create a period of additional crisis consideration for incident and crisis management groups. The exhibit shows two lines of impact, the major crisis without micro impacts steadily declining in severity, and possible spikes of risk and impact within the crisis when micro crisis events are added.

Understanding the Incident Management Plan Needs

When designing an IMP for the company, whether to meet specific program needs or to meet wider corporate requirements, it is important to map the probable risks an activity or organization may face. Risk mapping may take many forms, depending on the complexity and range of business and operating threats faced by a group. Granular-level threats will also be different from strategic ones. The company may choose to layer risk mapping, dealing with strategic risks for corporate consideration, and specific project risks for each business or project activity. Convergence of risks will occur between corporate and project levels as risks migrate between the two levels, each risk influencing how different levels and groups within a company are affected. Typical questions a company should ask when designing an IMP include:

- What is the risk tolerance level of the company?
- What risks are most commonly associated with the company, environment, or industry?
- When is the crisis event likely to occur?
- Where is the crisis event most likely to occur?
- How long is the crisis event expected to last?
- Is there likely to be forewarning of the event, or will it occur without any warning?

- What is the expected magnitude of the event—how significant will disruptions be?
- Are the company's resources sufficient to manage the event?
- How effective will government and support agencies be in responding to the crisis, and are they effective?
- How do threats to local employees compare to, or differ from, those to expatriates?
- In the event of such an emergency, how well would the organization be able to communicate with corporate offices, embassies, the host nation government, and other key agencies?
- What is the company's worst-case scenario associated with each crisis event?
- What secondary or associated risks will result from the crisis?
- Does the company have the expertise or resources to conduct adequate preparedness planning, or should the company seek support?

In order to determine the strategic threats a company might face across a range of risk factors, it is useful to map the impact each risk type will have on the organization as a whole. This is a natural precursor to the more focused risk evaluations on a project-by-project basis. There are various ways of illustrating risk impacts on a company, whether risk impacts are evaluated purely by the corporate offices, as illustrated in Exhibit 2.6, or a consensus is taken across multiple divisions or programs in order to assess the broader perspective of how risk types will impact different business activities, as illustrated in Exhibit 2.7.

Undertaking such macro risk evaluations will help guide management on which areas to focus on within the Business Continuity Management Plan, and what subcomponents should be covered within such plans as the IMP, evacuation and disaster response plans, repatriation guidelines, kidnapping and ransom responses, and

Risk Type	Probability	Impact Rating
Natural Disaster	1	Black
Pandemic	2	Red
Political Instability	4	Red
Damage to Reputation and Brand Image	2	Black
Kidnapping and Ransom	3	Amber
Fatality	3	Amber
Major Evacuation	3	Red
Major Industrial Accident	2	Red
Counterfeiting	1	Yellow
Commercial Espionage	1	Yellow
Fraud and Corruption	2	Yellow
Financial Risk	3	Red
Insurgency Attack	4	Red
Organized Crime	4	Yellow
Power Loss	2	Red
Terrorist Attack	5	Red
Labor Dispute	3	Green

Impact	
Rating	**Descriptive**
Black	Catastrophic
Red	Severe
Amber	Significant
Yellow	Minor
Green	Negligible

Probability	
Rating	**Descriptive**
5	Will Happen
4	Likely to Happen
3	Might Happen
2	Unlikely to Happen
1	Not Expected

EXHIBIT 2.6 Corporate Risk Evaluation

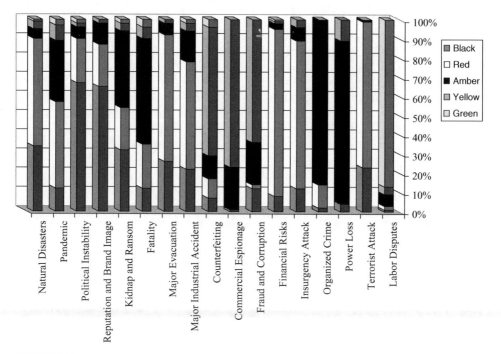

EXHIBIT 2.7 Consensus-Based Risk Evaluation

interface and resource planning. By drawing on the local perspectives of how a risk will impact a specific program or project, the IMP can be further refined to address unique impact ratings that might fall outside of the corporate standards. This can be covered as a generic impact value across the life span of the activity, or where appropriate further refinement can be conducted to address project stage-by-stage risk concerns and evaluations. It should be noted that while a local perspective is useful, managers may not have a refined understanding of risk nor the probability or impacts associated with threats and as such a degree of validation should be conducted by risk advisors.

Such evaluation tools provide managers with both a macro and a micro perspective of risk perspectives and impacts, with the color codes relating to risk levels. Once companies have designed a comprehensive IMP to meet the macro-level concerns, much of the material can be adjusted and realigned to suit unique operating environments or regions, reducing the effort required to create region- or project-specific IMPs—while still meeting the individual project requirements. At the outset of a locally produced IMP, mapping probable threats against project stages or work packages provides one method by which to rationalize the content of an IMP and to align it to specific portions of the business activity. This also concurrently identifies threat levels and trends that a business activity may face, as well as the impact levels a particular risk may have on a stage or work package within the project. The IMP can also assist wider Business Continuity Management Planning as a concurrent feature during IMP development, as illustrated in Exhibit 2.8.

Companies can also translate such project risk tables in terms of risk and probability impact mapping over the course of the project life span, as illustrated in

Risk Natures

Code	Risk Natures	Activity	Impact
A	Small Arms Fire	Site Clearance Work Package	High
B	Improvised Explosive Device		Extreme
C	Civil Disturbance		Medium
D	Tree Sitting		Medium
E	Theft		Low
F	Sabotage		Medium
G	Indirect Fire		High
H	Suspect Package		Low
I	Coercion		High
J	Espionage		Low
K	Monkey Wrenching		Low
L	Protests		High
M	Blockades		High
N	Sit-Ins		Low

Work Package Stages (Threats)

	Stage 1—Deforestation of Site			Stage 2—Foundation Laying			Stage 3—Utility Foundations			Stage 4—Construction of Buildings			Stage 5—Cabling and Power			Stage 6—Fixture and Fittings			Stage 7—Site Clearance		
	Codes	Prob.	Impact	Codes	Prob.	Impact	Codes	Prob.	Impact	Codes	Prob.	Impact	Codes	Prob.	Impact	Codes	Prob.	Impact	Codes	Prob.	Impact
Extreme Probability Risk Event Types	D,J,L	15	8	D,J,M	15	10	J	5	5	M	5	4	F,H,K,M	20	10	C,F,H	15	7	L	5	1
High Probability Risk Event Types	F	4	0	F	4	3		0	0	C,D,K	9	7	C	3	3		3	4			
Medium Probability Risk Event Types		0	0		0	0	E	3	1	B	2	5	J	3	4	M	1	1	C	2	3
Low Probability Risk Event Types	C	2	3	C	2	3	A,B	4	9	L	1	1	G	1	4	H	1	1	E	1	1
Negligible Probability Risk Event Types	B	1	5	B	1	5	B,M	2	10		1										
Stage Risk Probability Risk Rating		**22**			**22**			**14**			**17**			**26**			**19**			**8**	
Stage Impact Risk Rating			**19**			**21**			**25**			**17**			**21**			**12**			**5**

Individual Scoring

1	• Negligible
2	• Low
3	• Medium
4	• High
5	• Extreme

Group Scoring

10	• Negligible
20	• Low
30	• Medium
40	• High
50	• Extreme

EXHIBIT 2.8 Project Gantt Chart: Risk Mapping

89

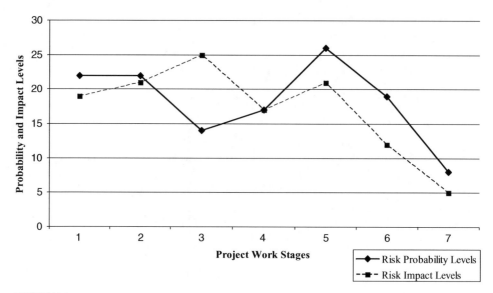

EXHIBIT 2.9 Statistical Risk Mapping

Exhibit 2.9, which demonstrates how the impact and probability ratings shown in Exhibit 2.8 can be migrated into numeric values and used to highlight periods of higher risk exposure to companies.

Companies may opt to invest more risk countermeasures or resources in periods of higher exposure, or place organizations on higher alerts for general security awareness or specific risk types. This can also define which elements of an IMP should be developed first if resources are constrained in terms of developing or tailoring such plans. The highest-impact or most probable risk natures should be dealt with first, with the least-impact, least likely risk natures being designed and implemented last.

Incident Management Plan Design and Implementation

The IMP should be supported at all levels, in terms of design, acceptance, implementation, and testing. The IMP has elements that are both live and static; however, familiarity with the plans is important to enhance the plans' positive effects and overall benefits to crisis response, and implementers should be exercised in their use in order to make responses better coordinated, as well as instinctive during high-stress situations, even if the content rarely changes. The design and implementation of the IMP should be collaborative where possible, following a simple three-step process:

1. Design and development
2. Review and testing
3. Adjustment and implementation

Design and Development

While many of the approaches within an IMP will be generic and governed by tried and tested methodologies aimed at a range of postulated threats, it is useful to draw on the multiple IMP stakeholders in terms of input, if resources and time permit, in order to support the effective design and development of such plans. This is especially relevant if unique local conditions require an adjustment to standard company approaches—particularly if operating conditions and local laws and customs play a significant role in determining the parameters of a response. In addition, while some methodologies may be pragmatically designed, the implications in terms of liability or administrative requirements may have consequences beyond the IMP authors' appreciation; therefore, a legal and administrative review may be required to offset secondary risks associated with managing an event. Human resources, legal counsel, and health and safety advisers may also bring value to the design and development of such plans, outside of typical security and management considerations. The collaborative design and development of such plans will inherently require more effort and time to achieve an agreed solution, but will also gain more buy-in from those responsible for using or supporting the IMP, as illustrated in Exhibit 2.10.

The input of stakeholders and users will also ensure that the IMP reflects the needs of those who will gain most value from it. The plans should be simple, clear,

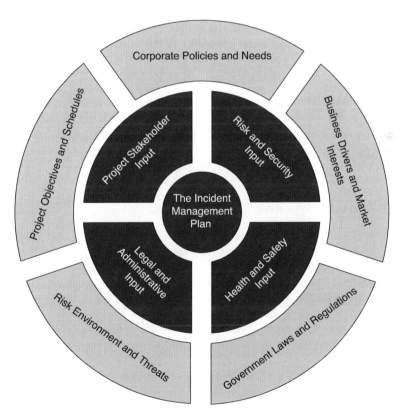

EXHIBIT 2.10 Design and Development

and unambiguous. The plans should also address real company issues and be aligned with actual threats such as hydrogen sulfide (H_2S) poisoning for oil-field services companies, or industrial accidents for construction companies. At times elements of the plan will be taken directly from the overarching Business Continuity Management Plan, as other components will have direct relationships with the implementation and functioning of the IMP—such as sections from the communications plan. Other elements may need to be refined to provide succinct and focused elements that relate only to the local responders or incident management team and their roles and responsibilities within the management of an emergency. The IMP at all times should seek to be succinct, specific, and user-friendly. Those risk types that have been identified within the risk evaluation phase, or needs analysis, should have specific responses connected to trigger points or trip wires, consistent with corporate policies and procedures but tailored to each unique operating environment.

Reviewing and Testing

Companies should factor in a period of review and testing for the IMP, whether as part of a companywide approach or through IMP test groups. There is significant value in drawing on the various stakeholders, users, and appropriate subcontractors to review the draft policies and plans in order to identify gaps or weaknesses. In addition, proving the effectiveness of such plans through management exercises (both practical and theoretical) will also identify where plans may not be pragmatic, may be overly complex or confusing, or may not sufficiently address the likely threats facing the company. For complex IMP components, the inclusion of external agencies may also be required during the review and testing phase (e.g., government agencies, military groups, local communities, or outsourced commercial support). This process of reviewing and testing will validate the IMP and ensure that the final version achieves the greatest success if an incident occurs. The first review and test should, under optimal conditions, be done prior to the plans being formally released. Management feedback loops throughout the use of the IMP during the project or plan life span should also be established to ensure that the plans are reviewed and improved on a scheduled or as-required basis, as illustrated in Exhibit 2.11.

Adjustment and Implementation

Once plans have been designed and tested, preferably with the participation and buy-in of all stakeholders and key user managers, final adjustments should be made prior to the IMP being formally released. The subsequent testing of plans through scheduled exercises, or indeed crisis events, will require continued adjustments and improvements to the IMP to reflect both the company's operational approach and the changing conditions of the risk environments in which the company operates. Continued reviews will keep the IMP applicable and will identify flaws, as well as gain greater understanding and buy-in for the IMP as a central tool for initial crisis response management. Confidence in its applicability will ensure that the plan is understood and indeed actually used during a crisis event. Collaboration from users and managers for the continued improvement of the plan, or subcomponents, also allows ideas and information to be channeled to the IMP custodian for appropriate adjustments, and supports a team ethos between field and corporate

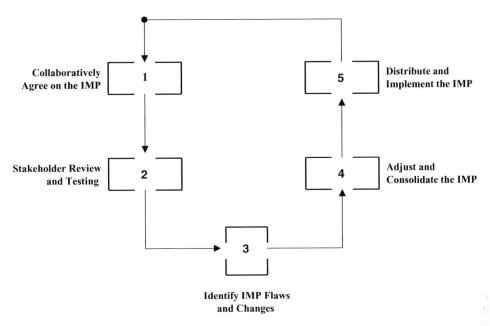

EXHIBIT 2.11 Review and Testing of the Incident Management Plan

offices—a relationship that will be vital during a crisis event. Implementation should be unambiguous, with a clearly defined final version being released to appropriate management and user staff. A series of management tabletop exercises might also be useful at the outset of the plan's release, as well as periodically to ensure skill and knowledge fade is prevented, and to allow plans to be improved with new concepts and approaches over time.

Incident Management Plan Policies and Procedures

The IMP should be aligned with the overarching policies and practices outlined within the overall Business Continuity Management Plan. Information flow should occur according to the communications plan. Organic and outsourced expertise and resources should be leveraged in conjunction with the organizational interface plan and the resource and procurement management plan. Interaction with media, families, and other groups should be guided by the public relations plan, and crisis response actions and decisions should conform with trigger plans and decision and authority matrixes. The IMP should also operate within the auspices of security management plans, standard operating procedures and tactics, techniques, and procedure policies. All policies, procedures, and plans should be complementary, with minimal duplication and overlap to avoid confusion, contradictory guidance, and wasted resources. Often the IMP and Business Continuity Management Plan will complement or leverage any company health and safety plans, as well as existing policies on dealing with the media or other operating practices; and companies may wish to provide some form of guidance to managers as to how the IMP will operate within the Business Continuity Management Plan, and what is expected of them during a crisis event.

The IMP may also work within the framework of security plans, which might determine how security and risk management is undertaken within a facility. A degree of tailoring may be required to merge the IMP into specific regional or task policies and plans. The IMP may also be supported by government response plans, and the points of connection should be defined and aligned to ensure that friction between internal and external plans or protocols does not occur. Modifications to the IMP should be done only as sanctioned by appropriate managers (or an IMP Custodian) in order to avoid conflicts with corporate interests, as well as to reduce the amount of deviation from response measures and information reporting formats.

Information Security

Some aspects of the IMP may be considered sensitive in nature, and consideration should therefore be given to who is permitted access to the plan. Other elements of the plan will be generic and intended for a wider audience, such as fire drills or suspect call responses, and managers should ensure that information and training are made available to the different levels of user audience. Where necessary, terms such as *restricted* and *unrestricted* can be applied to different elements of the IMP in order to ensure that managers share appropriate information with a wider audience, or restrict information to defined positions as required. Each recipient of the IMP is responsible for its safekeeping and for ensuring that no unauthorized copies are made.

Resourcing the Incident Management Plan

The IMP should be resourced with the appropriate policies and plans that guide and support the implementation of responses, as well as the technology required to effectively operate the IMP. The IMP is largely a human resource—driven activity, so the correct selection of response managers, with associated training and education, is required to ensure that the IMP can be adequately managed during a crisis. The IMP will also rely on technology, and the company should consider whether the IMP has sufficient resources to be effective in the event of a crisis—notably through the use of varied communication mediums, which will form a core component of the success of the IMP. The company should ensure that sufficient communication mediums and redundancies are available to flow information, guidance, and decisions throughout the organization. Connectivity and compatibility to supporting agencies are also important. The IMP itself may be posted within the company intranet, or hard copies may be held at office locations for use.

In order to be effective, risk assessments, security surveys and plans, and other components of the Business Continuity Management Plan should be undertaken so that the IMP operates within a supported environment. The resource limitations should also be known to management, as these will determine what parameters the IMP will operate in. Resources should be considered in terms of ensuring that the IMP is applicable and relevant, has the correct level of corporate buy-in and support, has adequate levels of practitioner education and training, has been correctly dispersed, and has the correct technological and physical materials required to make it work.

The Business Continuity Management Plan should also be resourced in terms of redundancy measures, materials, and protocols. Redundancies may apply to materials, infrastructures, or technologies. Companies may wish to ensure that information technology (IT) servers are located off the main site(s) to ensure that information storage is not directly affected by a facility crisis. Emergency or crisis response centers may also have secondary locations established, should the primary ones be within an affected area, and other crisis management resources may have backup components removed from normal facilities, including multiple-medium access to crisis and response plans.

Structuring Incident Management Plans

The IMP is designed to allow both first responders and managers within corporate offices, as well as field project locations to understand the risk natures and response measures appropriate to their company and its operations. The IMP provides logical and user-friendly response guidelines and information capture formats to support pragmatic incident management. The design of the IMP is an aspect of contingency planning; its implementation is a functional element of crisis management. The structure of the IMP will reflect the level of detail required by the company, as well as the complexity of the operating conditions a business activity is working under. In addition, the level of experience, capability, and reliability of those implementing the IMP should be considered, as clearer instructions and more comprehensive details may be required for a management element with limited experience in crisis management—especially for complex crisis natures. Where possible, the company should seek to retain a level of consistency in IMP structuring and approach methodologies across the group (where appropriate in terms of unique projects and environmental conditions), so that personnel moving between projects become familiar with how the plan is laid out and how it works—and that consistency of approach is maintained. The structuring of the IMP should consider five main elements:

1. Instructions
2. Management tools
3. Education
4. Information-gathering techniques
5. Response guidelines

Exhibit 2.12 illustrates some elements a company may wish to include within the IMP. The IMP should be designed to operate in isolation if necessary, despite working as a functional component of the Business Continuity Management Plan, as some user managers may not have access to supporting policies and plans, and the IMP is engineered to guide an inexperienced manager through a crisis quickly by the use of succinct and simple reference guides and instructions—reducing the need to refer to other documents in order to be effective. Where possible, elements of the Business Continuity Management Plan that are relevant to the IMP should be migrated into the plan to ensure consistency and to avoid unnecessary duplication of effort.

The policies, instructions, and threat overviews provide the user some instruction on how the IMP should be used, and the nature and aspects of the risks the company might face—placing the IMP into an understandable context. The data call templates

EXHIBIT 2.12 Structuring the Incident Management Plan

guide responders as to what information they would be seeking and passing through the crisis management structure, and the response guidelines illustrate what practical measures should be taken to bring control to the situation.

Incident Management Plan Policies and Instructions

The IMP's association with other aspects of the Business Continuity Management Plan should be clearly stated within the policies and instructions component. This will ensure that users are guided to the correct supporting policies and procedures that govern the implementation of the IMP (if they are not included within the IMP as stated). The IMP should not seek to duplicate unnecessarily those instructions, policies, plans, or procedures captured within other components of the Business Continuity Management Plan; however, it should briefly articulate how those elements guide the management of the IMP. The core subjects that might be covered for IMP usage are:

- Structure of the crisis management organization.
- Decision-making and authority matrixes.
- Alert states and response trigger points.
- Organizational interfaces and their part in the IMP.
- Communicating IMP activities through the communications plan.
- Leveraging resources through the resource and procurement plan.
- Reference policies, protocols, and other planning documents associated with the IMP.
- Reporting and record-keeping guidelines.
- Reference mapping and schematic usage.

As the IMP is designed to be a user-friendly document, the introductory elements should seek to be succinct and relevant. At most, these elements should introduce supporting policies and plans so that the user can be guided to these elements where required.

Incident Management Plan Cover Letter

For those companies that have no current IMP in place, it is important to advise personnel as to the rationale behind the creation of such a plan in order to avoid rumors and speculation, or at worst concern or fear within a workforce when such plans are developed or distributed. The following list provides a sample of some elements that might be included within such a cover letter:

- **Rationale.** In order to ensure the protection of our employees working and traveling worldwide, the company has approved the development of an IMP. The purpose of this plan is to enable personnel to respond in an organized and professional way to any incident that threatens the lives or health of the company's employees, or adversely affects its operations.
- **Context.** We have no reason to believe that the company or its employees are at any greater risk than other companies working in our industry, or in similar parts of the world. However, given political uncertainties around the world and the increasingly international nature of our business, we believe it is only prudent that we should seek to be as prepared as we can be.
- **Value.** The IMP is a functional element of the company's Business Continuity Management Plan, supporting local managers and first responders in understanding the nature of common risk types, as well as providing clear and pragmatic response guidelines to assist them in bringing control to a crisis event. The IMP is the first step in dealing with an issue, and bridges the response gap as the crisis response teams mobilize. The IMP is designed to deal with a range of incidents, whether they involve personnel or facilities or are associated with political unrest, natural disaster, medical emergency, criminal act, or otherwise.
- **Definition.** The IMP responsibility extends to any unexpected event that may have a significant impact on the company or its employees, or the community in which it operates, including political and security risks, medical emergencies, natural disasters, accidents, or any other event that might threaten the health and well-being of personnel, damage the reputation of the company, or cause impediments to business operations.
- **Utilization.** The IMP has elements by which to provide a brief insight into the types of risks the company and its employees may face, as well as pragmatic response guidelines and data call formats to support first responders and local managers in gathering accurate information and managing the first steps of an emergency. Each incident will require a tailored approach, although notification of designated incident and crisis response managers should occur as quickly as possible. The IMP is not designed to restrict sensible responses, but rather to act as a tool to support effective management.
- **Training.** The IMP will be supported with training for selected managers. Additional training may be provided for those exposed to new operating environments, or who may form an element of an incident management or crisis response team. This will be determined on a case-by-case basis.
- **Crisis Management.** Personnel should be aware that a detailed Business Continuity Management Plan is in place, and that the IMP forms a functional response component of this plan. Designated and experienced crisis managers will take control of an incident at the earliest opportunity, and all appropriate emergency response organizations will be incorporated within response plans, as well as leveraged during an incident itself.

The IMP introduction or cover letter should seek to allay any fears or concerns while placing the IMP into a broader context and crisis management framework. The author may be the CEO or a selected representative, and the recipients may be limited to incident and crisis response personnel, or the letter may be open to the entire organization.

Immediate Resource Mapping

While a function of the Business Continuity Management Plan, and in particular the resource and interface management plans, there can be value in providing a succinct resource mapping component to the IMP to ensure that managers are quickly directed to the most appropriate and reliable internal and external resources to help them to best manage a crisis event—especially at the local levels. Resource mapping should identify both usable and unavailable resource options so as to avoid time wasted pursuing those response groups that have been proven to be unreliable or unavailable during the contingency planning aspect of the risks management plan, as illustrated in Exhibit 2.13. Immediate resource mapping may cover a range of service areas, including but not limited to:

- Critical commercial support (utilities, power, medical, security, legal, etc.).
- Armed response or quick reaction forces.
- First line or surgical medical support.
- Medical evacuation support.
- Repatriation services.
- Emergency materials and resources.
- Transportation services (air, land, and maritime).
- Legal services.
- Explosives detection and clearance services.
- Kidnapping and ransom response services.
- Safe havens.
- Stress trauma support.
- Firefighting and emergency services.
- Security and guard services.
- Liaison and interpreter support.

Immediate resource mapping will also take into account the interface plan as well as the resource management plan (see Chapter 1), as they relate specifically to incident management. It is typically the crisis management elements that might mobilize the most significant resources to support the needs of a complex or large-scale crisis, and the IMP may therefore require a scaled-down version to enable the first stages of a crisis situation to be brought under control. Such simple reference guides may be placed onto an operations center wall, or within a simple flip chart as a reference document. They need to strike the right balance between providing sufficient guidance to reach the correct level of understanding and decision making versus providing so much data as to overwhelm and confuse incident managers.

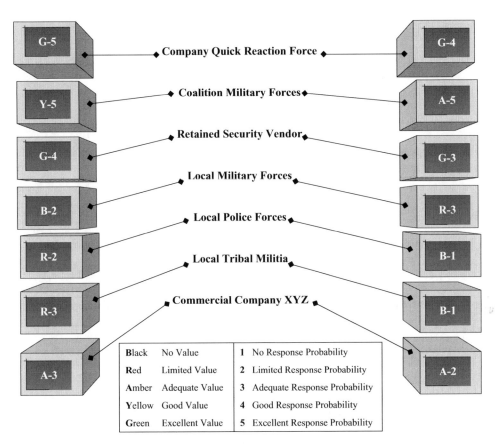

EXHIBIT 2.13 Incident Management Plan Immediate Resource Mapping

Incident Management Plan Communications and Tactical Resource Plan

Although the Business Continuity Management Plan should contain full communications and resource management plans, components specifically relevant to the IMP may be captured within an IMP communications and tactical resource plan, which is linked to the immediate resource mapping concept. The immediate resource schematics provide an indication as to the level or the reliability of support to be expected from different groups, guiding incident managers to the most reliable and capable groups, whereas the IMP communications and tactical resource plan provides a user guide as to which persons and groups provide support, as well as their specific contact details, as illustrated within Exhibit 2.14. Various models can be developed dependent on the size, nature, scope, and complexity of the company's operations, as well as the range of groups that are supporting or interacting with the company. Elements of the Business Continuity Management Plan's communications plan might be migrated into this model, as it applies to the IMP's requirements.

COMMON ALERT PROCEDURES The IMP should consider common alert procedures (CAP) as a method by which to cascade information both within the crisis

Organization	Name	Title	Tel. No.	E-mail	Fire	QRF	UXO	Medical	Aviation	Transport	K&R	Legal	Repatriation
Coalition Military								Support Matrix					
4th Infantry Brigade	Peterson	Colonel	123 - 5464644	CO@4Bde.com		✓	✓	✓					✓
5th Infantry Brigade	David Green	Colonel	123 - 4567888	Dgreen@sudan_mil.com			✓	✓		✓	✓		✓
4th Police Detachment	John Gillion	Lieutenant	123 - 6757575	OC@4RMP.com						✓	✓	✓	
Embassy													
U.S. Embassy	Paul Simons	RSO	123 - 9909000	rso@usembassy_sudan.com				✓			✓	✓	✓
U.S. Consul	John Collins	Legal Officer	123 - 9900009	j.collins@state.com				✓			✓	✓	✓
British Embassy	Sid Smith	Security Director	123 - 7676464	s.smith@fco.co.uk	✓			✓			✓		✓
Reciprocal Commercial Support													
Hill Construction Ltd	Kristen Marie	CoP	123 - 8657575	k.marie@hills.com		✓		✓				✓	✓
Pan's Electronics	Alex Jack	Project Manager	123 - 8657576	a.jack@pans.com		✓				✓			
Vll Helm Engineering Ltd	Amber Rose	Security Manager	123 - 8657577	a.rose@vil.com	✓	✓		✓		✓			
Alternative Company Projects													
Project 2	Julie Hiem	CoP	123 - 5674743	h.hiem@project2.com		✓		✓		✓			
Project 17	Fred Carney	Project Manager	123 - 9988777	f.carney@project17.com		✓				✓			
Local Government Agencies													
Law Enforcement	JimHarrington	Chief of Police	123 - 4568987	jharrington@jubapolice.com		✓		✓	✓			✓	
5th Republican Guard	Ali Mustafa	Colonel	123 - 5656565	a.mustafa@5aguard.org		✓	✓						
16th Infantry Brigade	Mohammed Jafz	Major	123 - 5555555	OC@16bde.org	✓	✓		✓	✓	✓			
Contracted Commercial Support													
Medical Clinic	St Francis	Emergency Room	123 - 999299	francis@emergency.com				✓	✓				
Aviation Support	FlyGreen	Operations	123 - 002020	operations@glygreen.com				✓	✓	✓			
Security Response	Shield	Tactical Operation	123 - 929281	TOC@shield.com		✓		✓		✓			✓
Local Law Firm	McKinney	Legal Officer	124 - 929292	Legal.officer@mckinney.com			✓					✓	

EXHIBIT 2.14   Incident Management Plan Communications and Tactical Resource Plan

management structure and to those employees or groups who might be affected by the emergency situation. CAP measures may include:

- E-mails
- Text alerts and pagers
- Phone calls
- Loudspeakers and broadcasting systems
- Radio or television alerts
- Alarm systems

The goal of the CAP is to get appropriate information to the right people quickly in order to both manage an emergency as well as reduce further risks to employees.

Initial Verbal Reporting

It is a fundamental aspect of the IMP to deliver clear and factual information to other elements of the company so that effective decisions can be made and response groups and resources can be mobilized. In addition, the dissemination of information will also assist in bringing control to a problem and avoid additional threats that could have otherwise materialized as a result of lack of control, or from erroneous reporting. The IMP should be designed to include data collection forms that match the risk types determined within the risk analysis section of the overall Business Continuity Management Plan (see Chapter 6). However, as with any plan, a degree of flexibility is always required, and a verbal briefing will often occur as a matter of expediency as written reports are being generated.

As a result, often a phone call will initiate the crisis response measures prior to any written reports being generated in accordance with IMP guidelines. The first phone call will trigger other response groups to mobilize and will set the scene for how an incident is managed. Getting logically presented and factual information across to other groups is imperative. The format shown in Exhibit 2.15 (used by the British police) captures within the simple acronym SAD CHALETS the typical aspects of information required that will provide effective first guidance to responding groups.

EXHIBIT 2.15   Verbal Reporting of Incidents: SAD CHALETS

- **Survey** the scene.
- **Assess** the situation and the risk implications.
- **Disseminate** information to the correct groups in the correct sequence.

- Casualties: Number, type, and condition.
- Hazards: Types, severity, impacts, and status.
- Access: Management control points, safe routes in, and reception centers.
- Location: Specific grid reference or prominent feature of the event.
- Emergency Services: What support is required.
- Type: Nature and type of crisis incident.
- Start Logging: Start collating information from the beginning of the event.

Such simple acronyms should be used within management centers and should be contained within the IMP to guide personnel in delivering the first verbal briefing as to the nature and circumstances of the crisis event.

The aim of the plan is to provide a simple, quick, and effective method by which both untrained and experienced professionals can assess whom to call for what support. Managers might also create e-mail distribution lists for internal dissemination of information, or for outward support requests so that known groups can be alerted quickly and concurrently. The immediate resource mapping is a more functional illustration as to how reliable support might be, acting as a prompt to determine which resources to call on. This plan might be a simplified and focused version of associated plans held within the Business Continuity Management Plan, and may combine several of those plans in a simplified cheat sheet format. Migrating duplicative information between plan elements effectively as they relate to different functional elements will ensure better consistency and reduce overall effort required to develop and sustain such plans.

Incident Management Plan Decision and Authority Matrix

While the Business Continuity Management Plan should contain a full decision-making and authority matrix to provide a clear structure by which to guide the different layers of company management, the IMP may have specific incident management guidelines in order to guide incident managers in determining what permissions they have, as well as whom they should contact in order to receive authority to take more impactful or strategic decisions. Clear limitations should be set as well intentioned activities can at times exacerbate a problem and defined parameters will negate some of these internal risks—this may be as simple as calling local emergency services, or more complex, such as alerting an embassy of an issue.

Although incident management is more tactical in nature, it may require the utilization of both internal and external resources during a period in which the more experienced crisis management elements are mobilizing and attempting to grasp the implications and the details of an emergency. Immediate notifications and resource usage should therefore be outlined to improve the efficiency of decision making, provide managers with the confidence to make critical and time-sensitive determinations, and also guide incident management to the people or groups they should be reaching out to for help. The format of decision-making and authority matrixes may reflect the structure and format illustrated in Chapter 1, and might be simplified or tailored to meet more tactical-level requirements.

Incident Management Plan Alert States and Trigger Response Plans

It is important for incident managers to be provided with simple guidance as to how to sensibly and effectively escalate a risk management posture to reflect threat indicators, or increasing levels of threat. It is also important to define the difference between a problem and a crisis, so that managers do not ignore a real crisis event, or conversely do not mobilize resources that far exceed a requirement, as this will quickly fatigue the crisis management responses. Frequently the determination between a problem and a crisis is a subjective one; however, some simple guidelines will assist those less experienced in identifying and managing crisis events.

The Business Continuity Management Plan will typically contain detailed alert states and trigger plans to meet a range of possible crisis scenarios; however, a simplified version can be useful within the IMP itself. Threat levels are often the key indicators of alert states, but threat levels can be extremely volatile and do not necessarily reflect actual risks to personnel, facilities, resources, or activities. Assessing alert states in terms of the threat and vulnerability will provide a more tailored and local alert state. This should be a continuous process of assessing the risk environment in which the company is operating, at local, regional, and national levels—rather than being purely associated with IMP requirements. Sound judgment forms the basis of a decision; however, the development of agreed alert states provides a common vocabulary, context, and structure for assessing and reacting to the threats that confront the company's people or project. In essence, these alert states provide a simple and effective way of conveying the severity of a situation to local, national, and corporate management in order to facilitate their decision-making process, as well as evidence and justify a response need. They also bring important consistency to the risk management approach. Alert states can also be used to trigger internal risk and security measures, increasing awareness, initiating contingency measures, and mobilizing resources to be positioned to enable the company to respond at appropriate levels to a particular need.

Alert states can be influenced by internal assessments, or may be influenced or guided by government, military, or civil assessments. There may be differences in what a government considers just reason to evacuate, and what commercial organizations see as the final trigger for a withdrawal. Businesses will bear the brunt of financial or project losses, whereas diplomatic warnings are more advisory and often not audience specific. Alert state risk assessments can also be tied directly to actions required and policies implemented. This will assist in a semi-automated process following the risk assessment. Alert states may vary from negligible to low, medium, high, or extreme. In each instance, an explanation of what drives the classification should be provided to avoid personal perspective or ambiguity, as well as what actions are required in association with alert states to reflect a change to risk levels. Tables may be complex or simple, depending on the complexity of the company requirement—although the IMP version should be as clear and focused as possible to reflect the user audience's knowledge, capabilities, and experiences. Exhibit 2.16 illustrates a simple table that might be used to guide first responders and incident managers through a simple and directed decision-making process connected to certain levels of risk probability. Numerical alerts can be used to guide managers to where they need to start taking action; alternatively, color coding is an option to making interpretation of risk levels easier for users.

Generic and macro-level trigger natures are illustrated in Exhibit 2.16; however, more specific triggers or trip wires may be defined by companies so as to provide granular-level guidance to staff. Organizations such as the U.S. Overseas Security Advisory Council (OSAC) advocate trip-wire planning for commercial organizations operating abroad. The OSAC advocates determining points at which certain risks—principally natural disasters, civil disorder and political unrest, terrorism, health and environmental threats, infrastructure weakness, and other facility or employee concerns—mobilize an organization into predetermined response measures (OSAC, "Tripwire Approach to Emergency Planning," May 11, 2008). Establishing trip wires or trigger points enables local managers, as well as corporate officers,

Natural Risk Types

Natural Risk Types	Increase Security or Safety Posture	Stand Up the IRT	Notify the CRT	Stand Up the CRT	Nonessential Operations Suspended	Essential Operations Suspended	Implement the IMP	Evacuate the Site or Area
Overland Floods	2	2	3	3	4	4	4	4
Earthquake	2	2	3	3	4	4	4	4
Forest Fire	3	2	3	3	4	4	4	5
Pandemic	2	2	3	3	3	4	4	4
Famine	4	4	5	5	4	5	4	5
Contamination of Water	2	3	4	4	5	5	5	5
Volcano	2	2	3	3	3	4	4	4
Hurricane	2	2	3	3	3	4	4	4
Tsunami	1	1	2	2	2	3	3	3

Man-Made Risk Types

Man-Made Risk Types	Increase Security or Safety Posture	Stand Up the Incident Response Team	Notify the Crisis Response Team	Stand Up the CRT	Nonessential Operations Suspended	Essential Operations Suspended	Implement the IMP	Evacuate the Site or Area
Industrial Fire	1	2	3	3	3	4	5	3
Industrial Hazard	1	2	3	3	3	4	5	3
Facility Intruder	2	3	3	4	3	4	5	4
Indirect Fire Hazard	3	3	4	4	3	3	5	3
Small Arms Hazard	1	2	2	3	3	3	5	3
Suspect Package	1	1	2	4	4	4	5	4
Unexploded Ordnance	1	4	4	4	4	4	5	4
Vehicle-Borne Explosive	1	1	2	3	3	4	5	4
Civil Disturbance	1	1	3	3	3	3	5	5

Alert States

1 Reports of a possible risk event occurring not evidenced but suspected.

2 Evidenced or substantiated reports of a risk event occurring in the near future.

3 Evidenced or substantiated reports of a risk event occurring in the immediate future.

4 Physical signs of the risk event occurring, precursors to a larger or more significant event.

5 The major risk event is under way.

EXHIBIT 2.16   Incident Management Plan Alert State Trigger Plan

to have clearly defined and unambiguous points at which decisions or actions are taken, whether they be major earthquakes, large-scale riots, pandemic alerts, fuel shortages, or water contamination threats. These specific trigger points or trip wires can include:

- Demonstrations that indicate growing social unrest, whether peaceful or violent in nature, especially if aimed at foreign workers, facilities, or other associated company activities.
- The media, host nation government, religious groups or leadership, or militia leaders preaching or actively spreading inflammatory propaganda or directives that could adversely affect the company, its personnel, or its facilities.
- A rapidly diminishing ability to gain accurate and timely information from local government organizations, foreign missions, and media agencies on local or regional events that could present threats to the company.
- Increasing levels of opportunistic criminal activity, especially if directed at specific ethnic or religious groups, genders, or business activities, locations, or facilities.
- Focused attention by organized crime on the company and its employees, activities, or facilities, or unwanted attention toward associated or similar commercial groups.
- Rising levels of insurgent, terrorist, or activist targeting, especially if directed toward the company or toward associated or parallel groups.
- Host nation, embassy, media, or other public announcements indicating an increase in specific threat types or pending crisis events.
- Sustained disruptions to basic infrastructure or utilities preventing the supply of clean water, gas, electricity, food, fuel, or other life-support essentials.
- Reliable reports of an imminent natural disaster—hurricane, typhoon, tsunami, wildfire, volcanic eruption, or flooding.
- Reports of a pending or occurring industrial or environmental disaster that could present toxic or physical hazards to personnel, as well as contaminate facilities, food or water supplies, or critical materials.
- An outbreak of contagious diseases that the local government or responding agencies do not have the resources, expertise, or medicines to treat.
- Rapid economic decline brought about by sanctions, civil unrest, coups, assassinations, or the turnover in host nation leadership, which might lead to local authorities being unable to maintain law and order.
- Political instability and loss of governance resulting from the abrupt replacement, detention, or arrest of key government officials, military leaders, political opponents, religious leaders, or other prominent figures.
- Similar organizations increasing security profiles, ceasing operations, closing facilities, rapidly evacuating personnel, or demobilizing activities.
- Foreign embassies and aid agencies declaring heightened risk alerts or withdrawing their presence from the area, region, or nation.
- The inability, lack of resources, or unwillingness for local or national security and law enforcement agencies to provide adequate protection to foreign workers and the company's interests.
- Rising levels of corruption, extortion, and legal liability risks presented by corrupt political leadership, which could result in detentions or imprisonment.

- Rapidly declining transportation capacities for road, rail, air, or maritime facilities, which could adversely affect the ability of company employees to evacuate the country.

Each company, and indeed project, should provide definitions and responses that are appropriate to its unique requirements and operating environment. The risk assessment conducted during the contingency planning aspect of the Business Continuity Management Plan's development should define what postulated threats are posed against a company or particular activity, and thus what should be included within the risk type category. The guidelines should be considered as such, guidelines, with common sense playing a critical role in how managers respond.

Alert Notification Systems

Companies may wish to develop alarm protocols and systems that will audibly or visually alert personnel to the severity of a risk, as well as actions taken to support the IMP. Common alarm systems will meet the requirements for a fire or common industrial risk; however, when companies operate within a more complex and dynamic risk environment, they may require a more detailed alert notification system. Exhibit 2.17 illustrates a highly simplified alarm status system that can be used to initiate immediate responses to a wide range of threats. More complex plans may be required to meet specific and high-impact risks, such as intrusion, indirect fire, unexploded ordnance, civil disturbance, industrial fires, hurricanes, floods, or other catastrophic hazards.

The alarm system will support immediate and accurate notifications for entire work sites, allowing the incident management team to focus more on managing the crisis than on managing large numbers of workers. Training, rehearsals, and education will be required to ensure that personnel know how to properly respond to alarm notifications when an incident occurs. Alarms may also be connected to specific tactical instructions for response groups, which might be specified within site security plans or other similar plans or policies. Mutual aid agreements between different organizations may also involve alert notifications being shared between different companies, whether verbal, e-mail, or through blog mediums.

Alarm	Audio Signal	IT Indication	Alarm Indication	Actions
Black	Radio, Siren, and Intercom	E-mail and Text	The risk is occurring.	Take cover immediately.
Red	Radio, Siren, and Intercom	E-mail and Text	The risk is imminent.	Move to shelters immediately.
Amber	Intercom	E-mail and Text	The risk is pending.	Prepare to move to shelters.
Local Green	Intercom	E-mail and Text	The immediate area is safe.	Work can resume at site.
Green	Intercom	E-mail and Text	The general area is safe.	Normal activities can resume.

EXHIBIT 2.17 Simple Alarm State Notifications

Incident Management Plan Information Capture Reports

The swift and accurate dissemination of information from the initial incident source to the incident response and crisis management teams is critical for the successful activation of appropriate personnel and the employment of the necessary crisis countermeasures: minimizing the potential damage an emergency event can cause. An important aspect of incident management is gathering accurate information in a timely manner in order to effectively implement response plans, as well as to feed information into the crisis management organization. Typically, information is disjointed, inaccurate, and sporadic during the early stages of a crisis event, significantly hampering the ability for managers to make sound decisions, mobilize the correct resources, and bring the greatest degree of control to the situation.

The establishment of layered communication measures is essential within both domestic and remote locations in order to ensure that effective information dissemination is available during crisis situations. A natural disaster can close down normal communication mediums, so alternative options should be available, such as satellite phones or independent and mobile Internet systems. A set of clearly established protocols and information dissemination points (see "The Communications Plan" in Chapter 1) will enhance the timely delivery of information, as well as ensure that the initial source of reporting is identified for future verification. Accuracy of reporting also reduces the potential for erroneous information and subsequent wasting of valuable time and resources. The use of focused reporting templates designed to prompt managers into asking the right questions and thus delivering more concise and detailed information to supporting organizations is also very useful (see Chapter 6). What may be an obvious question to one manager may not occur to another, so comprehensive information capture report templates can take away much of the confusion and effort for managers concurrently managing crisis response, while also feeding critical information to decision-making and support groups. The additional value of such capture reports is connected to post incident reviews and any company audits or investigations following an event.

Incident Management Plan Crisis Response Guidelines

Given the wide user audience for the IMP, companies should consider what guidelines are required for the lowest level of responder competence. More detailed explanations may be captured within a management section of the IMP, with more tactical guidelines being provided within the response section. Response guidelines walk a first responder or incident manager through logical methodologies and considerations for bringing control to a crisis event (see Chapter 5). The crisis response guidelines should be clear, simple, and as succinct as possible. They will provide a checklist of actions to take and options to consider while a crisis is in play. The response guidelines should be tabulated, as illustrated in Exhibit 2.18, so that responders can quickly move to the section pertinent to a specific event they are dealing with, rather than having to sift through volumes of non-applicable information during an emergency.

Crisis response guidelines should have associated information capture reports so that both elements work in a complementary fashion: the capture report gathering

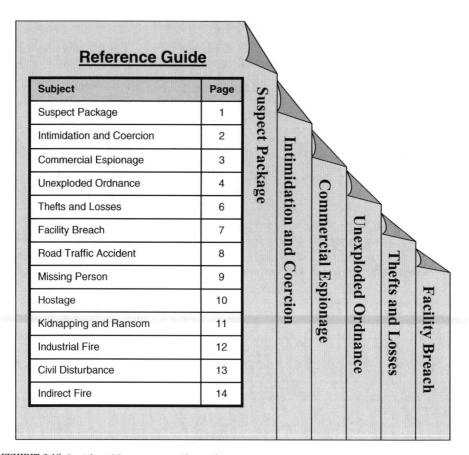

EXHIBIT 2.18 Incident Management Cheat Sheet

facts and the response guidelines providing effective response measures. Often a tear sheet approach allows managers to separate the response section required from the remainder of the IMP manual—allowing that section to be used in isolation.

Destruction Plans

A component of the IMP might include the identification of materials or information that might have to be destroyed if project staff need to depart a location quickly. Materials may include employment records (typically of locals), which could compromise personal safety and security, competitive business information, banking details, as well as security and intelligence materials. Some materials can be destroyed by burning, others by more technological methods such as using degaussing rings on IT hardware. Vehicles, communications, and other technologies and weaponry may also be elements of a destruction plan within certain environments. Clear authorities for destroying materials should be provided to ensure that managers understand their roles and responsibilities.

Incident Management Plan Risk Assessments

While typically a function of the crisis response team (CRT), it can in some instances be useful for the incident response team (IRT) to indicate how a crisis event may impact the company from a grassroots perspective. This will feed immediate concerns and information from the source of the event, to supplement the data response materials forwarded during the initial stages of a crisis event. A basic IMP risk assessment of how the event may affect the company can prove useful to support risk mitigation at all levels at the early stages of a crisis. Such assessments may include:

Immediate Concerns
- Is there an immediate risk to personnel?
- Is there an immediate risk to the company's reputation?
- What risks are presented to resources or facilities?
- Is there a risk to third parties?
- How long before any of these risks occur—how much time is there?

Situation
- What is the cause or motive of the risk event?
- Is it likely to get worse?
- Are other (different) threats likely to occur?
- What happened, where, and when?
- What effects are to be expected in the best case, likely case, and worst case?

Complicating Factors
- What legal implications are there?
- What media interest has been shown?
- What environmental factors will hamper the resolution of the problem?

The IMP risk assessment should not be confused with the responsibilities of the crisis response team and specialist responders, who should conduct more comprehensive risk assessments and evaluations during and following the crisis. The IMP risk assessment is a tool designed to provide a local perspective of the problems and impacts likely to occur that might fall outside of normal reporting formats within the IMP. While not a component of the IMP, the company should also link risk assessments to any recovery plans so that when the situation has sufficiently stabilized the company can begin to plan the resumption of normal operations.

Summary

The IMP is a functional component of the Business Continuity Management Plan. It leverages the policies, resources, and protocols contained within the Business Continuity Management Plan, but should be self-sufficient as a stand-alone plan, as some users may not have access to the wider instructions and guidelines provided within other company plans. The IMP should also be designed to meet two core goals: provide sufficient information prior to an emergency to place risks and responses into an understandable context for a wide user audience, as well as then offer simple, clear, and effective methods by which to capture and channel information, as well as empower local managers to deal with a wide range of crisis events. Training and rehearsals are critical for the IMP to be most effective, although commonly not all users will have the opportunity to be trained in its use, and therefore the plan should be as intuitive and pragmatic as possible.

The complexity and scope of an IMP will be determined by the nature, size, complexity, practices, and operating environments in which the company and its staff work. Simple versions of decision matrixes, resource plans, interface plans, and communications plans might be included to ensure that clear management and control practices are included. These are often diluted and focused versions of the same policies and plans contained within the more strategic corporate risk management plans. Where possible, information should be migrated from master plans and subcomponents to ensure consistency, as well as to reduce the level of effort required to develop and sustain such plans.

The IMP will assist the company in transiting from confusion to control and consolidation and recovery, as more experienced crisis managers are mobilized to support local staff and incident managers. The IMP should be a flexible and pragmatic tool, guiding without constraining management teams. Where possible, a custodian of master plans should be appointed (typically the Chief Security Officer), ensuring that consistency is retained as plans are tailored to suit unique geographic regions or projects, as well as channeling updates and enhancements to multiple users. The IMP may work to support project or business risk mapping activities, and should be reflective of the threats presented to each operating activity.

The design and development of plans should be as collaborative as possible, seeking buy-in and participation from the stakeholder population. Auditing and validations should occur to ensure plans remain in alignment with the corporate ethos and needs, and should not be permitted to become redundant after the initial effort and cost expenditures are made. Clear ownership and responsibilities should be attributed, and collaboration with external agencies should be undertaken to leverage resources, knowledge, and expertise. IMPs should reflect the company requirements, as well as outside influences like local laws and ordinances. The IMP may have repetitive components of other plans, but should be capable of operating in isolation.

CHAPTER 3

Crisis Management Structures

The structure of the company's divisions, departments, and geographic business interests, as well as any supporting security vendors or external agencies will govern the organization and membership of incident management and crisis response teams. The teams will typically be responsible for coordinating all activities during an emergency situation, both internally as well as managing and interacting with external groups, individuals, and agencies. The contingency plan should define the requirements expected of and from this team, their level of authority, what they are permitted to do, as well as seeking to identify the key personnel nominated to perform critical roles and any redundancies prior to any emergency event occurring (see Chapter 1).

It is important both within the company and especially within supporting agencies or vendors that the different levels of management focus and needs are clearly understood, and where possible documented. Corporate officers will require support in terms of strategic planning and business continuity and recovery requirements, while project managers will typically deal with more front-end-related issues, such as resolving immediate and granular-level requirements. Many focuses and needs will overlap, where both groups will be striving to reach the same overall goals, although perhaps with slightly different focus areas. The unique or nuanced focus areas associated with each group will determine what information or participation is required, and how they will respond. It is especially important that vendors understand the different needs and expectations of their clients in order to better support them—notably that the field office deals with the immediate requirements of the crisis while the corporate office typically assists with business continuity or recovery planning and other strategic-level issues.

Contingency planning presents an opportunity for the company to reduce the level of risk to its business activity as well as establish a viable plan to deal with problems while not under the pressure of a crisis event. While this opportunity should be exploited where possible, it requires time, energy and resources and many organizations pay lip service to the creation of a pragmatic and current business continuity plan, which often results in serious mismanagement during any subsequent incident. Those organizations that do plan ahead often avoid significant problems and respond in a manner that considerably reduces the impact of a crisis and supports overall business resilience. Companies should ideally take advantage of the time available prior to an emergency to design effective crisis response organizations and educate and train participants to respond to postulated or unexpected crisis situations with confidence and professionalism, rather than attempting to contend with developing such plans and structures, as well as educating responders, while concurrently meeting the needs of an ongoing emergency response.

It is arguable whether some groups should be considered a crisis management team or an incident response team. The defining point could be whether the group is focused purely on the incident in isolation or is responsible for dealing with matters outside of the event (i.e., effectively micro- or macro-level focus, decisions, and responsibilities). Typically, the crisis event will be dealt with at various levels, from the event source to the corporate executive level. In order to better coordinate activities and information, it is important that there occurs a management fusion at each level within the company, as well as with corresponding vendors, external agencies, or team members. The company should expect appropriate offices and management staff to be part of any response and information chain during a crisis, rather than being unadvised or ignorant of the situation. A separate joint venture interface plan can ensure that more accurate and timely information flows between the company and external groups, improving decision making and overall event awareness for a project team, as well as corporate officers.

Interorganizational Management

The company should, as part of the Business Continuity Management (BCM) Plan, determine what resources can be leveraged or outsourced to support incident and crisis management. Even major international companies will not have the expertise or past performance experience to manage every aspect of a crisis situation, and often governments or specialist organizations can bring expertise or considerable weight to bear that commercial organizations might not be able to match. Where possible and appropriate, the crisis management organization should seek to include government support and outsourced expertise as part of its crisis team composition. By predefining such supporting elements, the company might enhance contingency planning measures and make incident and crisis response measures more effective (i.e., exponentially increasing the response capabilities of the company), as well as actually reducing the costs required for contingency planning and crisis management.

The company should define with any external interfaces the preferences and requirements for communication traffic during an emergency situation. This also applies to contracted security vendor companies, as often the company project or program managers feel that their corporate offices are too involved in the tactical event and should not be directing response measures, or that they themselves have not been provided sufficient time to understand the scope and impacts of the problems before executive management begin asking questions and demanding or directing action. Conflicts within the company's own organization are common during crisis events; and subcontracted vendors supporting with such issues require clear guidelines and policies, as well as diplomacy and a balanced approach to multilevel requirements in order to understand from whom they should take direction, and how they should support the company's crisis response. Tiering the crisis management structure often helps companies understand the different focus areas as well as the spectrum of levels involved within a crisis event, as illustrated in Exhibit 3.1.

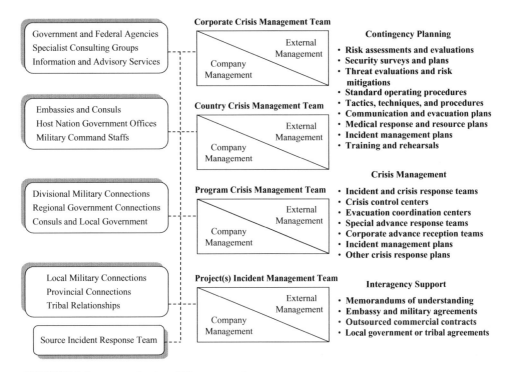

EXHIBIT 3.1 Interorganizational Management

The company, supporting agencies, and subcontracted security or crisis response vendors should collaborate, where possible, to determine the structure of the crisis response levels, functions, and responsibilities in order to align structures, policies, and procedures to best match crisis requirements. The event itself will also significantly influence the manner in which such response and management teams are established and how they operate. An example of a typical event chain of management functions follows:

- **First Responder.** The nonspecialist person or manager who might be first on the scene and will initiate the crisis response, as well as start information flows and control measures.
- **Source Incident Response Team (IRT).** A trained local incident control team or manager who might be first on site, or in close proximity to start to bring control to the crisis event.
- **Project IRT.** An incident response trained manager or team who will take from local responders the control over gathering information and controlling the tactical aspects of the crisis event.
- **Program Crisis Response Team (CRT).** A trained senior incident manager who might manage multiple aspects of the crisis event and mobilize local outsourced support, bridging the gap between incident management and crisis management.
- **Country CRT.** The first layer or true crisis management element that will support controlling the actual event in strategic terms, while also undertaking

peripheral crisis management functions and mobilizing in-country resources and outsourced support. They will often bridge the field and corporate levels.

- **Corporate CRT.** Senior-level crisis managers who will deal with strategic needs and issues for the company as a whole. They will sanction procurements and deal with public relations issues, as well as senior government agencies and special support groups.

While some organizations may have fewer levels within their crisis management structure, the three principle levels of the person at the scene, those dealing with the physical aspects of an emergency response, and the strategic crisis management element are nearly always found within a crisis event. The right balance of ownership, authorities, and operating parameters needs to be struck between the roles of the corporate and country office and those of the incident management teams. The key issues companies should consider are:

- The type, scope, and severity of the incident.
- How undertaking the role will undermine primary work functions for incident and crisis managers.
- The liability implications for those appointed to the tasks, are they the best choice to protect the company.
- Effectively managing the threat at the local, national, and corporate levels—focusing holistically on the implications of an event.
- Implementing standard operating procedures to reduce the risk probabilities.
- Implementing incident management plans (IMPs) to reduce the impacts of risk events and bring control to the situation.
- Implementing event-specific crisis response plans to augment and transition from incident management responses to full scale crisis management.
- Availability and experience of local management to handle an incident, determining early whether additional support is needed
- Identifying other supporting agencies that might be leveraged to assist with crisis management.
- Potential of the incident to have an effect on the company beyond the impacts of the actual event.

Companies will organize their crisis response teams based on a range of factors, including corporate structures, risk policies and management approaches, risk tolerance levels, geographic and industry influences, the ability and quality of government and other external support, as well as business partner or subcontracted security vendor participation. Each business activity may also bring unique requirements to the composition of a crisis team, either internally or in terms of outsourced support.

Crisis Leadership

An organization's BCM Plan is only as effective as the knowledge and capability of those employees or managers implementing the risk evaluations, mitigations, and crisis response measures contained within the plan. An important aspect of the BCM Plan, as well its tactical response element (the Incident Management Plan), is the education, rehearsal, and testing of key decision makers and response managers. The BCM Plan does not work in isolation of human decision making and participation, and while the policies and plans will certainly support more effective management responses, offering structure, guidance, and systems to help guide an organization through the wide spectrum of challenges they may face—it will invariably be the effectiveness of crisis leadership which governs how well, or indeed badly, an organization will fare.

Crisis management leadership contains many of the same skills and tenants as would be found within any leadership role. The main differences between typical management and a crisis decision making is the speed that decisions need to be made and the gravity of impacts associated with the decision. When considering crisis leadership the following principles should be considered:

- **Knowledge.** Crisis leaders should have the knowledge and experience to effectively manage a crisis situation. Crisis leadership requires swift, balanced, and decisive action. Responses should not be impaired by a lack of understanding, confusion, self-doubt (or indeed doubt in others), or the inability to formulate intuitive and innovative solutions based on a solid foundation of knowledge.
- **Information.** Decision making should be shaped by accurate and timely information. Decisions based on assumptions or speculation will invariably impede effective response measures and could exacerbate the problem. Understanding how to gather, process, understand, and utilize information quickly and effectively is a fundamental aspect of successful crisis leadership.
- **Confidence.** Crisis managers should have the confidence to take decisive action and to make informed judgments which are not undermined by self doubt or confusion. Confidence is based on the knowledge of how a crisis event unfolds and how to develop and implement structured, focused, and mature crisis solutions. Confidence also involves understanding your own, or organization's, limitations—and knowing when to seek support or guidance.
- **Practice.** Where possible (and appropriate) crisis leaders should seek to practice their management skills and associated responses to different forms of crisis events—whether it is a practical exercise or a management tabletop discussion. Practice will identify gaps and shortfalls as well as iron out any individual or group issues prior to an emergency occurring. Practice also develops knowledge, supports organizational structure, and creates confidence.
- **Structure.** Crisis leaders should develop a structured approach to their response to different forms of crisis events. Structure brings focus to what is often a confusing and dynamic leadership requirement. Structure also reduces confusion and doubt and engenders confidence within individuals and groups. Structure also reduces duplication of effort, identifies shortfalls and gaps in responses, and focuses multiple parties on meeting key issues.
- **Balance.** Crisis leaders should be decisive, but balanced in their approach to quickly formulating responses to often complex and challenging emergencies. The adage "less haste more speed" applies when considering rapid but balanced crisis management decision making.
- **Pace.** The pace of decision making should be measured and balanced, but reflective of the external drivers created by a crisis event—the speed of unfolding crisis events should be matched, or exceeded by the ability for managers to make effective decisions. Some crisis events will allow for a sedate pace of response,

others will require immediate decision making and action. Crisis leaders need to understand the tempo of response requirements and align their leadership style accordingly.

Establishing the ability for individuals to make mature, confident, and well-informed decisions will be pivotal for the success of the BCM Plan. The BCM Plan and its functional elements, such as the IMP and other crisis response plans (kidnap and ransom, evacuation, pandemic, and so on) are after all only a tool to support effective crisis leadership.

Organizational Crisis Leadership

Organizations are responsible for creating an environment in which effective crisis leadership can operate. Poorly structured and disorganized groups will struggle to successfully manage a crisis, even with highly competent and experienced crisis managers in place. The following organizational principles support effective crisis leadership.

- **Clear responsibilities.** The company should establish clear responsibilities within the crisis management organization to avoid duplication of effort, or gaps and shortfalls within crisis leadership responses. Clear responsibilities can also remove some of the internal company politics when a crisis occurs.
- **Training and education.** Companies should set aside time and resources to ensure that key crisis leaders are educated and trained in how to best manage a crisis event, and how to best utilize the policies, systems, tools, and protocols within the BCM Plan.
- **Practice and rehearsals.** Crisis management groups should practice crisis responses, whether this is a practical exercise or table top discussion. Practice and rehearsal creates familiarity with the BCM Plan, develops confidence in the plan as well as with the crisis management team, and identifies any shortfalls or friction points.
- **Empowering leadership.** Crisis leaders should be empowered to take decisive action within sensibly established parameters. Training and practice will create corporate confidence in empowering crisis teams and thus allow some elements of control to be decentralized, enabling more effective management to brought to a crisis situation at the local level. Crisis managers without the ability to make decisions or take action will be significantly undermined in their ability to successfully manage a crisis.
  - **Delegation.** As part of the empowering approach, management should seek to delegate (sensibly) to the lowest levels crisis decision making abilities so that a structured and streamlined management system is emplace, rather than a centralized, unwieldy, and ponderous crisis management structure. This forms a core component to empowering leadership.
  - **Authority lines.** Clear authority lines, permissions, and authorities should be in place to enable swift and sanctioned decisions within the crisis management organization. Managers should know who to ask for permission, rather than try to attempt to identify decision makers during a crisis event.
- **Established systems and supporting mechanisms.** Companies should create effective systems and supporting mechanisms prior to a crisis occurring which

will assist crisis leaders in logically guiding their decisions and supporting them in being efficient and effective in responding to an emergency. It will also ensure some degree of consistency in the response and provide confidence to managers that certain actions are automatically ongoing, and that defined information is being gathered and transmitted to predefined groups.

- **Innovation and flexibility.** Companies should understand that while crisis management systems and policies support crisis leadership, each crisis event will be unique and will require a tailored approach to achieving resolution. Innovation and flexibility are the cornerstones of effective crisis leadership—using established policies, plans, and protocols as tools, rather than crutches.
- **Leveraging.** Companies should always look both inward and outward to resources, knowledge, and capabilities which can be used to support effective crisis resolution. Those companies which do not leverage external resources will invariably miss opportunities to augment the effectiveness of their response.

Approach Methodologies

Crisis leaders should ask themselves "so what" when dealing with a crisis, taking each question and answer related to the crisis event to its natural conclusion. The "so what" principle will create multiple lines of consideration, with multiple subsets. Each line of consideration should be closed with an action point or decision. For example: An employee has been reported as involved in a car accident in Lagos Nigeria: the immediate lines of consideration may include:

- **When.** When did the accident occur.
- **Where.** Where did the accident occur.
- **What.** What happened.
- **Why.** Why did it happen.
- **Who.** Who was involved.
- **Support.** What needs to be done and what support is needed.
- **Management.** Who is taking charge of the event.
- **Risks.** What existing and new risks might be associated with the event.
- **Impacts.** What impacts, current and future are associated with the event.

Following a logical structure of gathering information and making effective decisions crisis leaders may adopt the "so what" approach to determine action points and decisions. So answers will provide answers to other questions and so duplication can be easily avoided. For example:

1. **When did it occur.** We don't know when the accident occurred; so what—we need to establish the time as injured employees may be at risk; so what—we need to speak with someone with accurate information; so what—how do we get accurate information on the situation?

    Action points. Use the crisis communications plan and the mediums of mobile phone, e-mails, or text messaging. Use the information sources of chiefs of party or security managers, other employees, friends, family, police station, or hospitals.

2. **Where did it occur.** We need to establish where the accident occurred; so what—the roads are poor and medical support is remote and limited; so what—we need to possibly extract them from the site and find get them to good medical treatment; so what—how do we do this?

> *Action Points.* Determine the location of the accident in relation to road, air or maritime casualty extraction routes as well as companies which might be able to support the medical extractions. We need to find hospitals or medical centers which could provide the correct level of medical treatment. We need to determine how payment is made and whether any insurance policies are in place.

3. **What happened:** We need to establish what happened; so what—it will determine the extent of injuries as well as any associated legal implications; so what—we need to establish the facts?

> *Action Points.* See points one and two. Also consider legal risks and implications and possible defense support requirements associated with being arrested or investigated within Nigeria.

And so forth. . . .

Each set of action points might also result in a "so what" scenario. For example, if no insurance policies are in place how can payment be made to ensure that medical treatment will be administrated to injured employees, or how can air evacuation options be utilized and who can make the decision and how can the company be engaged and paid? While the "so what" approach appears obvious and based on simple common sense, it is surprising how often obvious yet highly impactful issues are missed during a crisis situation. As such this form of approach can help crisis leaders ensure that they move through complex thought processes in a logical and comprehensive manner.

Education and Training

Education and training creates the conditions in which individuals and groups can successfully utilize sound BCM Plans, as well as have the confidence to step outside of established policies and plans to meet unique challenges which the BCM Plan may not have fully addressed. The following forms of education and training are available to develop and sustain the skills and capabilities of an organization's crisis leaders.

- **Formal Instruction.** Formal instruction may take the shape of a focused training course for crisis leaders on risk and security management issues, whether conducted as part of a series of modules or as a condensed package.
- **Mentoring Programs.** Mentoring programs may be formal or semiformal with experience, and trained crisis leaders mentoring less experienced team members so that cross-pollination of skills and knowledge occurs.

- **Shadowing and Transitioning.** Crisis leaders may delegate or transition responsibilities over a defined period to ensure that new crisis leader incumbents have a period of indoctrination prior to fully assuming responsibilities.
- **Tabletop Exercises.** Management leadership exercises and discussions can be used to run a crisis management team, and individuals, through their paces as a low cost, high value training medium.
- **Discussion Groups.** Discussion and working groups or forums can provide a valuable medium whereby information and ideas are shared and friction points or shortfalls are identified and resolved.
- **Instructional Manuals.** Training manuals can be used (often in conjunction with other education and training mediums) to educate crisis leaders on their own role, as well as how an organization will function and respond to a crisis.
- **Web-Based Training.** Web-based education and training mediums can be used to meet the needs of a dispersed crisis management team.
- **Train the Trainer.** Creating internal capability through a *train the trainer* scheme can improve the knowledge and capabilities of the instructor, while also creating a pyramid effect of capability within a wider group.
- **Activation Exercises.** Activation exercises can be used to determine the ability for individuals and the crisis management team to effectively respond to a crisis event. This tests both the mechanisms for activation, as well as the competence of individuals and the wider group in terms of response.

There is no miracle answer for how crisis leadership should work, nor necessarily a way of predicting, nor assessing after the event whether the individual or group leadership approach used was the most effective way of managing a particular crisis. Establishing a solid platform from which good decisions can be made should be the principle goal of companies and organizations. In addition, corporate leadership should bear in mind that it is better to make some form of decision, rather than make no decision at all in the event of a crisis—recovery is invariably preferable than inaction.

Supporting Crisis Management Groups

Once established, it is important that the IMP and Business Continuity Management Plan as a whole is managed and sustained correctly. Access to materials should also be readily available to the incident and crisis response groups, regardless of the location of staff or operations. The following concepts can provide useful management approaches for managing and accessing risk and crisis management materials:

- **Intranet Access.** Consideration should be given to placing response guideline materials on the company intranet in order to permit access from any geographic region at any time. This also allows materials to be downloaded in bulk, rather than tying up e-mail servers, and also reduces the risks of version control issues.
- **Security Permissions.** Certain access privileges should be restricted to key staff only. A clear access control policy and portioned material segments should be established.
- **Data Capture Tools.** The establishment of data capture tools, recording crisis events, details, and other important information, can support trend analysis

and risk forecasting, as well as provide evidence of problems and solutions undertaken to support business activities.

- **Fusion Point.** The company should determine a fusion point in both management and storage terms in order to ensure that materials are effectively managed, new materials collated and utilized, and redundancies avoided. This will also ensure consistency of applications and standards, because these can become quickly lost as multiple managers tailor their own reports and policies to suit their unique operating conditions.

Establishing a common access system will enable real-time reporting, easy updates and reviews of materials, collaborative initiatives to pool and consolidate concepts and materials, as well as the ability to establish crisis-specific management files as they occur. The tracking of trends and statistical data is also more easily managed with a shared management system (see Exhibit 3.2, which demonstrates how projects can feed in information to a central custodian in order to collate and analyze information).

Such information can then be easily converted into statistical data in order to determine whether trends are being set for specific projects or threat natures in general (see Exhibit 3.3).

A range of organizations might be available and positioned to support incident and crisis management teams in managing an emergency situation. Some groups, such as the Overseas Security Advisory Council (OSAC) and Security Information Service for Business Overseas (SISBO), can support the development of networks and forums to identify and avoid risks abroad, as well as leverage other commercial groups' capabilities and expertise during an emergency. Embassies, law

Man-Made Crisis Events	Project 1	Project 2	Project 3	Project 1	Project 2	Project 3	Project 1	Project 2	Project 3	Project 4	Project 5	Project 6	Totals
	Jan–Mar08			Apr–June08			Jul–Sep08			Oct–Dec08			
	Quarter 1			Quarter 2			Quarter 3			Quarter 4			
High-Value Thefts ▪	3	2	1	1	1	0	6	7	2	1	2	4	30
Civil Disturbances ▪	1	0	0	0	0	0	3	4	9	3	4	2	26
Labor Disputes ▪	1	2	0	1	1	0	0	2	0	0	6	0	13
Workplace Violence ▪	12	1	0	11	0	0	32	4	0	8	0	1	69
Workplace Accidents ▪	3	0	0	6	2	1	12	2	1	5	2	1	35
Robberies ▪	6	0	1	3	1	0	4	0	0	7	0	1	23
Auto Thefts ▪	9	2	1	4	1	0	4	1	1	8	2	0	33
Breaking and Entering ▪	3	0	0	1	0	0	1	0	1	3	0	0	9
Sabotage ▪	0	0	0	0	0	0	1	0	0	0	0	0	1
Small Arms Fire ▪	9	1	0	4	2	1	3	2	1	8	2	0	33
Indirect Fire Attacks ▪	3	0	0	1	0	0	0	0	1	3	0	1	9
Natural Crisis Events	Jan–Mar08			Apr–June08			Jul–Sep08			Oct–Dec08			
Floods ▪	2	3	1	1	0	0	0	0	0	0	2	1	10
Forest Fires ▪	0	0	0	0	0	1	2	1	0	0	0	0	4
Earthquakes ▪	0	0	1	0	0	0	0	0	0	0	0	0	1
Sandstorms ▪	0	0	0	0	0	0	1	1	0	1	0	0	3

EXHIBIT 3.2 Crisis Data Capture Tools

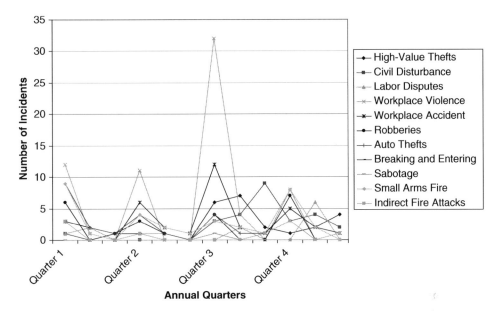

EXHIBIT 3.3 Man-Made Event Data Tracking

enforcement, emergency services, and military organizations may also be available to support the crisis management team in governmental terms. Contracted commercial support, whether logistical services such as maritime, land, or air transportation services, medical support, or security and legal provision, may also form components of a supporting agency plan. The company should determine what resources and capabilities can be leveraged as a noncost element, as well as what needs can be met only by contracted support in order to bridge any shortfalls or gaps in organic capability.

Response Buildups

Each crisis event will define what management resources are required to bring control to a situation. The entire crisis management organization may not be required on every occasion, and only those individuals or groups whose contributions and participation are required to effectively manage a crisis situation should be mobilized. Exhibit 3.4 illustrates a possible buildup of a crisis response organization following an event. At any stage the company may turn off the crisis response measures if the situation is resolved, or if it transpires that there is in fact no threat or crisis. Defining the difference between a problem and crisis is important in order to create the right expectations and perspectives, ensure that emergencies are correctly managed, and make certain that crisis and incident response organizations are not unduly fatigued. Typically, the response buildup starts from the bottom (e.g., the first responders identifying an issue and alerting their management chain, with information moving upward as more senior and experienced management are mobilized to respond to the threat). Preferably, if the company has a robust intelligence capability and risk mitigation system in place, threats will be identified prior to occurrence and the

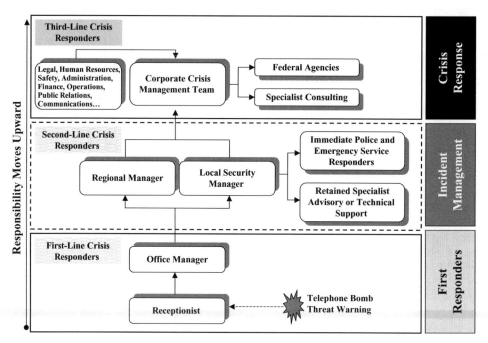

EXHIBIT 3.4 Response Buildup

process can be driven from the top down, especially if the crisis is a strategic issue such as relating to public relations or financial and brand issues.

Depending on the configurations adopted by the company when designing the crisis response organizational structure, as well as where the event strikes in terms of immediate hierarchy involvement, there may be a series of quickly escalating response levels flowing from the point of occurrence upward and outward to the most senior levels of the crisis response organization. If a crisis is brought under control and the impacts are neutralized, some elements of a crisis response organization might not be involved, or may be quickly stood down. Escalation of participation should be driven by the need to manage an event and offset its effects, rather than to generate immediate or unnecessary involvement of all participants within the plan.

Crisis Management Structures

Each company will define the composition and structure of its own crisis response group dependent on the nature, size, and scope of the organization, as well as the operating regions and risk types it is exposed to. The tiering of response groups creates an effective command-and-control chain that meets both corporate and field requirements, as well as reflecting the size and complexity of response needs. Four basic layers might be found within a typical crisis response organizational structure:

1. Corporate
2. Country
3. Program
4. Project

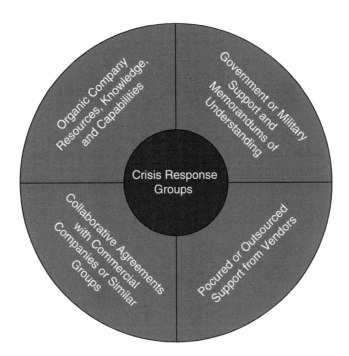

Crisis Response Groups

Organic Company Resources, Knowledge, and Capabilities

Government or Military Support and Memorandums of Understanding

Collaborative Agreements with Commercial Companies or Similar Groups

Pocured or Outsourced Support from Vendors

EXHIBIT 3.5 Crisis Response Organizational Structuring

A company should consider the value or determining participation from external groups in support of crisis response measures at each level, as well as drawing on its own knowledge, resources, and capabilities. Both parent and operating region governments and military or law enforcement agencies can provide considerable support during crisis events, often bringing influence or capabilities far outside of a commercial organization's area of expertise—although these should not be relied upon. The company might also wish to consider collaboration arrangements where mutual support is offered to other groups in return for reciprocal levels of assistance during a crisis event. The engagement of specialist subcontracted vendors is also an area where the company may wish to identify, retain, or contract support for services outside of its area of competence (see Exhibit 3.5).

The following information captures some layers of crisis response structures as well as key participant leadership that might be found within a crisis response organization.

Corporate Crisis Response Team

The corporate CRT is responsible for strategic risks and issues that affect the company as a whole, as well as for mobilizing resources and financial assistance to support the overall management of the crisis event. The corporate CRT may also liaise with government agencies in order to leverage support and will contract with outsourced advisory groups and resources to bridge gaps within the organization's capabilities. The corporate CRT will also liaise with corporate partnering companies and subcontractors in order to ensure that all appropriate measures are being taken, in terms of operational support as well as business continuity and recovery, legal, liability, reputational, and media liaison. The corporate CRT will also liaise and advise investors and shareholders as to the situation, to mitigate the effects of speculation, rumor, and erroneous reporting.

The corporate CRT should ensure that any partner companies or subcontractors that fall under the umbrella of the business activities CRT are informed of response activities, and also conform to agreed response measures (especially media management). The corporate CRT should also ensure that any subcontracted security vendors provide the appropriate levels of support throughout the incident, supplying both operational services, as well as capturing information and performing in a manner that reflects the standards and ethos of the company. In addition, the corporate CRT will ensure that human resources, media, and legal groups are linked between vendor and teaming companies to coordinate any information releases or responses.

Most important, the corporate CRT will ensure that information sharing with employee families as well as support and care for any persons involved in the incident are appropriately addressed. In addition, direct support to families and repatriation measures will be established and coordinated to support the country CRT. The corporate CRT will mobilize all human resources, media, government, and legal specialists in order to offer support, guidance, and management of the incident and personnel in practical resource terms, as well as mobilizing resources necessary to support a crisis event and deploy specialists and support staff to augment country management initiatives. The corporate CRT will have overall decision-making authority and will be responsible for strategic planning and senior-level liaison. The corporate CRT will also typically guide business recovery measures and decision making once the situation has stabilized. Following an incident, the corporate CRT will be responsible for capturing all information, decisions, and details in order to conduct an audit of the incident, as well as provide instructions on any policy or procedural changes. This team will also determine whether the business or operational activity remains viable, or whether business approaches require change.

Country Crisis Response Team

The country or national CRT is typically comprised of the most senior managers responsible for a geographic region, typically led by the country or general manager or chief of party. The country CRT will coordinate all national-level activities and support as the focal point of regional crisis management. The country CRT has the local expertise and relationships to mobilize resources and support in-country to deal practically with an incident, on behalf and under direction of the corporate CRT. The country CRT will normally provide expert advice and recommendations to both corporate and program CRTs, and also coordinate all support in the area from both internal and external resources, including military, diplomatic missions, law enforcement, and other supporting or commercial organizations. The country CRT will focus information flow from the program incident response team (IRT) to the in-country subcontracted security vendors and teammates, as well as act as the coordination point for tactical and strategic-level advice, requirements, decision making, and actions.

The country CRT may also act as the national reception team for evacuations, and may deploy supporting company resources from other projects to meet resource gaps for an affected group. In addition, the country CRT may locally contract supporting vendors to provide medical, transportation, security, legal, and life support needs. The country CRT will also liaise closely with teammates and subcontractor management to bring coordination to a multiple-participant response, ensuring that all crisis management needs are being met and that information is shared among affected parties. The country CRT may also initiate local reciprocal or mutual aid agreements, as well as memorandums of understanding.

A country CRT may be led by the most senior commercial manager and security or risk adviser for the region, and will typically be the group that establishes or evaluates national and subordinate crisis response plans and policies. The team should therefore be intimately familiar with each subordinate program or project and should be capable of supporting operational decision making from a local perspective, as well as relaying detailed and personalized information upward to the corporate CRT.

Program Incident Response Team

The program incident response team (IRT) will often bridge the gap between incident management and crisis response, dealing concurrently with both the event effects as well as considering strategic issues. The program IRT might, depending on the size and complexity of the program as well as the scope and nature of the team's appointment, either focus more on strategic-level or crisis management initiatives or, if more tactically aligned, concentrate on managing the granular aspects of the emergency situation. The focus area of the program IRT will also depend on whether the program has been directly affected and the team is dealing with emergency requirements firsthand, or they are supporting a subordinate project experiencing a crisis situation. The program IRT will use both the IMP and more detailed and event-focused response plans as guidelines.

The program IRT is principally led by the most senior security consultant or company program manager within the program. If a company or vendor security manager leads this team, this security manager typically does so in close partnership with the senior company program manager. The point at which management decision making transfers from the program manager to the security manager must be defined in order to streamline decision making—as often the program manager will initially lead decision making during the opening stages of a crisis, up until the crisis has reached a certain stage when operational or security and safety decision making becomes more important. The program IRT manager and staff must ensure that all security staff and supporting military, medical, and other external service support groups are directed to assist the local incident response team commander in order to effectively evacuate personnel and assets from the risk area, as well as ensure that any medical support is readied to receive casualties. In addition, the program IRT will often integrate any vendor's or teaming partner's staff into the existing program IRT, ensuring they complement each other's efforts and avoid duplication or unnecessary confusion or friction.

The program IRT's secondary function is to notify all company management chains of the incident in order to initiate the country and corporate CRTs. At appropriate junctures, the program IRT manager will provide documented accounts (in predetermined formats) as to the status and details of the incident, as well as formal serious incident reports. The program IRT may also assess the risk implications to support decision-making requirements (see IMP Risk Assessment Reports in Chapter 6). Any subcontractor program IRTs should be expected to conduct similar reports and documentation concurrently, liaising with its own country CRTs. The program IRT will typically report directly to the country CRT.

Project Incident Response Team

The project IRT may be led by an experienced security manager, or the project manager in the absence of a security professional. A transition of control may also occur if both a project manager and a security manager are within the project team, with the security professional assuming a command role, rather than an advisory role, only if the risk exceeds certain limits—typically where security and safety are central to the nature of the emergency situation. These limits should be clearly defined to avoid friction and ambiguity of leadership roles during a crisis event. Typically the project IRT will focus on dealing with the actual crisis event, leveraging support from program, country, and corporate crisis management structures in order to mobilize resources outside of the project's organic capabilities. The project IRT may deploy response groups within its structure and may also instigate local agreements and support capabilities within defined plans and protocols. They will be the main users of the IMP and may under emergency circumstances implement more complex crisis response protocols and plans, such as emergency evacuations and disaster response plans.

The project IRT is normally tactically focused, rather than dealing with the strategic and non-tangible aspects of the crisis, such as reputation and liability concerns, although managers should be aware of the implications their actions and the crisis event may have further up the chain of responsibility, and should act to mitigate these risks where possible or appropriate. The project IRT will, however, be responsible for feeding information, insights, and guidance to more senior management teams so as to ensure an accurate representation of the event to support sound decision making, as well as making sure that threat and impact evaluations are fed throughout the crisis management structure. The size, complexity, and makeup of the project management team will determine the degree of autonomy and responsibility the project IRT will have.

Special Response Teams

A special response team (SRT) may be mobilized to support the corporate CRT in dealing with strategic crises, such as public relations and media advisers, legal counsel, or investigative services, or they may be deployed to the region or area in which a crisis is occurring in order to bring knowledge, experience, and additional capabilities to bear to support incident management groups. The configuration and objectives of an SRT will depend on the nature of the crisis, as well as the operating environment in which an event is occurring. The SRT may be highly specialized, such as advisers in kidnapping and ransom situations, legal counsel, or technology consultants, or may be more tactical in nature, such as security consultants and disaster and evacuation response managers. A series of SRT options may be defined within the contingency planning component of the Business Continuity Management Plan in advance of a crisis event occurring, and may require retainer fees or preagreed contractual and operating arrangements. Conversely, an SRT may be cre-ated ad hoc to meet unique and unplanned crisis events, requiring the mobilization of either in-house or outsourced support.

Composition of Crisis Response Teams

The composition of the crisis and incident response teams should reflect the person-nel required to analyze and deal with any events, from the management or command elements to specialist advisers. Hierarchy and politics should not be an aspect of management selection; rather, responsibilities should be attributed based on com-petence, knowledge, and experience. The role of the crisis or incident management team is to be in a position to respond effectively to postulated threats or actual events in a timely manner, implementing and adjusting where necessary predefined response policies and plans.

Top management commitment is critical for the success of this team; the outcome of a crisis not only affects business success and corporate interests, but perhaps more importantly can impact the lives and the jobs of employees—people who are reliant on the skills of management to see them, and at times their families, through a crisis event. The various levels of CRTs and IRTs will flow information and recommendations up to the corporate management or executive board while having autonomy of decision making within certain agreed and defined parameters. The level of decision making, responsibility, and authority will vary from corporate down to project teams, as well as down to the event IRT. As much responsibility as possible and appropriate should be forced downward to enable local managers to be empowered to contribute to the management and control of emergencies—while still being answerable to corporate management. The IMP provides a guideline for all levels of management, supported by more focused and comprehensive plans for singular, complex, and high-impact events. When considering a generic crisis response organization, however, the following appointments or groups may form components of a crisis and incident management structure for the company:

- Crisis management team commander
- Crisis team coordinator
- Physical and risk security manager
- Technical security manager
- Special response team leader
- Administration manager
- Intelligence or information officer
- Liaison officer
- Communications manager
- Public relations officer
- Legal counsel
- Human resources department
- Health and safety department
- Stress trauma adviser
- Reception team manager
- Finance officer
- Investor relations officer

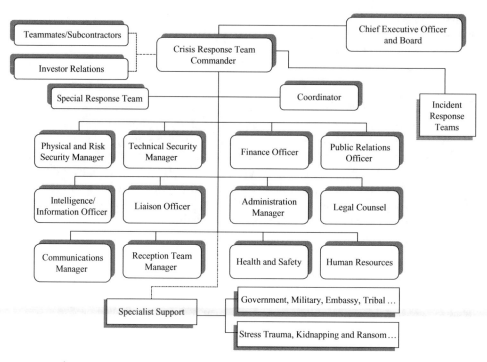

EXHIBIT 3.6 Crisis and Incident Response Structures

Invariably a host of supporting staff will accompany this core group in support of implementing plans, requirements, and activities. Some elements will be provided in-house, while others may be outsourced. The composition of a CRT should reflect the crisis event and the impacts it might have on individuals experiencing the risk, as well as the implications it might have on the company. Exhibit 3.6 illustrates possible group compositions.

Each company or group should define the nature, scope, and parameters of the roles and responsibilities within its response organization, driven by business as well as operational needs. The titling of each appointment may be adjusted to reflect the image, nature, and ethos of the company, as well as the status of those holding the appointments. Some companies will soften titles in order to reflect the ethos and branding of the group, while others will choose more militaristic titles to define the roles and responsibilities of the appointments. The following sections capture some concepts as to the nature of crisis management team responsibilities.

Crisis Management Team Commander

The chair of the crisis response group, or crisis management team commander (CMTC), will oversee the development and implementation of the company's Business Continuity Management Plan, as well as its separate components, including the IMP. The CMTC will also be responsible for ensuring that plans are distributed and that appropriate levels of education, training, evaluation, and rehearsals are conducted prior to a crisis event occurring. The CMTC will be responsible to the chief executive officer (CEO) in all matters related to preparing for and dealing with a crisis situation.

The CMTC typically makes executive decisions based on the advice and information provided from relevant subject matter experts, both within the company crisis response group and supporting company departments, as well as from external advisory agencies. CMTCs should be selected for their ability to make calm and analytical decisions under high-stress conditions, based on the company's ethos and corporate objectives, and balancing these with a clear understanding of the wider issues.

The CMTC should be able to conduct concurrent activities and absorb and respond to information in a dynamic, logical, and pragmatic manner. Following an incident, the CMTC should oversee the conduct of a comprehensive review of all policies and measures in order to update the risk management program. The CMTC should be supported by a second in command who takes over in the CMTC's absence and provides support and advice during intensive incidents. This post may be held by, or report directly to, the CEO and board officers of a company.

Crisis Team Coordinator

The crisis team coordinator (CTC) supports the functional activities of the CMTC and will conduct quality assurance checks on policies, plans, and procedures on a scheduled basis, or following a crisis event. The coordinator will also ensure that the plan has been distributed and disseminated appropriately, particularly for oversees or high-risk operations. Accountable for scheduling and evidencing training and testing of the plan, the coordinator will also prepare the Crisis Control Center or Tactical Operations Center for use.

The CTC may also monitor political and security risks as they affect the company and its business activities, tracking risks and alerting management to possible threats. The appointment may also ensure that coordination and arrangements are established with supporting groups, especially if response plans are to be amalgamated or used in tandem. This appointment might be held by the chief security officer or the CSO's deputy.

Physical and Risk Security Manager

The physical and risk security manager is responsible for risk management advice as well as physical security measures and the management of security personnel and resources. This manager is typically the chief security officer (CSO) of a company and will provide both strategic and tactical advice and guidance to the CMTC, if the security manager is not undertaking that appointment himself or herself.

This appointment will implement response plans and provide guidance to supporting groups in terms of practical requirements and activities. The security manager might also instigate emergency response groups to bring control to the situation, or implement risk countermeasures. This appointment will typically entrust the practical command of response teams to well-trained and experienced subcommanders, who will deal firsthand with any incidents from the incident control point. This post looks at both strategic and tactical impacts and ramifications, and advises the CMTC directly to ensure that best courses of action and decision making are possible.

Technical Security Manager

The technical security manager is responsible for the technical aspects of security, providing specialist advice and guidance on technology systems that might be used as part of the contingency plan and crisis management response procedures. Typically, the technology security manager reports to the physical and risk security manager (i.e., CSO) in order to most effectively utilize any technical assets available to mitigate risks or gather and collate information required for decision making.

The technical security manager for technology-related crisis events (i.e., cyber security risks) may take precedence and directly advise the CMTC. The technical security manager should be supported by specialist personnel who will oversee and utilize a range of information technology and security technology equipment.

Special Response Team Leader

The special response team (SRT) can provide companies with invaluable assistance in supporting the establishment of an immediate management focal point at the beginning of a crisis situation, managing emergency requirements on behalf of the company, advising local managers on response protocols and decision-making requirements, and ensuring that accurate information and support requests are channeled quickly and effectively back to corporate offices. SRTs should be engineered to assist in bringing swift resolutions to issues, regardless of the geographic region or operating conditions. They should be proven problem solvers, capable of dealing with a raft of issues and challenges in a focused and clinical manner, and leveraging all available local resources to support problem rectifications. SRTs may be used domestically or for foreign business activities. Under some circumstances, the SRT may assume control of a situation, reporting directly to the CMTC.

The SRT should provide high-grade management support, as well as proven operational and tactical services. The team should be positioned to assess the holistic problems facing a project, and quickly design effective and innovative mitigation and recovery measures. The SRT team leader will often be an expert in the field and as such undertakes roles clearly defined by the company, especially if SRT team services are outsourced by the company. A variety of services may be offered, including:

Operational management	Medical care and repatriations
Intelligence gathering	Health and safety
Communications and information technology	Stress trauma services
Legal services	Risk and security evaluations
Public relations services	Security provisions
Investigations	Structural damage control
Liaison and mediation	Workplace violence
Industry expertise	Kidnapping and ransom situations
Evacuation management	

Administration Manager

All events require the accurate collation and documentation of information as well as the practical mobilization of resources and support to deal with a crisis event. The administration manager may be tasked with providing document control, gathering facts and details of those involved in the event, booking flights, allocating and making available monies to procure resources (through the finance officer), identifying internal and external resource providers, plus a myriad of other mundane but essential tasks.

The administration manager is responsible for taking action on the logistical and procurement aspects of a crisis response, allowing other participants to focus on strategic or tactical activities that will rely on adequate administrative support. The administration manager may have responsibility for resource and procurement plans, although guided by the crisis response tacticians as to what might be required in terms of resources and scheduling in order to meet each unique crisis event.

Intelligence or Information Officer

The intelligence or information officer acts as the central point for all intelligence data, compiling information into an easily usable medium. This person should provide advice and guidance in order to ensure that decisions are based on accurate and up-to-date information. This person should liaise with other intelligence or information agencies to provide mutual support, including government, military, or commercial agencies. The intelligence or information officer should be supported with an intelligence department or outsourced support (where appropriate) providing all necessary task and administrative assistance.

The intelligence or information officer provides the tools for effective decision making and risk evaluations. Typically, the intelligence or information officer will report to both the CSO and the CMTC, providing tactical decision-making support; forecasting future risks leading onward from the crisis event, as well as their implications for long-term impacts; and supplying information and assessments to support a resumption of operations.

Liaison Officer

The liaison officer (LO) is responsible for interfacing with any external agencies needed to support the immediate response to an incident, as well as sustained support for long-term crisis events. The LO may identify any external assistance required, including embassies, military forces, militias, tribal groups, and other government offices. The LO will typically act on behalf of the CMTC providing an initial notification of support required to these groups, and reporting their readiness to the CMTC. The IMP or other crisis response plans may define the actions taken by the liaison officer under certain crisis situations to make sure that support is quickly leveraged and that activities are conducted quickly and effectively.

The LO will act as the intermediary between external support or advisory agencies and the CMTC during and after the incident, depending on its severity and nature. The liaison officer should also work closely with the physical and risk security manager to ensure that coordination of measures and advice is achieved. For some organizations this function will be undertaken by the physical and risk security manager as a concurrent duty. The LO is typically familiar with the operating area and is attuned to the local conditions, as well as providing an established network of local relationships that can be exploited to support company interests.

Communications Manager

The communications manager is responsible for identifying the availability and reliability of multiple communication mediums within all business operating regions, and identifying shortfalls and gaps that might undermine crisis response requirements. The communications manager is also responsible for ensuring that communication mediums are compatible with supporting agencies, enabling interorganizational operability.

The communications manager is responsible for ensuring the accurate and timely delivery of information to relevant personnel. This manager acts as the focal point for all incoming and outgoing information, assisted by a communications department that will manage communications infrastructure equipment. It is the communications manager's role to ensure that multiple levels of communication are available to support the crisis response measures, and that a full and accurate list of points of contact is available both internally and externally for use during the crisis event, as well as for any subsequent audits or investigations. The communications manager will retain a log of communications traffic during the incident in order to provide immediate and accurate updates, as well as an auditable trail of actions and information for postincident audits or investigations.

Public Relations Officer

The public relations officer should track business activities that might result in a public relations or crisis communications event, as well as monitor media capabilities and resources in those countries where the company has the highest public exposure. The company should preidentify a spokesperson to deal with verbal and written media requirements and determine whether a spokesperson may be required also at the site of the crisis event.

The public relations officer will typically brief the CMTC and CEO on the requirement for the company to make public statements, as well as the content and method of delivery. The public relations officer is responsible for controlling the content, timing, and issue of all statements to the media, monitoring media coverage of the incident, and assessing the impacts to the business venture and company as a whole. The public relations officer will also advise the CMTC and CEO as to hostile and friendly media organizations and individual reporters, as well as controlling access of media groups to employees and their families, especially if injuries, fatalities, or kidnappings have occurred.

While not necessarily an integral part of the crisis management team, the public relations officer should be a well-trained intermediary or spokesperson between the organization and the media or civic leaders—providing useful assistance in the positive delivery of information, enhancing the image of the organization externally, as well as contributing indirectly to employee morale. Personnel from within the public relations department may also be involved in dealing with sensitive personal issues (related to employees or their families), as well as issues requiring discretion and compassion when dealing with families and the local community. In addition, they may brief personnel on how to manage media inquiries.

Legal Counsel

Crisis situations may have legal implications or impacts, either directly in terms of the legal ramifications and requirements following the detention of employees by foreign governments, or indirectly in terms of liability risks following investigations or claims made against the company for negligence or damages. Legal counsel may be necessary to evaluate and mitigate the possible implications of a crisis event and the liability exposure the company faces. The legal counsel will guide the CEO and CMTC as to the ramifications of an incident, assisting management teams in identifying the best courses of action to mitigate these risks. Within new or difficult operating environments, the legal counsel may be tasked with identifying host nation legal resources (in advance of an incident) that might be of assistance to the company in the event of a crisis, as well as liaising with appropriate embassy officials as required. An aspect of contingency planning, and indeed in certain circumstances incident management, a local law firm may be retained to represent the company, being more familiar with local laws and the nuances of the host nation's legal system.

The legal counsel may be responsible for reviewing public announcements in terms of liability risks to the company or its officers. They should also advise on the legal aspects of negotiations, payment of ransoms or protection money, and the passage of information to law enforcement agencies in the country involved with a crisis. The legal counsel may determine legal responsibilities to victims and their families, including the payment of any compensations or insurance policies. They should advise crisis managers on report content in order to safeguard both the company and its employees. The legal counsel may advise the CEO and CMTC as to the structure, content, and access restrictions of reports and other information, especially if sensitive or inflammatory in nature.

Human Resources Department

The human resources department will be responsible for the accounting of all personnel within or adjoining a crisis situation, ensuring that accurate records of who is involved within the crisis, as well as their next of kin details, are properly managed. They will retain rosters of the whereabouts of personnel, especially during evacuation scenarios—advising the CMTC so that a full and accurate head count can be conducted and sustained. This is especially important for remote or high-risk locations where the threat of losing accountability of personnel can be significant and catastrophic. They will establish systems that track and manage the movement of personnel, working with operational managers for the conduct of routine travel within a project area.

The human resources department may be tasked with providing regular briefings to families of employees affected by a crisis, ensuring that regular meetings are conducted to keep them abreast of the situation. The department may also arrange for providing support, whether monetary, advisory, or compassionate, for families or victims. They may also support the CMTC and CEO in monitoring the morale and welfare of employees, and gathering personal details from the IRTs on injuries and fatalities, as well as missing persons.

Health and Safety Department

The health and safety department will play a key role regarding risks that might result from industrial accidents, whether causing the crisis event or occurring as a result of the initial incident. In addition, health, hygiene, and other aspects more relevant to health and safety will be important considerations in terms of the holistic approach to risk management during a crisis event, especially in natural disasters or pandemics. Primacy of roles in terms of security, health, and safety should be considered based on the nature and impact of the threats faced during a crisis. Consequently, primacy of leadership may change depending on the nature of the incident; for one form of crisis the health and safety officer may report to the security adviser, whereas for another the situation may be reversed. The CMTC may also have each report independently, depending on circumstances, to enable both perspectives to be accurately represented.

Stress Trauma Adviser

Crisis situations, whatever their nature, have the potential to cause psychological damage to those directly and indirectly involved in the event. Often even those on the periphery of an event are affected. It may be advisable for companies to consider including a stress trauma adviser as part of the crisis management team, whether recruited from internal resources or through outsourced support. Stress trauma advisers can provide specialist advice and guidance on how to prevent emotional contagion, provide critical stress debriefings or crisis intervention group sessions, and minimize court settlements for emotional damage claims.

This post should work closely with the legal counsel and public relations officer, and report directly to the CMTC. Companies should also consider that whereas many stress trauma measures are well intentioned, research into the Lockerbie bombing (1988 terrorist aircraft attack resulting in the deaths of several hundred passengers) and the *Herald of Free Enterprise* disaster (1987 British ferry capsizing that resulted in the drowning of almost two hundred passengers) has failed to empirically determine whether these measures caused more good than harm. A careful balance between offering meaningful support to employees and their families and exacerbating the problem further should be carefully considered. Only those qualified and sanctioned by the company should provide stress trauma support.

Reception Team Manager

The requirement to evacuate personnel and materials from project sites to a safe location within a country—or in the most extreme cases evacuating all personnel and high-value assets under emergency conditions from a country—will require personnel to operationally and administratively manage the movement of people and resources from their work sites to reception centers and evacuation points. If a crisis situation warrants a local or national evacuation, the crisis team may need to create a subgroup: the corporate advance and reception team (CART). This team should be prepared and equipped ready for dispatch to a region, nation, or bordering country to support the safe and controlled evacuation of company personnel and assets from the crisis event. The CART may be considered a special advance response team in that it deploys to assist local managers in dealing with a crisis.

The CART lays the groundwork for evacuation and relocation activities. It may be designed to meet either natural disaster risks or man-made crisis threats. Typically, it consists of a senior company representative and support and administrative staff, although for man-made crises a security component may be added. Operating under a reception team manager, its function is to manage the reception of evacuees at a regional safe haven, and where necessary support the evacuation by air, land, or maritime means to a final safe location. A chain of reception centers may be established to ferry personnel and assets from the point or area of risk. The team's tasks include the booking of hotels, transportation, and follow-on flights; providing a focal point for liaison with external organizations; dealing with medical care and emergencies; procuring and preparing offices for the continuation of business; media management; accounting for all personnel and their status; and reporting to corporate-level management on the general situation. Security components may also be required to protect reception centers and evacuation points if the area is susceptible to physical risks.

Finance Officer

In the event of a crisis, money may be required to lease or procure services and resources. The finance officer is responsible for ensuring that appropriate funds are available to meet urgent crisis requirements and that procurements can be authorized quickly and effectively to support effective incident and crisis response measures. The finance officer may sanction aspects of a procurement or resource plan, or may approve new procurement requirements driven by unique crisis needs.

The finance officer may also be required to prepare plans for obtaining any ransom money in the denomination required during kidnapping and ransom situations, advising the CMTC on relevant currency or exchange regulations; identifying sources for the covert collection, transportation, and storage of cash; as well as to arrange for the recording of the serial numbers of banknotes for a kidnapping or extortion incident. The finance officer may also sanction leasing aviation assets for evaluations, procuring medical or security services to deal with casualties, or procuring resources or services to enhance facility security resources, or manage other crisis costs.

Under all circumstances, the financial officer must maintain oversight over company fiscal arrangements, authorizing funds expended in the course of any crisis events. The financial officer will be required to establish the procedures used in accounting for money and in protecting information relating to its intended use. The financial officer should also be available for postincident reviews to provide an expense history related to the affected operations, as well as the forecasted implication in expenditure and incurred costs associated with a crisis response.

Investor Relations Officer

The company may appoint an investor relations officer to ensure that the company's investment interests are protected during a reputational crisis event. The company's value in the marketplace in general, as well as with shareholders and investors, may be damaged during a crisis event, and the company should seek to mitigate those risks by providing briefings, advisories, and forums in which confidence can be regained and sustained. The investor relations officer can also advise the CEO as to any subsequent crises that might befall a company in terms of public confidence and fiscal issues, as share values are often undermined by crisis events.

Incident Management Structures

The crisis event may be tactically managed by several layers of incident response teams. The event incident response team manager may be a working group engineer, an office manager, or a local security specialist—typically working within a remote or small work site. The project incident response team manager is typically more experienced, and where possible trained and qualified in crisis management, and is often the operations or facility manager or security manager within a project task. In some cases, higher levels of management such as the program element will also perform an incident response function, although for larger projects their responsibilities may straddle both incident management and crisis response.

The focus of the incident response element will be to maintain the safety of personnel and high-value resources, as well as deal with injured persons or damaged infrastructures and equipment. While their primary focus will be the security and safety of personnel and critical assets, this can be best achieved only by informing relevant crisis agencies of the situation in order to leverage additional support, both in operational terms and for management, administration, and logistical support. The incident response group should have tactical, decision-making authority in order to bring control to a situation and reduce impacts while preventing an escalation of the crisis; however, it should be directly managed and supported by the program or country crisis response team.

The company should seek to empower incident management groups with clearly defined roles and responsibilities, enabling them to make decisions with confidence through knowledge and clear guidelines and instructions. Flexibility and innovation are often required, as each crisis event is unique, and lateral thinking is often necessary to manage an event. Incident management teams might fall into one or all of the following categories:

- **Strategic.** Focused on the long-term implications of the event, the leveraging of unique high-profile support, evaluation of further risk factors that might cascade from the point of crisis, and dealing with all peripheral matters not directly associated with the actual resolution of the emergency situation itself.
- **Operational.** Focused on safeguarding both personnel and critical resources during the crisis event, as well as any resulting micro crises. Typically this team comprises the management team who are supporting the tactical component and mobilizing initial resources while also interfacing with the crisis management teams. Often, but not always, the operational element is somewhat removed from the actual event.

- **Tactical.** Focused on operational responses to the specific event in order to safeguard the well-being of personnel, as well as protect critical assets, during a crisis event. Typically, tactical elements are directly involved with the incident itself (i.e., helping at the site of a road traffic accident, dealing with a civil disturbance, managing a casualty, evacuating personnel from a flooded area, and so forth).

Crisis Control Center

The company should either establish a permanent facility in which to manage crisis events (if the frequency and scope of crises facing its business activities warrant such an investment) or develop and pre-position portable crisis management resources to quickly establish a temporary crisis control center within an operating area. Alternatively, a virtual crisis management center may be more preferable in terms of cost and ease of management. It is critical that resources enable the crisis team to communicate with multiple groups, both those dealing with a crisis at the point of the emergency as well as those leveraged or contracted to support the resolution of a crisis. Multiple mediums for communication are often required, as the crisis event may have affected one or several communication lines. The following considerations are offered to assist companies in provisioning an effective crisis control center:

Communications
- Landlines, satellite phones, and mobile phones
- Fax machine
- Videoconferencing

Information Technology
- Computers and printers
- Internet connectivity
- PowerPoint and monitors

Management
- Status boards and personnel rosters
- Action plans and operational instructions
- Management and interface structures
- Action boards and personnel status tracker
- Implemented plan tracker
- Intranet management site

Information
- Intelligence reports
- News channels (television and radio)
- Intelligence briefing boards
- Ongoing directives
- Status reports
- Threat reviews

Documents
- Business Continuity Management Plan
- Security plans and exhibits
- Agreements and contact lists

Mapping and Imagery
- Regional and local maps
- Satellite and aerial photography
- Schematics and floor plans

Facilities
- Conference rooms and offices
- Private briefing room
- Secure area for security materials

Administrative Support
- Photocopier machine
- Satellite and aerial photography
- Schematics and floor plans

Ancillary Equipment
- Stationery supplies
- Rubber gloves and plastic bags
- Medical stores
- Air-conditioning or heating
- Beds and showers
- Securable cabinets
- Paper shredder
- Access control (locks)
- Food and water
- Power and lighting

Access to the crisis control center should be restricted to only appropriate persons, and should be locked if the center is not operated during certain hours. Access to intranet sites or other information technology storage facilities or mediums should also be restricted and monitored. The location and resources available to the crisis control center, whether sited within the affected area or positioned outside of an impacted area, will determine what resources are required, as well as the level of security needed to secure this critical facility.

Monitoring Crisis Management Programs

A Business Continuity Management Plan and its constituent elements should be considered a living entity, subject to growth and change. While the company may develop an all-encompassing IMP to meet a wide spectrum of typical operating challenges, tailoring and updates of the IMP will often be required to ensure that the plan retains its accuracy and effectiveness for each operating activity and region. An intelligence-driven policy will govern how the procedures are amended, adapted, or revised. The changing and evolving external socioeconomic and geopolitical influences should be used in concert with internal and external monitoring evaluations and validations, ensuring that security measures and crisis response arrangements reflect the current threats and that the potential for complacency within the company is minimized. Changing supporting structures or management elements should also be incorporated within aspects of the Business Continuity Management Plan and supporting components such as the IMP, reflecting fluctuating and evolving organizational structures, capabilities, and focuses (i.e., notably if stages within a project see significant differences in approach requirement).

An internal monitoring or assessment team can be used to test, evaluate, and exercise personnel in their responsibilities, ensuring that corporate policy is being effectively implemented at all levels, as well as identifying any areas for change or improvement. Enhancements should be collaboratively sought from both corporate and field levels. Such a monitoring team is also useful in the formal assessment of personnel, contributing to the evaluation of a crisis management structure as well as key individuals within it.

External monitoring teams allow a fresh and impartial validation on how well formulated and relevant the current security policies and plans are. They can also contribute in a consultancy role, offering suggestions to the executive management on policy amendments and alternative methods of implementing security arrangements. External monitoring can be through unannounced spot checks, exercises, or allocated assessment periods, and can be conducted concurrently with management exercises in the IMP's utilization.

External consultants may also be required to offer guidance on how to amend or adapt the Business Continuity Management Plan and IMP following a crisis incident. Many organizations, having successfully managed a crisis, slip into a state of complacency, believing that they now have the expertise to overcome any future crises (Ian I. Mitroff and Christine M. Pearson, *Crisis Management: A Diagnostic Guide for Improving Your Organization's Crisis-Preparedness*, Jossey-Bass, 1993, p. 23). Companies should seek to learn from a crisis event and improve their response policies, procedures, and mechanisms to better manage any subsequent crises.

Summary

The crisis response plans are only as good as those managers and users who implement them. Companies that pre-design their crisis and incident response structures will be better placed to respond instinctively and in an organized and rehearsed manner to any crisis event that might befall the company. Training and practice will provide confidence and familiarity for managers undertaking such roles. Redundancies should also be in place to account for absent decision makers or critical support staff. Complex and dispersed company groups should also seek to establish mechanisms by which different groups converge to provide integration and collaboration, rather than working independently of each other. Consistency of management approach should not impede innovation and tailored approaches, but will provide an invaluable framework from which managers can draw ideas, plans, and materials, as well as expertise and resources.

Companies should consider crisis response organizations in a holistic manner, tracking a typical crisis situation through the varied groups of people who will be involved—from the secretary who takes a call to the company CEO who briefs the media and investors. Each group will have both overlapping and unique focuses, interests, and needs. The points of convergence should be designed to meet multiple party interests, while group-specific policies and plans should be designed to integrate directly or peripherally into the group's overall approach. The leveraging of external agencies should be a key component of contingency planning, and external advisers or specialists should be included in the crisis management structure. Understanding how to build up the crisis management organization to meet stages within generic or unique risks will also avoid unnecessary fatigue and wasted resources, delivering the right help at the right levels at the right times.

CHAPTER 4

Scope of Risk

Companies operating both within their conventional business settings and in more unique operating environments will be presented with a wide scope of tangible and intangible risks. Executive leaders, project and business managers, and risk and security professionals must understand the nature, scope, probability, and impact that a varied spectrum of risks challenging their corporate interests and business activities can have, so that threats can be avoided or mitigated through sound contingency planning. Understanding the scope of risk also enables companies to better manage crisis events, as the direct and associated effects of a risk will be more fully understood and planned against before they occur. Establishing a scope of risk effectively creates a risk register, both in generalized forms and more specifically engineered to a particular region or project area. Given that incident managers or local users may not have visibility of the entire Business Continuity Management (BCM) Plan, it can be useful to provide succinct overviews within the incident management plan (IMP) as to the risk types and natures so that incident managers can place a crisis event into a broader and more understandable context. This might be considered an educational or advisory aspect of an IMP.

If companies subcontract the development or implementation of the IMP to outsourced vendors, it is also important that those subcontractors can also place risks into a company-specific and commercial context, as risks will be perceived differently between organizations and result in unique impacts for each company. In addition, companies should also be mindful of how risks impact their teammates and subcontractors, as a direct risk presented to their activity or personnel may have significant impacts on peripheral groups, which will in turn affect their operations. Company tolerance levels also vary and risks may create ripple effects where the initial cause creates new risk types and impacts. Mapping the outward effects of a risk event and how the event affects both the company, associated groups or individuals will enable more productive business continuity and recovery, as illustrated in Exhibit 4.1.

The IMP should *not* seek to provide a specialist understanding of any particular risk type, as each element will be unique and may require significant training or experience within a particular industry field. Rather, the IMP might have a section designed to illustrate some general risk forms that are most likely to affect the incident management team—from those with tangible or physical effects that can be measured more easily in terms of impact to those that are more nebulous in their causes or effects (i.e., supporting the awareness that many risks bridge the gap between hard and soft effects). By assisting incident managers in seeing the holistic

Workplace Violence—Physical Threats		
	Nature	**Impacts**
Physical Assault	Punching, kicking, or biting	Bruising, breaks, infections, concussion, organ damage
Knives	Hacking, slashing, or stabbing	Punctures, lacerations, organ damage, arterial injuries
Firearms	Hitting or shooting	Organ damage, arterial risks, breaks, severe traumas
Property Damage	Personal property damage	Fire, sabotage, breakages, contiminations of materials, or structures
Jostling	Pushing, shoving, or tripping	Breaks, bruising, intimidation, and physical and psychological harm
Substance Violence	Spitting, thrown acids or drinks, poisoning	Burns, infections, and poisoning

Workplace Violence—Nonphysical Threats		
	Nature	**Impacts**
Physical Threats	Assault, guns, or knives	Depression, fear, poor performance, and workplace absence
Intimidation	Open threats or innuendos of violence	Depression, fear, poor performance, and workplace absence
Coercion	Subtle threats or innuendos of violence	Illegal actions, depression, fear, and poor performance
Harrassment	Pestering, irritants, inappropriate attention and remarks	Resentment, violence, depression, and poor performance
Embarrassment	Demeaning actions, statements, or insinuations	Fear, poor performance, and workplace absence
Substance Violence	Spitting, thrown acids or drinks, poisoning	Burns, infections, and poisoning

EXHIBIT 4.1 Workplace Violence Risk Mapping

risk picture, companies can better operate within corporate tolerance levels, achieving desired business goals and more effectively implementing risk management policies, plans, and procedures. The IMP should seek to meet certain principles in order to be effective (see Exhibit 4.2).

The following risks will be addressed within this chapter in order to provide an overview of risk types, as well as an indication of the spectrum of risk natures that might face a company's operations, whether domestically or internationally based:

Man-Made Risk Types
- Espionage or information security breach
- Kidnappings and ransoms
- Hostage situations
- Domestic terrorism (monkey wrenching)
- Power blackouts
- Road traffic accidents
- Complaints

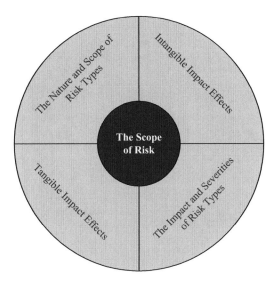

The Scope
of Risk

The Nature and Scope of
Risk Types

Intangible Impact Effects

Tangible Impact Effects

The Impact and Severities
of Risk Types

EXHIBIT 4.2 Principles to Scoping Risks

- Muggings or robberies
- Missing persons
- Civil unrest
- Arrest and detention
- Pending arrest or detention and exit denial
- Loss of sensitive or high-value equipment
- Unexploded ordnance and mines
- Indirect or direct fire attacks
- Suspect calls
- Workplace violence
- Threats, coercion, and extortion
- Facility intrusion
- Chemical, biological, or radiological threats
- Small arms fire
- Complex or armed attacks
- Medical emergencies
- Repatriations of remains
- Explosive attacks or sabotage
- Suspect packages and letters
- Bomb threats
- Vehicle-borne improvised explosive devices
- Sabotage
- Family liaison
- Media management
- Computer-related incidents
- Disciplinary issues
- Office, facility, or hotel fires
- Labor disputes

Natural Risk Types
- Floods
- Earthquakes
- Pandemics
- Tsunamis (tidal waves)
- Hurricanes and tornadoes
- Volcanoes
- Sandstorms
- Landslides
- Forest fires

Security and Safety Awareness

An important precursor to the IMP is the training and education of employees operating either domestically or within foreign operating environments. Companies may wish to expand IMP training to include hostile environment briefings or training in order to illustrate the typical risks employees traveling to, or operating in, a new or challenging environment may face, and thus assist them in avoiding many of the issues that could befall them, but may fall outside of their common experiences or understanding. Often corporate policies and plans may not be provided to a wider audience as a complete product, but instead only appropriate sections are furnished to employee users. Therefore, each plan should contain the relevant information to allow it to operate in isolation to achieve its objectives, whether geared toward a domestic audience familiar and comfortable with their cultural or environmental surroundings or toward an audience operating within a new or unfamiliar territory.

Companies should consider at what level they should educate and train staff in order to provide the appropriate foundations for the IMP. Layered training within an organization will often be appropriate, as a sizable company will typically have a small proportion of staff exposed to certain levels of risk or specific risk types, while the wider group will be exposed to more generic levels and types of risk. Some groups may require a cursory level of education and training, while others may require a more comprehensive training regime. The function of hostile environment or security awareness training can have broad objective parameters, or may be focused on a particular operating environment. Some common themes that may be covered are:

- Typical risk types and impacts.
- Assessing and evaluating risk.
- Situational awareness and travel security.
- Cultural sensitivity and awareness.
- Social, religious, political, and gender norms.
- Regional infrastructures and support structures.
- Medical and health impacts.
- Risk mitigation techniques and emergency responses.

Hostile environment (or traveler's safety) training will often act as both supportive and preemptive measures for the IMP. Some company staff may not be aware that there are approximately 300 religions in nearly 200 independent countries world-wide, all with their own unique characteristics and risk factors. Some countries are led autocratically, others through democratically elected or monarchical systems. In some countries gender equality is a given, whereas in others women have diminished social roles. Shaking hands or showing feet in some cultures is offensive, while folding your arms in other cultures indicates that you are paying attention. In some countries free speech is a right, whereas in others public expressions of opinion can result in imprisonment. Taking photographs in some countries may lead to arrest; in others, drinking alcohol is forbidden. Companies may therefore wish to precede the IMP with some form of security or safety awareness training so that personnel will understand the cultural and environmental context in which the IMP is set.

Crisis Management Training

In order to be most effective, companies should invest the time and resources to ensure that management is prepared to face the range of risks it may face as an organization or as an individual project. The value in training managers can be expressed as follows:

- Allows managers to be self-sufficient and structure and develop their own plans.
- Supports managers in identifying risks prior to an emergency occurring, enabling better risk mitigation measures.
- Enables an effective response to crisis situations—bringing control and understanding more quickly to an event.
- Allows local managers to understand how best to leverage organic and external resources and capabilities.
- Provides validation of plans and policies (i.e., helps to sustain such plans over the course of the project's life span).
- Provides confidence, familiarity, and buy-in from users and stakeholders.
- Demonstrates duty of care and corporate governance and responsibility.
- Improves interagency cooperation and relationships.
- Supports better business practices (i.e., makes for more productive and profitable pursuits).
- Gains greater buy-in from users and stakeholders.
- Engenders a collaborative approach and positive contributions to mitigating risks and dealing with crisis events.

Stages of Disasters

It is also useful for the user of the IMP to understand the typical stages of a disaster situation so as to place the risk implications into a chronological sequence and time context. The following provides simplified explanations as to the different stages of disaster situations:

- **Acute Phase.** The acute phase—the disaster itself—is the phase when most casualties occur. In natural disasters this may be short—for example, minutes (earthquakes) to hours or a few days (floods, hurricanes) or long and drawn out (famine, epidemic). A war is effectively a continuing disaster, but since fighting often shifts around an area, parts of the country may be in the immediate post-disaster phase while others are still in the acute phase. The IMP typically addresses the effects of the acute phase.

- **Immediate Postdisaster Phase.** During this phase the high and immediate casualty rate is usually replaced by a steady but declining toll of injury and death. The main medical problems are generally the treatment of injuries. In earthquakes and hurricanes, the majority of those who are going to survive are found within 12 hours of the disaster. Most of those injured will have been treated in the first 24 to 32 hours. This period is typically when crisis response teams (CRTs) start to transition responsibilities from the incident response teams (IRTs).

- **Intermediate Phase.** In natural disasters (or individual events in a man-made disaster, such as a massacre), this typically begins after three to five days, and tends to peak at 10 days. It is the period when the diseases brought about by acute exposure (to heat or cold), lack of clean water supplies, and poor sanitation appear, as people are often crowded together in temporary shelters. It is characterized by a rise in acute respiratory infection and diarrhea. Toward the end of this period, diseases such as dysentery, cholera, typhoid, and hepatitis become more common. Measles may also occur, and the lack of food and the ability to cook it may begin to seriously affect the more vulnerable employees, leading to higher malnutrition rates and decreased resistance to infection. The CRT will typically be fully in effect by the intermediate phase.

- **Late Phase.** This is usually the phase in which actual business or operational recovery begins. The timing of the start of this phase and its duration are extremely variable and depend on many factors, such as the health care infrastructure and what damage has been suffered; availability of shelter, clean water, and food; and the diseases endemic to the area. It is in this period that business recovery starts and CRTs start to demobilize and typically transition responsibilities back to project management. It is also the phase during which post incident reviews might be conducted and policies and plans amended to reflect any shortfalls or necessary changes in response or requirements.

This chapter is not intended to be inclusive of all risk types, nor how they might flow under different conditions, or how they might affect an organization within different environments, but is designed to illustrate *some* examples of risk natures that might form the educational or advisory section within a company's IMP. These should be succinct versions of those threats covered within a risk evaluation section (or risk register) within the Business Continuity Management Plan, but engineered to meet the needs of a wider user audience. Industry-specific examples should be incorporated to reflect the unique requirements of a company or specific business activity.

Man-Made Risks

Companies may face a range of man-made risks, dependent on their profiles, business environments, operating methodologies and practices, and risk tolerances. Man-made risks such as war, intrastate conflicts, political instability, organized and opportunistic crime, and insurgency and terrorist acts can present some of the same problems seen with natural disasters: weakened social infrastructures, fires, famine, and disease. In addition, man-made risks bring personal risks to companies, their personnel, and facilities: muggings, kidnappings, bombings, shootings, organized attacks against facilities or individuals, and unexploded ordnance and mines. Social and political instability can also result in demonstrations, riots, and the targeting of both foreigners and their facilities or activities. Man-made threats may also shift from area to area, constantly changing the dynamics of a company's risk level, and therefore require an up-to-date appreciation of the environment in which a business is operating, as well as a flexible and focused IMP that can meet the multifaceted nature of man-made risks.

Man-made risks may also include espionage by criminal groups or government agencies, a lack of power or basic facilities and amenities, increased risks from road traffic accidents, and unforeseen problems that might result from detention, legal, or medical issues. Corruption, coercion, intimidation, and the inability to communicate between company groups or with a parent government may also result from man-made risks, as well as industrial or environmental hazards. Companies will often find that the ability of government emergency response organizations to effectively manage the wide-ranging impacts of man-made risks during the early stages of the events are somewhat limited, as they may be attempting to cope with associated problems connected to an event. Conversely, host nation government groups may be part of the problem. Like natural disasters, a man-made crisis may disrupt communication systems, emergency services, transportation and supply chains, and public utilities. The IMP therefore provides the company a degree of self-reliance during a period where external support may be limited or disjointed—while government and support agencies are mobilized to respond to widespread and often multifaceted crisis situations. The following sections provide some examples of typical man-made risks a company may face, as well as associated risk implications that may need to be managed.

Espionage or Information Security Breach

Commercial or industrial espionage includes the acquisition of sensitive commercial or government information through both legal and illegal means in order to steal, use, or acquire data that will give illegally gained competitive advantages in technological or brand capacity, or undermine another group's business activities or reputation. Espionage can be an unethical but legal act if information is gathered from discarded materials that come into the public domain. This may include riffling through the trash in order to find sensitive documents. Industrial espionage may also use both unethical and illegal means to gain information by theft of trade secrets, the use of bribery and blackmail, seduction and pretense, human and technological surveillance, and violence and intimidation. Industrial espionage may be undertaken by criminal groups, businesses, or governments, or in some cases by insurgent and terrorist organizations, and often occurs during a tendering or product development period.

Companies should identify which activities and individuals are most at risk from espionage and review the policies, procedures, and training in place to safeguard information and materials. The company should develop standard operating procedures to protect sensitive information through policies and physical and technological security measures. The IMP will provide the initial alert and response measures if an information breach is reported.

The risk of espionage can occur in any country or political state, within the West or in a newly independent republic (either a totalitarian state or freely elected democracy). In order to minimize the threat of industrial espionage, a company should advise personnel that there is always a risk, especially during business negotiation periods or when designing new products. As a result, any sensitive information or documents should be identified and protected; that is, staff should be advised never leave sensitive documents lying around—always keep them with you. Hotels and hotel safes can, and in some countries definitely will, be searched. Personnel should assume their hotel rooms, telephones, and in some cases long-term accommodations are bugged with electronic devices. Personnel should seek to use their cell phones as opposed to the hotel phones, preferably on the balcony. Personnel should also assume their e-mails will be intercepted; their content should be sanitized where possible.

Electronic files or documents should be saved on a secure hard drive that is Pretty Good Privacy (PGP) encrypted, and ideally only on company assets. An alternative to the hard drive of the laptop/desktop is an external hard drive, which itself should be secured when left unattended. File sharing should also be managed appropriately so as to ensure that only those personnel requiring and authorized to have such information have access. A need-to-know policy should be applied. Veiled speech or prearranged code words should be used on radio networks and when communicating by telephone so as to ensure operational security. When using the telephone to make calls that may include classified information when or relaying sensitive information, individuals must use their utmost capability to ensure they cannot be overheard by third-party individuals.

Sensitive or classified information may be used by unauthorized persons to undermine an organization's business interests or project activities, or physically target facilities, supplies, or personnel. Information security should reflect the risks posed if such information were to fall into the wrong hands. Consequently, all potentially classified or sensitive documentation and notes should be disposed of by burning or shredding, and not be discarded in trash bins. This includes commercially sensitive information, personnel data, rosters, plans, schematics, telephone lists, reports, surveys, and schedules. Classified material may come in the form of documentation, data, slides, photographs, and communications traffic. All personnel should be aware of their surroundings when discussing sensitive or classified information on the radio networks (which are usually non-secure) or by telephone (which is even less secure). Besides electronic forms of eavesdropping, impromptu or casual eavesdropping may also occur.

While industrial espionage generally takes the form of technological infiltration or physical searches, personnel should be aware that it may take the form of a personal interrogation. To this end, it is advisable to be wary of members of the opposite sex who wish to talk after several drinks, in either a seductive or a companionable manner. When traveling abroad, it is inadvisable to become inebriated in unknown company, as it may expose you to unnecessary physical risk. Personnel should decline a drink that they have not seen poured unless the dispenser is known and trusted.

Kidnappings and Ransoms

Kidnapping is the forceful taking away or transportation of persons against their will, or without the consent of their legal guardian. Kidnapping often includes some form of imprisonment by the captor. Kidnappings are typically associated with crime or political activists; however, they can also include instances where persons give up their freedom to religious groups (if deemed harmful), the detention of a spouse against his or her will, abducting a child during parental disputes, the abduction of a bride to marry the abductor (if against the will of her guardians), or holding hostage a person to force another to commit an act against their will (coercion). This section of the IMP is designed to outline the nature and complexity of a kidnapping and ransom event. The IMP is not designed to manage such a crisis, only to ensure first response measures are taken until the transition to specialist crisis managers can occur.

Kidnapping, detention, and extortion are now some of the fastest-growing crimes against companies in the developing world, with around 15,000 reported incidents worldwide each year as of 2007. Kidnapping and ransom situations are highly specialized areas; they can be short-term risk events or may last many years as captives are held for considerable amounts of time. There are two main forms of typical kidnappings: the commercial and the ideological. The commercial kidnapping is conducted purely for monetary gain; the ideological kidnapping is for political or religious reasons. In some instances, commercial and ideological rationales may overlap, with a commercial or criminal kidnapping being conducted as a means to sell captives onward to a religious or political group for financial gain, or where such groups kidnap persons to acquire funding for their cause.

Commercial kidnapping is the most common risk type and comes in various forms—from criminal opportunists who kidnap an individual from the street and make the person withdraw money from a cash machine, to fake kidnappings where families are informed that a member has been kidnapped and money is demanded for their alleged release. More organized kidnappings target wealthy persons; individuals or groups plan the kidnapping in detail, which often results in much larger release costs. It is in the interest of commercial kidnappers to release their captives after ransoms are paid in order to perpetuate the business opportunity within this criminal industry sector. Commercial kidnappings are usually shorter in duration than ideological kidnappings and more frequently result in the release of the victims. Political or religious groups might engage in kidnappings in order to make a public statement, to deter government or commercial activities, to effect the release of persons from detention, or to achieve other political or religious demands. In the worst cases, captives are killed publicly, with media releases to achieve a group's goal. Often demands are made of governments rather than corporations or families. Ideological kidnappings tend to have a longer duration, unless the planned intention is to kill the captive from the outset.

The speed and quality of decision making and the immediate actions taken in the initial stages of a kidnapping incident are likely to have a significant influence on the outcome for both the individual and the associated company. The immediate implementation of the IMP therefore can play a critical role in ensuring the safe return of the captive. A transition from the IMP activities to corporate risk management response will occur at a point when specialist kidnapping and ransom consultants can assume the management responsibilities for the incident. If operating within a hostile location, immediate notification of supporting Western or local military authorities might assist with the immediate recovery of kidnapped persons through roadblocks and quick response intercession, before the victim can be removed from the area. Key initial IMP actions taken after a kidnapping include:

- Ensure hostage safety.
- Use external governmental or military agencies (if appropriate).
- Establish the company's negotiation policy.
- Understand the ransom policy and parameters.
- Carry out agreed policies and procedures with local authorities.
- Ensure family support policies and measures are in place.

Companies should use only a trained specialist to undertake any negotiations with kidnappers, not general managers or corporate executives. It is important to determine a negotiation strategy in terms of whether to negotiate, make payment, or seek alternative solutions. This will be done outside of the IMP parameters. The involvement of external parties is also a factor that requires consideration, in terms of providing time for law enforcement investigation or requesting government or military support. The extent of control permitted by external parties is also an important consideration—some government agencies may impose restrictions on the involvement of other groups in the situation, and such restrictions, or indeed the participation of government, could in some instances undermine the victim's chances of safe release. In addition, often the kidnappers' initial ransom demand is too high. It is invaluable to have experienced and trained professionals determine whether to negotiate in order to provide the company, and/or family, a measure of future protection by reducing the kidnappers' expectations and demonstrating that no further funds will be available if the hostage is not released. For commercial kidnappings, the contingency planning policy should set a target settlement figure and the level of an initial offer.

It is important for companies to understand that it is not only the captive individual and family who are affected by a kidnapping and ransom situation; the future safety and welfare of other company employees, the reputation of the company, its ability to continue business within the kidnap environment, and the company's market image and employees' image of the organization are also at risk. In addition, the manner in which a kidnap and ransom situation is managed may have adverse effects on the company's relationship with the host nation authorities. These requirements and considerations provide an introduction to some elements that the company's leadership should consider during a kidnapping and ransom event:

- **Verify the Kidnapping.** Company management should explore all alternative explanations, including confirming that the individual is not just late or lost and has not been in an accident.
- **Brief Personnel.** The company should brief all likely recipients of a call from the kidnappers, ensuring that the communicator is ready to ask "proof of life" questions on receipt of the initial call. The company should choose a dedicated telephone to use for communications with the kidnappers.
- **Gather Information.** Companies should consider attaching a recording device to telephones to ensure that all instructions and information are received and evidence is gathered. If no recording equipment is available, the company

should ensure that the person receiving or conducting any calls from the kidnappers makes full written notes as soon as possible afterward. Original tapes and letters sent by kidnappers may also be important evidence. Letters and envelopes should be touched only at the extreme corners and should be placed in plastic envelopes for photocopying and then transferred to normal envelopes and secured for eventual handover to police. Tapes should be copied immediately and originals secured. Transcripts and translations should be made as soon as possible.

- **Control Information.** The number of copies made of any information should be kept to a minimum, and strict security control should be applied by delegated company management. Permission should be given by appropriate persons before any material is handed over to local police or other authorities.

- **Initial Negotiations.** The initial response to the kidnappers should not include any commitment to, or comment on, monetary or other demands. The person who is in contact with the kidnappers should indicate that other management elements are en route who have decision-making authority. At all times this person should be conciliatory with the perpetrators, as this allows the company time to establish an approach plan and also allows experts time to be deployed to the management location in order to best manage the incident. Proof of life will also be required to confirm the well-being of the kidnapped employee.

- **Media Handling.** If the incident is known to the media, the company must monitor media reporting. Press inquiries should be referred to corporate headquarters for the public relations manager (spokesperson) to handle. If questioned, local managers might be authorized to admit that there is a kidnapping, stating that, because life is at risk, it would be wrong to make any additional comment. Companies should seek the media's understanding and sympathy in the matter, and request that they act responsibly, as it is in the best interests of the hostage and family. No details should be provided on the company's intentions or negotiation activities, contacts, liaison with law enforcement agencies, or the hostage, other than identity and any demands made by the kidnappers.

- **Family Liaison.** The family of any victim will be shocked and in need of advice, information, support, and administrative assistance from the company. Immediate support must be provided wherever they are located. A responsible party from the company must obtain the captive's information, health, and other medical details that may not already be known, as well as recent photographs. In exceptional circumstances, families may need to be relocated to friends or relatives, although the preferred solution is to move a friend or member of the company to stay with the family. The company should ensure that regular liaison and briefings are carried out by a manager trusted by the family. The representative should brief the family on the full facts and the likely sequence of events, while not being overly optimistic. The representative should avoid discussing rumors or speculation, or indicating that the incident is likely to be over in a short time. The company or external kidnap and ransom consultants should also warn family members of possible pressure tactics by kidnappers (e.g., threats or upsetting letters or videotapes from the hostage).

If personnel within a company are exposed to high levels of kidnap threat, some useful guidelines can be provided as part of a hostile environment training program. This can be in the form of risk avoidance measures, such as understanding what levels of threat an individual may be exposed to, knowing where safe locations and routes are to reduce the probability of kidnapping, reporting suspicious activity, varying schedules and routes, maintaining information security, and remaining vigilant when in high-risk areas or situations. Personnel should be advised that the majority of kidnappers are seeking a reward and only view their captives as a commodity, bearing no personal ill will toward the victim, and that the majority of kidnappings are resolved without injury to the victim. If personnel are unfortunate enough to be kidnapped, some simple guidelines can improve their situation during the event, such as:

- Hostages should not discuss religious or political matters, but remain neutral at all times.
- Hostages should seek to personalize themselves by discussing family and loved ones.
- Hostages should accept any food or water given, and be passive and non-confrontational.
- Hostages should rest as much as possible and be aware of their surroundings, noises, sights, and smells in order to provide information to authorities on release.

The IMP will support immediate kidnapping and ransom response needs, provide a critical flow of information to the CRT, trigger a corporate kidnapping and ransom response plan, and initiate the mobilization of specialist groups. The manager should refer to the Business Continuity Management Plan section relating to kidnapping and ransom, or typically contact the head of the corporate or country crisis response team directly if a kidnapping occurs. Incident managers should also consider the implications of the kidnapping in terms of the safety of other employees within the area or region. An increase in the company's overall security posture may be advisable under some circumstances if the kidnapping is potentially a precursor to additional threats.

Hostage and Hijacking Situations

Hostage or hijack situations involve the unlawful detention of an individual or group. The distinction between a hostage and kidnapping situation is that the location of the victim is typically known during a hostage situation, and that hostage events are typically resolved more swiftly than a kidnapping event. Hijacking is typically the taking of hostages when in transit, either when individuals or groups are in land-based vehicles, maritime vessels, or aircraft. Hijackers may be motivated by many of the same motives as kidnappers. Hostage situations may involve disgruntled employees, personal disputes, criminals, or in the most extreme cases activists, insurgents, or terror groups.

The nature of the operating environment will determine the approach used to manage a hostage or hijacking situation. Hostage negotiation is a specialist field, and company managers should not enter into discussions with the perpetrators. The following considerations should be applied to hostage situations:

- What are the motives or agendas of the individual or group?
- Does the individual or group have a history of undertaking hostage situations? If so, what were the outcomes?

- Who has been taken hostage, and what is the victim's mental and medical condition?
- Was the hostage targeted specifically or indiscriminately?
- Has this been planned, or was it spontaneous or unintentional?
- Are the perpetrators armed and violent?
- Have the perpetrators made realistic or unrealistic demands?
- How effective are local law enforcement and other agencies in dealing with hostage situations?
- Are other personnel at risk?
- Has the area been cleared and cordoned off?

Domestic Terrorism (Monkey Wrenching)

Special-interest extremists or domestic terror organizations present some unique challenges to companies operating at home, or less frequently abroad. Many of the threats faced through the criminal activities of such groups will apply to other risk areas, although domestic terrorism provides some peculiarities in the nature and impact of the threats posed. While many companies focus on the more common risk types, it is useful to consider the more significant domestic challenges typically overlooked within risk management considerations, but which can result in significant impacts upon commercial and government activities at home. Domestic terrorist groups represent challenges that span a broad spectrum of political, environmental, economic, and social issues.

Domestic terrorism is typically defined as the unlawful use, or threatened use, of violence by a group or individual based and operating entirely within a defined country or its territories without foreign direction, and which is committed against persons or property with the intent of intimidating or coercing a government or its population in alignment with political or social objectives. Domestic terrorism might be classified in terms of special-interest extremists, or right- and left-wing extremist groups. Such groups have caused hundreds of millions of dollars of direct and indirect cost to government and commercial organizations worldwide, as well as contributing to social discord, which undermines business goals and market confidence. The IMP will play a key role in alerting the company to possible extremist activities, as well as managing responses to activists or groups targeting the company, its personnel, facilities, or interests.

Special-interest terrorism differs from traditional right- and left-wing terrorism in that extremist special-interest groups seek to resolve specific issues, rather than achieve a wider political change. Such groups focus on environmental, antiwar, animal rights, and antinuclear issues, attempting to bring about change through public focus or by creating economic risks that undermine a targeted business or project activity. Right-wing terrorist groups often adhere to the principles of racial supremacy and embrace antigovernment, antiregulatory beliefs. Often these groups will operate under a nation's laws of free speech, while creating social tensions based around race and religion. Right-wing extremism is of significant concern to governments and businesses, as issues can quickly become volatile and encompass broad sections of a populace or workforce. Left-wing groups are focused on revolutionary socialist doctrine and focus more on capitalism and imperialism issues. Their goals are typically to bring about change through revolutionary rather than political measures, focusing on major institutions or government programs.

Domestic terror or activist groups are often comprised of dedicated but often transient members who float between various activist organizations and who use a combination of crude and sophisticated methodologies to undermine commercial or government activities through the targeting of public image and reputation, as well as facilities, materials, and personnel. Such groups often seek to illicit public support through symbolic and high-impact activities, some of which are illegal and on occasion result in significant damage and financial loss. On rarer occasions, members might engage in violence against individuals or groups, whether psychological or physical. It is important for companies to understand the methodologies employed by domestic terrorist groups in order to protect personnel, facilities, resources, and activities. By determining the typical and atypical methodologies used by domestic terrorist groups, companies are better placed to develop risk management policies, procedures, and internal training programs, as well as leverage external government and commercial organizations and their capacities in order to protect the group's holistic business needs.

Domestic terrorist groups are often imaginative and will adapt their approach methodologies to suit each new campaign or event. Some groups are well organized and will conduct detailed planning in order to gain the most effective results from their activities, to the extent they may run training and education classes in order to maximize individual activists' impacts. Groups can also be flexible and therefore unpredictable in nature, taking advantage of changing circumstances, or exploiting opportunistic gaps or weaknesses. While many events are designed to have a broad impact, some groups can be very selective and focused in their targeting, and may pursue a singular course of action with distinct focus in order to achieve their desired results. Many domestic terrorist groups will also seek to avoid obvious management structures and will have a degree of decentralized control, although all groups have a permanent or semipermanent leadership core. During events, ringleaders may be designated to incite or channel the larger protest group, and spokespeople may be preselected to ensure the message is imparted according to the strategic objectives of the campaign. Typically, groups are guarded and suspicious and will seek to retain operational secrecy to protect against government or commercial investigations. Small groups with well-established and proven members will typically retain control of key information, undermining the ability of law enforcement or companies to map all threat aspects as part of a strategic countermeasure plan.

It is important for companies engaged in, or associated with, business activities that might attract attention from such groups to develop an IMP that deals with the common as well as unique risks such organizations or individuals present. The following section captures known approach methodologies used by domestic terrorist groups targeting commercial and government activities that illicit their campaign focus. Exhibit 4.3 illustrates some risk forms that are associated with domestic terrorist groups.

The following provides a summation of typical operating practices by domestic terrorist groups:

- **Intelligence Gathering.** Domestic terrorist groups might engage in distinct intelligence gathering activities of project offices, project sites, and individual employees. Subversion of employees or subtle intelligence gathering techniques within social contexts may be employed in order to gather company or project

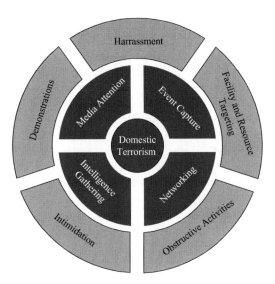

EXHIBIT 4.3 Domestic Terrorist Methodologies

information. Activists may join work crews or office staff in order to embed themselves within an organization and gain access to restricted information, be better able to support campaign planning, or be better placed to undertake acts of sabotage. Subterfuge may also be used to gather information through misrepresentation and deceit, with activists placing fact-finding calls or posing as postal workers or sister office staff in order to seek addresses and other sensitive information. Subversion of employees may also occur with the leveraging of disgruntled former or current employees to gather strategic information for their activities, enable smear campaigns, or facilitate sabotage.

■ **Media Attention.** Some groups may seek to leverage local, national, and international media attention in order to undermine the principles and values of the target business activity, as well as tarnish the company's reputation and image. In addition, media attention enables activist groups to garner additional support from those supporting their specific causes. Media attention can be gained through articles, publications, radio, television, demonstrations, and more aggressive singular events. Media attention through staged or contrived incidents can also be used to create a situation where the target company or its employees respond to a situation in a manner that undermines their reputation, credibility, and objectives. Media attention provides an exponential multiplier to the group's activities.

■ **Demonstrations.** Many extremist groups use public demonstrations through high-profile or project areas in order to gain exposure, as well as impede business activities. Demonstrations may be singular events lasting hours, or may be protracted, lasting days to months and evolving into site occupancy (e.g., tree sitting). Demonstrations are typically nonviolent and involve chanting, banners, and costumes. Media organizations will have been alerted by organizers to the event, and contrived situations may be arranged to embarrass or elicit reactive responses from the target group. Demonstrations may also involve the symbolic burning of items, or the activists leaving obstructive or unpleasant items such as manure and tree stumps at the target site.

- **Facility Targeting.** Individuals or groups may target project facilities or offices in order to harass employees, gain media attention, or impede business. Activists may attempt to seek covert or overt entry into facilities through deception or force, and may attempt to remove sensitive information or items from facilities. In addition, activists may deposit obstructive items, or resort to unpleasant pranks such as placing manure or prawns into air vents to create unpleasant odors. Fire alarms may be activated and hoax bomb threats placed to create tension and fear, and to undermine business activities. Air vents may be blocked and air-conditioning units disabled to spoil working conditions. Convention centers may be targeted with helium balloons being released with activist slogans. Intruders may also seek to enter executive offices in order to deliver a psychological message. Damage to facilities may also be undertaken to create fear and tension in employees, as well as impede business and incur costs for the targeted group.
- **Intimidation.** Extremist groups may target individuals, their families, or residences in order to harass or intimidate employees. Activists may be highly focused and channel resources into a single target, rather than attempting to target multiple persons. The status of the targeted individual may also not be relevant, from an executive board member to a janitor, as the effects of intimidation will cascade through an entire organization. Employees may be followed overtly or covertly, and may be heckled, challenged, and subjected to physical and verbal abuse. Residences may be the object of demonstrations, harassment, and damage. Family members may be subjected to intimidating attention to the point of children being approached at school with inflammatory remarks being made regarding their parent's employment.
- **General Harassment.** Activists may undertake a regime of pranks or general harassment in order to create tension, fear, embarrassment, and frustration. Mail may be redirected from homes to other addresses, black sheets of paper may be faxed to disrupt business communications, pornographic or homosexual materials or subscriptions may be forwarded to business addresses, and prank calls may be placed to disrupt communications. Paint may be smeared onto vehicles, oil placed onto the windscreens of cars, and fuels tampered with.
- **Event Capture.** Activist groups may seek to gather information through video and photography, as well as voice recordings to be used either as part of their media campaign or in order to enable them to seek legal proceedings against their target or police authorities. Event capture also enables activists to defend themselves against prosecution.
- **Networking.** Extremist groups may seek to leverage other groups that have similar ideals or goals in order to increase the impact of an organized event or campaign. The mapping of relationships against the interests of the activity will assist a potential target company in identifying other organizations that might become involved in a campaign or an event.
- **Resource or Asset Targeting.** Sabotage or property destruction (monkey wrenching) is a tool used by some activists to damage or destroy high-value materials or resources in order to slow or stop business, as well as undermine the profitability of a business venture. Psychologically, such activities also create fear and tension within a workforce and may result in inadvertent injuries. Sabotage

is typically aimed at strategic or high-value items, seeking long-term damage or impediments to the project goals. Psychological damage, even through inference, may also be an approach methodology that undermines a project's achievements.

■ **Obstructive Activities.** Extremist groups may seek to impede business goals by obstructing either company project or administrative activities. Individuals or groups may place themselves in the way of machinery or access points in order to create physical blockades, on occasion chaining themselves to fences, posts, cattle grids, or each other (blockades). Individuals may also climb trees to prevent felling of the trees within construction or logging areas (tree sitting), using simple to complex structures that might enable a long-term presence, which poses a difficult and dangerous challenge to police authorities seeking to safely evict protesters. Vehicles, barrels, concrete blocks, and tree stumps may also be used in order to restrict movement and access to areas or facilities in order to impede business. Activists may also seek to enter facilities, resulting in sit-ins in public areas, or the occupancy of boardrooms or other sensitive and symbolic areas.

Companies should consider whether their business goals and activities, individual employees, or sections of their workforce might illicit the attention of such domestic terrorist groups, and how the approach methodologies of such groups might affect the company and its employees. While many of the approaches used by domestic terrorist or activist groups are relatively passive, some nonphysical activities can result in tension and fear, and on occasion aggressive attention focused on resources or people can result in substantial structural, resource, and reputational damage—or worse, injuries or fatalities to staff by extremist groups seeking more direct and robust techniques to further their sociopolitical objectives. The IMP should contain measures by which to mitigate the immediate effects of domestic terrorist groups as part of a wider risk management approach.

Power Blackouts

Power blackouts and rolling blackouts involve a disruption of electric power supply and may result from a large-scale loss of electricity supply to an area, which can stem from a defect in a power station, damage to a power line or other part of distribution system, a short circuit, or the overloading of electricity systems. Blackouts are also associated with a range of natural disasters, or may be the result of infrastructure targeting by disruptive groups. Blackouts are also very common in developing countries where the increase in demand for electricity exceeds the increase in electric power generation, and may result in scheduled or predictable losses of power, or periodic and unscheduled occurrences. Blackouts can have security and safety implications that within some environments may necessitate IMP responses, such as:

■ Food and water storage supply risks (as well as accessing water through pumps).
■ Medical equipment or medicine storage risks.
■ Security equipment utilization disruption—cameras, alarms, lights, and access control.

- Communication disruptions.
- Life-support disruptions: cooking, cleaning, heating, showers, and other basic amenities.
- Critical business operation disruptions.
- Transportation infrastructure effects.

Companies should consider having an organic power source (generator) and sufficient spare fuel to provide critical power during short- or medium-term outages. Essential supplies such as flashlights, batteries, portable radios, portable water, and dried food supplies should be available as part of an emergency goods supply. Freezers will be inoperable and thawed foods or medicines will spoil, so freezer doors should be kept shut to prolong the usability of frozen goods. Appliances should be turned off during a blackout, and additional battery life for information technology (IT) resources, as well as backup facilities, may be a worthwhile investment. Travel should be restricted, as traffic signals and road lighting might be affected, increasing the risks of a road traffic accident. Building elevators, ATMs, shops, and other services may also be affected. Blackouts might also result in other risks such as looting, fires, and impaired emergency response services, and the IMP should reflect the types of risks posed to each project if a power failure occurs.

Road Traffic Accidents

The highest risk in terms of injury within any business environment, even high-threat regions, often comes from road traffic accidents (RTAs). An RTA may result from poor driving standards, difficult road conditions, or as a secondary risk following an attack. It is important that policies and procedures reflect the risk of road travel relevant to a particular country, region, or threat environment. Some considerations that might be useful when considering the risk impacts of an RTA are:

- What are the risks associated with the local road conditions?
- What is the level of competence of local national drivers?
- What threats are faced from hostile groups?
- What threats are faced from security measures required (in terms of driving) to avoid hostile persons or group threats?
- What are the local laws governing actions following an RTA?
- How do local laws conflict with security risks from hostile persons or groups?
- What is the impact of an RTA, especially if a local national is injured or killed?
- What is the action following an RTA within a safe, medium-risk, and high-risk location?
- What special training is required to mitigate driver risks?

Companies should also consider the serviceability of vehicles, as the degree of mechanical reliability and structural safety of locally leased or procured vehicles may render them unsuitable or unsafe for company use. Companies should also ensure that vehicles are properly equipped with breakdown equipment and emergency stores (e.g., medical kits, water, food, communications, spare tires, flashlights, and so on). A well-trained local driver may mitigate some of the risks associated with RTAs, providing a liability buffer between the company and the event. Companies should also consider whether vehicles are suitable for the road conditions, and what emergency equipment should be included within each vehicle. Typical risk factors associated with driving might include:

- Collision resulting in injuries and damages.
- Overturned or damaged vehicle resulting in trapped occupants.
- Arrest and liability following an accident.
- Violent response by the community as a result of injured locals, livestock, or property.
- Passengers being made vulnerable to criminal or insurgent threats.
- Passengers being stranded due to inoperable vehicles.
- Loss of high-value or sensitive materials due to vehicle damage or abandonment.
- Media or reputational issues connected to vehicle accident.

Hostile environment training should also acquaint personnel with vehicle security awareness. Where possible, the vehicle should look as if locally owned, the interior should also be clean so that suspicious items can be more easily identified, valuables should be locked in the trunk, no logos or markings should be visible, and vehicles should be parked within well-lit and secured areas where possible. In some environments, vehicles should be checked for tampering, and in some countries fuels may be contaminated or watered down, causing engine failure.

In the event of an RTA, the incident manager should utilize the IMP data forms and guidelines to ensure that all facts are gathered quickly in order to assess the extent of the risks remaining to personnel, as well as their impacts. If required, liaison with legal representation should be conducted to offset liability, and persons should be collected and transported to medical attention or a safe location if appropriate. Adherence to local laws should be implemented, unless such courses of action place the personal safety of individuals at risk. Witness statements and reports should be collated and an investigation conducted. Compensation should be made where appropriate. Disciplinary action should be taken when blame lies with the driver, and repairs should be made to any damaged assets.

Complaints

Complaints made by governments, local authorities, other companies, communities, groups, or individuals may result in reputational and liability risks to the company. They may also generate resentment and ill will from local communities and workforces, which could result in peripheral threats to business activities, such as widespread labor disputes, or in severe cases, to threats posed directly to personnel and assets. Complaints may be related to employment conditions and terms, labor disputes, business arrangements and contracts, the leasing of vehicles or facilities, damage resulting from accidents, contaminant spills, contract awards, or construction tasks. Complaints may also result from disputes over right of passage or land ownership claims. Complaints may be substantiated with documentary, material, or pictorial proof, or may be based only on verbal assertions.

It is important that complaints are dealt with quickly and effectively in order to safeguard a company's reputation, as well as its operations. It is also important to assess the possible impacts of the complaint, as well as its implications in terms of generating additional risks. The IMP should ensure that all complaints are documented, and where appropriate, investigated. An initial response to complaints should be provided as part of the IMP to indicate that action has been taken. For those complaints that could result in serious impacts to the company or might create media interest, reports and responses should be routed through the legal and public relations departments with crisis management components assuming responsibilities for onward investigations and actions from the local or incident managers. Resolution of complaints, whether responding to claims or paying compensations, should be done in a measured but timely manner.

Muggings or Robberies

Robbery or mugging is a risk faced in any part of the world. Companies should advise their personnel to avoid areas with high crime rates or hostile ethnic populations, as well as educate them as to personal security awareness. This can be especially relevant in poor countries or where ethnic or gender groups may be exposed to higher levels of risk. Personnel should avoid demonstrating their wealth, should carry limited cash or valuable items, and should always seek to remain in public and well-lit spaces. If robbed or mugged, people are generally advised not be aggressive, but hand over their money and possessions without resistance, remaining calm so as not to excite the robber. Typically robberies are motivated by crime rather than a personal grudge, and most criminals will depart after being given money or valuable items.

The IMP will be reactive following a robbery or mugging, with an emphasis on post incident response measures. Preemptive training, briefings, and policies will be key in enabling personnel to identify and avoid risks. The following techniques may minimize the risk of being a victim of economic crime:

- Holding bags in both hands may render people more vulnerable.
- Remain in well-lit and crowded areas where possible to reduce vulnerability.
- If suspicious individuals show unwanted attention, seek a crowded area and an official person.
- The company may choose to place certain areas out of bounds and provide emergency contact numbers to mobilize support.
- In some instances the company many provide transportation between work and living areas to reduce the risks of robbery or assault.
- Do not necessarily trust persons stating they are police officers; always ask for identification.

Unique local factors may also be prevalent, and some governments and law enforcement agencies may be working with the criminals. The IMP should be designed to respond to generic risks, as well as meet unique local factors.

Missing Persons

People disappear for many reasons. Some choose to disappear for personal reasons, only to return shortly afterward. Others may have been involved in an accident, or in the most serious cases the person may have been detained by local government officials or abducted by criminal groups. It is important to ascertain the reason for the disappearance as quickly and accurately as possible, as this will determine the manner in which a response is conducted. The absent person may have a neurological illness that can cause them to become lost, or they may not know how to identify themselves. The person may be suicidal and seeking a remote location to spare the family from discovering the body. In some instances the person may be seeking to take advantage of better employment or living conditions elsewhere. The absent person may be seeking to avoid prosecution, may have joined a cult or gang, or may be seeking to avoid an abusive partner or parent. The person may be returning home following a family loss, or as a result of famine or other types of disasters. The missing person may also have been threatened, kidnapped, sold to slavery, or been forced to marry.

Typically persons are not considered missing until they have been absent for over 24 hours, although in remote, hostile, or disaster-struck regions the period of absence may be much shorter before the possibility of being missing is considered. It will be important for managers to determine the possible cause of the absence, where the person might be, and what risks that person might be facing. Any routes and schedules associated with the person, as well as the details of those who might have been accompanying the person should be sought. The IMP is a tool used to manage the first indications that a person may be missing, establish whether the cause is known, and mobilize the correct response groups to locate absent personnel.

Some cultures or environments will be more prone to employees choosing to be absent from work or being susceptible to risks that result in their disappearance. This might include a culture of absenteeism, higher levels of travel risk or illness and injury, or natural hazards such as flooding that might prevent employees from attending work. High levels of crime or social disorder may also prevent persons from traveling, or might result in individuals or groups leaving an area of risk until troubles subside. Understanding these factors will enable managers to determine whether absence is an indicator of a common issue, or should trigger the crisis management team in responding to a missing (rather than absent) person event.

Civil Unrest

Civil unrest might include demonstrations, riots, parades, or sit-ins. The disruption of public services may be the original cause of the disorder, although more typically the cause of such issues are related to economic stagnation, severe inflation, devaluation of currency, man-made or natural disasters, severe unemployment, oppression, political scandal, or, in some countries, sporting events. Civil unrest can affect the conduct of operations and possibly the safety of personnel on an immediate or possibly long-term basis. It is important that the immediate and long-term risks are identified and managed to safeguard the company, its personnel, its activities, and its resources. Civil unrest may be focused against a government, social or ethnic group, or specific companies, industries, facilities, or individuals. Often civil unrest events can quickly escalate into chaos, and a loss of law and order might occur. Widespread damage to property and assets, looting, theft, and attacks against groups or individuals may also result—targets often include shops, cars, restaurants, state-owned institutions, and religious buildings. The following risks may be present during a civil disturbance:

- Arrest and detention.
- Physical violence and attacks.
- Fires and arson.
- Looting and theft.
- Sabotage and vandalism.
- Loss of public utilities and governance.
- Impairment of health and emergency services.
- State and government agency response measures.
- Employee fear and intimidation.
- Business confidence and operational productivity.
- Supply chain assurance and material security.

The disruption of social infrastructures and public utilities such as water, fuel, and electricity may occur; in addition, the loss of public communication mediums may occur as a secondary effect of civil unrest, and such secondary effects may exacerbate the initial cause of the civil unrest. Riots are usually characterized by disorganized groups engaged in sudden bouts of violence, vandalism, and crime. In some instances riots are well organized, with ringleaders directing the larger crowd and inciting violence. Usually peaceful protestors may be caught up in a moblike frenzy, and spectators might be at risk from police response measures. The company should seek to forecast events that could result in civil unrest, and should create response plans, led initially by the IMP, by which to protect local and expatriate personnel, as well as facilities and resources.

Arrest and Detention

There are some countries in which poor political relations, civil disorder, and corruption of government and law enforcement agencies are prevalent, and innocent travelers may be unlawfully detained. Detention typically refers to a state or government holding a person in a particular area either for interrogation, as punishment for a suspected crime, or as a precautionary measure while investigating a potential threat posed by that person. Any form of imprisonment can be called detention, although the term is associated with persons who are being held temporarily without a warrant or charge. Imprisonment implies that a determination of guilt has been made, and that the detainee will serve a custodial sentence. The period of detention may be short, or may last months to years. The conditions in which a detainee may live will also vary depending on the political and social systems prevalent within the country. The following factors should be considered when undertaking such discussions:

- What are the facts of the arrest or detention?
- Is the detainee guilty?
- What risks does the detainee face while in prison?
- Can the detainee be released on bail?
- What types of punishment are associated with the alleged or actual crime?

- Can pressure be brought to bear using legal or embassy support?
- Who in the host nation government or agency is dealing with the case?
- What does the detainee need while in custody (food, cigarettes, medicines)?
- When can the detainee be visited?
- When is the court date?
- Are others at risk of arrest following the detention?
- Ensure that a lawyer is present during interviews and questioning.
- Advise the person never to sign any document without a lawyer present, nor admit to any guilt.

The company should have prepared plans by which to deal with both the lawful and unlawful detention of employees by foreign government agencies, as well as anticipated detention risks. The company should also consider the implications of detentions of similar groups or businesses as an early warning for risks the company might face. Detentions may occur as a result of a business arrangement or practice, the ownership of unauthorized information or materials, following involvement in a civil disturbance, for political or religious reasons, as a result of an alleged or actual crime, on the basis of alleged spying or espionage, for social transgressions, or to protect an individual from a group or community. Management discussions should be held, where possible, with local governments to establish policies and agreements on how to deal with such incidents quickly and effectively.

Pending Arrest or Detention and Exit Denial

Local managers should consider the risks that are associated with the pending arrest or detention of personnel, or measures used by government agencies to deny exit. Pending detention or exit denial may be associated with imminent legal actions, investigations, commercial or political disputes, or corruption issues. Such risks presented to an individual may be transferred to other members of the organization and may escalate past the initial problem to become more significant and far-reaching. In some countries, exit visas may also be denied due to shifting government policies or personalities, causing short-term disruptions to travel, rather than presenting actual risks.

The IMP is designed to respond to the threat or possibility of detention, or the likelihood or actual denial of exit from a foreign country. Local managers should take the following actions for either risk type:

- Alert legal counsel.
- Determine the risks posed to the person or group.
- Determine whether any charges or allegations have merit, and the possible punishments associated with such allegations.
- Notify the embassy, if appropriate.
- Reassure the person as well as the family.
- Determine what risks are presented to the remainder of the group or organization.
- Determine who is responsible (within government) for the issue, and possible agendas.

- Ensure that any questioned person is always accompanied, preferably by a lawyer.
- Determine the requirements to meet any legal conditions necessary to allow exit.

Hostile environment training can prepare employees for possible detention scenarios, including asking detaining persons for official credentials and identity papers, passing those details on to embassies or company representatives, and not offering resistance or bribes. The IMP should be tailored to meet the typical problems facing employees within a certain operating environment, as well as be linked to the resource or interface plan so that legal assistance or local fixers can be deployed to secure the early release of a detained person. The IMP should seek to create a situation whereby the employee avoids arrest (if appropriate and legal), or can depart from the region safely and lawfully. Inaction by managers or the assumption that matters will resolve themselves can result in employees being exposed to unnecessary and avoidable levels or risk, discomfort, and concern.

Loss of Sensitive or High-Value Equipment

The loss of sensitive or high-value materials, equipment, or information can have significant operational, liability, and licensing implications for companies. Companies should identify which materials, resources, and equipment might be considered sensitive or of high value, and attribute measures by which to protect such items. Risks may include:

- Espionage
- Loss
- Theft
- Damage
- Destruction

Once companies have defined which materials or items are considered critical for their operations, or impactful on their wider interests, measures should be engineered to protect them. The value may be tangible, such as a fiscal value or operational necessity, or intangible, such as a liability or reputational risk. If espionage, loss, theft, damage, or destruction occurs, the company should consider the following:

- Establish the nature and details of the material or item.
- Determine the impact of the crisis event, both direct and peripheral.
- Confirm the last location and owner responsible for the material or item.
- Gain written reports from the person to whom the item was assigned.
- Confirm whether the item was destroyed, or was left intact at the scene.
- Liaise with appropriate authorities to recover the item, or confirm destruction.
- Take appropriate actions to mitigate the risks associated with the loss of the item, especially for communications- or intelligence-sensitive materials.
- Confirm that standard operating procedures were followed (i.e., provide a post incident report).

- Take post incident measures to prevent reoccurrence.
- Undertake disciplinary measures where appropriate.
- Take logistical and financial measures as appropriate.

The IMP is designed to meet the immediate response measures if espionage, loss, theft, damage, or destruction occurs. It is also designed to convey detailed information to decision-making and support groups so that materials or items can be quickly recovered, or countermeasures be implemented to negate risk effects. The IMP can also assist in making the necessary adjustments to the company's business or operating approach and activities to reflect the implications of lost materials or information.

Unexploded Ordnance and Mines

Unexploded ordnance (UXO) presents a threat to personnel, materials, and facilities due to explosive hazard risks. There are hundreds of millions of unaccounted-for mines worldwide, typically along disputed borders or areas of historical hostility. These mines continue to present serious risks to the local populace as well as to companies operating abroad. Threat areas are rarely, if at all, properly marked. Clearance of movement corridors and work sites is often a challenge to projects seeking to operate safely within a region. Ordnance is also subject to drift, often being moved seasonally by rivers, or shifting with landslides. The scattering of explosive ordnance can make locating materials difficult to impossible, and shifting sand and dirt can mask or uncover minefields. In some instances, buildings and other structures may also be booby-trapped, with explosives inadvertently detonated by unintended victims.

Companies should advise their staff on UXO awareness, including how to recognize explosive ordnance and minefields, whether marked with Western symbols, or with tin cans or sticks by the local communities. Companies should also invest time and resources in training staff in how to avoid risks presented by UXOs, as well as what to do if inadvertently caught in a minefield. The following guidelines should be provided to staff to avoid explosive hazard threats:

- Avoid areas that have in the past been mined, or have been the scene of fighting—they are typically mined.
- Conduct a threat assessment for areas of doubt in order to evaluate the risks of UXO or mines within a work site or mobility corridor.
- Do not pick up attractive items or attempt to retrieve souvenirs from battlefields—they may be booby-trapped.
- Do not attempt to remove obstacles that are blocking your vehicle's route, as they may be booby-trapped.
- Avoid isolated and uninhabited buildings, as they may be booby-trapped.
- Avoid buildings that might have been bombed, as they may have unexploded ordnance and are also likely to be structurally unsound.
- Avoid areas that have not been cultivated by locals, or that have discarded packaging materials in the area.

As part of a hostile environment training package for those companies with staff operating in countries with mine threats, security awareness will assist in mitigating many of the threats personnel will face. Staff should be instructed to always check with local authorities or local leaders as to any known mine threats, especially if leaving well-used roads or tracks. Where possible, personnel should keep to well-used pathways, tracks, and roads, although they should still be observant for unusual indentations or bumps in the ground. If a mine detonates in close proximity to personnel, they should be advised that there will likely be more mines in the vicinity, and that they might be within a minefield. Personnel who suspect or know they are in a minefield should be advised to:

- Do nothing, stay still, remain calm, and wait for assistance.
- Retrace your steps if you can clearly identify them, or use vehicle tracks if visible.
- Only if you are under immediate attack or dealing with a casualty with life-threatening injuries, you may use a knife or a stick and prod gently at a 45-degree angle over a three-foot-wide path in front of you in order to identify the edge of any possible mines, creating a safe path out of the risk area.

The IMP should be used as a secondary component to any advisory instructions or training provided to deployed staff. Company policies on safe movement and restricted areas should also be a key component to operating within areas known to contain mines or other explosive hazards. The IMP provides guidance to managers if staff find themselves within a suspected or known minefield, enabling the safe and controlled extraction of personnel from a threat area. Separate instructions should be provided to staff operating in areas with unexploded hazards as part of a separate safety awareness package.

Indirect or Direct Fire Attacks

An indirect fire (IDF) attack is one in which a device such as a rocket or mortar round is fired by launching the round into the air with the aim of it landing on, or near, its target. On striking the ground, the round will detonate, creating a blast wave and throwing shrapnel in all directions, or may not detonate, resulting in unexploded ordnance hazards. There may be no warning of an incoming round, and if a round explodes near personnel or facilities it should be assumed that several more rounds may be inbound.

A direct fire attack is one in which a round is fired directly at the target from a weapon such as a pistol, rocket-propelled grenade, missile, rifle, or machine gun. Indirect fire attacks provide easy targeting opportunities for hostile groups and have been used by terrorists and insurgents for several decades. In Northern Ireland, terrorist organizations used mortars and rockets to attack military bases with great effect and little risk to the instigators. The ability to target areas or specific structures from a distance and remotely from the weapon system reduces the risk to the user, while concurrently making threat-reduction measures difficult to implement by security forces, especially in urban areas, where the risk of a retaliatory strike (counter-battery) incurring collateral damage reduces response effectiveness as well as deterrence to hostile groups.

The risks faced by a company from IDF attacks vary, depending on the operator's skill in targeting effectively (hitting what is being aimed at or getting a general area strike pattern), the size of the target area, the equipment used, and any secondary threats that could result from the attack, especially for facilities with combustible materials (notably oil and gas refineries and storage areas). The risks associated with IDF attacks include:

- Damage to structures or buildings.
- Resulting industrial hazards.
- UXO clearance, fires, and explosions.
- Follow-on small arms fire or complex attacks.
- IDF fragmentation hazards (primary and secondary).
- Casualty management and evacuation procedures.

Companies can provide adequate risk mitigation and countermeasures to reduce the effects of IDF risks, including bunkers, overhead protection, safe havens, compartmentalization of work sites with blastproof walls, blast films for windows, muster procedures, and medical management areas. An effective warning system and the education of personnel as part of a hostile environment training package are also useful, advising personnel to immediately take cover if they are warned of incoming fire or hear explosions, staying close to the ground and avoiding areas that might pose a shrapnel or explosive hazard.

The effective use of an IDF attack is often hindered by a lack of effective command, control, and communications necessary for coordinated attacks. As a result, IDF attacks are rarely coordinated with the accuracy and timeliness necessary to cause maximum impacts. Many groups tend to favor shoot-and-scoot tactics, necessitating quick and therefore inherently inaccurate setup, with a minimum number of rounds fired before moving away from the firing area quickly to avoid being apprehended. IDF attacks present an area risk to companies and can also undermine business activities, as personnel may spend many hours in shelters while the risk is present, which can be both fatiguing and demoralizing. The IMP is designed to provide a systematic manner by which to respond to IDF threats, protecting personnel and allowing business operations to resume quickly and safely once the threat has passed.

Suspect Calls

Suspect calls can be made for a variety of reasons. Callers may be seeking to cause alarm, panic, or confusion within an organization for competitive business reasons; to disrupt operations; or to warn of an impending crisis. Suspect calls can also be made as pranks by teenagers and others, or as hoaxes by disgruntled or fired employees. Suspect calls may be directly threatening (such as bomb threats), and may suggest risks to specific personnel, groups, facilities, resources, or activities. Suspect calls can be highly disruptive and can cause uncertainty and fear within a workforce. Companies should therefore seek to determine the nature, scope, and authenticity of the call as quickly as possible. Some of the following guidelines should be provided to personnel receiving suspect calls:

- What was the nature of the call—threat, warning, or other?
- What was the content of the call—what was said, what will happen, when and where will it happen?
- Was the caller male or female?
- Was there more than one caller?

- Was there a regional or ethnic accent?
- Where there any voice characteristics—lisp, stutter, or slang used?
- Was the caller calm or irate?
- What was the approximate age of the caller?
- Was the caller educated or unrefined in use of language?
- Did the caller sound familiar—did the person know things only employees might know?
- Was there a caller ID number from the call?
- Were there any background noises that might indicate where the call was made?

Local managers and incident response teams should notify law enforcement agencies (if appropriate for their operating environment) and consider the following factors associated with suspect calls:

- Does the call sound credible?
- Is there a history of such calls? If so, how often have such calls been made, and what resulted from previous calls?
- Is there a code word to authenticate a real caller—has this been established as a protocol?
- Is there an immediate threat, or is there time to mobilize the CRT?
- What type of threat does this event pose to personnel, facilities, and business activities?
- Is this threat from an individual, a group, or an organization?
- Can the call be traced through the local telephone company?
- Can future calls be recorded?
- Are the police appropriate resources to leverage to respond to this type of situation?
- What measures should be taken to protect the company and its personnel?

The IMP should be considered the first step in dealing with a suspect call. If the call indicates an imminent threat, such as a bomb or armed attack, the IMP should consider whether it is appropriate to evacuate a facility or increase the security posture as a result of the call. Local managers must balance the need to take such calls seriously, but not have business activities continually and unnecessarily derailed by prank or hoax calls. Suspect calls may trigger other elements of the IMP and the broader Business Continuity Management Plan if deemed credible.

Workplace Violence

Employers have a general duty to provide employees with work and a workplace free from recognized hazards that are causing, or are likely to cause, death or serious physical harm. Workplace violence prevention has generally been accepted as falling under the auspices of this general duty when hazards:

- Represent a significant risk to employees in a unique or unpredictable concurrence of circumstances.
- Are known to the employer and are considered hazards in the employer's business or industry.
- Are ones that the employer can reasonably be expected to prevent.

Workplace violence is unique as a business hazard, because unlike other hazards the company might face it does not involve a work process or specific operating environment, but instead is an act committed by a person—whether an employee, an ex-employee, a customer, a family member, or a client of the company. Workplace violence can have a significant impact on both personnel safety and operational productivity, as well as resulting in serious legal and liability issues for the company. Workplace violence can quickly reduce group morale; increase workforce absenteeism, stress, and retention and recruiting issues; and bring negative publicity and reputational challenges. Risks can range from verbal abuse or inferred threats to simple assaults, aggravated assaults, robberies, thefts, hostage taking, hijackings, rapes, sexual assaults, shootings, and fatalities.

Risk mitigation can be provided through effective screening, vetting, and hiring processes, a no-weapons policy within the workplace, adequate security policies and staffing, as well as advisory training programs for managers and staff. Managers should be trained to spot the warning indicators of possible workplace violence risks, typically associated with some form of stress, and the IMP should provide guidance on immediate actions if indicators or actual events occur. The IMP should be linked to both conflict resolution measures as well as IRT and external agency response measures. The following policies and management measures will help reduce workplace violence probabilities and impacts:

- Effective recruitment policies and procedures, including background checks.
- A no-weapons policy within the workplace.
- Training for staff and management.
- Effective security policies and staffing.
- An interface and response plan with local police agencies.
- Conflict resolution training for key managers.
- Termination policies and plans—especially for high-risk or susceptible personnel.
- Risk audits to assess stress levels and workplace violence probability levels and response measures.

An employee exhibiting the following symptoms is not necessarily an individual who is prone to violence; however, violence is always a possibility when these warning signs are evident. These indicators are typical of an employee in difficulty; they strongly suggest that some kind of immediate intervention is needed:

- **Excessive Tardiness or Absences.** Beyond simply missing work, an employee may also reduce the workday by leaving early or departing the work site without authorization, or present numerous excuses for otherwise shortening the workday.
- **Increased Need for Supervision.** Employees typically require less supervision as they become more proficient at their work. An employee who exhibits an increased need for supervision, or whom the supervisor must spend an inordinate amount of time managing, may be an individual who is signaling a need for help.
- **Reduced Productivity.** If a previously efficient and productive employee experiences a sudden or sustained drop in performance, there is reason for concern. This is a classic warning sign of dissatisfaction.

- **Inconsistency.** As in the case of reduced productivity, an employee exhibiting inconsistent work habits may be in need of intervention. Employees are typically quite consistent in their work habits, and if this changes, the manager has reason to suspect the individual is in need of assistance.
- **Strained Workplace Relationships.** Many of the classic behavioral warning signs may be identified under this category. If a worker begins to display disruptive behavior in the workplace, it is imperative that the manager intervene as quickly as possible to diffuse a potentially violent situation.
- **Inability to Concentrate.** This may indicate a worker who is distracted and in trouble. Employee counseling is indicated.
- **Violation of Safety Procedures.** This behavior may be due to carelessness, insufficient training, or stress. If an employee who has traditionally adhered to safety procedures is suddenly involved in accidents or safety violations, stress may be indicated.
- **Changes in Health or Hygiene.** An employee who suddenly disregards personal health or grooming may be signaling for help.
- **Unusual Behavior.** As mentioned previously, a sustained change in behavior is often an indication of an employee in difficulty. Common sense is the best judge of this issue. Workers are typically familiar with the personalities of their peers and are often quick to notice significant changes.
- **Fascination with Weapons.** This is a classic behavioral warning sign that should be easily recognized by coworkers and managers.
- **Substance Abuse.** It is important that every organization have some methodology in place to identify and assist an employee who has become the victim of drug or alcohol abuse.
- **Stress.** Stress is a serious and widespread problem in the workplace. As with substance abuse, an organization should have procedures in place to identify workers who are victims of stress and provide an effective intervention program.
- **Excuses and Blaming.** This is a classic behavioral warning sign that is often easy to identify but just as often ignored by managers. A worker who engages in this behavior is often signaling for assistance, and requires counseling and, possibly, professional intervention.
- **Depression.** Depression is a common ailment, and an individual suffering from depression is not necessarily prone to violence. If, however, the depression is evident for a sustained period of time, professional intervention is recommended, because a violent outcome is always a possibility.

Many of these indicators for managers are alternative ways of interpreting the key behavioral warning signs associated with potential violence. They are almost always warning signs of an employee who requires help. An astute manager will often be quite aware of these indicators through experience and instinct. These tools, experience and instinct, are valuable components of good management, and any employee who exhibits one or more of these indicators must be assumed to be in need of assistance or intervention. The IMP is designed to enable managers to understand what measures should be taken if warning indicators are present, or in more serious cases, if personnel are responding in an aggressive or violent manner to other employees.

Threats, Coercion, and Extortion

Coercion is the practice of compelling a person to behave in an involuntary manner (either through action or inaction), by the use of threats, intimidation, or some other form of pressure or force. Extortion occurs when a person either unlawfully obtains money, property, or services from a person, entity, or institution through coercion or intimidation, or threatens a person, entity, or institution with physical or reputational harm unless they pay money, or property (or is profiting in some other manner). Threats, coercion, or extortion of company staff or subcontractors can be detrimental to the safety and welfare of individuals, as well as to the productivity of the business activity as a whole. Critical personnel or entire workforces may not attend work if perceived to be at risk, and employees may feel forced to undermine the company by actively participating in illegal or unethical activities if they or their families are threatened. Isolated threat or coercion events, even when perpetrated by individuals or based on a hoax, can have widespread and dramatic effects on the morale of entire workforces and the success of both micro- and macro-level business activities, even when driven by individual and group perceptions rather than by a clinical assessment of risk. The company should consider the following when facing such threats:

- Consider the welfare of the employee and overall workforce morale.
- Consider the implications to corporate reputation and business continuity.
- Obtain all available details about the incident.
- If it appears a credible extortion, threat, or coercive event, mobilize the CRT.
- Identity of perpetrators, their motive, credibility, capability, and likely intentions.
- Conduct a detailed analysis of the threat: to kill, injure, or kidnap personnel or to sabotage, damage, or steal equipment or intellectual property.
- Establish the implications if the threat were to be carried out.
- Establish whether dialogue can be established without increasing the threat.
- Determine what external government and specialist resources might be required.
- Gather information on any other existing or previous similar threats and their outcomes.
- Consider the legal and long-term business implications of conceding to demands.
- Review the capability of local law enforcement agencies to act to eliminate the threat; confirm they are not involved.

It is important for companies to make a determination of the nature, extent, and likelihood of a threat or coercive risk, taking into account the welfare and safety of employees, corporate reputation, and the business continuity requirements. Typically, such risk elements are identified by or reported to local managers, and in coordination with the company's security manager, a pragmatic threat assessment should be undertaken, balancing the likelihood of the threat being implemented against the impacts the threat will have on the individual or group, as well as the company operations. While the safety of employees is paramount, companies must also consider the legal liabilities in the event of a threat being carried out. The company must also evaluate whether coerced individuals are assisting (albeit unwillingly) criminal groups to protect family members, are seeking financial compensation for false claims, or are indeed at any real risk.

Threats may be made to specific individuals or as a blanket statement to communities or particular groups. Threats and coercion may also be used as a business vehicle by unscrupulous companies seeking to deter competition. In some countries, criminal threats are often masked under the auspices of insurgency and terrorism. Companies should seek to determine the motive behind threats and coercion. Understanding the nature, likelihood, and scope of any postulated threat can be developed, in part, by establishing the gender, race, age, education level, voice characteristics, and mental or emotional state of the person making the threat, whether in person or by telephone. Any mention of a demand for money or other concessions will also assist in determining the nature and extent of the risk, confirming the motive, credibility, capability, and likely intention of the perpetrator(s).

The company may wish to review security arrangements of employees, consider withdrawal or relocation of those most at risk, and determine mitigation measures to enable business to continue. Options may include ignoring any demands, attempting to deflect the perpetrator(s) by entering a dialogue in order to cause a delay without actually dismissing the demand, and negotiating for local government or community support. Companies may also consider threatening to withdraw from operations in the area, thereby laying off the local workforce; this move might generate external resolutions, as a wider community is detrimentally affected. Law enforcement agency assistance may be sought, with the intention to plan an operation to arrest the perpetrator(s) during negotiations or a pretense of payment. Alternatively, modifications to operating procedures can be implemented to avoid or mitigate the risks. The IMP will assist local managers in gathering clear and detailed information as to the nature of the risk, enabling companies to quickly distinguish real from perceived risks posed by these threats, educate affected employees, as well as take remedial actions to protect staff and the business activity at risk.

Facility Intrusion

A facility breach may be due to unintentional intrusion by ignorant trespassers—for example, as a result of the facility being on traditional trade or migration routes by nomads—or it may be done by opportunistic and unrefined criminal elements seeking to pilfer materials; by organized crime seeking to steal high-value assets; or by insurgents, terrorists, or special-interest group activists seeking to kidnap employees, damage critical infrastructures, or make a public statement to support their cause. Intrusion may be slowed by physical security structures and manpower provided to protect a facility, and alerts may come from human or technological measures. Typically the security plan for a facility or critical infrastructure will outline the measures used to deter, detect, delay, prevent, and respond to an intrusion. Where mature security plans and policies are not in place or a non-security-trained manager is in charge of the first stages of a response, the IMP will play a crucial role in providing guidance to assist in managing the situation until law enforcement or other response agencies can deploy and resolve the situation.

In the event of a physical security breach of a facility, it is important that both immediate and interim-term risks are identified, understood, and mitigated. The nature of the intrusion will largely determine the actions taken (i.e., if intruders are armed or unarmed; if they intend to harm individuals, steal property, or damage infrastructures). The following common threats are posed by facility intrusion:

- Physical or psychological threats to personnel, including assault, intimidation, and kidnapping.
- Threats to critical infrastructures: explosive hazards, vandalism, and contamination.
- Theft or damage to assets and other materials.
- Espionage and data theft.
- Corporate reputation and image risks.
- Disruption to operational and business productivity.
- Sit-ins or unlawful occupancy of areas or work spaces.
- Liability and legal risks.

In addition, the nature of security policies and resources in place to protect a facility will also guide the response measures (e.g., mature or inadequate policies and plans, and a robust and armed security force or an insubstantial and unarmed response force). Long-term risks will be the responsibility of the crisis response group, who should address shortfalls and gaps within any security plan and associated policies and resource levels. Local site or incident managers should determine the following facts as the basis of their response decision paths:

- Where has the breach occurred?
- When did it occur?
- Are intruders armed and violent?
- How many intruders are there? Is their location known? What do they look like?
- What is their intent, and what other threats might be posed by the intruders?
- Can organic security resources counter those of the intruders?
- What level of support is available from government or other agencies?
- What personnel are at risk, and can they be secured?
- What resources of infrastructures are at risk, and can they be secured?

The IMP should complement a mature and well-constructed security plan where possible. The IMP should be tied to standard operating practices and preprepared security response protocols to ensure that security personnel, or other employees, carry out immediate actions upon notification of a security breach. Where security plans and resources are not in place, the IMP should be focused on ensuring the safety of personnel and the protection of vulnerable or high-value resources or assets, while guiding law enforcement or other resources to the point of threat.

Chemical, Biological, or Radiological Threats

The likelihood of a chemical, biological, radiological (CBR), or (or in extreme cases) nuclear attack is remote. However, the probability of such threats, whether delivered through advanced delivery mechanisms or through radioactive dirty bombs, will likely increase over time as terrorist organizations seek to obtain weapons of mass destruction. In addition, common explosives mixed with toxic chemicals can create makeshift chemical threats. Indicators that a chemical or biological attack has taken place might be groups of people displaying unusual behavior, and dead birds or animals in close proximity. Mist, clouds, or pools of unusual liquid or abnormal smells should be treated with suspicion; in places that have sensor equipment, an alarm may sound.

The symptoms of a chemical attack may include pinpointed pupils and dimness of vision, red or irritated eyes and skin, choking and coughing, vomiting, nausea, and convulsions or seizures. Chemical agents may be heavier than air and sink into gullies, craters, and low-lying areas. The correct response is to cover the mouth and nose, move away from the area, and decontaminate with the use of water or other specialist materials. The effects of a biological attack may not be seen immediately, as they take time to develop after exposure, but may include a number of indicators, such as flulike symptoms, shortness of breath, vomiting, and diarrhea. If personnel believe they have been attacked with a biological agent, they should cover their noses and mouths, move out of the area, and seek immediate medical help.

Exposure to radioactive material is not (typically) immediately life-threatening, and the danger diminishes with the distance placed between the source and the individual. Personnel should be aware that dust and debris may carry radioactive materials that can be ingested or absorbed through the skin. Again, personnel should cover their noses and mouths and move away from the area, washing off dust and debris at the earliest opportunity. The effects of a nuclear attack will be immediately apparent and devastating. The effect of a nuclear detonation would be heat, blast, and radiation. Nuclear detonations that take place in the atmosphere create an electromagnetic pulse (EMP), which will seriously damage electronic devices connected to power sources or antennas. This includes communication systems, computers, electrical appliances, and automobile or aircraft ignition systems. The damage could range from a minor interruption to actual burnout of components. Most electronic equipment within 1,000 miles of a high-altitude nuclear detonation could be affected. Battery-powered radios with short antennas generally would not be affected. Although an EMP is unlikely to harm most people, it could harm those with pacemakers or other implanted electronic devices. If personnel are in the area of a nuclear detonation and are uninjured, they should leave the area and place themselves upwind of the blast to avoid radioactive fallout.

Although the threats associated with chemical, radioactive, and biological risks are significant, there are some simple measures that can be taken to help protect personnel and facilities:

- Cover the mouth and nose with a wet cloth.
- Seal a building or room by closing air vents, windows, and doors using adhesive tape to prevent contaminants from entering.
- Move to higher ground, as dust and other gaseous toxins will settle.
- Drink only bottled water and sealed or protected food.
- If in a vehicle, personnel should close all windows and vents, and turn off air-conditioning.
- Personnel should move upwind of any event location as soon as safely possible.

The IMP should be designed to offer simple and pragmatic advice and guidance to allow personnel exposed to chemical radioactive or biological threats, whether makeshift and unrefined or more conventional in nature. Measures should be pragmatic and should not alarm personnel—the IMP aims to implement measures by which to reduce contamination hazards, as well as create safe conditions for personnel to weather a crisis until government agencies can respond.

Small Arms Fire

Small arms fire is the use of rifles or handguns against a target, whether person, vehicle, or structure, presenting a personal and psychological risk to employees, as well as secondary hazards if fired within areas with highly combustible materials. The caliber and velocity of the rounds as well as their composition and nature will determine the level of damage this form of threat may pose to personnel or facilities. Typically, smaller-caliber rounds will not penetrate commercial vehicle armoring, although explosive or armor-piercing rounds will. In addition, munitions can pose an indirect threat if fired indiscriminately, or can create secondary hazards if they ignite explosive or flammable materials. Small arms fire can also present a risk in countries when the firing of weapons is associated with demonstrations or festivals, as rounds may land with sufficient force to cause injuries.

Small arms are typically divided into shoulder-fired weapons and handguns. Handguns are subdivided into revolvers and semiautomatic pistols. Revolvers have a cylinder that holds five or six rounds of ammunition that can be loaded individually or with a speed loader. A semiautomatic pistol is loaded with a magazine that can hold up to 17 rounds. Semiautomatics have a higher rate of fire than a revolver. Handguns are easy to conceal, which poses an additional threat as they may not be immediately visible to staff. A limitation of handguns is that although a round will travel a considerable distance and inflict injury, they are not typically accurate beyond 100 feet. Shoulder-fired weapons include rifles and machine guns, which have greater power and range and a higher rate of fire than a handgun. Typically, a rifle is effective at 300 yards (three football fields) or more, while a bipod-mounted machine gun can be effective past 800 yards. One of the limitations of rifles is they are not as concealable as handguns, so it is much easier to determine when a person is carrying one.

Hostile environment training and security procedures will play a more significant role in enabling staff to respond to small arms threats, as the threats are typically short-lived (unless associated with a complex attack), and consequently immediate personnel responses will play a greater role than a management response. That said, the IMP will provide simple response guidelines in order to support management decision making in the event that a group or facility comes under threat from small arms fire.

Complex or Armed Attacks

A complex attack is when a hostile person or group uses several forms of attack against a target concurrently. For example, the perpetrator may detonate improvised explosive devices (IEDs) to slow or damage vehicles, then engage immobilized vehicles with rocket-propelled grenades and small arms fire once vehicles are stationary. The complex attack typically aims to kill or injure as many people as possible, significantly damage critical infrastructures, or enable instigators to effect a kidnapping.

Such attacks are usually more thoroughly planned than other forms of risk and are typically aimed at a specific target rather than being opportunistic in nature, due to the complexity of planning and the resources required. Complex attacks are typically planned well in advance of the event and may result from companies setting trends that enable hostile groups to plan specific operations, or be associated with a notable event or visit. Effective risk mitigation and security planning will form the basis for avoiding complex attacks. Training and other contingency planning factors will largely determine how a company weathers a complex attack.

Where the threat of a complex attack is likely, companies will have typically engaged security companies to provide personnel to safeguard facilities and employees. Typically, the security plan for a facility, as well as the policies and protocols that guide security personnel, will play a pivotal role in responding to a complex attack threat. The IMP, however, will provide non-security professionals some guidance on how to respond to a complex attack, especially relevant if no contracted security organization has been engaged.

Medical Emergencies

Companies should ensure that appropriate levels of organic (in-house) medical support exist for emergency requirements for projects operating in remote and hostile locations, as well as that some form of medical evacuation measures are in place to relocate staff to adequate clinics or hospital facilities, especially in countries where such facilities are unreliable or absent. A comprehensive medical plan, including treatment plans, casualty evacuation, and repatriation policies and procedures, should be developed to support companies in managing injuries or fatalities effectively, as shortfalls in response effectiveness will reduce injury management measures, as well as have significant moral and liability repercussions. Medical emergencies can range from broken limbs to heat- or cold-weather-related injuries, workplace accidents, heart attacks and strokes, or in more volatile regions injuries from gunfire, explosives, or toxic hazards. The stabilization of a casualty, no matter what the cause of illness or injury, will be critical in increasing the victim's likelihood of recovery while more competent medical services are mobilized to support the crisis.

Medical response plans should be integrated with military and government agencies to augment the effectiveness of a response (see the interface and resource management plans in Chapter 1). In addition, companies may wish to engage medics or emergency medical technicians (EMTs) to provide appropriate day-to-day health and welfare support services for all project and support staff, as well as first-line stabilization of more serious casualties. The integration of a highly trained medical emergency responder capable of providing practical first-line response to injured personnel, in terms of airway, breathing, circulation, CPR, bleeding, immobilization of spinal injuries or bone fractures, and defibrillation using automatic external defibrillators (AEDs) will significantly enhance the survivability of project staff suffering from postincident injuries. EMT personnel will also be better placed to notify receiving medical centers of prearrival requirements (information or notifications provided by security staff to receiving medical centers).

An emergency medical evacuation plan should be developed that includes specialist medical evaluation providers, as well as medical insurance carriers. Management should evaluate the quality and competence of medical facilities and staff within the local area, as well as how quickly and effectively they can respond to a work site accident. Procedures for calling on the assistance of external support agencies should be developed, as well as a method by which to notify a casualty's family of a problem. Once the casualty has been admitted to a medical center, local management should maintain track of the patient's status, as well as any follow-on requirements. The IMP should be designed not necessarily to instruct local managers and the IRT on how to treat casualties (although some form of basic first aid is always useful), but how to quickly implement a medical response plan as a component of the Business Continuity Management Plan. For local arrangements the IMP may contain a succinct version of a more detailed medical response plan, pertinent to a specific project's needs.

Repatriations of Remains

While not actually a specific risk type, rather the result of a crisis, repatriations can present a threat to the company if poorly managed. The repatriation of an employee's remains can be a challenging and emotive task for a manager under the best of circumstances. Often repatriation will be managed by a CRT, rather than by an IRT, as the movement of any remains will typically occur over a more protracted period of time. That said, the initial actions taken under the IMP will support the overall process, as the IRT will typically manage the first stages of a fatality event. When the fatality has occurred within a remote area, or in a country with limited infrastructures, repatriation can become significantly more difficult, and often an IRT will play a more involved role within the first stages of a repatriation. It is important that repatriations are effectively managed through every stage of the crisis, not only to reflect the moral obligation a company may have to the deceased and the loved ones, but also to safeguard the employee's insurance claim, as well as protect the company from reputational and liability suites.

Repatriations will differ in nature and complexity, depending on the company, its location, and the insurance requirements and support mechanisms in place. The condition of the deceased, both at the time of death and due to any deterioration that might occur during the repatriation process itself, will also affect the nature and impact of the process. Repatriations may consume considerable amounts of a management team's time and resources, as there are considerable procedural and documentation requirements to move a person's remains both in-country and across international borders. The following considerations should be included in repatriation:

- **Possession Considerations.** Ensure that all personal effects are collected and inventoried by appropriate managers. All valuable effects should travel in the casket with the deceased. Inventories should travel with the casket, with copies held by the country CRT.
- **Religious Considerations.** Management should confirm the religion denomination and requirements of the deceased, requesting support in terms of blessings in accordance with particular beliefs.
- **Communication Considerations.** Management may wish to close down lines of project communications to enable the CRT to personally notify the family, preventing erroneous information from being transmitted from the site of the incident. Media inquiries should be routed through the public relations division.

Employees should be advised as to the situation as quickly as possible and appropriate.

- **Contribution Considerations.** Under some circumstances it might be appropriate to gather contributions for the family. The company may wish to arrange a bank account for money to be deposited into.

- **Travel and Escort Considerations.** The deceased should be escorted to the family to ensure that all problems are solved en route. A travel plan should be written to minimize errors. A contracted funeral director will require the following information: the deceased's name, passport number, nationality, and passport issue location.

- **Embalming and Autopsies.** Definitive requirements for autopsies should be established to protect the deceased's insurance policy. Formal notification of a requirement prior to embalming should be gained from the insurer. Embalming is typically a requirement prior to air transportation and should be conducted *after* the autopsy, as it would interfere with results.

- **Clothing Considerations.** On completion of the autopsy and embalming process, suitable attire should be placed on the deceased. This should be taken with the escorts and should reflect cultural requirements. Body shapes may also change noticeably after death or an autopsy, and dressing a corpse can be problematic.

- **Pay Considerations.** Remaining wages should be paid immediately to the family. Bank account details should be confirmed to ensure that the deceased's bank account has not been frozen and the next of kin can receive the outstanding wages immediately.

- **Insurance Considerations.** The corporate CRT should confirm whether an autopsy is required. If one is required, the deceased should not be embalmed until the autopsy is complete. Local, regional, or national autopsy facilities should be identified. International facilities may be required, en route to the deceased's family location, to conduct any autopsy. Clear guidelines should be issued by the corporate CRT to meet insurance requirements.

- **Documentation Considerations.** The family will be required to provide a letter of authority for the conduct of an autopsy. Marriage licenses and other proofs of relationship will be required for insurance purposes. The contracted funeral provider assisting with the movement of the deceased must have all necessary documentation e-mailed in advance, and, in addition, must have specific information on the family's contracted funeral provider in order to secure an air waybill permitting onward air travel. All hard copies should be sent with the deceased.

- **Medical Considerations.** The family must be informed that the deceased may require an autopsy and must be embalmed in order to permit travel on civilian airlines. Medical documentation must be secured from the relevant appropriate person.

- **Travel Requirements.** The aircraft number, departure point, departure date, departure time, arrival point, and arrival time must be documented so that multiple groups can be coordinated within the process.

It is imperative that the IRT receives appropriate guidance in order to safeguard the family's emotional and insurance welfare, as well as the company's reputational and liability exposure. The IMP initiates the requirements of a repatriation; however, more matured policies and officers should quickly assume responsibility for this form of crisis situation. Repatriations can easily go wrong, and strict management is required to move a deceased's remains across international borders.

Explosive Attacks or Sabotage

An improvised explosive device (IED) is a device placed or fabricated in an improvised manner that incorporates destructive, lethal, noxious, pyrotechnic, or incendiary chemicals and is designed to destroy, disfigure, distract, or harass. They may incorporate military stores, but are normally devised from nonmilitary components. IEDs have become increasingly popular with criminal, insurgent, and terrorist groups in hostile locations, especially where law enforcement and social controls are poor and where munitions are readily available. IEDs can have significant impacts on a company and its business interests by directly presenting risk to personnel and facilities, as well as creating an atmosphere of fear that undermines business continuity. IEDs are a relatively simple way to cause significant casualties to vehicles and/or personnel. Often they are placed or carried to areas of high population density, such as marketplaces, job centers and employment lines, or other public gatherings. IEDs can also be used to damage critical infrastructures (as part of a facility intrusion), with hazards formed from both the blast and fragmentation threats (see the next section, Suspect Packages and Letters). Command wire, radio control, or mechanical activation; human delivery; and directional initiation or timer devices can be used to set off the devices. IEDs take many forms, from explosives disguised in Coke cans to vehicle-borne explosive devices.

Delivery methods include being placed at the point of detonation, often either hidden or disguised, and being placed in vehicles or made to appear harmless. Suicide bombers, either pedestrian or vehicle-borne, or in rarer instances waterborne, might be used. Typical threat areas include the undersides of bridges, road embankments, road junctions and corners, underpasses, curbs, potholes, standing water, and culverts. IEDs are simple to manufacture, can be created in large numbers, and can be linked together to create a daisy-chain effect leading to simultaneous explosions. While not notably effective against armored vehicles (although ball bearings used as a fragmentation hazard do penetrate B6 armor), the blast and fragmentation hazard against soft-skinned vehicles and people can be dramatic. IEDs can also be placed at project sites, waiting for site visits, and can be left in place for long periods pending detonation. They can cause significant damage to critical infrastructures and can result in secondary hazards such as explosions, fires, and toxic materials release.

As a precursor to the IMP, hostile environment training should be considered as a tool for preparing personnel deploying to regions exposed to such risks. When selecting a hotel, travelers should, as an example, request a room between the third and fifth floors that faces away from main roads or other places that allow vehicular access to the hotel. This reduces possible blast effects from roadside bombs and places the occupant's room at a location that will be accessible to most countries' fire departments, yet is high enough above the ground as to minimize the risk of someone throwing an explosive object into the room. If a suspect package or identified IED has been found, personnel should be advised not to touch the device. They should note its location and details and evacuate the immediate area—up to

1,500 feet, depending on the size of the device. Personnel should always seek to place hard structures between a device and themselves as well as any evacuation routes, as even at a distance danger remains from falling debris, blast waves, and fragmentation hazards. In the event of a detonation, personnel should be wary of falling debris and broken glass, which may become secondary projectiles. After an explosion has occurred, clouds of resulting smoke and dust can contain particles of asbestos and fiberglass, which can be harmful if inhaled. Explosions may also result in fire hazards, and all power, gas, and water supplies should be turned off if possible. Other training may include searching vehicles for explosive devices, safe parking measures, high-risk locations (e.g., culverts, bridges, crossroads), and other factors that will reduce the risk exposure to personnel.

The IMP allows local managers to quickly and effectively clear a risk area, confirm the details of the device, and mitigate initial and subsequent threats to personnel and facilities. If a detonation occurs, the IMP will support the immediate management of the crisis as well as confirm that no secondary devices have been planted by hostile groups, especially at command or muster points.

Suspect Packages and Letters

Packages left unattended by owners cause concern as potential explosive hazard threats, regardless of whether they contain harmful materials. Harmless or innocently left packages often significantly disrupt project operations as facilities are cleared of staff, work is impeded, and explosive ordnance teams respond to deal with any prospective explosive hazards. In hostile regions, suspect packages can also be used to waste the time of security personnel, or to elicit attention from security groups in order to enable hostile groups to conduct an ambush, effectively baiting the security forces to a location of choice.

Explosive devices pose a significant risk to facilities, especially if the devices are strategically placed, such as within an area of high staff use or on a vulnerable aspect of the facility's structure (see the earlier Explosive Attacks or Sabotage section). All personnel should be educated to be constantly vigilant against the threat of suspect packages or IEDs. Personnel should be instructed to report any suspicious items quickly to appropriate authorities. The risk area posed by suspect package hazards depends on the size and nature of the explosive materials used. Secondary threats from materials packed around explosives (nails, chemicals) can also cause additional damage. Often explosive hazards are placed at points that cause additional threats, such as adjacent to combustible materials or at critical infrastructure points. The IMP is designed to allow organizations to quickly and effectively respond to a suspect package threat, safely ascertaining whether the package has been innocently left or it poses a real hazard. The plan brings swift control to the situation, feeds information to responding groups, and enables business to resume more expeditiously. Exhibit 4.4 illustrates six guidelines that should be followed when evacuating an area in which an IED or suspect package has been reported.

Suspect letters can be classified within the same category as a suspect package, although there are some differences in the manner in which the device may be detonated, as well as the objectives of the assailant. While a suspect package may be triggered remotely or through tampering, typically suspect letters are designed

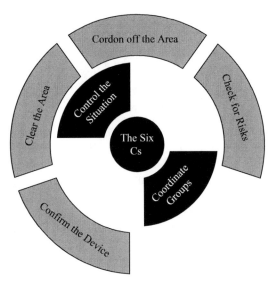

EXHIBIT 4.4 The Six Cs

to withstand movement through a postal system without detonation, only causing damage when opened by the intended victim. Although the danger zone of a suspect letter will be constrained by the size of the explosive materials, it can still cause injuries or even fatalities. In addition, other hazards such as anthrax can theoretically be placed within a small device, causing more harm than the explosive materials alone. Suspect letters reduce the risk exposure of the assailant, as the perpetrator does not need to place or deliver the materials, and they are therefore common mediums for presenting threats to individuals or organizations by more advanced terrorist organizations.

Bomb Threats

The majority of bomb threats are hoaxes or unfounded suspicions of risk. Bomb threats can be used as a tool for disrupting business or operations, causing fear and uncertainty within workforces, as well as allowing the perpetrator to observe response protocols for future targeting plans. When determining whether to respond to a bomb threat, it is useful to consider the capabilities of groups and their objectives, as well as previous trends and impacts that an explosive hazard might present both directly to the facility and its employees, as well as to the surrounding populace. It is also important to remember when clearing facilities, especially large and complex sites, that the time taken for the responding external agencies (i.e., police, army, and so forth) to search an unfamiliar location can be considerable; for example, it took 200 explosives police and military technicians with 50 explosives detection dogs 14 hours to search a football stadium in the United States before a recent political rally, as opposed to 30 minutes for trained stadium staff who were familiar with the area (Houston Police Conference, August 6, 2008). Often, therefore, it is more effective for the site to be broken into manageable sections, with those most familiar with the area (i.e., the company staff) searching for items or materials that are out of place, as such items may not be deemed suspicious by external groups, who conversely may consider mundane items suspect and create additional confusion during a response.

Vehicle-Borne Improvised Explosive Devices

Vehicle-borne improvised explosive devices (VBIEDs) are an increasingly commonly used weapon by terrorists groups to target facilities, vehicles, or people. Vehicles may be loaded with explosives and driven by suicide bombers to the point of detonation, or may be remotely triggered. In some instances vehicles may also be driven by innocent drivers who have been coerced to drive the vehicle to the point of detonation. Vehicles can range from bicycles to large tankers. Secondary hazards might originate from fuels carried within vehicles, or chemicals that form a crude chemical delivery threat. Explosives come in a variety of forms, from mortar shells to plastic explosives. Additional components such as ball bearings may be packed around explosive materials to create additional damage. Explosives may also be disguised within door frames or other structural components of a vehicle. A VBIED poses an additional element of risk compared to an IED in that it is mobile and often delivered by a suicidal fanatic.

A detonated VBIED causes a range of threats to personnel and facilities, originating from the initial explosion. An explosion is a sudden release of energy caused by a rapid chemical reaction, which usually turns a solid into heat and gas. The rapidly expanding hot gas created by the reaction pushes the surrounding air out in front of it, thus creating a pressure wave, known as the *blast wave*. The effects of an explosion will depend on the power, quality, and quantity of the explosive material used. There are six basic effects that result from an explosion:

1. **Fireball.** The ball of fire created as part of the explosive process is very local to the seat of the explosion and is short-lived; however, it can cause injuries and fires.
2. **Shattering.** This effect is local to the seat of the explosion, is normally associated with high explosives, and damages local structures and objects.
3. **Primary Fragments.** These are the fragments of the device and the packaging that are in close contact with the explosive charge. They are propelled at high velocity over a great distance. The primary fragments cause casualties and damage at a greater distance than the secondary fragments.
4. **Blast Wave.** This is the very fast-moving high-pressure wave created by the rapidly expanding gas of the explosion. It can bounce off hard surfaces and can be channeled down corridors and elevator shafts.
5. **Ground Shock.** Ground shock is produced by the effect of the explosion impacting the ground local to the seat of the explosion, sometimes creating a crater. The shock wave can damage pipes, cables, and other structures.
6. **Secondary Fragments.** These are the fragments that have been created by the blast wave imparting pressure on material unable to withstand the extreme pressure. The material that forms secondary fragments includes glass, roof slates, timber, and metal frames. These fragments can cause significant injuries and damage to the surrounding area.

Security standard operating procedures and security plans will be used to mitigate the probability of a VBIED occurrence. This may come in the form of physical security structures, policies, and security personnel. The IMP typically deals with the immediate measures taken *following* a detonation, or supports such measures if a suspect vehicle has been identified prior to detonation.

Sabotage

Sabotage can include a range of risks to companies, employees, and operations. Sabotage may be conducted through vandalism or pranks, or may be related to disgruntled employees. It may be done by companies or groups with competing interests, or by criminal elements, either organized or opportunistic. It may be conducted by special-interest groups, hostile foreign governments and agencies, insurgents, or terrorists. Acts of sabotage may be subtle, with acts designed to draw attention to an agenda without causing significant damage or long-term disruptions, or may be catastrophic in nature (such as the use of IEDs). Sabotage may also be used as a tool for extortion, or in some cases may be focused on undermining the credibility and reputation of an individual or group. The following considerations should be weighed in the threat area of sabotage:

- What are the goals and motivations of the saboteurs?
- Does the threat of sabotage place employees or other groups at physical risk?
- Can it result in damage to machinery and equipment, materials and resources, structures and systems, or technology infrastructure and communications mediums?
- What secondary effects may result from the sabotaged element (e.g., explosive hazards, toxic leaks, infrastructure failure, resource contamination, supply chain, and business disruptions, etc.)?
- What costs in terms of damages and disruptions are connected with the act?

Family Liaison

Like repatriations, family liaison is a product of a crisis, although an area which if badly managed can create considerable damage at both personal and corporate levels. Typically, incident managers will not liaise with families following a crisis event, that being the purview of a CRT representative, typically those trained or experienced in dealing with sensitive or emotive issues. However, under some circumstances a trained or experienced family liaison representative may not be able to deploy to a family's location in a timely manner, requiring local incident managers to act in this capacity. The family of any victim may be shocked, distraught, confused, and under considerable stress. Families will require a clear and unambiguous briefing, and may also require emotional and financial support, as well as administrative assistance and specialist advice and counseling. Immediate support must be provided wherever a family may be located. Family liaison representatives should be clear and direct when delivering bad news. Often family members will misunderstand information, or may absorb only some of the elements of a briefing rather than all of the key details being delivered. Representatives should not be overly optimistic, should state clear facts, and should avoid speculation and assumptions. Family liaison representatives may advise family members to stay with close friends or relatives and may need to keep families abreast of the health and well-being of affected employees, insurance issues, and other matters connected to an incident.

The company should provide clear details as to the circumstances and status of a crisis event in which the family's loved one is involved, the health status or circumstances of death of the employee, what actions the company is taking in terms of repatriation and investigations, what financial arrangements have been made to meet the preliminary needs of the family, and any other support that might be offered. Regular updates should be provided where appropriate, and counseling services or support lines should be identified and proffered where appropriate. The IMP is not designed to prepare local managers in terms of family liaison functions, but to provide advice and guidance if they are approached by distraught, grieving, or worried families, or if more experienced family liaison support is not immediately available due to geographic, safety, or travel restrictions.

Media Management

Another by-product of a crisis, media management can form the basis of significant secondary risks to the company if not professionally managed. The company will typically impose strict guidelines and policies on media management, both in-house and for subcontracted vendors or business teammates. Interaction with media in terms of verbal and written briefings should be closely managed to ensure that there is clear and accurate representation of facts through authorized and appointed representatives. Dealing with the media is an art, and inaccurate representation can undermine both the company and the vendor. A clear set of policies should be established so that all employees understand the protocols of dealing with media inquiries, whether face-to-face or via the Internet or phone calls. Part of the Business Continuity Management Plan should include the appointment of a media spokesperson at both corporate and project levels (see Chapter 3). In the event of an incident, media queries should be directed by the IRT to the CRT and the embedded public relations representative. The public relations department should develop prewritten scripts for likely incidents to ensure that detailed and factual presentation of information is available. This will reduce management strain during a crisis and will assist with the focus and delivery of information. Any area of interest from the media or any comments made should be recorded in order to advise the company and the vendor corporate offices as to media interests or possible intentions and story angles. Companies may also wish to identify or engage public relations companies for high-profile or high-impact events as a contingency planning measure.

Media inquiries may be overt, with media persons identifying themselves, or may be covert, with persons asking questions under pretense, often in social settings. Consequently, personnel should be advised not to discuss sensitive matters in public forums or with strangers. Personnel should also be advised to be polite to the media, not to mislead or lie, but conversely not to be engaged in protracted conversations that could be misrepresented. Local personnel should be advised to use such phrases as:

- "I am not the right person to speak to on this matter; our public relations manager will be better positioned to assist you."
- "As you can understand, this is a sensitive matter and erroneous reporting may endanger people; I would ask that you not place people at risk."

- "Our crisis management team is dealing with the emergency, and as soon as the facts are known we will share these with you."
- "It is not in the best interests of the families to speculate on who has been injured or killed; I would ask you to respect their feelings and allow us to notify the families with confirmed facts, rather than report assumptions or speculation."

The IMP is not designed to assist local managers in dealing with the media, unless the company authorizes them to do so, but is designed to assist local managers in directing media inquiries to appropriate company spokespersons, as well as in reducing any harmful effects media activities may have under certain circumstances.

Computer-Related Incidents

The rapid advancement of computer technology has been matched with an equally swift development of computer-related crimes. In the past, computer viruses were generally passed between users via floppy disks. Therefore, computer-related crimes could be easily reduced through the purchase of software from reputable sources or by not copying programs onto floppy disks. Modern technology now allows criminals to enter a computer system or network through the Internet, e-mails, memory sticks, or direct insertion (i.e., placing a disk loaded with a virus directly into a computer). If a worm or virus is suspected, the easiest way to resolve the problem is to reformat the hard drive, copying saved files. Personnel should be advised that typically computers are illegally accessed through Internet connections and that the longer the laptop or computer is online, the longer criminals have to access and install viruses or worms, or to steal valuable or sensitive data. The laptop or computer should be disconnected when not in use and should have antivirus programs installed. Companies should always have redundant material backup systems to safeguard materials storage.

Information technology (IT) crime can be utilized as a tool for industrial espionage, or can simply be an opportunistic activity by malicious or voyeuristic individuals or hackers. This can be economically motivated through identity theft or part of an organized criminal network. There are three types of computer crime:

1. Unauthorized use of a computer (e.g., stealing passwords, accessing a computer).
2. Creating or releasing malicious programs.
3. Harassment and stalking in cyberspace.

As part of an IT security policy, IT specialists should erect protective measures to safeguard IT infrastructure, as well as offer advisory services or training for employees. Some common methods by which to protect IT resources include:

- Keep laptops and computers locked at all times when not in use.
- Use passwords that are a random selection of upper and lowercase letters, numbers, and symbols (do not save passwords on your computer).
- Be sure all downloads and attachments opened are from a trusted source (never open an attachment with a file name ending in .exe or .vbs, nor an attachment that has a double file extension—a three-letter code at the end of a file name, such as jpg or vbs).

- Omit personal or sensitive information sent over unsecured lines (including phone numbers and e-mails, whether business or personal).
- Use an Internet service provider that scans all e-mails for viruses with antivirus software.
- Send information over a landline connection rather than wireless networks.
- Encrypt information and place the transmitter as far away from exterior walls and windows as possible to further reduce risks.

Malicious computer crimes are usually instigated in order to disrupt or destroy information technology systems, whether they are specific computers, service providers, or targeted web sites. The most common malicious computer crimes are carried out through the introduction of viruses or worms into an operator's system. These can be introduced as part of a sabotaged commercial program, as an e-mail attachment, or via floppy disk data. More aggressive methods of introducing malicious programs can be through the active intrusion into a victim's computer, such as:

- Distributing software and updates via downloads from the Internet.
- Creation of viruses that are then delivered inside macros in Microsoft Word.
- Malicious computer programs that can be delivered as attachments to e-mails.

All data and document files from disposed of IT materials should be erased as a deterrent, and a Wipe Info program should be used to overwrite all free space on the hard disk when a computer is being disposed of, making it difficult to recover data and document files. Disabling the hard disk by removing the integrated circuits or destroying the hard drive also prevents computer criminals from gaining useful information from a redundant computer.

The IMP is not designed to necessarily manage an IT breach (although IT responders may have a technical IMP in place), as this will typically require specialist support to manage a crisis and does not often present direct risks to personnel safety. While an IT security breach may not be considered a crisis in terms of safety, it can present catastrophic risks to a company if its infrastructure is damaged, or if valuable information is stolen or copied. The IMP should provide some sensible guidance on how to notify the appropriate support so that the problem can be more effectively resolved using technical support services.

Disciplinary Issues

Every company will face an occasional employee disciplinary issue, whether it merits a caution or is serious enough to warrant a dismissal or arrest. Disciplinary issues can be related to performance, ethics, substance abuse, possession of illegal materials or items, inappropriate interaction with other employees' clients or partners, or theft, fraud, and espionage issues. Disciplinary issues present a series of challenges and threats to companies, including:

- Legal implications, such as lawsuits, claims, and charges.
- Reputational threats associated with ethics, performance, and market confidence.

- Violent response by personnel, either those being disciplined or those connected to an event.
- Subsequent immoral actions taken by disgruntled employees.

Disciplinary actions may be verbal if minor, or may require formal counseling and written warnings. The following general guidelines might be applicable in some instances:

- If minor, verbally address the discipline matter—with clear directions for resolution and onward requirements.
- If major (and appropriate), provide a written warning, detailing how rules or regulations were breached, with clear objectives and impacts of any reoccurring breaches.
- If personnel are to be released from contract, a written warning with clear policies on extracting personnel from the project site must be provided and implemented.
- It should be noted that personnel may react with anger or violence. In some instances, security personnel should be present or available if the manager may be at risk.
- Witnesses should be present in order to attest to the conduct of parties in case a subsequent legal action occurs.
- The nature of the incident should be documented and stored appropriately.
- Warnings should be considered sensitive in nature, and not discussed outside of appropriate parties.

Common dangers faced by businesses are malicious or criminal activities of former employees who leave a company with access codes and passwords, or have installed malicious viruses within a server. Employees may also react with violence (see the Workplace Violence section earlier in this chapter) during a counseling session. The IMP should be designed to determine the nature of any offense as well as how managers should approach disciplinary issues.

Office, Facility, or Hotel Fires

Office, facility, or hotel fires can present unique risks depending on the operating region in which they occur. In some countries, firefighting equipment cannot reach above the third floor of a structure, presenting additional risks to the occupants. In addition, the safety standards in different countries vary, increasing the risks of fires rapidly spreading and not being brought under control by water sprinklers or other fire-retardant appliances. For companies operating in high-rise buildings, the ability of personnel to safely evacuate from the higher floors may also present challenges. Companies should develop pragmatic and rehearsed fire drills to ensure that personnel instinctively know how to respond to protect themselves during such a crisis event. Facilities may also have additional hazards that might be triggered by a fire, including combustible materials, toxic hazards, and serious structural risks that might occur. Personnel should also receive a fire briefing upon starting work at a new office complex, should understand where alarms are situated, and should also walk escape routes and be shown where muster points are located. The following provides simple measures by which personnel can increase the likelihood of a safe escape during a fire, thus supporting the IMP:

- Review the floor plans of the office block, facility, or hotel; ask for a copy of the evacuation plan if available.
- Locate nearby fire alarms and fire extinguishers.
- Practice unlocking and opening the windows in your room or office. Look outside to see if you could escape without injury.
- Learn the layout of your room, facility work area, or office floor, and know how to unlock your door in the dark. This will help prepare you for quick evacuation at night or during a power outage.
- Place your room keys/office keys on a nightstand/desk where you can find them quickly. Take your room key/office key with you when you evacuate in case emergency exits are blocked by fire and you must return to your room/office.
- Sound the fire alarm and alert neighbors and other workers on your floor of the emergency.
- Close doors behind you to prevent the spread of flames within the office space, work area, or hotel floor.
- Walk to safety via the nearest fire exit. If you encounter smoke en route, crouch or crawl low to the ground. Do not stand up, as you may be overcome by the smoke or toxic fumes.
- Feel any doors with the back of your hand. If the door feels unusually warm or hot, do not open it—the fire may be right outside. If the door is not warm or hot, open it slowly. Be prepared to close the door quickly if smoke rushes in.
- Once you are safe from danger, locate the nearest phone and inform the front desk, hotel, or switchboard operator of the emergency.
- If trapped and the phone works, call the hotel or switchboard operator—explain that you are trapped in your room or office and are in need of rescue.
- If trapped, fill a bathtub or sink (if available) with water and wet your towels and sheets. You may also use water to cool the walls; use a wastebasket or ice bucket to help bail water. Use a restroom if a bathtub or sink is unavailable.
- To seal the room/office doorway from smoke, put wet towels or sheets at the bottom of the door. If you have wide duct tape, seal the entire doorjamb. Stuff any vents with wet towels or sheets, or tape a magazine over each vent to prevent smoke from entering.
- Make your location more visible to firefighters; hang a sheet out the window. Do not use the sheet to climb down from your room or office.
- If smoke enters the room, use a blanket or sheet to make a tent over your head, put your covered head out the window, and breathe clean air. If your window does not open, you may have to break it with a chair or drawer. Break the window only as a last resort.
- If smoke can enter your room/office from outside, close the window immediately and keep it closed. Make this observation before breaking a window.
- Do not take the elevator; if you attempt to take the elevator in a fire, you may become trapped. The elevator may also take you to the floor where the fire is. Use the stairs to walk to the bottom floor of the hotel, office, or facility. Hold on to the handrail as you go so as not to be knocked down by someone behind you, or by the impact of any explosions that might occur.

- If you encounter smoke or fire on lower levels, return to your room/office. Call the hotel or facility switchboard operator and explain that you are trapped.
- If you cannot make it back to your room/office, walk to a floor with clearer air and attempt to find another emergency exit. As a last resort, climb the stairs to the roof.

Companies should provide fire briefings to staff to support the IMP, which allows local managers more time to focus on quickly gathering information to assist the safe evacuation of personnel, as well as a more effective response by emergency services rather than herding staff to exits. The IMP element should focus on determining the location and nature of the fire, extracting personnel from danger, and notifying any emergency responders of the situation and details. The following elements should be considered by company first responders and incident managers during an office, facility, or hotel fire:

- **Nature, Location, and Extent.** What type of fire is it? Are there additional hazards such as toxic chemicals, explosive materials, or other contaminants that emergency responders need to be aware of? Where is the fire? Is it contained, or has it spread?
- **Fire Response Measures.** What measures are in place to deal with the fire (e.g., sprinklers, fire-suppressing gases, fire doors)? How do they operate? Are they working?
- **Additional Risk Areas.** Are any areas particularly at risk from the fire? What impacts will the fire have if it reaches those areas (e.g., explosive, toxic, structural dangers, risks to personnel)?
- **Mustered Personnel.** Have all personnel been accounted for? Where are they? Where are the emergency muster points?
- **Missing or Trapped Personnel.** How many personnel have not been accounted for? Are any personnel trapped? If so, where?
- **Casualties.** Are there injuries? If so, how many? What is the status and severity of the casualties?
- **Materials.** Is there any sensitive, high-value, or critical material or information that needs to be retrieved? Where is it located? What is the nature of the material? What value is placed against it, and what are the impacts if it is lost?

The emergency services will typically quickly take control of a crisis situation on arrival in most countries; however, local managers will have a better understanding as to the situation when firefighters arrive and can provide a quick, accurate, and focused briefing to enable responders to more effectively take control of a situation. Local managers will also better understand out-of-the-norm factors such as toxic or combustible material hazards, as well as the number, status, and location of personnel. The IMP should be considered a bridging tool between the company and emergency responders, supporting the transfer of response to external agencies.

Labor Disputes

Labor disputes may be wide-ranging and affect the provision of utilities, emergency services (e.g., medical, fire, hospital), law enforcement, and governance services. Labor disputes may also be connected to industry-specific areas, such as rail, air, and maritime transportation, causing disruptions to supply chain management, as well as the provision of services essential for the safety and security of company staff. Labor disputes may also be localized to a specific industry sector (e.g., mining, farming, industry, production, finance), or a specific work activity or site—involving employees striking or undertaking disruptions, or threats of disruptions, to business operations.

Labor disputes are typically organized by unions, political parties, or local leaders. The risks presented by such disputes can involve the full spectrum of other man-made risks, from coercion, intimidation, threats, and violence aimed at individuals to blockades, property damage, and espionage, as well as more unique practices such as disrupting business through overt or covert means. Labor disputes are usually connected to employment conditions, pay, benefits, downsizing, or other financial and social factors.

Natural Risks

Natural risks such as floods, hurricanes and earthquakes present their own challenges to incident management and CRTs. Some natural disasters can be predicted and planned for, especially if an area is susceptible to specific risk types (e.g., a city is constructed on a fault line, a work site is built next to a river, or a facility is located in a region prone to hurricanes). However, often little if any warning is available to prepare companies and their employees for individual events; in these cases, the IMP plays an important part in allowing first responders and follow-on management teams to best mitigate natural disaster risks. Natural disasters can also trigger a range of man-made risks, such as civil disturbances, looting, and loss of public utilities. Floods are characterized by extensive damage to property and agriculture, with significant loss of life immediately after the event, often with long-term health impacts due to damage to social infrastructures, resulting diseases, and contaminated water supplies. Earthquakes present many similar problems; however, there are generally more fatalities and injuries immediately after an earthquake due to fires and collapsing buildings, with fewer medium- and long-term health risks than floods. Other natural disasters such as widespread famine can present additional endemic challenges—for example, malaria, measles, cholera, dysentery, typhus, and dengue. The impacts of these crisis events often create significant logistical, infrastructural, and communications challenges for companies, and can lead to an increase in criminal activity and social instability, especially in areas where social infrastructures and governance are already fragile.

Companies often find that the ability of government emergency response organizations to effectively manage the wide-ranging impacts of a natural disaster during the early stages of the event is somewhat limited, as the event will have typically disrupted communications, transportation, and supply chains. The IMP therefore provides the company with a degree of self-reliance during a period when external support will be limited or disjointed—while government and support agencies are mobilized to respond to widespread and often multifaceted crisis situations. The following sections provide some examples of typical natural risks a company may face.

Floods

Flood effects may be limited to a local event affecting an individual community in a low-lying area or adjacent to a river, or may be widespread, affecting entire river basins. Floods may occur in a matter of minutes (i.e., flash floods), or may develop slowly over a period of days. Flash floods often have a dangerous wall of water that carries rocks, mud, and other debris, can sweep away buildings, vehicles, and other structures in its path, and occur with little sign of the rainfall that initiated the event. Overland flooding occurs outside a defined river or stream, such as when a levee is breached. Overland flood effects can be limited, or can engulf an entire city resulting in catastrophic levels of devastation. Flooding can also occur when a dam breaks, or when water is channeled without warning along small streams, gullies, creeks, culverts, dry streambeds, wadis, or low-lying ground that might appear harmless in dry weather.

Companies should ensure that weather warnings are tracked and local advisories regarding safe and unsafe areas are identified. Personnel should avoid dry riverbeds, low-lying areas, and valleys during storms. Upon notification of a flood warning, managers should ensure that all electrical appliances, water, and supplies are moved above ground level. Where possible, water barricades should be constructed using sandbags against doorjambs and cracks, or around buildings and valuable materials. During a flood, personnel should avoid streams, drainage channels, canyons, and other areas known to flood suddenly. If flash flooding is a possibility, personnel should be moved immediately to higher ground or to the top level of a building. Managers should track radio and television broadcasts to stay abreast of the situation, and to listen for local emergency alerts or instructions if caught within a flood-stricken area. You can post your status and requirements for emergency services using sheets, paint markings, or other indicators as to the number of personnel within a facility, any injuries that require treatment, and special assistance required.

If personnel need to leave a facility, they should not walk through more than six inches of moving water, as the water velocity can cause them to fall. In addition, moving water can disguise holes or hidden obstructions that could result in injury. If movement through water is necessary, still-water areas should be selected and a stick should be used to check depth, identify holes, or discover underwater obstructions. Individuals or groups being evacuated should be tied to one another on a safety line and should be aware of the threats from power lines and debris hazards. Personnel should not attempt to drive vehicles through a flooded area if the water is higher than the bottom of the door, as such levels will likely cause the vehicle to stall or lose traction. One foot of water will float most vehicles, and two feet of rushing water can carry most vehicles downstream.

Once the initial effects of a flood have abated, the IRT should continue to monitor radio and television broadcasts to track secondary flood hazards as well as emergency response instructions. Special attention should be paid to whether water supplies have been contaminated and whether there has been damage to transportation and medical infrastructures. Personnel should avoid floodwaters, as water may be contaminated by oil, gasoline, raw sewage, or, in extreme cases, decaying carcasses. Water may also be electrically charged by underground or downed power lines. Personnel should also be wary of areas where floodwaters have receded; roads may be weakened and could collapse under the weight of a vehicle. Buildings also may have been structurally weakened and may collapse or have concealed threats. The IMP is designed to support incident managers during the initial stages of a flood, taking action to increase the safety of personnel, as well as the protection of critical infrastructures where possible.

Earthquakes

Earthquakes are caused by tectonic plate movements that make the ground shift or vibrate, resulting in fires, gas leaks, collapsed buildings, flooding due to ruptured pipes, damage to bridges and other structures, and the shattering of fragile or glass structures. Earthquakes can consist of a sequence of foreshocks and aftershocks. Commonly, public utilities and communications are disrupted by severe earthquakes, as are emergency services. The IMP is designed to address the immediate preparation for and response to an earthquake event, reducing the probability of injuries to personnel and damage to facilities.

Although some areas have government-led risk management structures and protocols in place to identify pending earthquakes and respond to the subsequent hazards, there is typically only a few moments of warning to allow preparation. The initial response to a warning must therefore be well practiced and proven in order to be effective. Prior to the earthquake occurring, personnel should seek to secure all loose possessions, especially large, heavy, and breakable items. A safe location should have been identified as part of the contingency plan to accommodate personnel. If no such facility is available, personnel should seek refuge under sturdy tables or door frames. Where possible, gas supplies should be turned off and open flames should be quenched. If outside during the earthquake, personnel should drop to the ground and take cover until the shaking stops, covering their heads with their arms, and positioning themselves away from glass, windows, outside doors, and walls. Doorways should be used only if they are known to be strongly supported. If outdoors, personnel should be advised to stay outside and move away from buildings, streetlights, and utility wires until the shaking ceases. The greatest danger exists near building exits and alongside exterior walls. Personnel should be advised that the ground movement during an earthquake is seldom the direct cause of injury.

Personnel in a moving vehicle at the time of the earthquake should stop as quickly as safety permits and remain within the vehicle. Vehicles should not be stopped near buildings or under trees, overpasses, or utility wires. Once the shaking has ceased, vehicles can be used at slow speeds and with caution—avoiding roads, bridges, or ramps that might have been damaged by the earthquake. After an earthquake, aftershocks may occur, as well as secondary hazards such as fires, floods, explosions, or tsunamis. Personnel should be aware that gas leaks might result in fires and that many of the symptoms of floods and hurricanes will be prevalent. Any personnel trapped within collapsed buildings should not light a match or move about and disturb any dust or debris; rather, they should cover their mouths with handkerchiefs or clothing and tap on a pipe to assist rescuers in locating them. Personnel should shout only as a last resort, as shouting can cause them to inhale harmful materials and become exhausted. The IMP is designed to support local managers and the IRT leading up to and during the first effects of an earthquake, prior to crisis management structures and groups mobilizing.

Pandemics

A disease outbreak or pandemic is the occurrence of incidences of disease in excess of what would normally be expected within a defined community, geographical area, or season. An outbreak may occur in a restricted geographical area, or may extend over several countries. The risk period may be short (lasting several days or weeks) or may be protracted (lasting months or years). A single case of a communicable disease long absent from a population or caused by an agent (e.g., bacterium or virus) not previously recognized in that community or area, or the emergence of a previously unknown disease may also constitute an outbreak that should be reported and investigated.

If a project or company staff are operating within an area subjected to an epidemic or disease outbreak, management should listen to the news to ascertain the extent of the disaster and follow any instructions on gathering within reception centers, as well as safety precautions. Where appropriate, personnel should cross-reference the disease against their medical records to determine whether they have been inoculated or are vulnerable to infection. If project staff members have not come into contact with the disease or carriers, personnel should evacuate the area immediately and seek medical attention as a precautionary measure. The probability of infection can be minimized by avoiding infected areas, drinking bottled water, maintaining personal hygiene standards, and avoiding certain animals that may act as disease carriers. Local managers should consider:

- Has anyone within the company been infected?
- Is it safer to evacuate personnel, or is it safer to remain in place?
- How long will people be permitted to leave the area by local authorities?
- Can the local authorities manage the situation? Do they have the capacity and expertise?
- Are there sufficient resources to remain in place—notably food and water?
- Can vaccines and medicines be mobilized to support the management of the pandemic?
- Are there other threats that might result from the pandemic—civil disorder, utility disruptions, or interruption of essential material deliveries?

The IMP is designed to limit exposure to possible infection, as well as reduce the health and contamination impacts if personnel are infected. The IMP should support swift and sensible decision making as to the immediate courses of action that projects should take following a pandemic notification. Crisis management structures should be quickly alerted and assume responsibility for pandemic response following an event triggering the IMP and IRT.

Tsunamis (Tidal Waves)

Tsunamis, also known as seismic sea waves or tidal waves, result from a series of enormous waves created by an underwater disturbance such as an earthquake (the most common cause), landslide, or volcanic eruption, occurring with little if any warning. A tsunami can move hundreds of miles per hour in the open ocean and strike land with waves as high as 100 feet (or more). Areas are at greater risk if they are less than 25 feet above sea level and within a mile of the shoreline. There may be several waves of differing strengths, and different shorelines can experience varying tsunami sizes even within a few miles. Managers residing within a coastal area should be cognizant of the risk of tsunamis in connection with earthquakes. Radio or television alerts may provide some forewarning, leading to personnel moving to higher ground to avoid the worst of the effects. A further indicator may be water receding away from the shoreline. Following a tsunami, project staff should stay away from a flooded area until advised that it is safe to return. The same hazards as for flood will be prevalent, including underwater hazards, structural damage, loss of public utilities, contamination, and electrical risks. The most common impact resulting from a tsunami is drowning.

The IMP should provide immediate support in terms of reacting to a tsunami notification, as well as during and following an event. The IMP is designed to reduce personal risk exposure to a tsunami's effects by providing the company with an immediate response protocol that removes personnel from harm's way, where possible. The IMP should also include a mechanism where personnel report their location to the incident response manager so that recovery measures can be implemented for those stranded within a flooded area, and injured or missing personnel can be identified.

Hurricanes and Tornadoes

A hurricane is a type of tropical cyclone, which is a generic term for a low-pressure system that generally forms in the tropics. It is an intense tropical weather system of strong thunderstorms with a well-defined surface circulation and maximum sustained winds of 74 miles per hour (119 km/h) or greater. Sustained winds are defined as a one-minute average wind speed measured at about 33 feet above the surface. Hurricanes are categorized according to the strength of their winds. A category 1 hurricane has the lowest wind speeds, while a category 5 hurricane has the strongest. These are relative terms, though, because lower-category storms can sometimes inflict greater damage than higher-category storms, depending on where they strike and the particular hazards they create. Tropical storms can also produce significant damage and loss of life, typically due to flooding.

A tornado is a violently rotating column of air that is in contact with both a cloud base and the surface on the earth. Tornadoes come in many sizes, but are typically in the form of a visible condensation funnel, whose narrow end touches the earth and is often encircled by a cloud of debris. Most tornadoes have wind speeds of about 110 miles per hour, are approximately 250 feet (75 m) across, and travel a few miles before dissipating. Some attain wind speeds of more than 300 miles per hour (480 km/h), stretch more than a mile (1.6 km) across, and stay on the ground for dozens of miles (more than 100 km).

The IMP is designed to provide immediate response measures for company facilities and personnel to reduce the risks and impacts presented by hurricanes and tornadoes. Facilities located in areas with a history of severe weather conditions may install permanent storm shutters to offer protection for windows. Alternatively, boarding up windows offers an emergency solution. Surrounding trees and shrubs should be well trimmed to prevent debris from damaging the property or personnel, and loose and clogged rain gutters and downspouts should be cleared. The company may designate a safe room and stock such a facility with a disaster supply kit—water, nonperishable food, medications, and lighting.

During a hurricane or tornado, personnel should avoid windows, skylights, and glass doors, as debris and strong winds may shatter such structures. Personnel should move to a safe area, such as an interior office, a closet, or a bathroom on the lower level of the facility. In case of flooding, electricity should be turned off at the main circuit breaker. If the facility loses power, major appliances should be turned off, such as the air conditioner and water heaters, to reduce damage. Personnel should not leave a safe location when in the eye of a hurricane, but must wait until the storm has passed over, since there will be a short period of calm, followed by a rapid increase in wind speed from the opposite direction.

Following a hurricane or tornado, personnel should remain indoors until official notifications have been issued indicating that it is safe to leave the property. Personnel should be advised not to touch fallen or low-hanging wires and to stay away from puddles with wires in or near them. Many of the same conditions resulting from floods or earthquakes will be prevalent, with weakened structures, contaminated water, and a loss of social infrastructures. The IMP should provide guidelines to local managers and incident response groups so that they can prepare for pending hurricane and tornado events, limit the danger to personnel and facilities during the crisis, and recover safely once the storm has passed to safe areas or emergency muster points designated by government authorities.

Volcanoes

A volcano is a mountain that opens downward to a reservoir of molten rock below the surface of the earth. When pressure from gases within the molten rock becomes too great, an eruption occurs. Eruptions can be either quiet or explosive; there may be lava flows, flattened landscapes, poisonous gases, and flying rock and ash. Because of their intense heat, lava flows create significant fire hazards and can destroy all structures in their paths. Typically, lava flows are slow moving, and personnel can move out of their way. Ash flows can occur on all sides of a volcano, and ash debris can fall hundreds of miles downwind of the volcano. Dangerous mudflows and floods can occur in valleys leading away from volcanoes, striking with little warning. Typically, mature crisis management plans are in place for projects operating within the shadow of a volcano. The IMP plays an important role in the first actions taken during an eruption, enabling personnel to deal with the common risks that accompany volcanic eruptions, including:

- Earthquakes and tsunamis
- Mudflows and flash floods
- Landslides and rockfalls
- Ashfall and acid rain

During a volcanic eruption, personnel should try to leave the affected area using an established evacuation plan (if advised by authorities), avoiding downwind areas and river valleys downstream of the volcano. If caught indoors, personnel should close all windows, doors, and dampers; put all machinery inside a garage or barn; and bring all animals and livestock into closed shelters. If personnel are outdoors, they should seek shelter indoors as quickly as possible. If subjected to ashfall, personnel should seek protection by wearing long-sleeved shirts and long pants, goggles to protect vision, and a damp cloth to assist with breathing.

Following a volcanic eruption, personnel should stay out of an affected area, as the effects of a volcanic eruption can be experienced many miles from the main event, including mudflows, flash flooding, forest fires, and high-temperature ash flows. When safe to do so, roofs should be cleared of ash, as it can result in structural collapse. The IMP should be designed to provide guidance if a volcanic eruption is imminent so as to enable managers to make the determination whether to evacuate or to remain in place, and help them reduce the possible risks associated with falling debris and other associated hazards. The employment of mature crisis response plans should quickly follow a volcanic eruption.

Sandstorms

Sandstorms, recognizable as large clouds traveling over the ground, occur frequently in most deserts. Some sandstorms last only a matter of hours, whereas some, like the Seistan desert wind in Iran and Afghanistan, blow constantly for up to four months. The IMP provides guidelines for project staff operating in such regions in order to allow them to protect themselves, their facilities, as well as valuable or vulnerable resources in the event of a sandstorm.

Prior to a sandstorm occurring, windows, vents, and skylights should be closed to prevent dust from entering facilities. Vehicles should be turned off (unless especially prepared) to avoid damaging the engines. If personnel are required to operate outside, they should be advised to lubricate their nostrils with petroleum jelly (if available) to prevent the mucus membranes from drying out, tie cloths over their noses and mouths, and wear goggles to protect their vision. Personnel should also remove contact lenses, tuck in clothes (tops into pants, pants into socks) to prevent burns from the sand, and wear long sleeves and trousers. Visibility may become extremely limited, and groups should be attached together by ropes to prevent personnel from become disoriented and lost. If personnel are lost or trapped in a sandstorm, they should seek shelter in buildings or rock outcroppings, or if no natural shelters are available, they should lie down and wait out the storm. If trapped in vehicles, engines should be switched off and vents closed. Following a sandstorm, personnel should be advised to rehydrate and wash off dust particles (especially from under the fingernails). The IMP should be used to provide clear guidance during the notification period pending the arrival of a sandstorm, as well as during the sandstorm event itself.

Landslides

A landslide is a phenomenon that includes a wide range of ground movement, such as rockfalls, deep failure of slopes, and shallow debris flows. Although gravity's action on an oversteep slope is the primary reason for a landslide, there are other contributing factors affecting the original slope stability. Landslides may also follow heavy rains or earthquakes. Deforestation may also contribute to landslides, which may vary from minor movements to major slope failures that can carry large buildings downslope. Indicators of potential landslides include changes to the landscape, such as changing patterns of storm-water drainage on slopes (especially the places where runoff water converges) and land movement. Small slides and flows may occur as a precursor to larger earth movements. Doors or windows stick or may also jam for the first time; new cracks may appear in plaster, tile, brick, foundations, outside walls, or walkways; or stairs may begin to pull away from buildings. In addition, slowly developing and widening cracks appear on the ground or on paved areas such as streets or driveways. Underground utility lines may break, and bulging may appear at the base of a slope. Water may also break through the ground surface in new locations; fences, retaining walls, utility poles, or trees may tilt or move; and a faint rumbling sound that increases in volume may be noticeable as the landslide event approaches. The ground may start to shift in the direction of the slope, and unusual sounds such as trees cracking and boulders striking together may indicate moving debris.

Personnel should be advised to avoid steep slopes, especially close to mountain edges, near drainage ways, or bordering natural erosion valleys. When a landslide may be imminent, personnel should be advised to stay alert and awake, since many debris flow fatalities occur when people are sleeping. If project staff are in areas susceptible to landslides and debris flows, the IMP may include policies or guidelines for departing the area at the first indication of a potential landslide. After a landslide, personnel should stay away from the slide area and follow directions broadcast on local news or television stations. Additional hazards include flooding, damaged roadways, and damaged public utilities, such as broken gas pipes. Managers should check the building foundations, chimneys, and surrounding land for damage, as structural dangers may pose additional postevent hazards. The IMP should be designed to guide managers as to the immediate actions taken when the first indicators occur, as well as during and immediately following a landslide event.

Forest Fires

Forest fires and wildfires are very common in many places around the world. Forested areas are particularly susceptible to wildfires, especially where climates are sufficiently moist to allow the growth of trees but feature extended dry or hot periods. Forest fires are particularly prevalent in the summer and fall, as well as during droughts when fallen branches, leaves, and other material can dry out and become highly flammable. Wildfires are also common in grasslands and scrublands and are most severe on days with strong winds, which help increase the tempo and intensity of fires. Forest fires present significant risks to urban areas bordering forested or grassland areas, as well as facilities and travelers caught in the fire's path. Forest fires fall into three basic categories:

1. **Wildfire.** An unplanned and unwanted fire, including unauthorized human-caused fires, escaped wild land fire use events, escaped prescribed fire projects, and all other wild land fires.
2. **Wild Land Fire Use.** The application of the appropriate management response to naturally ignited wild land fires to accomplish specific resource management objectives in predefined designated areas.
3. **Prescribed Fire.** Any fire ignited by management actions to meet specific objectives.

The common causes for such fires include human carelessness, arson, volcanoes, heat waves, drought, lightning, and industrial accidents. The effects can be devastating and can quickly overwhelm emergency responders attempting to extinguish the fires. The propagation of a fire has three mechanisms that managers should be aware of (if operating within regions susceptible to forest fires):

1. **Crawling Fire.** A fire that spreads via low-level vegetation (e.g., bushes, grass, and scrub).
2. **Crown Fire.** A fire that spreads across the top branches of trees. Crown fires can spread at an incredible pace through the top of a forest. They can be extremely dangerous to all inhabitants underneath, as they may spread too fast to be outrun, particularly on windy days.
3. **Jumping Fire.** A fire that produces burning branches and leaves that are carried by the wind to start distant fires. A jumping fire can be carried over roads, rivers, or even firebreaks.

The IMP should be designed to support companies whose facilities or work sites operate within regions that suffer from forest fires. Prior to a forest fire event, companies should undertake the following measures as part of their contingency planning phase:

- Consult with your local fire department regarding the measures required to make the facility more fire resistant.
- Check for and remove fire hazards in and around the facility, such as dried-out branches, leaves, and debris.
- Develop fire response plans and rehearse these with personnel and local authorities.
- Learn fire safety techniques and teach them to employees.
- Make sure every floor and all working areas have smoke detectors.

During a forest fire event, the local or incident response manager should undertake the following simple activities to increase the protection of personnel and facilities:

- Monitor local radio stations in order to understand where the fire is located, and which areas are affected by the downwind effects—in terms of smoke hazards as well as the direction in which the fire is moving.
- Prepare personnel to evacuate along prescribed escape routes once the location and direction of travel are known.
- Remove all outdoor furniture, tarps, and other combustible material from the facility exterior; these present a flammable hazard for jumping fire threats.
- Close all doors in the facility; shut off gas valves and pilot lights; and remove flammable drapes, curtains, awnings, and other window coverings.
- Keep lights on to aid visibility in case smoke fills the facility.
- If sufficient water is available, turn sprinklers on to wet the roof and any waterproof valuables to reduce the risks of ignition.
- Limit the time spent outdoors until conditions improve to avoid breathing in harmful smoke.
- Turn off air exchange units that bring air in from the outside if they are worsening indoor air quality.

The IMP is designed to protect facilities from being susceptible to fire hazards during a forest fire crisis, as well as help determine the point at which personnel evacuate if the fire comes into immediate proximity of the facility. The guidance and instructions provided by government authorities should be followed at all times; however, companies can increase the levels of awareness and response to their employees during such events by developing simple and sensible response measures and protocols.

Summary

The common and unique risk factors facing an organization range considerably, whether the group operates within a familiar domestic setting, or whether they have a widespread global footprint. The perception of risk, the nature of the organization itself, the structure of a company's risk board or council, as well as the competence and resource parameters of a security department and IRT and CRT response groups all play a significant part in how risks are planned for and managed. External influences, such as a company's exposure in terms of risk and activity profile, the stability of the operating environment, industry-specific business vulnerabilities, and the importance of reputation, also play a key role in defining how much detail and preparation go into developing a comprehensive Business Continuity Management Plan, as well as the components that make up such a plan—including the IMP.

This chapter has briefly touched on a wide spectrum of risk types (both principle and by products of a crisis) that a company might face, from the common everyday-risks such as road traffic accidents and disciplinary issues found within most domestic businesses to those risks that might be typically associated with more volatile environments (e.g., third-world or post-conflict regions)—explosive hazards, armed attacks, and kidnapping and ransom risks. By succinctly outlining both generic and unique risk types, the IMP helps users to place risks into an understandable context, significantly enhancing the ability to use the response guidelines, ask the right questions, and deliver the right information in the information collection reports.

The educational or advisory aspect of the IMP illustrated in this chapter provides a Risk Register for companies, and empowers local managers and the IRT to work with a sufficient level of understanding, enabling better business resilience and quicker recovery following a crisis event. Such information should be supported, where possible and appropriate, with training and rehearsals so that the guidelines and responses provided in the response section (see Chapter 5) can be implemented with the greatest effectiveness.

Incident Response Guidelines

Each crisis event will involve unique factors that will affect how the initial and often inexperienced first-line responders or ad hoc response groups respond, as well as how the follow-on and typically predefined and experienced incident and crisis management teams (CMTs) will manage to an event. It is problematic to attempt to completely define predetermined response plans and management guidelines, as each situation will be unique and each response guideline will require the necessary degree of flexibility needed to reflect the fluid management and operational requirements of each crisis event. That said, companies can plan ahead and determine the most likely risk events, as well as a sensible set of response options that can be used to guide less experienced managers through what is often a confusing and highly stressful situation, or provide a quick checklist for those with more experience to ensure complacency does not set in and uniformity of response measures are maintained.

Response guidelines should be considered as such: guidelines. They should not be considered restrictive, unless the implementing staff requires clear and strict instructions for dealing with particular crisis events. They effectively provide a sensible first responder and manager handrail which ensures that advice and guidance is offered where needed, and specific instructions are provided where necessary. It also ensures that key management requirements are not missed during an emergency, and that a logical and structured approach to resolving a situation is provided. Common sense and sound leadership at all times should take precedence. In addition, companies might wish to consider including a liability exemption for such documents, as such guidelines cannot prevent a crisis from occurring, and are not surefire measures by which to prevent injuries, property loss, or damage. These guidelines are purely mitigation tools for individuals to use during an emergency, helping focus a response and bring control and structure to often confusing situations. Response guidelines are useful for even the most experienced of crisis professionals, as they provide a checklist to walk a manager through response considerations as an event occurs, providing focus, structure, and consistency. Additional elements can then be added to enhance the response measures as required. Those drafting response guidelines should also consider the environment in which such documents will be utilized—often fast moving, high stress, and under considerable pressure. Therefore, the response guidelines should contain enough information to bring understanding to the user, without requiring significant time to read through and implement recommendations or gather information.

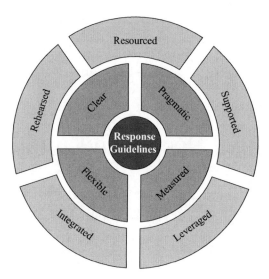

EXHIBIT 5.1 Response Guidelines Principles

Response guidelines support the company in developing uniformity and transparency across the organization, ensuring that the basic tenets of response are understood and applied evenly, within what can often be complex and compartmentalized organizations. They can also be used in conjunction with information capture reports, helping managers both practically deal with a problem, as well as share critical information between multiple participants (see Chapter 6). These policies and procedures also evidence the company's efforts to manage its risks, and can form an important aspect of its duty of care approach. In addition, such measures might offset business risks, as well as reputational and liability risks if a crisis event results in a subsequent investigation or lawsuit. Such response guidelines are not designed to constrain innovation or lateral thinking, but should be configured to provide the foundations of a response system, as well as share simple and useful procedures for managing crisis events in the best way possible. The principles that should be applied when developing response guidelines are illustrated in Exhibit 5.1, and should conform to the following considerations:

- **Resourced.** The response guidelines should have the correct resources available to allow plans to be implemented, in terms of education for users as well as the materials needed to implement responses.
- **Supported.** Response guidelines should be supported by all management levels in order to ensure that activities have prior buy-in and that consistent approaches are in place.
- **Rehearsed.** Ideally, response measures will have been practiced prior to an emergency so that managers and users are familiar and comfortable with the guidelines and requirements.
- **Integrated.** Integration both within the company and with external agencies is critical to ensure that response guidelines are effective. Technological integration is also required.

- **Leveraged.** Response guidelines should seek to leverage organic and external resources and capabilities in order to augment a user group's capabilities and capacity.
- **Flexible.** Response guidelines should be inherently flexible in order to meet the unique factors that invariably accompany each crisis event. They should guide, rather than be rigidly enforced.
- **Measured.** Response guidelines should provide a calm, measured, and mature response to crisis events, reducing panic or knee-jerk reactions.
- **Clear.** Response guidelines should be clear and easy to follow—meeting the knowledge, capabilities, and experiences of a wide and diverse user audience.
- **Pragmatic.** Response guidelines should be pragmatic and realistic. They should provide the right level of support to resolve a problem—simplicity and realism are vital.

The following response guidelines offer *suggestions* for how simple and user-friendly management protocols can be developed to meet the requirements of a wide user audience, for a variety of threats a company or organization might face. Each guideline should be considered as an isolated tool, providing sufficient instructions and prompts to assist first responders and crisis managers in dealing with singular events. A degree of repetition will be evident within some guideline protocols as each management response guideline should be self contained and able to operate in isolation. At the end of each guideline response is a blank organization contact list that can be used to guide managers to the correct organizations to liaise with, alert, or mobilize for each type of risk event. This should be linked to the Business Continuity Management Plan communications and interface plans and should be simple enough for those not trained or experienced in applying crisis management policies and procedures to use effectively, but should also be designed to support a range of incident response and crisis management teams as well. It should be remembered that these plans will need to be clear, simple, and succinct when used in order to offer guidance to managers while they concurrently face the stresses and challenges of coping with the crisis event itself. Companies should seek to tailor such responses to suit their corporate policies and objectives, making plans short or more detailed depending on their need and level of risk, as well as the business activity and its operating environment.

Aspects of the response guidelines and data call section will be repetitive of other components of the Business Continuity Management Plan. This is necessary in some areas so that each section can operate in isolation, if required. The aim of this chapter is to provide readers a series of cheat sheets that can be directly copied, and then enhanced or modified to suit particular company or operating environment requirements.

Vehicle-Borne IED Incident Management

Incident Management Guidelines

A vehicle-borne improvised explosive device (VBIED) will be in the form of a static vehicle or a mobile/static suicide bomber, set on a timer, set on a tilt mechanism, or remotely detonated. Standard operating procedures should be in place to limit the opportunities for unauthorized vehicles containing explosives to enter a secured area. This will include both physical measures (barriers, gates, guards) and policies and procedures (see appropriate security plan for the project).

In the event of a VBIED incident occurring, the following points should be addressed:

✓ Action Points

1. Stand up the Incident Management and Crisis Response Teams using the SAD CHALETS system.
2. Move to the predefined Security Alert Status, in which all security personnel are mobilized.
3. Take shelter (lie down, move behind or into a hard structure, move away)—refer to *explosive hazard distances* diagram for details.
4. Establish a casualty management point.
5. Assist casualties and walking wounded—provide Casualty Reports as per Communications Plan.
6. Establish an *Incident Control Point* (ICP) to coordinate responses and meet external response groups—notify responding agencies of the location and of safe routes into the site.
7. Confirm there are no secondary devices—conduct a security sweep.
8. Implement the six Cs:
   - **Confirm.** Confirm the presence of the suspect device. This should be a one-person task (if appropriate) and needs to be done from a distance whenever possible. Maximum use should be made of hard cover and spotting equipment through such means as binoculars or scopes.
   - **Clear.** Clear the area around the device of all personnel, working from the device outward, to a distance of 900 feet. Maximum use should be made of hard cover, such as buildings. No one should be in clear sight of the threat area.
   - **Cordon.** Cordon off the 900-foot danger area and set up an Incident Control Point (ICP) for follow-on agencies to meet at. Personnel who are being cleared from the area should be checked at random to deter additional threats.
   - **Control.** Control the cordoned-off area to ensure that only authorized access is achieved. Only emergency services should be allowed to breach the cordon through the control point. Any breaches of the cordon should be reported immediately to the Incident Response Team (IRT) Commander.

- **Check.** All personnel stationed on the cordon should check their immediate area for secondary devices and hazards. Any suspicious items should be reported to the situation commander, and their position should be marked.
- **Coordinate.** Commercial companies will rarely manage an explosive hazard in isolation from external government or military support. Therefore, effective coordination between company and external management and response teams is critical for the safe resolution of the situation.

9. Send out security alerts according to the crisis Communications Plan to notify staff to avoid the area if traveling.
10. Mobilize the Quick Response Force (QRF) if appropriate to mitigate possible secondary attacks.
11. Notify medical facilities and support agencies (see Communications Plan).
12. Carry out a roll call of all employees and personnel.
13. Begin a running log of events as they occur, recording activities.
14. Do not divulge the names of casualties until their next of kin have been notified.
15. Provide a Serious Incident Report (SIR) if required.
16. Cordon off the site of a detonation—this is relevant for any forensic investigations, as well as to mitigate the threat from any secondary devices or unexploded ordnance.
17. Consider alternative business locations for future business operations in the area.
18. Increase security measures—conduct a full investigation of the incident using all agencies and methods available.
19. Forward all information through the correct communication channels, and update where necessary.
20. Provide an *Incident Management Plan (IMP) Risk Assessment Report* as soon as possible.

See also Cordoning Incident Management.

Key People to Call (see the IMP Communications Plan)

Group	Yes/No	Group	Yes/No
Medical organization		Organic QRF	
Military interface		Crisis response team	
Embassy or consulate		Security provider (vendor)	
Police, fire, or ambulance		Other groups	

Casualty Incident Management

Incident Management Guidelines

It is essential that full and accurate information is gathered in order to most effectively report and deal with a medical emergency. Inaccurate reporting can undermine the level of support a casualty may receive.

In the event of a casualty evacuation, the following steps should be taken:

✓ Action Points

1. Stand up the Incident Management and Crisis Response Teams using the SAD CHALETS system.
2. Ensure that the details of the casualty and the person's condition are accurate and detailed; confirm, then confirm again.
3. Determine what support is required, and notify the relevant medical facilities and organizations.
4. If appropriate, notify the appropriate consulate/embassy/military organizations (see Communications Plan).
5. If the medical evacuation involves going into hostile areas, notify a quick response security team to escort and assist in the evacuation.
6. Continue reporting of the situation to ensure best support levels and information sharing is achieved.
7. Maintain contact with medical teams to receive updates on the casualty status.
8. Notify the casualty's family when appropriate, typically through corporate crisis management teams.
9. Determine if continued operation in the area of the incident will result in more casualties—consider alternatives.
10. Make attempts at retrieving any lost or damaged sensitive materials or equipment.
11. If the party is ambulatory, move the casualty out of harm's way and make the person as comfortable as possible. If the party cannot be moved, establish a secure perimeter around the injured person.
12. Notify manager in charge.
13. Establish the cause of the injury and how this might pose other risks—industrial accident, industrial risk, hostile groups, natural event, and so on.
14. Maintain contact with the medical team on scene to receive updates and to ensure proper care is being taken.
15. Begin to record information in the record of events log, and provide an injury or accident report.
16. Forward all information through the correct communication channels, and update where necessary.

Key People to Call (see the IMP Communications Plan)			
Group	Yes/No	Group	Yes/No
▪ Medical organization		▪ Organic QRF	
▪ Military interface		▪ Crisis response team	
▪ Embassy or consulate		▪ Security provider (vendor)	
▪ Police, fire, or ambulance		▪ Other groups	

Missing Person Incident Management

Incident Management Guidelines

In high-risk locations, a failure to report in or communicate with managers may result in staff being reported and considered missing within a very short time frame. In typical operating environments, the term *missing* is usually applied only after the person has been out of contact for more than 24 hours (36 hours in a low-risk area).

In the event of a missing person incident, the following steps should be taken:

✓ Action Points

1. Stand up the Incident Management and Crisis Response Teams using the SAD CHALETS system.
2. The appointed manager is to establish facts with the last person to be in contact with the missing person.
3. Inform the appropriate consulate/embassy/law enforcement or military agencies.
4. Check with local hospitals to see if the person has been admitted.
5. Check with local police stations to see whether the person has been arrested or reported injured.
6. Ascertain the last known whereabouts of the person and who, if anyone, the individual was with.
7. Check personnel records to see if the person has a medical condition, or a history of losing consciousness as well as any medical risks the person might face.
8. Contact all possible locations (business and personal) where the person may have visited, or where the individual may now be.
9. Determine whether security teams or personnel can search areas or locations where the person might be.
10. Consider the use of a local investigator who could be of assistance in locating the person or determining what has happened.
11. Liaise with the person's family through an appointed manager.
12. Appoint a media spokesperson and prepare statements if necessary.
13. Keep a running account of the situation, updating as things occur; retain reports, and distribute information.
14. Begin to record information within the record of events log.
15. Forward all information through the correct communication channels, and update where necessary.
16. Provide an *IMP Risk Assessment Report* as soon as possible.

Key People to Call (see the IMP Communications Plan)			
Group	**Yes/No**	**Group**	**Yes/No**
▪ Medical organization		▪ Organic QRF	
▪ Military interface		▪ Crisis response team	
▪ Embassy or consulate		▪ Security provider (vendor)	
▪ Police, fire, or ambulance		▪ Other groups	

Road Traffic Accident Incident Management Data Call

Incident Management Guidelines

Road traffic accidents can be relatively mundane events in some environments, or quickly escalate into significant events in others. Local laws and environmental conditions can have a significant impact on how injured personnel are managed and moved to safety, as well as the repercussions if local persons are injured or local materials are damaged. Road traffic accidents that would typically not be considered serious in Western countries can lead to loss of life or long-term imprisonment in others. Staff should be aware of any peculiar laws and requirements of the country they are operating in, as well as any safety precautions and areas in which they should be self-reliant in order to effectively deal with an accident.

In the event of a road traffic accident occurring, the following steps should be taken:

✓ Action Points

1. Notify the Incident Management and Crisis Response Teams using the SAD CHALETS system.
2. Determine the extent of injuries of those involved (if any).
3. Find out where injured parties were taken and whether the injuries warranted hospitalization.
4. Determine if local authorities or personnel are involved, and if the occupants of the vehicle are being charged with a crime.
5. Establish the location and status of company vehicle, and arrange for the retrieval of the vehicle and any company property if it is immobile.
6. Notify the embassy if company staff have been arrested or detained.
7. Notify the embassy if local nationals have been injured or killed.
8. Begin to record information within the record of events log.
9. Consider a compensation plan if the cause of the accident resulted from employee error.
10. Liaise with local police authorities to seek their support (if appropriate).
11. Be sure to completely and accurately fill out the *Driver Accident Report Form* (see Data Capture Reports section).
12. Forward all information through the correct communication channels, and update where necessary.
13. Conduct an IMP Risk Assessment if the incident is serious, with significant implications.

Key People to Call (see the IMP Communications Plan)			
Group	**Yes/No**	**Group**	**Yes/No**
▪ Medical organization		▪ Organic QRF	
▪ Military interface		▪ Crisis response team	
▪ Embassy or consulate		▪ Security provider (vendor)	
▪ Police, fire, or ambulance		▪ Other groups	

Facility Physical Security Breach Incident Management

Incident Management Guidelines

A physical security breach of a facility, whether in a remote, hostile, or permissive environment, may pose a range of risks to the company. Managers should consider the nature and intent of the breach, as well as the possible goals and motives of the intruders.

In the event of a physical security breach occurring, the following points should be addressed:

✓ Action Points

1. Stand up the Incident Management and Crisis Response Teams using the SAD CHALETS system.
2. Establish the nature of the breach (criminals, youths, activists, terrorists) and associated risk levels and types.
3. Elevate alert status and post guards around the area; start roving patrols.
4. Notify local government, military, and law enforcement organizations.
5. Determine where the breach occurred and secure the point of entry.
6. Confirm an Incident Management Control Point to receive external security agencies; notify them as to safe routes in.
7. Perform a role call of all personnel; identify any missing staff.
8. Close down and secure all facilities; if necessary, move personnel to safe havens.
9. Perform an inventory of all weapons, equipment, and documents, if appropriate.
10. Determine the consequences of the breach and begin mitigation to prevent future security breaches.
11. Employ bomb-sniffing dogs if appropriate, and clear muster points for possible hazards.
12. Provide status reports to organic and external security groups.
13. Conduct a sweep of the area for unauthorized intruders and devices.
14. Confirm whether intruders are still present; if so, track and monitor their movements if possible.
15. Maintain a flow of information to organic and external security groups.
16. Write a complete, detailed report of the breach.
17. Forward all information through the correct communication channels, and update where necessary.
18. Provide an *IMP Risk Assessment Report* as soon as possible.

Key People to Call (see the IMP Communications Plan)			
Group	Yes/No	Group	Yes/No
■ Medical organization		■ Organic QRF	
■ Military interface		■ Crisis response team	
■ Embassy or consulate		■ Security provider (vendor)	
■ Police, fire, or ambulance		■ Other groups	

Kidnapping and Ransom Incident Management

Incident Management Guidelines

Kidnapping is a specialist area and must be treated with the utmost professionalism and sensitivity. The distinction between a hostage situation and kidnapping situation is that the location of the victim is not known during a kidnapping situation. In certain environments, the ability to recover kidnapped persons might be possible using Western military force support to cordon off or search areas, if the proper incident management policies, agreements, and standard operating procedures are in place. In other environments, it will be the sole responsibility of a kidnapping and ransom team to recover kidnapped persons.

In the event of a kidnapping, the following (initial) steps should be taken to ensure the safety of the victim:

✓ Action Points

1. Stand up the Incident Management and Crisis Response Teams using the SAD CHALETS system.
2. Liaise with appropriate consulate/embassy and nearby police or military commander if authorized.
3. Be sure that a kidnapping has indeed occurred; explore all possible explanations for a missing person (see missing person guidelines).
4. Confirm where the victim was last seen, and with whom; get a full statement of events, as well as what the victim was wearing.
5. Determine whether the victim has any medical conditions, and ascertain the state of the person's mental health.
6. Start a log of events and update it as events transpire.
7. Alert expert consultants and negotiators (if sanctioned).
8. Notify the victim's family (if sanctioned).
9. Limit information given to the media for the well-being of the victim.
10. Choose a telephone to be used when talking to kidnappers, and attach a recording device if possible.
11. Retrieve personal file of victim so that "proof of life" questions can be verified.
12. Do not indicate to kidnappers that police have been notified (if appropriate).
13. Promise nothing, but be conciliatory.
14. Allow the experts to do their job once they arrive on scene.
15. Take notes and record details such as voice, age, timbre, race, and gender of kidnappers.
16. Take statements from anyone who may have witnessed the event; obtain a description of kidnappers, vehicles, and other details.
17. Place all evidence in plastic bags; handle corners only to avoid damaging fingerprints.

18. Forward all information through the correct communication channels, and update where necessary.
19. Provide an *IMP Risk Assessment Report* as soon as possible.

Key People to Call (see the IMP Communications Plan)			
Group	**Yes/No**	**Group**	**Yes/No**
▪ Medical organization		▪ Organic QRF	
▪ Military interface		▪ Crisis response team	
▪ Embassy or consulate		▪ Security provider (vendor)	
▪ Police, fire, or ambulance		▪ Other groups	

Media Management Incident Management

Incident Management Guidelines

Only those appointed to deal with the media should offer comments to these agencies. Nothing said is ever off the record. Inappropriate comments or observations can cause considerable damage to the company, its employees, or its operations. Always refer to a higher authority prior to speaking to media persons.

If an incident occurs that is brought to the attention of the media, or that necessitates the attention of the media, the following guidelines should be followed:

✓ Action Points

1. Stand up the Incident Management and Crisis Response Teams using the SAD CHALETS system.
2. Contact the company spokesperson as a point of contact for the media.
3. All statements given to the media should be developed by the public relations department to ensure that accurate and factual information is being delivered.
4. All employees should be briefed to direct all questions to the appointed company spokesperson, and to resist making comments to the media.
5. Do not deliberately lie to the media; if necessary, limit information for the well-being and safety of any victims that may be involved in an incident.
6. Request that the media act responsibly and do not endanger employees by releasing information that might pose risks or cause avoidable harm or distress to families.
7. Always seek advice or guidance from appointment managers.
8. Use the following statements if necessary:
   - "An appointed representative will answer your question to ensure that you are provided with the correct facts."
   - "Please provide me with your contact details, and the appropriate person will assist you in this matter. I am unable to comment at this time."
   - "Please act responsibly so as not to endanger personnel or cause harm or distress to personnel's families."
9. One spokesperson should be appointed by the company as a point of contact for the media, and if necessary another should be on-site at the scene of the incident.
10. Forward all information through the correct communication channels, and update where necessary.
11. Provide an *IMP Risk Assessment Report* as soon as possible.

Key People to Call (see the IMP Communications Plan)			
Group	**Yes/No**	**Group**	**Yes/No**
▪ Medical organization		▪ Organic QRF	
▪ Military interface		▪ Crisis response team	
▪ Embassy or consulate		▪ Security provider (vendor)	
▪ Police, fire, or ambulance		▪ Other groups	

Detention and Arrest Incident Management

Incident Management Guidelines

Detention or arrest within some cultures can present significant challenges for both the person as well as the company. It is important to ensure that the detainee's status and location are determined as soon as possible. Embassies should also be advised to create an environment of official transparency to safeguard the detainee's well-being.

In the event that an employee or a subcontractor has been arrested or detained, the following immediate steps should be taken:

✓ Action Points

1. Stand up the Incident Management and Crisis Response Teams using the SAD CHALETS system.
   - Determine the needs and mobilize company legal support.
   - Mobilize local legal representation if already established.
   - Request corporate direction.
   - Determine the requirements and mobilize initial external agency support or intercession.
2. Notify detainee's supervisor.
3. What are the risks faced by the detainee? Is the detainee safe or in danger? Provide bail if possible.
4. What are the name, rank, branch, and position of the senior government official dealing with the case?
5. When is the date for the court hearing? When can the detainee receive visitors?
6. Notify the appropriate consulate or embassy.
7. Arrange for legal representation if not part of an established protocol—if necessary through the embassy.
8. Determine the seriousness of the alleged crime and possible punishments.
9. Ascertain the identity of the aggrieved party, and what compensations may be required if the detainee is convicted.
10. Ascertain specifics of the arresting authority: agency, location, arresting officers, managers, risks associated with agency.
11. Determine what can be done to rectify the situation to the satisfaction of aggrieved party and arresting authority.
12. Determine what, if any, company property and/or documents have been confiscated during the arrest, and arrange for retrieval if possible.
13. Were persons injured or killed? Has livestock or property been damaged?
14. Arrange to have comfort items made available to the detainee (i.e., food, water, blankets, clothing, etc.) as well as items useful for bartering while in prison (e.g., cigarettes, cash, food).
15. Does the detainee require medicines, and is the person vulnerable to any health issues?

16. Forward all information through the correct communication channels, and update where necessary.
17. Provide an *IMP Risk Assessment Report* as soon as possible.

Key People to Call (see the IMP Communications Plan)			
Group	**Yes/No**	**Group**	**Yes/No**
■ Medical organization		■ Organic QRF	
■ Military interface		■ Crisis response team	
■ Embassy or consulate		■ Security provider (vendor)	
■ Police, fire, or ambulance		■ Other groups	

Hostage Situation Incident Management

Incident Management Guidelines

The speed and quality of decisions and actions taken during the initial stages of a hostage situation are likely to have a significant influence on the outcome. The distinction between a hostage situation and a kidnapping situation is that the location of the victim is known during a hostage situation. The nature of the operating environment will also determine the approach used. Hostage situations may involve disgruntled employees, personal disputes, criminals, or in the most extreme cases activists or dissidents. Hostage negotiation is a specialist field, and company managers should not enter into discussions with the perpetrator.

In the event that an employee or subcontractor is being held hostage, the following immediate steps should be taken:

✓ Action Points

1. Stand up the Incident Management and Crisis Response Teams using the SAD CHALETS system.
2. Notify appropriate law enforcement, military, and government agencies for immediate assistance.
3. Establish the location of the incident, as well as details of perpetrator(s).
4. Secure the area if possible; contain the hostage situation to prevent escape or exposing other parties to follow-on risks:
    - Close off all vehicle exit routes to prevent the perpetrator and hostage vehicle from escaping (use unmanned vehicles if necessary to block routes).
    - Lock exit doors and routes to prevent escape by foot.
5. Cordon off the area to prevent other employees being taken hostage; clear area of all staff:
    - Send out notifications (e.g., e-mail, phone, and text).
    - Seal access routes.
6. Establish a line of communication with the perpetrator; do *not* try to negotiate—inform the perpetrator that someone is en route who is authorized to make decisions.
7. Provide floor plans, maps, and other details to law enforcement upon arrival.
8. Establish an Incident Control Point and safe access routes, notify external agencies, and organize a reception to lead them into the location via a safe route.
9. Forward all information through the correct communication channels, and update where necessary.
10. Provide an *IMP Risk Assessment Report* as soon as possible.

Key People to Call (see the IMP Communications Plan)			
Group	**Yes/No**	**Group**	**Yes/No**
■ Medical organization		■ Organic QRF	
■ Military interface		■ Crisis response team	
■ Embassy or consulate		■ Security provider (vendor)	
■ Police, fire, or ambulance		■ Other groups	

Suspect Call Incident Management

Incident Management Guidelines

Suspect calls might result from a prank caller seeking to disrupt operations, cause concern or friction within an organization, or in the most extreme cases warn companies of a pending crisis event. All calls should be taken seriously, although crisis response measures should be put into action only for those calls deemed valid, as most calls have no substance. This will reduce response fatigue while still addressing calls that meet established company criteria for assessing the probability of the call being genuine.

In the event that a suspect call is received, the following actions should be taken:

✓ Action Points

1. Inform the local manager responsible for security and safety; if necessary, escalate upward to the regional or corporate Incident Management and Crisis Response Team using the SAD CHALETS system.
2. Notify appropriate law enforcement, military, and government agencies if appropriate.
3. Ensure a full record of the call was made (see Data Capture Reports).
4. Take the details of the caller (i.e., age, race, gender, accents, emotional status, remarks and threats, background noises, etc.).
5. Determine the nature and risk presented from the call; implement response plans according to risk natures identified and deemed valid.
6. Can the call be traced? If so, implement a trace and alert the police.
7. Can the call be recorded? If so, record the call.
8. Forward all information through the correct communication channels, and update where necessary.
9. Provide an *IMP Risk Assessment Report* as soon as possible.

Key People to Call (see the IMP Communications Plan)			
Group	**Yes/No**	**Group**	**Yes/No**
▪ Medical organization		▪ Organic QRF	
▪ Military interface		▪ Crisis response team	
▪ Embassy or consulate		▪ Security provider (vendor)	
▪ Police, fire, or ambulance		▪ Other groups	

Civil Unrest Incident Management

Incident Management Guidelines

Civil unrest may be isolated and short-term events, or be widespread and long-lasting crisis situations. Civil unrest can involve the direct or indirect targeting of foreign personnel and local employees, office and project sites, resources and assets, as well as personnel and materials in transit. Crime and social disorder are often associated with such situations. Personnel may also be exposed to risks associated with police responses if caught within a crowd or riot event.

In the event that a civil unrest situation occurs, the following immediate steps should be taken:

✓ Action Points

1. Stand up the Incident Management and Crisis Response Teams using the SAD CHALETS system.
2. If required, establish a *Crisis Response Center* and local Incident Management Team.
3. Alert security personnel—appropriate security response measures should be taken, enhancing security alert states and measures.
4. Alert supporting military and external agencies; request advice and support from embassies, consuls, and other government groups.
5. Gather all available intelligence on the situation from:
   - External agencies
   - Local workforce
   - Media
   - Subcontractors
   - Other companies
6. Determine the nature, tempo, scope, and impacts of the civil unrest situation.
7. Initiate reciprocal reporting agreements with other commercial groups.
8. Determine which groups, facilities, and resources are most at risk.
9. Secure facilities, materials, and resources.
10. Send local employees and workforces home if it is safe to do so.
11. Move nonsecurity personnel to safe havens or securable areas.
12. Conduct a muster of all personnel within a safe haven, and account for missing personnel.
13. Move personnel away from crowds and out of sight if necessary. Personnel are to stay away from windows or other apertures, and stay behind solid structures.
14. Ensure that personnel are moved away from combustible or flammable materials.
15. Consider the implementation of an evacuation plan if required or appropriate.

(continued)

(*continued*)

16. Forward all information through the correct communication channels, and update where necessary.
17. Provide an *IMP Risk Assessment Report* as soon as possible.

Key People to Call (see the IMP Communications Plan)			
Group	Yes/No	Group	Yes/No
▪ Medical organization		▪ Organic QRF	
▪ Military interface		▪ Crisis response team	
▪ Embassy or consulate		▪ Security provider (vendor)	
▪ Police, fire, or ambulance		▪ Other groups	

Unexploded Ordnance or Suspect Package Incident Management

Incident Management Guidelines

The mishandling of a suspect package or unexploded ordnance (UXO) can result in injury or death, in addition to the loss of forensic evidence. Such materials may be left in small bags, might be disguised as rubbish bags or placed in Coke cans, might be portions of partially detonated munitions, or might be booby-trapped materials. At all times, incident managers should consider the safety of the persons involved in the operation, the integrity of the evidence, the requirement not to touch the suspect package or item, the need to quickly and safely clear the area, and the need to pass on information so that specialist responders can deal with the situation.

In the event that a suspect package or UXO situation occurs, the following immediate steps should be taken:

✓ Action Points

1. Stand up the Incident Management and Crisis Response Teams using the SAD CHALETS system.
2. Initiate a site evacuation plan if required. Consider threats posed by moving personnel—ensure that escape routes are not exposed to UXO or suspect package risks. Determine whether it is safer to have personnel remain where they are or move.
3. Do not use radios or mobile phones near the device.
4. **Confirm:** Confirm it is an explosive package. Do not touch it, and remember the five Ws:
   - What have you found? Get a description—size, shape, color, wires visible; take photos if possible and do not approach or touch.
   - Where was it found? Provide a 10-figure grid reference or other reference point.
   - When was it found? Get time and date.
   - Why are you there?
   - Whether it has been moved or touched.
5. **Clear:** Clear the area to ensure the safety of personnel; no one should be in line of sight of the package. The following elements should be considered:
   - Radio transmissions only at a safe distance: handheld, vehicle fitted.
   - Mark the route to the UXO or suspect package.
   - Establish an Incident Control Point to notify external agencies of location and safe route in.
   - Wedge open doors (allow clear access and exit for personnel).
   - Evacuate personnel to safe locations; conduct musters to identify missing persons.
   - If using a bomb shelter area, ensure that the building has previously been surveyed by a structural engineer as being capable of providing protection from a nearby explosion.

(continued)

(continued)

6. **Cordon:** Cordon off the area until emergency services arrive to assume control:
   - Establish correct cordon distances (see Exhibit A).
   - Ensure that all personnel, including security, are out of line of sight of the package or material.
   - Ensure that personnel are not at risk from secondary hazards.
   - Ensure that personnel are behind hard cover if possible (concrete walls).
   - Ensure that personnel are not observing the incident from behind windows (blast effects).
   - Ensure that personnel are upwind if chemical or other such hazards are present.

7. **Control:** Control the situation until relieved or the emergency services arrive:
   - Control the scene and area.
   - Establish safe routes and control points.
   - Ensure that all persons are not in line of sight of the materials (900 to 1,500 feet away).
   - Ensure that the control room is aware of any action you take; be accurate with your information.

8. **Check:** Check the area for other threats as well as evidence:
   - Check for secondary hazards.
   - Ensure that the location is protected for police investigations.
   - Save evidence, if any, on the site.
   - Secure the area.
   - Consider other potential and present hazards.

9. **Coordinate:** Commercial companies will rarely manage an explosive hazard in isolation from external government or military support. Effective coordination between company and external management and response teams is critical for the safe resolution of the situation.

10. Assess any damage to the site following an explosion. Also implement the casualty response procedures.

11. Forward all information through the correct communication channels, and update where necessary.

12. Provide an *IMP Risk Assessment Report* as soon as possible.

Key People to Call (see the IMP Communications Plan)

Group	Yes/No	Group	Yes/No
Medical organization		Organic QRF	
Military interface		Crisis response team	
Embassy or consulate		Security provider (vendor)	
Police, fire, or ambulance		Other groups	

EXHIBIT A   Explosive Hazard Table (Guidelines Only)

Threat Description	Explosive Capacity (TNT Equivalent)	Threat Distances	Outdoor Evacuation Distances
Pipe Bomb	5 lb or 2.3 kg	70 ft or 21 m	850 ft or 259 m
Briefcase/Suitcase Bomb	50 lb or 2 kg	150 ft or 26 m	1,850 ft or 564 m
Small Car Bomb	500 lb or 227 kg	320 ft or 98 m	1,500 ft or 475 m
Large Car Bomb	1,000 lb or 454 kg	400 ft or 122 m	1,750 ft or 534 m
Passenger Van Bomb	4,000 lb or 1,814 kg	600 ft or 195 m	1,750 ft or 838 m
Small Moving Van Bomb	10,000 lb or 4,536 kg	860 ft or 263 m	3,750 ft or 1,143 m
Moving Truck Bomb	30,000 lb or 13,608 kg	1,240 ft or 375 m	6,500 ft or 1,982 m
Semitrailer Bomb	60,000 lb or 27,216 kg	1,500 ft or 457 m	7,000 ft or 2,134 m

Source: Michael Blyth, *Risk and Security Management: Protecting People and Sites Worldwide.* Copyright © 2008 John Wiley & Sons. Reprinted with permission of John Wiley & Sons.

Suspect Letter Incident Management

Incident Management Guidelines

The mishandling of suspect mail can result in injury, death, and the loss of forensic evidence. Suspect letters may contain explosive or other hazardous substances intended to harm personnel or disrupt operations. Letters may be small, but can result in serious injuries if detonated. Letters are typically designed to detonate only when opened, as explosive mail travels through postal systems to reach an intended target. At all times, incident managers should consider the safety of the persons involved in the operation, the integrity of the evidence, the requirement not to touch the suspect letter, the need to quickly and safely clear the area, and the need to pass on information so that specialist responders can deal with the situation.

In the event that a suspect mail situation occurs, the following immediate steps should be taken:

✓ Action Points

1. Stand up the Incident Management and Crisis Response Teams using the SAD CHALETS system.
2. Do not attempt to bend the item (letter bombs are normally stiff and difficult to bend). Greasy marks and unusual odors may indicate explosive substances.
3. Do not put the item in water or in any other liquid, nor tamper or interfere with the letter in any manner.
4. Examine the item with X-ray equipment or metal detector, if possible.
5. Put the item in a dry place, away from glass and metal (to avoid injury from flying particles if there is an explosion).
6. If a garden or adjacent spare ground is available, place the letter inside a container with a lid (if possible, both made of wood or plastic).
7. If no garden or spare ground is available, place the contained letter in an uninhabited basement. If no garden, spare ground, or uninhabited basement is available, place the item in an isolated room, preferably without windows. If the room has windows, these should be opened.
8. Persons should be prevented from approaching within 75 feet of the suspect letter, no matter where it has been placed.

The immediate area should be cordoned using the five Cs:

9. **Clear:** Clear the area to ensure the safety of personnel; no one should be in line of sight of the package. The following elements should be considered:
   a. Radio transmissions only at a safe distance (e.g., handheld, vehicle fitted).
   b. Establish an Incident Control Point to notify external agencies of location and safe route in.
   c. Wedge open doors (allow clear access and exit for personnel).
   d. Evacuate personnel to safe locations; conduct musters to identify missing persons.

10. **Cordon:** Cordon off the area until emergency services arrive to assume control:
    a. Establish correct cordon distances, approximately 75 feet.
    b. Ensure all personnel, including security, are out of line of sight of the package or material.
    c. Ensure that personnel are not at risk from secondary hazards.
    d. Ensure that personnel are behind hard cover if possible (concrete walls).
    e. Ensure that personnel are not observing the incident from behind windows (blast effects).
    f. Ensure that personnel are upwind if other such hazards are likely.
11. **Control:** Control the situation until relieved or the emergency services arrive:
    a. Control the scene and area.
    b. Establish safe routes and control points.
    c. Ensure that all persons are not in line of sight of the materials.
    d. Ensure that the control room is aware of any action you take; be accurate with your information.
12. **Check:** Check the area for other threats as well as evidence:
    a. Check for secondary hazards.
    b. Ensure that the location is protected for police investigations.
    c. Save evidence, if any, on the site.
    d. Secure the area.
    e. Consider other potential and present hazards.
13. **Coordinate:** Commercial companies will rarely manage an explosive hazard in isolation from external government or military support. Therefore, effective coordination between company and external management and response teams is critical for the safe resolution of the situation.
14. Assess any damage to the site following an explosion. Also implement the casualty response procedures.
15. Forward all information through the correct communication channels, and update where necessary.
16. Provide an *IMP Risk Assessment Report* as soon as possible.

Key People to Call (see the IMP Communications Plan)			
Group	**Yes/No**	**Group**	**Yes/No**
▪ Medical organization		▪ Organic QRF	
▪ Military interface		▪ Crisis response team	
▪ Embassy or consulate		▪ Security provider (vendor)	
▪ Police, fire, or ambulance		▪ Other groups	

Destruction of Sensitive Materials Incident Management

Incident Management Guidelines

Should an evacuation of a project location occur under circumstances where materials or data must be left behind, a *destruction plan* will be required to ensure that commercial and operational materials are made inaccessible to persons illegally occupying or searching the location after staff has departed.

In the event that sensitive materials must be destroyed, the following immediate steps should be taken:

✓ Action Points

1. Stand up the Incident Management and Crisis Response Teams using the SAD CHALETS system.
2. Confirm which materials cannot be saved or transferred prior to evacuation.
3. Confirm that all destruction plan participants understand what materials must be destroyed, and allocate final destruction tasks.
4. Confirm that destruction or sanitizing technologies are available to enable the destruction plan (prepare in advance where necessary).
5. Confirm any centralized destruction areas.
6. Ensure that participating managers confirm when materials have been destroyed or sanitized; record using a destruction report (see Exhibit B).
7. Retain records of all materials destroyed; send to the appropriate crisis response team.
8. Report all materials that could not be destroyed, including the content as well as any business or security implications.
9. Forward all information through the correct communication channels, and update where necessary.
10. Provide an *IMP Risk Assessment Report* as soon as possible.

Key People to Call (see the IMP Communications Plan)			
Group	**Yes/No**	**Group**	**Yes/No**
▪ Medical organization		▪ Organic QRF	
▪ Military interface		▪ Crisis response team	
▪ Embassy or consulate		▪ Security provider (vendor)	
▪ Police, fire, or ambulance		▪ Other groups	

EXHIBIT B   Sensitive Material Destruction Example

Destruction Report—Items Sanitized or Destroyed

Material Description	Copy Type	Unit	Location	Destruction Method	Responsible	Destroyed
▪ Commercial Data	Soft Copy	Computer 2	Office 3	Magnetic Wipe	IT Manager	√
▪ Commercial Data	Soft Copy	Computer 6	Office 12	Magnetic Wipe	IT Manager	√
▪ Local Employment Records	Hard Copy	File Cabinet 3	Office 12	Fire Bin	HR Manager	√
▪ Security Plans	Hard Copy	File Cabinet 6	Office 2	Fire Bin	Security Manager	√
▪ Intelligence Reports	Soft Copy	Computer 9	Office 2	Magnetic Wipe	Intelligence Manager	√
▪ Intelligence Reports	Soft Copy	Computer 11	Office 2	Magnetic Wipe	Intelligence Manager	√

Destruction Report—Items NOT Sanitized or Destroyed

Material Description	Copy Type	Unit	Location	Risk Implications and Recommendations
▪ Security Plan—Site Zulu	Hard Copy	File Cabinet	Office 4	Compromise existing security—increase security posture.
▪ Local Employment Records	Soft Copy	Computer 1	Office 12	Risk presented to local employees—report to police.
▪ Commercial Data	Soft Copy	Computer 21	Office 16	Commercial espionage—report to police.
▪ Intelligence Report	Hard Copy	Wall	Office 14	Operating policy risk—report to military.

Repatriation Incident Management

Incident Management Guidelines

The repatriation of a deceased's remains can be challenging under the best of circumstances. Where resources are limited and infrastructures poor, repatriations can consume considerable time and resources. Regardless of the effort required, it is vitally important for repatriations to be conducted effectively and quickly, both to meet the morale obligations of the company and to protect the family's interests. Errors in a repatriation can cause unnecessary emotional distress, void a family's insurance policy, and undermine the reputation of a company, as well as increase its liability.

In the event of a repatriation incident occurring, the following points should be addressed:

✓ Action Points

1. Stand up the Incident Management and Crisis Response Teams using the SAD CHALETS system.
2. Possession considerations:
   - Collection of personal effects is carried out by appropriate manager.
   - A signed inventory of personal effects is taken by appropriate manager.
   - Ensure that all nonappropriate information is identified within the possessions.
   - All personal effects (e.g., rings, etc.) should travel with deceased in the casket.
   - All nonpersonal effects should be sealed in a box and sent with the casket, if possible (with escort).
   - Copies of all documents kept with Administrative Manager with copies sent to the corporate office.
3. Religious considerations:
   - Confirm religion and any religious requirements during immediate time after death.
   - Request a chaplain to offer blessings soon after death (at appropriate location).
   - Conduct a ceremony at all locations to mark his/her passing; request priest if necessary.
   - Confirm requirements with tribal elders or other appropriate persons.
   - Have order of service, plus photos taken/sent to family.
4. Communication considerations:
   - Shut down all phones and Internet services to prevent family being informed through inappropriate source(s).
   - No one should speak to the media, as this should be handled by the company Media Department or spokesperson.
   - An "all hands" should be conducted as soon as possible to allow people to know what is occurring, and so as to avoid rumors.

- The IRT management should confirm with the CRT who is speaking to the relevant homeland office so that communications are passed effectively to the family.
5. Travel and escort considerations:
    - The deceased should be escorted to the family to ensure that all problems are solved en route.
    - Clearance and passport/Department of Defense details must be given to relevant military personnel for military flights.
    - A travel plan should be written and distributed to minimize errors and ensure that coordination is achieved.
    - The following information will be required by the contracted funeral provider for onward flight bookings: deceased's name, passport number, nationality, and passport issue location.
6. Clothing considerations: On completion of the autopsy and embalming process, suitable attire should be placed on the deceased. This should be taken with the escort and should reflect cultural requirements.
7. Pay considerations:
    - Remaining wages should be paid immediately to the family.
    - Bank account details should be confirmed by the corporate office to ensure that the deceased's bank account has not been frozen and the next of kin can receive the outstanding wages immediately.
8. Insurance considerations:
    - The Corporate CRT is to confirm whether an autopsy is required. If one is required, the deceased should not be embalmed until the autopsy is complete. Local, regional, or national autopsy facilities should be identified. International facilities may be required, en route to the deceased's family location, to conduct any autopsy. This may be through military, embassy, or commercial providers.
    - The Corporate CRT is to confirm with the insurance broker the specific requirements to be included in any report.
    - Clear guidelines should be issued by the Corporate CRT to meet insurance requirements in order to guide the doctors on the language to be used and specific clauses to be included.
    - Clear guidelines should be issued by the Corporate CRT on the wording requirements of any serious incident and postincident reports that may be used as part of the insurance claim documentation.
9. Documentation considerations:
    - The family will be required to provide a letter of authority for the conduct of an autopsy.
    - Marriage license and other proof of relationship will be required for insurance purposes.
    - The contracted funeral provider assisting with the movement of the deceased must have all necessary documentation e-mailed in advance. In addition, it must have specific information on the family's contracted funeral provider in order to secure an air waybill permitting onward travel.

(continued)

(*continued*)

- All hard copies should be sent with the deceased. Electronic copies of information will be required by the international funeral contractor and the Corporate CRT.

10. Medical considerations:
    - The family must be informed that the deceased may require an autopsy and must be embalmed in order to permit travel on civilian airlines.
    - Medical documentation must be secured from the relevant military or other appropriate persons, and sent as per all other documentation requirements.

11. Repatriation requirements (travel): Flight details from the country of incident to the external airport should be recorded and distributed. The following flight details will be required to coordinate movement and funeral services: military or commercial aircraft number, departure point, departure date, departure time, and arrival point.

12. Repatriation requirements (in country administration):
    - Administrative Manager is to provide all necessary documentation to the military or appropriate civil authorities. Copies of all paperwork are to be held on electronic media for shipment and referral.
    - All documentation that will travel with deceased will be copied (front and rear page of passport, etc.) where appropriate.
    - A final compilation is to be forwarded to the Security Manager and Corporate CRT for reference and storage.
    - Copies will also be required for the contracted international funeral service provider. This will be sent in advance of the deceased leaving the point of departure. This will allow administrative requirements to be conducted efficiently and hasten any governmental and shipping requirements.
    - All hard copies of documentation will be carried by hand by an escort and delivered to the international funeral contractor, which will provide its own escort to take the deceased to the family.
    - An electronic inventory of the deceased's possessions is to be retained by the local IRT Manager.
    - A hard copy inventory of the deceased's possessions is to be placed with the deceased.
    - A hard copy inventory of the deceased's possessions is to be carried by the escort.
    - The name, address, and contract details of the next of kin and the company are to be placed on the casket.

13. Repatriation requirements (escort duties):
    - Contact international funeral provider upon arrival at next stop.
    - Assist with the release of deceased from relevant military or appropriate commercial authority care into the custody of the international funeral contractor.
    - Provide the international funeral contractor with all hard copy documentation.

- Ensure that all necessary documents are processed properly.
- Arrange for the bulk personal possession items of the deceased to be moved with escort onto the final flight.
- Ensure that any excess luggage charges are paid for by the international funeral contractor and billed to the company.
- Inform local IRT or Country CRT manager of all timings and key activities, so that they can relay the information on to the deceased's family.
- Confirm flight times for the onward move to deceased's home location with IRT or Country CRT manager, so that they can inform the relevant people.
- Confirm that the air waybill is prepared by the international funeral contractor and that the deceased's funeral home details have been confirmed and the funeral home is ready to collect the deceased.
- The Consignee's address and name details are to be placed on the coffin.

14. Deceased documentation required: passport, Department of Defense card, copy of contract, death certificate, statement of record of recognition of deceased, chronological records of medical care, initial casualty report, funeral director authority for release, and inventory of possessions; all hard copies must travel with the deceased.

See also Cordoning Incident Management.

Key People to Call (see the IMP Communications Plan)			
Group	Yes/No	Group	Yes/No
▪ Medical organization		▪ Organic QRF	
▪ Military interface		▪ Crisis response team	
▪ Embassy or consulate		▪ Security provider (vendor)	
▪ Police, fire, or ambulance		▪ Other groups	

Domestic Terrorism or Special-Interest Groups Incident Management

Incident Management Guidelines

Domestic terrorists or special-interest groups may focus on companies for a variety of reasons, typically due to the nature of a business activity that falls within their area of interest. Domestic terrorist groups are generally nonviolent toward individuals (although can cause alarm and might engage in intimidation), but do often damage property and destroy materials, which in itself can present a physical risk. Such groups leverage the media as a tool to promote their causes and should be managed with care so as not to further their agendas.

In the event of a domestic terrorism incident occurring, the following points should be addressed:

✓ Action Points

1. Stand up the Incident Management and Crisis Response Teams using the SAD CHALETS system.
2. Secure the facility to prevent access by unauthorized personnel.
3. Alert the local police and request assistance.
4. Determine the immediate objectives of the group:
   - To steal information.
   - To sabotage materials, facilities, or equipment.
   - To illicit media attention.
   - To instigate a physical or verbal response from employees or managers.
   - To gain access to sensitive areas, or stage a sit-in within offices or work sites.
   - To barricade or impede access to areas.
   - To intimidate, threaten, or harm employees.
   - To plant harmful or hazardous materials.
   - To conduct prank activities (i.e., disruptive in nature).
5. Do not physically touch any activists or their possessions if possible.
6. Avoid inflammatory remarks or heated discussions.
7. Ask persons to leave a premises or work site politely, and inform them of any laws or regulations they are breaking.
8. Do not discuss company activities, policies, or plans.
9. Record the group's or individual's activities using cameras or closed-circuit TVs as part of investigation and legal response requirements.
10. Record their activities and note any risks posed to personnel, facilities, or materials.
11. Secure offices, laptops, and sensitive information if an intruder has been reported.
12. Engage other elements of the IMP if specific threats are presented (assault, intimidation, fire, damage, espionage, etc.).
13. Send regular situation reports to the Crisis Response Team.
14. Provide an *IMP Risk Assessment Report* as soon as possible.

Key People to Call (see the IMP Communications Plan)

Group	Yes/No	Group	Yes/No
▪ Medical organization		▪ Organic QRF	
▪ Military interface		▪ Crisis response team	
▪ Embassy or consulate		▪ Security provider (vendor)	
▪ Police, fire, or ambulance		▪ Other groups	

Espionage Incident Management

Incident Management Guidelines

Espionage can be conducted by individuals, groups, or governments in order to gain commercially sensitive information. Espionage can take many forms, either covert or overt, and can have significant impacts on a company, especially during a tendering phase of a business pursuit. Espionage can be conducted within the parameters of the law, or may be illegal. It can be geared to commercial activities, as well as operational functions.

In the event of an espionage incident occurring, the following points should be addressed:

✓ Action Points

1. Stand up the Incident Management and Crisis Response Teams using the SAD CHALETS system.
2. Determine what has occurred:
   - When did it happen?
   - Where did it happen?
   - Who was involved?
   - What information or materials were stolen or divulged?
   - What implications does this have to the company?
3. Secure facilities or sensitive materials to prevent further losses.
4. Take a statement from the individual reporting the event.
5. Determine whether any laws have been broken.
6. Determine who might be or is responsible:
   - Group or organization.
   - Individuals involved.
7. Determine whether persons are at physical risk following the event; stop any activity that might be compromised if persons are at risk.
8. Alert police or federal agencies if urgent in nature.
9. Provide an *IMP Risk Assessment Report* as soon as possible.

Key People to Call (see the IMP Communications Plan)

Group	Yes/No	Group	Yes/No
▪ Medical organization		▪ Organic QRF	
▪ Military interface		▪ Crisis response team	
▪ Embassy or consulate		▪ Security provider (vendor)	
▪ Police, fire, or ambulance		▪ Other groups	

Site Occupation or Sit-Ins Incident Management

Incident Management Guidelines

Site occupation or sit-ins may occur for a variety of reasons. Domestic terrorists or special-interest groups may seek to stage a public protest, labor disputes may result in employees disrupting work, and local communities or nomadic tribes may seek to publicly illustrate concerns or disagreements with the company by occupying areas, offices, or work spaces. Site occupation or sit-ins may be peacefully conducted, or may be violent in nature. Durations of occupancy may be short, or may be for long periods of time, especially if personnel cannot be evicted safely.

In the event of a site occupation incident occurring, the following points should be addressed:

✓ Action Points

1. Stand up the Incident Management and Crisis Response Teams using the SAD CHALETS system.
2. Secure the facility to prevent access by additional unauthorized personnel.
3. Secure areas that are being occupied by unauthorized persons to prevent other areas being invaded. Secure offices, laptops, and sensitive information.
4. Clear the areas of employees, notify personnel of the situation, and avoid mixing staff and authorized persons where possible.
5. Alert the local police and request assistance in order to evict persons.
6. Determine other threats presented by the individuals or groups:
   - To steal information.
   - To sabotage materials, facilities, or equipment.
   - To illicit media attention.
   - To instigate a physical or verbal response from employees or managers.
   - To gain access to sensitive areas, or stage a sit-in within offices or work sites.
   - To barricade or impede access to areas.
   - To intimidate, threaten, or harm employees.
   - To plant harmful or hazardous materials.
   - To conduct prank activities (disruptive in nature).
7. Passively attempt to escort persons from the area or building. Do not engage in aggressive measures unless essential. Such activities should be undertaken by security staff only.
8. Avoid inflammatory remarks or heated discussions.
9. Ask persons to leave a premises or work site politely; inform them of any laws or regulations they are breaking.
10. Do not discuss company activities, policies, or plans.
11. Record the group's or individual's activities using cameras or closed-circuit TVs as part of investigation and legal response requirements.

(continued)

(continued)

12. Record their activities and note any risks posed to personnel, facilities, or materials.
13. Forward an *IMP Risk Assessment Report* when possible.

Key People to Call (see the IMP Communications Plan)			
Group	**Yes/No**	**Group**	**Yes/No**
▪ Medical organization		▪ Organic QRF	
▪ Military interface		▪ Crisis response team	
▪ Embassy or consulate		▪ Security provider (vendor)	
▪ Police, fire, or ambulance		▪ Other groups	

Sabotage Incident Management

Incident Management Guidelines

The sabotage of a facility or equipment can be through common vandalism damaging or making resources inoperable or faulty, or may be through focused and well-planned activities by organized crime, insurgency, special interest groups, or terrorists. Sabotage may be dramatic in nature, resulting in catastrophic effects, or may be subtle and difficult to detect. Sabotage may place personnel at risk, may disrupt operations or may result in structural failure or other secondary risk effects.

In the event of a sabotage incident occurring, the following points should be addressed:

✓ Action Points

1. Stand up the Incident Management and Crisis Response Teams using the SAD CHALETS system.
2. Lock down the facility or work site, alert personnel, and move employees to safe areas or safe havens if necessary.
3. Mobilize security personnel to secure access points and high-value areas; all area movements are to stop until response measures are completed.
4. Conduct security sweeps and searches to locate any additional acts of sabotage, as well as search for saboteurs.
5. Determine what has been sabotaged:
   - Machinery and equipment.
   - Materials and resources.
   - Structures and systems.
   - Technology and communications.
6. Are the saboteurs still on-site? Can they be detained by security or police agencies?
7. Are the saboteurs violent? Are they armed? How will they respond if apprehended? What risks are associated with the individuals themselves?
8. Determine what risks are connected to the act:
   - Explosive
   - Failure
   - Disruptive
   - Toxic
   - Structural
   - Information
9. What risks are presented to personnel directly, or as a result of secondary hazard?
10. Raise the alert status and security posture of the facility to the predefined planning level, and mobilize security staff, closing down access control points and securing buildings.

(continued)

(continued)

11. Alert law enforcement agencies to investigate or prosecute groups or individuals.
12. Cordon the affected area or resources to enable an investigation to be conducted; do not contaminate the area in terms of forensics requirements.
13. Document and photograph sabotaged materials, assets, or structures.
14. Provide an *IMP Risk Assessment Report* as soon as possible.

Key People to Call (see the IMP Communications Plan)			
Group	Yes/No	Group	Yes/No
■ Medical organization		■ Organic QRF	
■ Military interface		■ Crisis response team	
■ Embassy or consulate		■ Security provider (vendor)	
■ Police, fire, or ambulance		■ Other groups	

Demonstrations Incident Management

Incident Management Guidelines

Many groups will use public demonstrations to gain media exposure, as well as impede business activities. Demonstrations may be singular events lasting hours, or may be protracted, lasting days to months and evolving into site occupancy (e.g., tree sitting). Demonstrations are typically nonviolent and involve chanting, banners, and costumes. Demonstrations may also involve the symbolic burning of items, or the leaving of obstructive or unpleasant items such as tree stumps or manure. In the most extreme cases, demonstrations may lead to an escalation in violence and may turn into riots.

   In the event of a demonstrations incident occurring, the following points should be addressed:

✓ Action Points

1. Stand up the Incident Management and Crisis Response Teams using the SAD CHALETS system.
2. Establish the temperament of the demonstration: Is it violent, disruptive, intimidating, or peaceful?
3. Establish the agenda and objectives of the individuals or groups: Who are they, what do they want to accomplish, and how?
4. What risks are presented to personnel directly, or as a result of secondary hazards?
5. Lock down the facility or work site; alert personnel and move employees to safe areas or safe havens if necessary.
6. Raise the alert status and security posture of the facility to the predefined planning level and mobilize security staff, closing down access control points and securing buildings.
7. Mobilize security personnel to secure access points and high-value areas; all area movements are to stop until response measures are completed.
8. Conduct security sweeps and searches to locate any acts of sabotage, as well as search for demonstrators.
9. Alert law enforcement agencies to manage demonstrators; indicate whether any unlawful acts have been conducted and the temperament of the demonstration.
10. Cordon off the affected area or resources in order to contain the demonstration where possible and appropriate.
11. Document and photograph the demonstration in case an investigation or legal action is required post event.
12. Provide an *IMP Risk Assessment Report* as soon as possible.

Key People to Call (see the IMP Communications Plan)			
Group	**Yes/No**	**Group**	**Yes/No**
▪ Medical organization		▪ Organic QRF	
▪ Military interface		▪ Crisis response team	
▪ Embassy or consulate		▪ Security provider (vendor)	
▪ Police, fire, or ambulance		▪ Other groups	

Pending Detention or Exit Denial Incident Management

Incident Management Guidelines

Exit denial or pending detention may be associated with imminent legal actions, investigations, commercial or political disputes, or corruption issues. Such risks presented to an individual may be transferred to other members of the organization and may escalate past the initial problem to become more significant and far-reaching in nature. In some countries, exit visas may also be denied due to shifting government policies or through personalities, causing short-term disruptions to travel, rather than presenting actual risks.

In the event of a pending detention or exit denial incident occurring, the following points should be addressed:

✓ Action Points

1. Stand up the Incident Management and Crisis Response Teams using the SAD CHALETS system.
2. Alert local legal counsel and seek advice and intercession where appropriate.
3. Determine the risks posed to the person or group.
4. Gather the full and accurate details of the allegation or issue: Provide clear, honest, and detailed facts. Avoid assumptions or opinion when reporting information to the CRT.
5. Determine whether any charges or allegations have merit, and the possible punishments associated with such allegations.
6. Notify the embassy, if appropriate.
7. Reassure the person as well as the person's family.
8. Determine what risks are presented to the remainder of the group or organization.
9. Determine who is responsible (within government) for the issue, and possible agendas.
10. Consider relocating personnel or groups within the country to provide additional time to determine the facts and prepare for any risks that might occur.
11. Ensure any questioned person is always accompanied, preferably by a lawyer.
12. Determine the requirements to meet any legal conditions required to allow exit.
13. Provide an *IMP Risk Assessment Report* as soon as possible.

Key People to Call (see the IMP Communications Plan)			
Group	**Yes/No**	**Group**	**Yes/No**
■ Medical organization		■ Organic QRF	
■ Military interface		■ Crisis response team	
■ Embassy or consulate		■ Security provider (vendor)	
■ Police, fire, or ambulance		■ Other groups	

Complaints Incident Management

Incident Management Guidelines

Complaints made by governments, local authorities, other companies, communities, groups, or individuals may result in reputational and liability risks to the company. They may also generate resentment and ill will from local communities and workforces that could result in peripheral threats to business activities, such as widespread labor disputes or, in severe cases, to threats posed directly to personnel and assets. Complaints may be related to employment conditions and terms, labor disputes, business arrangements and contracts, the leasing of vehicles or facilities, damage resulting from accidents, contaminant spills, contract awards, or construction tasks. Complaints may also result from disputes over right of passage or land ownership claims.

In the event of a complaint incident occurring, the following points should be addressed:

✓ Action Points

1. Stand up the nominated incident manager using the SAD CHALETS system. Mobilize the Crisis Response Team only if the incident is significant, with immediate and high-impact risk implications.
2. Establish whether there is documented evidence to substantiate a complaint.
3. Establish immediate risks associated with a complaint:
   - Physical
   - Operational
   - Liability
   - Reputational
   - Relationship
4. Take written statements from the person or group making the complaint.
5. Take written statements from those accused of a wrongdoing.
6. Seek legal assistance if appropriate.
7. Notify law enforcement agencies if a civil issue.
8. Make no admission of guilt or responsibility until all facts are known and authorized persons determine the course of action.
9. Ensure that all information is accurately documented.
10. Take disciplinary or compensation actions within permitted parameters of authority.
11. Provide an *IMP Risk Assessment Report* as soon as possible.

Key People to Call (see the IMP Communications Plan)			
Group	**Yes/No**	**Group**	**Yes/No**
▪ Medical organization		▪ Organic QRF	
▪ Military interface		▪ Crisis response team	
▪ Embassy or consulate		▪ Security provider (vendor)	
▪ Police, fire, or ambulance		▪ Other groups	

Blackouts and Power Loss Incident Management

Incident Management Guidelines

Power blackouts and rolling blackouts involve a disruption of electric power supply and may result from a large-scale loss of electricity supply to an area, which in turn can result from a defect in a power station, damage to a power line or other part of distribution system, a short circuit, or the overloading of electricity systems. Blackouts are also associated with a range of natural disasters, or can be a result of infrastructure targeting by disruptive groups. Blackouts are very common in developing countries where the increase in demand for electricity exceeds the increase in electric power generation, and may result in scheduled or predictable losses of power, or periodic and unscheduled occurrences.

In the event of a power loss incident occurring, the following points should be addressed:

✓ Action Points

1. Stand up the Incident Management Team using the SAD CHALETS system. Alert the Crisis Response Team only if significant risks or additional effects are expected.
2. Turn off all appliances and utilities and turn on emergency generators (if available).
3. Determine the cause of the blackout, and evaluate the risks the cause itself might present.
4. Gather all staff and move outside, or to an area with lighting.
5. Stop work activities and reduce movements or travel.
6. Raise the alert status and security posture of the facility to the predefined planning level and mobilize security staff, closing down access control points and securing buildings if at additional risk.
7. Protect heat-sensitive medical equipment or medicine storage facilities.
8. Alert staff outside of the facility or affected area.
9. Determine the extent and coverage of the blackout and what critical services and utilities it affects.
10. Take appropriate actions to address secondary risks or resulting casualties.
11. Provide an *IMP Risk Assessment Report* as soon as possible.

Key People to Call (see the IMP Communications Plan)			
Group	Yes/No	Group	Yes/No
▪ Medical organization		▪ Organic QRF	
▪ Military interface		▪ Crisis response team	
▪ Embassy or consulate		▪ Security provider (vendor)	
▪ Police, fire, or ambulance		▪ Other groups	

Loss of Sensitive or High-Value Materials Incident Management

Incident Management Guidelines

The loss of sensitive or high-value materials, equipment, or information can have significant operational, liability, and licensing implications for companies. Companies should identify which materials, resources, and equipment might be considered sensitive or of high value and attribute measures by which to protect such items. Risks may include espionage, loss, theft, damage, or destruction.

In the event of such an incident occurring, the following points should be addressed:

✓ Action Points

1. Stand up the Incident Management and Crisis Response Teams using the SAD CHALETS system.
2. Establish the nature and details of the material or item, and determine how it was lost.
3. Determine the impact of the loss or damage to sensitive or high-value materials: both direct and peripheral.
4. Confirm the last location and owner responsible for the material or item.
5. Gain written reports from the person to whom the item was assigned.
6. Confirm whether the item was destroyed or was left intact at the scene or work site.
7. Liaise with appropriate authorities to recover the item or to confirm destruction.
8. Take appropriate actions to mitigate the risks associated with the loss of the item, especially for communications- or intelligence-sensitive materials.
9. Confirm that standard operating procedures were followed; provide a postincident report.
10. Provide an *IMP Risk Assessment Report* as soon as possible.

Key People to Call (see the IMP Communications Plan)

Group	Yes/No	Group	Yes/No
▪ Medical organization		▪ Organic QRF	
▪ Military interface		▪ Crisis response team	
▪ Embassy or consulate		▪ Security provider (vendor)	
▪ Police, fire, or ambulance		▪ Other groups	

Indirect Fire and Direct Fire Attacks Incident Management

Incident Management Guidelines

An indirect fire (IDF) attack is one in which a device such as a rocket or mortar round is fired by launching the round into the air with the aim of it landing on or near its target. On striking the ground, the round will detonate, creating a blast wave and throwing shrapnel in all directions; or it may fail to detonate, resulting in unexploded ordnance hazards. There may be no warning of an incoming round, and if a round explodes near personnel or facilities, several more rounds may be inbound.

In the event of an indirect or direct fire attack occurring, the following points should be addressed:

✓ Action Points

1. Stand up the Incident Management and Crisis Response Teams using the SAD CHALETS system.
2. Sound the alarm to notify personnel of incoming risks (use appropriate alarm type).
3. Move personnel to bunkers or other hardened shelters, if safe to do so.
4. Alert personnel outside of the affected area who may be moving toward the risk area.
5. Raise the alert status and security posture of the facility to the predefined state and mobilize security staff, closing down access control points and securing buildings.
6. Conduct a role call of all personnel; account for missing persons.
7. Alert supporting agencies: military, police, or other.
8. Close down the facility, secure access control points, and prepare for possible secondary attacks.
9. On completion, manage casualties and damage.
10. Conduct a UXO sweep prior to allowing staff to resume duties.
11. Determine the damage in terms of:
    - Indirect fire (IDF) damage to structures or buildings.
    - Resulting industrial hazards.
    - UXO damage, fires, and explosions.
    - Follow-on small arms fire or complex attacks.
    - IDF fragmentation hazards (primary and secondary).
    - Casualty management and evacuation procedures.
12. Provide a postincident report and an *IMP Risk Assessment Report* (if applicable) as soon as possible.

Key People to Call (see the IMP Communications Plan)			
Group	**Yes/No**	**Group**	**Yes/No**
▪ Medical organization		▪ Organic QRF	
▪ Military interface		▪ Crisis response team	
▪ Embassy or consulate		▪ Security provider (vendor)	
▪ Police, fire, or ambulance		▪ Other groups	

Workplace Violence Incident Management

Incident Management Guidelines

Workplace violence can have significant impacts on both personnel safety and operational productivity, as well as result in serious legal and liability issues for the company. Workplace violence can quickly lower group morale and increase workforce absenteeism, stress, retention, and recruiting issues, as well as bring negative publicity and reputational challenges. Risks can range from verbal abuse or inferred threats to simple or aggravated assaults, robberies and thefts, hostage taking, hijackings, rapes and other sexual assaults, shootings, and fatalities.

In the event of a workplace violence incident occurring, the following points should be addressed:

✓ Action Points

1. Stand up the Incident Management and Crisis Response Teams using the SAD CHALETS system.
2. Determine who is at risk, and move them out of confrontational situations or the risk area.
3. Determine what risks are present:
   - Is the aggressor physically or verbally violent?
   - Does the aggressor have a history of violence?
   - Is the aggressor armed in any way?
4. Mobilize local security and or police to intercede immediately, restraining the provocateur if necessary (as a last resort).
5. Attempt to diffuse the situation, if safe and appropriate.
   - Always work with others rather than in isolation.
   - Avoid aggressive postures or inference.
   - Suggest to the aggressor to come back later to discuss with senior management, in order to diffuse the situation and enable police to respond.
6. Avoid confrontational discussions; placate the aggressor, if possible and appropriate, while police or security personnel respond.
7. Are others at risk? Clear the area if required.
8. Provide a postincident report as soon as possible.

Key People to Call (see the IMP Communications Plan)			
Group	**Yes/No**	**Group**	**Yes/No**
▪ Medical organization		▪ Organic QRF	
▪ Military interface		▪ Crisis response team	
▪ Embassy or consulate		▪ Security provider (vendor)	
▪ Police, fire, or ambulance		▪ Other groups	

Chemical, Biological, or Radiological Attack Incident Management

Incident Management Guidelines

The likelihood of a chemical, biological, or radiological (CBR) attack is remote. However, the probability of such threats, whether delivered through advanced delivery mechanisms or through radioactive dirty bombs, will likely increase over time as terrorist organizations seek to obtain weapons of mass destruction. In addition, common explosives mixed with toxic chemicals can create makeshift chemical threats. There are a number of indicators that a chemical or biological attack has taken place, such as groups of people displaying unusual behavior or dead birds or animals in close proximity. Mist, clouds or pools of unusual liquid, or abnormal smells should be treated with suspicion; in places that have sensor equipment, an alarm may sound.

In the event of a CBR incident occurring, the following points should be addressed:

✓ Action Points

1. Stand up the Incident Management and Crisis Response Teams using the SAD CHALETS system.
2. Determine the scope and nature of the threat.
3. Determine where the center of the incident is, as well as any downwind hazards.
4. Instruct personnel to cover their mouths and noses with wet cloths to avoid breathing in contaminants.
5. Seal buildings or rooms by closing air vents, windows, and doors using adhesive tape to prevent contaminants from entering.
6. If safe to do so, move personnel to higher ground, as dust and gaseous toxins will settle.
7. Instruct personnel to drink only bottled water and protected food.
8. If in vehicles, personnel should be instructed to close all windows and vents, and turn off air-conditioning.
9. Personnel should move upwind of any event location as soon as safely possible.
10. Personnel outside of an affected area should be notified so they will not be exposed to avoidable risk.
11. Casualty and other risk hazards or effects should be managed according to the IMP.
12. Provide an *IMP Risk Assessment Report* as soon as possible.

Key People to Call (see the IMP Communications Plan)			
Group	**Yes/No**	**Group**	**Yes/No**
▪ Medical organization		▪ Organic QRF	
▪ Military interface		▪ Crisis response team	
▪ Embassy or consulate		▪ Security provider (vendor)	
▪ Police, fire, or ambulance		▪ Other groups	

Complex Attack Incident Management

Incident Management Guidelines

A hostile person or group may use several forms of attack against a target concurrently. The complex attack typically aims to kill or injure as many people as possible, significantly damage critical infrastructures, or enable instigators to effect a kidnapping. Such attacks are usually more thoroughly planned than other forms of risk, and are typically aimed at a specific target rather than being opportunistic in nature due to the complexity of planning required and the resources required. Effective risk mitigation and security planning will form the basis for responding to complex attacks.

In the event of a complex attack incident occurring, the following points should be addressed:

✓ Action Points

1. Stand up the Incident Management and Crisis Response Teams using the SAD CHALETS system.
2. Mobilize all security personnel, and implement security response protocols.
3. Notify all employees, and move staff to safe areas/havens if possible.
4. Lock down all access control points and facilities to restrict unauthorized movements.
5. Raise the alert status and security posture of the facility to the predefined state and mobilize security staff, closing down access control points and securing buildings.
6. Notify supporting military or police agencies; nominate an incident control point (ICP) and safe route into the area.
7. Locate aggressors and establish a cordon with security response groups.
8. Determine the size and composition of the aggressor group, and relay the information to security response personnel.
9. Determine the agenda and objectives of the aggressor group, and instigate countermeasures.
10. Implement other aspects of the IMP as they relate to the incident.
11. Provide an *IMP Risk Assessment Report* as soon as possible.
12. Provide a postincident report when the crisis is over.

Key People to Call (see the IMP Communications Plan)

Group	Yes/No	Group	Yes/No
■ Medical organization		■ Organic QRF	
■ Military interface		■ Crisis response team	
■ Embassy or consulate		■ Security provider (vendor)	
■ Police, fire, or ambulance		■ Other groups	

Family Liaison Incident Management

Incident Management Guidelines

Local or incident managers will not generally liaise with families following a crisis event, that being the responsibility of a crisis response team representative, typically those trained or experienced in dealing with sensitive or emotive issues. However, under some circumstances a trained or experienced family liaison representative may not be able to deploy to a family's location in a timely manner, requiring local incident managers to act in this capacity. The family of any victim may be shocked, distraught, confused, and under considerable stress. Families will require a clear and unambiguous briefing, and may also require emotional and financial support, as well as administrative assistance and specialist advice and counseling.

In the event of a family liaison incident occurring, the following points should be addressed:

✓ Action Points

1. Stand up the Incident Management and Crisis Response Teams using the SAD CHALETS system.
2. If approached by family members, seek authority and guidance from corporate offices on what information can be relayed, and in what format.
3. Ensure that any information passed to the family is accurate and has been confirmed (double-check).
4. Be clear and unambiguous, avoiding words that could be confusing or misunderstood.
5. Do not make assumptions, and do not offer opinions, false expectations, or unwarranted hope: Be clear and concise, and only use facts.
6. Seek appropriate support if dealing with distraught family members; seek support from police agencies and counselors if passing on bad news.
7. Recommend that relatives or friends stay with the family to offer support.
8. Be aware of media interest and the risks and challenges it will pose—for both the company and the family.
9. Document any discussions, and relay the facts to the CRT.
10. Identify the family's needs and request support prior to making any commitments.
11. Provide an *IMP Risk Assessment Report* as soon as possible.

Key People to Call (see the IMP Communications Plan)			
Group	**Yes/No**	**Group**	**Yes/No**
▪ Medical organization		▪ Organic QRF	
▪ Military interface		▪ Crisis response team	
▪ Embassy or consulate		▪ Security provider (vendor)	
▪ Police, fire, or ambulance		▪ Other groups	

Office, Facility, or Hotel Fires Incident Management

Incident Management Guidelines

Office block, facility, or hotel fires can present unique risks depending on the operating region in which they occur. In some countries, firefighting appliances cannot reach above the third floor of a structure, presenting additional risks to the occupants. In addition, the safety standards in different countries vary, increasing the risks of fires rapidly spreading and not being brought under control by water sprinklers or other fire-retardant appliances. For companies operating in high-rise buildings, the ability of personnel to safely evacuate from the higher floors may also present challenges; companies should develop pragmatic and rehearsed fire drills to ensure that personnel instinctively know how to respond to protect themselves during such a crisis event. Facilities may also have additional hazards that might be triggered by a fire, including combustible materials, toxic hazards, and serious structural risks that might occur.

In the event of an office, facility, or hotel fire incident occurring, the following points should be addressed:

✓ Action Points

1. Stand up the Incident Management and Crisis Response Teams using the SAD CHALETS system.
2. Alert the emergency services, and pass on details as to the nature of the emergency as well as details on personnel, materials, secondary hazards, and casualties.
3. Determine the nature, location, and scope of the fire.
4. Determine any secondary hazards that might be present (e.g., toxic, flammable, or explosive).
5. Muster personnel, and move them to a safe location upwind of the fire and outside of any explosive hazard area.
6. Cordon off the area and prevent spectators from blocking evacuating personnel or emergency response agencies.
7. Alert adjoining buildings or facilities of the risk, and support a local evacuation of the risk area.
8. Account for missing or trapped persons, and determine where they might be.
9. Manage any casualties; apply triage where necessary.
10. Determine whether any critical information or materials might be damaged, and alert emergency responders as to the nature and rationale for exposing responders to risks in retrieving such materials.
11. Determine any threats outside of the fire event, especially in hostile environments. Apply appropriate security and safety measures to mitigate peripheral risks.
12. Apply other elements of the IMP as required.
13. Provide an *IMP Risk Assessment Report* or postincident report as soon as possible.

Key People to Call (see the IMP Communications Plan)			
Group	Yes/No	Group	Yes/No
▪ Medical organization		▪ Organic QRF	
▪ Military interface		▪ Crisis response team	
▪ Embassy or consulate		▪ Security provider (vendor)	
▪ Police, fire, or ambulance		▪ Other groups	

Threats, Coercion, and Intimidation Incident Management

Incident Management Guidelines

Coercion is the practice of compelling a person to behave in an involuntary manner either through action or inaction, by the use of threats, intimidation, or some other form of pressure or force. Extortion occurs when a person either unlawfully obtains money, property, or services from a person, entity, or institution through coercion or intimidation, or threatens a person, entity, or institution with physical or reputational harm unless they are paid money or property. Threats, coercion, or extortion of company staff or subcontractors can be detrimental to the safety and welfare of individuals, as well as to the productivity of the business activity as a whole. Critical personnel or entire workforces may not attend work if they perceive themselves to be at risk, and employees may feel forced to undermine the company by actively participating in illegal or unethical activities if they or their families are threatened.

In the event of a coercion incident occurring, the following points should be addressed:

✓ Action Points

1. Stand up the Incident Management and Crisis Response Teams using the SAD CHALETS system.
2. Establish which individuals or groups are at risk.
3. Establish who is the perpetrator or group that is threatening the individual, group, or organization.
4. Establish the perpetrator's agenda, motivation, and goals, and determine what implications these have on personnel, activities, and facilities.
5. Establish the nature and impacts of the risk, as well as the probability of occurrence:
   - Is it an empty threat?
   - Is it a real threat?
6. Take precautions to safeguard individuals, groups, and facilities while police and other response groups are mobilized.
7. Inform the police, providing as much detail as possible.
8. Establish whether other individuals, groups, or facilities might be at risk, and alert any at-risk groups.
9. Collect any evidence of the threats made for investigation and possible prosecution.
10. Increase the security and safety posture in locations at risk.
11. Implement any associated IMP policies.
12. Provide an *IMP Risk Assessment Report* as soon as possible.

| Key People to Call (see the IMP Communications Plan) ||||
Group	Yes/No	Group	Yes/No
■ Medical organization		■ Organic QRF	
■ Military interface		■ Crisis response team	
■ Embassy or consulate		■ Security provider (vendor)	
■ Police, fire, or ambulance		■ Other groups	

Mugging or Robbery Incident Management

Incident Management Guidelines

Robbery or mugging is a risk faced in any part of the world. Companies should advise their personnel to avoid areas with high crime rates or hostile ethnic populations, as well as educate them as to personal security awareness. This can be especially relevant in poor countries or where ethnic or gender groups may be exposed to higher levels of risk. Personnel should avoid demonstrating their wealth, should carry limited cash or valuable items, and should always seek to remain in public and well-lit spaces. A person who is robbed or mugged is generally advised not to be aggressive, but to hand over money and possessions without resistance, remaining calm so as not to excite the robber. Typically robberies are motivated by crime, rather than a personal grudge, and most criminals will depart after being given money or valuable items.

In the event of a robbery incident occurring, the following points should be addressed:

✓ Action Points

1. Stand up the Incident Management Team using the SAD CHALETS system. Inform the Crisis Response Team only if serious injury occurred or if sensitive materials were stolen.
2. Determine whether anyone was injured, physically or psychologically.
3. Seek medical assistance if injuries occurred, and counseling if appropriate.
4. Determine what was stolen: its value to the individual as well as the company.
5. Inform the police, providing:
   - Date, time, and location of occurrence.
   - Injuries resulting from the event.
   - Items stolen.
   - Description of the assailant.
   - Any history associated with the area or individual of assaults and robberies.
6. Review the security measures or advisory briefing for the area in which the crime occurred.
7. Determine whether risks are posed to employees inside and outside of the facility.
8. Provide a detailed incident report if the event occurred on company property.
9. Increase security measures if the incident occurred on company property.

Key People to Call (see the IMP Communications Plan)			
Group	Yes/No	Group	Yes/No
▪ Medical organization		▪ Organic QRF	
▪ Military interface		▪ Crisis response team	
▪ Embassy or consulate		▪ Security provider (vendor)	
▪ Police, fire, or ambulance		▪ Other groups	

Small Arms Fire Incident Management

Incident Management Guidelines

Small arms fire is the use of rifles or handguns against a target, whether a person, vehicle, or structure, presenting a personal and psychological risk to employees, as well as secondary hazards if fired within areas with highly combustible materials. The caliber and velocity of the round as well as its composition and nature will determine the level of damage this form of threat may pose to personnel or facilities. Typically smaller-caliber rounds will not penetrate commercial vehicle armoring, although explosive or armor-piercing rounds will. In addition, munitions can pose an indirect threat if fired indiscriminately, or can create secondary hazards if they ignite explosive or flammable materials. Small arms fire can also present a risk in countries when the firing of weapons is associated with demonstrations or festivals, as rounds may land with sufficient force to cause injuries.

In the event of a small arms fire incident occurring, the following points should be addressed:

✓ Action Points

1. Stand up the Incident Management and Crisis Response Teams using the SAD CHALETS system.
2. Determine whether a hostile activity is under way:
   - Directly targeting individuals or facilities.
   - Indirect gunfire within a broad zone.
   - Celebratory gunfire from festivals.
3. Determine whether the gunfire is effective—is it hitting the intended targets, or is it indiscriminate?
4. Move personnel to safe areas or havens if permissible.
5. Initiate security response groups if appropriate.
6. Secure the facility; close all access points and lock buildings.
7. Inform all employees: Instruct them where the threat is and direct them to safety.
8. Alert external response groups to intercede: military, police, and commercial QRFs.
9. Implement other aspects of the IMP as appropriate.
10. Provide an *IMP Risk Assessment Report* as soon as possible.

Key People to Call (see the IMP Communications Plan)

Group	Yes/No	Group	Yes/No
▪ Medical organization		▪ Organic QRF	
▪ Military interface		▪ Crisis response team	
▪ Embassy or consulate		▪ Security provider (vendor)	
▪ Police, fire, or ambulance		▪ Other groups	

Floods and Tidal Waves Incident Management

Incident Management Guidelines

Flood effects may be limited to a local event, affecting an individual community in low-lying areas or adjacent to a river, or may be widespread, affecting entire river basins. Floods may occur within a matter of minutes (flash floods), or may develop slowly over a period of days. Flash floods often have a dangerous wall of water that carries rocks, mud, and other debris and can sweep away buildings, vehicles, and other structures in its path, occurring with little sign of the rainfall that initiated the event. Tsunamis, also known as seismic sea waves or tidal waves, result from a series of enormous waves created by an underwater disturbance such as an earthquake, landslide, or volcanic eruption, and occur with little if any warning. A tsunami can move hundreds of miles per hour in the open ocean and strike land with waves as high as 100 feet (or more).

In the event of a flood or tidal wave incident occurring, the following points should be addressed:

✓ Action Points

1. Stand up the Incident Management and Crisis Response Teams using the SAD CHALETS system.
2. Determine the location of the risk, as well as the direction and the speed of the water's travel in order to evaluate the likely affected risk area.
3. Move personnel to high ground if possible. If remaining in buildings, utilities should be switched off and materials moved to the higher levels.
4. Centralize food, water, and other essential stores in an area that is protected from floodwater. Fill up bathtubs and containers with water at the start of a flood. Expect to be self-reliant for several days.
5. Avoid areas that might channel floodwaters (e.g., low-lying ground, wadis, riverbeds, valleys, etc.).
6. If time permits, use water barriers (e.g., sandbags, etc.) to seal doorjambs, cracks, windows, and the like to stop or slow water entering facilities.
7. Place indicators for emergency responders that personnel are trapped in buildings by using sheets, paint, and so on, stating numbers, casualties, and any support needed.
8. Monitor radio stations to track the event and its possible effects.
9. Avoid walking through moving water, as it can sweep personnel off their feet and disguise hidden hazards.
10. Avoid moving through flooded regions due to contamination and health hazards.
11. Do not drive through a flooded area, as it will disguise holes and hazards, and two feet of moving water can sweep vehicles downstream.
12. Drink only bottled or stored water; utilities may have been contaminated.

(continued)

(*continued*)

13. Be aware of secondary hazards: Pipelines (gas, water, sewer) may have been ruptured, power cables may have electrified water, and crime and health hazards may increase.
14. Implement other aspects of the IMP as appropriate.
15. Provide an *IMP Risk Assessment Report* as soon as possible.

Key People to Call (see the IMP Communications Plan)			
Group	Yes/No	Group	Yes/No
▪ Medical organization		▪ Organic QRF	
▪ Military interface		▪ Crisis response team	
▪ Embassy or consulate		▪ Security provider (vendor)	
▪ Police, fire, or ambulance		▪ Other groups	

Earthquakes Incident Management

Incident Management Guidelines

Earthquakes are caused by tectonic plate movements that make the ground shift or vibrate, resulting in structural damage that can cause fires, gas leaks, collapsed buildings, flooding due to ruptured pipes, damage to bridges and other structures, and the shattering of fragile structures. Earthquakes can consist of a sequence of foreshocks and aftershocks. Commonly, public utilities and communications are disrupted by severe earthquakes, as are emergency services.

In the event of an earthquake incident occurring, the following points should be addressed:

✓ Action Points

1. Stand up the Incident Management and Crisis Response Teams using the SAD CHALETS system.
2. Move personnel to a prearranged safe location. If no such facility is available, personnel should seek refuge under sturdy tables or door frames.
3. Where possible, gas supplies should be turned off and open flames should be quenched.
4. When warned of an earthquake potentially occurring, personnel should seek to secure all loose possessions, especially large, heavy, and breakable items.
5. During the earthquake, personnel should drop to the ground and take cover until the shaking stops, covering their heads with their arms, and positioned away from glass, windows, outside doors, and walls.
6. If outdoors, personnel should be advised to stay outside and move away from buildings, streetlights, and utility wires until the shaking ceases.
7. If in a moving vehicle at the time of the earthquake, personnel should stop as quickly as safety permits and remain in the vehicle. Vehicles should avoid stopping near buildings or under trees, overpasses, and utility wires.
8. After an earthquake, aftershocks may occur, as well as secondary hazards such as fires, floods, explosions, or tsunamis. Personnel should be aware that gas leaks might result in fires.
9. Personnel trapped within collapsed buildings should not light a match or move about and disturb any dust or debris; rather, they should cover their mouths with handkerchiefs or clothing and tap on a pipe to assist rescuers in locating them.
10. Account for missing staff, manage injuries, and report as per other IMP instructions.
11. Other elements of the IMP should be instigated as appropriate.
12. Provide an *IMP Risk Assessment Report* as soon as possible.

Key People to Call (see the IMP Communications Plan)			
Group	Yes/No	Group	Yes/No
■ Medical organization		■ Organic QRF	
■ Military interface		■ Crisis response team	
■ Embassy or consulate		■ Security provider (vendor)	
■ Police, fire, or ambulance		■ Other groups	

Pandemics Incident Management

Incident Management Guidelines

A disease outbreak or pandemic is the occurrence of incidences of disease in excess of what would normally be expected within a defined community, geographical area, or season. An outbreak may occur in a restricted geographical area, or may extend over several countries. The risk period may be short, lasting several days or weeks, or may be protracted, lasting months or years. A single case of a communicable disease long absent from a population or caused by an agent (e.g., bacterium or virus) not previously recognized in that community or area or the emergence of a previously unknown disease may also constitute an outbreak and should be reported and investigated.

In the event of such an incident occurring, the following points should be addressed:

✓ Action Points

1. Stand up the Incident Management and Crisis Response Teams using the SAD CHALETS system.
2. Determine the affected area and nature of the pandemic: Are project staff or operations within or near an affected area? Have personnel just returned from the affected area?
3. Determine the response actions being taken by government or other groups: Are they effective?
4. Determine whether anyone within the company has been infected.
5. Evaluate whether it is safer to evacuate personnel or to remain in place.
6. How long will local authorities permit people to leave the area?
7. Can the local authorities manage the situation? Do they have the capacity and expertise?
8. Are there sufficient resources to remain in place, notably food and water?
9. Can vaccines and medicines be mobilized to support the management of the pandemic?
10. Are there other threats that might result from the pandemic: civil disorder, utility disruptions, and interruption of essential material deliveries?
11. Should the local workforce be sent home? What instructions of support can be offered?
12. Evaluate what resources are required to move project staff to a safe location.
13. Implement other aspects of the IMP as required.
14. Provide an *IMP Risk Assessment Report* as soon as possible.

Key People to Call (see the IMP Communications Plan)			
Group	Yes/No	Group	Yes/No
▪ Medical organization		▪ Organic QRF	
▪ Military interface		▪ Crisis response team	
▪ Embassy or consulate		▪ Security provider (vendor)	
▪ Police, fire, or ambulance		▪ Other groups	

Hurricanes and Tornadoes Incident Management

Incident Management Guidelines

A hurricane is a type of tropical cyclone, which is a generic term for a low-pressure system that generally forms in the tropics. It is defined as an intense tropical weather system of strong thunderstorms with a well-defined surface circulation and maximum sustained winds of 74 miles per hour (119 km/h) or greater. Tropical storms can also produce significant damage and loss of life, typically due to flooding. A tornado is a violently rotating column of air that is in contact with both a cloud base and the surface on the earth. Tornadoes come in many sizes, but are typically in the form of a visible condensation funnel, whose narrow end touches the earth and is often encircled by a cloud of debris. Most tornadoes have wind speeds of 110 miles per hour (177 km/h), are approximately 250 feet (75 m) across, and travel a few miles before dissipating.

In the event of a hurricane or tornado incident occurring, the following points should be addressed:

✓ Action Points

1. Stand up the Incident Management and Crisis Response Teams using the SAD CHALETS system.
2. Determine the location, direction, and speed of travel of the storm to evaluate which areas are most susceptible to risk (although changes in direction can occur).
3. If time permits, facilities should seek to board up windows as an emergency solution if storm windows or shutters have not been fitted.
4. Personnel should be moved to a nominated safe room with stocks of emergency stores: water, nonperishable food and medications, and lighting. Or personnel should move to a safe area, such as an interior office, or a closet or bathroom on the lower level of the facility.
5. Personnel should avoid windows, skylights, and glass doors, as debris and strong winds may shatter such structures.
6. Personnel should not leave a safe location when in the eye of a hurricane, but must wait until the storm has passed over; since there will be a short period of calm, followed by a rapid increase in wind speed from the opposite direction.
7. In case of flooding, electricity should be turned off at the main circuit breaker. If the facility loses power, major appliances, such as the air conditioner and water heaters, should be turned off to reduce damage.
8. Personnel should be advised not to touch fallen or low-hanging wires, and to stay away from puddles with wires in or near them if leaving buildings.
9. Monitoring of radio stations will provide information as to the storm's passage, as well as emergency response measures being taken.

(continued)

(continued)

10. Other aspects of the IMP should be carried out as appropriate (regarding flooding, landslides, pandemics, etc.).
11. Provide an *IMP Risk Assessment Report* or status report as soon as possible.

Key People to Call (see the IMP Communications Plan)			
Group	Yes/No	Group	Yes/No
■ Medical organization		■ Organic QRF	
■ Military interface		■ Crisis response team	
■ Embassy or consulate		■ Security provider (vendor)	
■ Police, fire, or ambulance		■ Other groups	

Volcanoes Incident Management

Incident Management Guidelines

A volcano is a mountain that opens downward to a reservoir of molten rock below the surface of the earth. When pressure from gases within the molten rock becomes too great, an eruption occurs. Eruptions can be quiet or explosive; there may be lava flows, flattened landscapes, poisonous gases, and flying rock and ash. Because of their intense heat, lava flows create significant fire hazards and can destroy all structures in their paths. Ash flows can occur on all sides of a volcano, and ash debris can fall hundreds of miles downwind of the volcano. Dangerous mudflows and floods can occur in valleys leading away from volcanoes, striking with little warning. The common risks that accompany volcanic eruptions include earthquakes and tsunamis, mudflows and flash floods, landslides and rockfalls, and ashfall and acid rain.

In the event of a volcanic eruption occurring, the following points should be addressed:

✓ Action Points

1. Stand up the Incident Management and Crisis Response Teams using the SAD CHALETS system.
2. During a volcanic eruption, personnel should leave the affected area using an established evacuation plan (if advised by authorities), avoiding downwind areas and river valleys downstream of the volcano.
3. If caught indoors, personnel should close all windows, doors, and dampers; put all machinery inside a garage or barn; and bring all animals and livestock into closed shelters.
4. If personnel are outdoors, they should seek shelter indoors as quickly as possible.
5. If subjected to ashfall, personnel should seek protection by wearing long-sleeved shirts and long pants, goggles to protect vision, and a damp cloth to assist with breathing.
6. Following a volcanic eruption, personnel should stay out of an affected area, as the effects of a volcanic eruption can be experienced many miles from the main event, including mudflows, flash flooding, forest fires, and high-temperature ash flows.
7. When safe to do so, roofs should be cleared of ash as it can result in structural collapse.
8. Monitoring of radio stations will provide guidance as to the situation, any advisory alerts and instructions, and any governmental response measures.
9. Personnel should avoid areas susceptible to channeling floodwaters, as dangerous mudflows and floods can occur in valleys leading away from volcanoes, striking with little warning.
10. Other aspects of the IMP should be instigated where required.
11. Provide an *IMP Risk Assessment Report* as soon as possible.

Key People to Call (see the IMP Communications Plan)			
Group	Yes/No	Group	Yes/No
▪ Medical organization		▪ Organic QRF	
▪ Military interface		▪ Crisis response team	
▪ Embassy or consulate		▪ Security provider (vendor)	
▪ Police, fire, or ambulance		▪ Other groups	

Sandstorms Incident Management

Incident Management Guidelines

Sandstorms are recognizable as large clouds traveling over the ground, occurring frequently in most deserts. Some sandstorms occur for only a matter of hours, whereas some, like the Seistan desert wind in Iran and Afghanistan, blow constantly for up to four months. The IMP provides guidelines for project staff operating in such regions in order to allow them to protect themselves during a sandstorm, as well as protect their facilities and valuable or vulnerable resources.

In the event of a sandstorm incident occurring, the following points should be addressed:

✓ Action Points

1. Stand up the Incident Management Team using the SAD CHALETS system. The Crisis Response Team should be alerted only if the event is likely to result in threats to personnel or significant disruptions to operations.
2. The location, direction, and speed of traveling sandstorms should be determined in order to evaluate which areas will most likely be affected.
3. Prior to a sandstorm occurring, windows, vents, and skylights should be closed to prevent dust from entering facilities.
4. Vehicles should be turned off (unless especially prepared) to avoid damaging their engines.
5. If personnel are required to operate outside, they should be advised to lubricate their nostrils with petroleum jelly (if available) to prevent the mucus membranes from drying out.
6. Personnel should be instructed to tie cloths over their noses and mouths and to wear goggles to protect their vision when exposed to the sandstorm.
7. Personnel should also be instructed to remove contact lenses, tuck in clothes (tops into pants, pants into socks) to prevent burns from the sand, and wear long sleeves and trousers.
8. Visibility may become extremely limited, and groups working outdoors should be attached together by ropes to prevent personnel from become disorientated and lost.
9. Personnel should be mustered within a defined space and missing persons accounted for.
10. Other elements of the IMP should be implemented as appropriate.
11. Provide an *IMP Risk Assessment Report* as soon as possible.

Key People to Call (see the IMP Communications Plan)			
Group	Yes/No	Group	Yes/No
▪ Medical organization		▪ Organic QRF	
▪ Military interface		▪ Crisis response team	
▪ Embassy or consulate		▪ Security provider (vendor)	
▪ Police, fire, or ambulance		▪ Other groups	

Landslides Incident Management

Incident Management Guidelines

A landslide is a phenomenon that includes a wide range of ground movement, such as rockfalls, deep failure of slopes, and shallow debris flows. Landslides may also follow heavy rains or earthquakes. Changes to the landscape may indicate an imminent landslide, such as changing patterns of storm-water drainage on slopes (especially the places where runoff water converges) and land movement. Small slides and flows may occur as a precursor to larger earth movements. Doors or windows stick or may also jam for the first time; new cracks may appear in plaster, tile, brick, foundations, outside walls, or walkways; stairs may begin to pull away from buildings. In addition, slowly developing and widening cracks appear on the ground, or on paved areas such as streets or driveways. Underground utility lines may break, and bulging may appear at the base of a slope. Water may also break through the ground surface in new locations; fences, retaining walls, utility poles, or trees may tilt or move; and a faint rumbling sound that increases in volume may be noticeable as the landslide event approaches. The ground may start to shift in the direction of the slope, and unusual sounds such as trees cracking and boulders striking together may indicate moving debris.

In the event of a landslide incident occurring, the following points should be addressed:

✓ Action Points

1. Stand up the Incident Management and Crisis Response Teams using the SAD CHALETS system.
2. Personnel should be advised to avoid steep slopes, especially close to mountain edges, near drainage ways, or in natural erosion valleys.
3. During a landslide warning, personnel should be advised to stay alert and awake, since many debris flow fatalities occur when people are sleeping.
4. If project staff are in areas susceptible to landslides and debris flows, consideration should be given to departing the area as the first indicators of a possible landslide occur.
5. After a landslide, personnel should stay away from the slide area, following directions from local news or television stations.
6. Additional hazards include flooding, damaged roadways, and damaged public utilities, such as broken gas pipes.
7. Managers should check the building foundations, chimney, and surrounding land for damage, as structural damage may pose additional postevent hazards.
8. Personnel should be mustered, and missing staff must be accounted for.
9. Other elements of the IMP should be instigated as appropriate.
10. Provide an *IMP Risk Assessment Report* as soon as possible.

Key People to Call (see the IMP Communications Plan)			
Group	Yes/No	Group	Yes/No
▪ Medical organization		▪ Organic QRF	
▪ Military interface		▪ Crisis response team	
▪ Embassy or consulate		▪ Security provider (vendor)	
▪ Police, fire, or ambulance		▪ Other groups	

Forest Fires and Brush Fires Incident Management

Incident Management Guidelines

Forest fires or wildfires are very common in many places around the world. Forested areas are particularly susceptible to wildfires, especially where climates are sufficiently moist to allow the growth of trees, but feature extended dry or hot periods. Forest fires are particularly prevalent in the summer and fall, as well as during droughts when fallen branches, leaves, and other material can dry out and become highly flammable. Wildfires are also common in grasslands and scrublands and are most severe on days with strong winds, which help increase the tempo and intensity of fires. Forest fires present significant risks to urban areas bordering forested or grassland areas, as well as to facilities and travelers caught in the fire's path.

In the event of a wildfire incident occurring, the following points should be addressed:

✓ Action Points

1. Stand up the Incident Management and Crisis Response Teams using the SAD CHALETS system.
2. Prior to a forest or bush fire occurring, managers should:
   - Consult with the local fire department regarding the measures required to make the facility more fire resistant.
   - Check for and remove fire hazards in and around the facility such as dried-out branches, leaves, and debris.
   - Develop fire response plans, and rehearse these with personnel and local authorities.
   - Learn fire safety techniques and teach them to employees.
   - Make sure every floor and all working areas have smoke detectors.
3. During a forest fire event, the local or incident response manager should undertake the following simple activities:
   - Monitor local radio stations in order to understand where the fire is located, and which areas are vulnerable to the downwind effects, in terms of both smoke hazards as well as the direction in which the fire is moving.
   - Prepare personnel to evacuate along prescribed escape routes, once the location and direction of travel is known.
   - Remove all external furniture, tarps, and other combustible material from the facility exterior; these present a flammable hazard for jumping fire threats.
   - Close all doors in the facility, shut off gas valves and pilot lights, and remove flammable drapes, curtains, awnings, or other window coverings.
   - Keep lights on to aid visibility in case smoke fills the facility.
   - If sufficient water is available, turn sprinklers on to wet the roof and any waterproof valuables to reduce the risks of ignition.

(continued)

(*continued*)

- Limit the time spent outdoors until conditions improve to avoid breathing in harmful smoke.
- Turn off air exchange units that bring air in from the outside if they are worsening indoor air quality.

4. Provide an *IMP Risk Assessment Report* as soon as possible.

Key People to Call (see the IMP Communications Plan)

Group	Yes/No	Group	Yes/No
■ Medical organization		■ Organic QRF	
■ Military interface		■ Crisis response team	
■ Embassy or consulate		■ Security provider (vendor)	
■ Police, fire, or ambulance		■ Other groups	

Summary

Incident response guidelines should be clear, simple, and reflective of the policies of the company and the operating environment in which a project is operating. Companies should invest the time and resources to tailor each response type to suit their own corporate requirements, as well as ensure they pragmatically reflect the conditions under which such response will operate. Buy-in at all levels is required to ensure that such guidelines will be utilized, and where necessary followed. Entirely independent action by local managers or isolated incident response teams will add confusion and a lack of consistency in responding to threats, although at all times a degree of flexibility is required to reflect the shifting and unique risks each event will pose. Training and rehearsals will provide the necessary confidence and familiarity with plans for varied levels of users to be capable of implementing procedures; this can be done by management through tabletop exercises or by larger groups of staff with practical exercises.

This chapter is not designed to be a definite and exhaustive guide to how a company should respond to a particular risk type; rather, it provides a framework and concept for how companies might choose to structure a functional aspect of the IMP aimed principally at first responders, while also supporting more experienced crisis managers. Companies may choose to make response guides more succinct, or conversely may provide additional depth to reflect the experience and competency levels of their user audience. Companies should seek to design a master template for each risk type, and then permit a degree of local tailoring by individual projects. Many risk types have not been included in this chapter, and companies should map their risk environments so as to ensure that all contingency requirements are met.

CHAPTER 6

Crisis Information Capture Reports

The inability to effectively gather and share information is a frequent management failure during many crisis events both within the incident response group actually managing the emergency at the point of crisis and in terms of those other elements within the company seeking to support and respond to the problem. Information flow is often slow, inaccurate, and poorly presented, reducing the ability of an organization to effectively understand and manage a crisis. The flow of information both within the project group and to corporate officers and external agencies is vital for the success of incident management as well as the overall crisis response. Information flow among teammates, vendors, and external groups is also important; multiple plug-in points should share relevant information for a unified management approach to aid in making the right decisions and allocating the right resources.

The company and contracted or supporting groups should establish a simple and effective reporting system, with defined reports and communication channels to ensure that information gets to the right people at the right time and is factual and usable. A variety of reports may be required, depending on the nature and scope of the emergency situation facing the company, as well as dynamics within the company organization, contracted groups, and supporting agencies. At times a single crisis event may require a series of reports to meet different macro- and micro-level crisis natures in order to be effective; at times an amalgamated report that includes various constituent elements of an incident management plan (IMP) may need to be created during an emergency to reflect unique emergency situations, reducing management repetition and making reporting more efficient and effective.

Reports should be designed to support, not hinder or burden, incident response and crisis management teams that will be concurrently dealing with the physical effects of a crisis, while also communicating critical information to supporting groups. They should be simple, focused, and succinct. For ease, information can be broken into two basic categories: a report and a return. The distinction between a *report* and a *return* is subjective. However, fundamentally, a report can be considered a medium by which managers provide information, assessments, and recommendations, whereas a return purely provides requested statistics or hard data. While both project teams and teammates or vendors might initially perceive the establishment of a range of documents to meet report and return requirements to be an additional administrative burden, in retrospect most managers during and following a crisis find that a defined reporting structure with predefined templates makes information management easier over the course of the crisis, as well as after the incident when historical data is required for post incident reviews or investigations. In addition, sensible report structuring systems can also remove repetitive and duplicative efforts within the organization overall, permitting managers to focus more time and resources on dealing with the actual crisis itself. For some events, information from both categories will be included within one document.

A sound reporting structure with sensible and pragmatic information requirements will support all management levels and groups in establishing a more efficient organizational process for mature and effective crisis management responses. Consistent templates and materials flowing through company, partner, or vendor structures enable more effective decision making, and provide a monitoring mechanism to track and manage accountability and performance within incident and crisis management teams. Reporting chains should also have nodal points, where several sets of information flow into an incident or crisis manager, who generates a consolidated report and forwards that report to a series of other recipients. This process reduces e-mail or telephone traffic and best coordinates information management, as illustrated in Exhibit 6.1. A mature company Business Continuity Plan (and IMP) will have a raft of standardized reports and returns that the company can modify to suit its own needs, reducing the burden on the company when establishing new reporting structures or templates for additional business activities.

To avoid reports and returns becoming burdensome during periods of high-tempo operations or crisis events, they should be focused and cleanly structured. The use of annexes for sections might also allow management to focus only on the areas of interest to them rather than having to sift through volumes of data to get to their area of interest. This level of detail is typically not required during the use of the IMP, but will be needed at times for the crisis management (sustained) phase, or for post incident reviews. The use of web-hosted reporting can support regular updates and ensure that information can be more effectively shared between multiple users and stakeholders – rather than through typical email traffic. Reports and returns typically reflect generic needs, risk issues, operational activities, incident management and crisis responses, the delivery of services, manpower levels, and significant events. For the IMP, reports and returns are focused on delivering critical

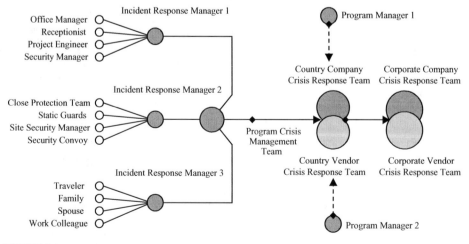

EXHIBIT 6.1 Information Flow Management

operational, risk management, and time-sensitive information. Exhibit 6.2 illustrates some principles that should be considered when developing crisis information capture report templates for a company or specific business group:

- **Focused.** Information capture reports should be focused on particular crisis scenarios and provide information essential for various layers of management to make effective decisions.
- **Channeled.** Reporting of crisis information should be channeled along efficient paths of communication, with defined nodal points and consolidation points. Restrictions should apply along channels where necessary.
- **Rehearsed.** In order to be effective, training and rehearsals should be conducted on the use of template reports and the methods by which to quickly gather information.
- **Resourced.** Resourcing, like all other aspects of the Business Continuity Management (BCM) Plan, will define whether managers can operate and communicate effectively.
- **Integrated.** Reporting of information should integrate all information sources, as well as ensure that all stakeholders, both within and external to the company, are included.
- **Simple and Clear.** Report templates should be simple and clear, reflecting the breadth of experience, knowledge, and capabilities of the user audience.
- **Pragmatic.** Reports should be pragmatic tools, engineered to achieve results through the timely and accurate dissemination of information. They should help, not hinder the user.
- **Intuitive.** It should be assumed that many of the user audience will not have received training on the use of the reports, so the reports should be as intuitive as possible to enable ease of use.
- **Flexible.** Every crisis situation will be different, and reports should provide guidelines and a logical system for gathering information, but should be not constraining or restrictive.

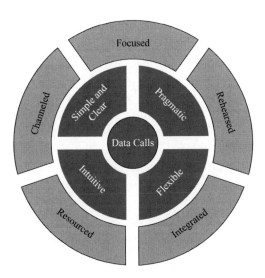

EXHIBIT 6.2 Crisis Information Capture Report Principles

IMP reports and returns should be standardized where possible and appropriate, as this ensures that information is presented in the same manner, contains the same forms of content, and meets the same objectives across multiple divisions, projects or operating regions. However, while consistency in structure and content is important, companies should seek to have reports reflect the operating environment and risk natures a project may be facing. The documents created and implemented should seek to support, not hinder, business activities; thus, only those matching a risk-specific need should be used. They should act to prompt considerations specific to an incident or emergency type in the same fashion as the response guidelines, walking users through a logical sequence in order to ensure that the right information is collected and shared among the incident and crisis response groups.

Immediate Verbal Reporting (SAD CHALETS)

Often crisis responders will initiate a crisis notification through a verbal briefing. As such, it is imperative that a clear and accurate verbal briefing is provided to initiate the IMP, supporting any written materials forwarded within the following data call sheets. This should be structured in a uniform and logical format so that personnel are guided through the key information components that will best enable resources to be mobilized and decisions to be made. The acronym SAD CHALETS, used by British police departments, is a tried and tested list of subject matter areas that first responders should address when briefing the IRT and CRT, as well as external emergency or response groups:

S   **Survey** the scene.
A   **Assess** the situation and the risk implications.
D   **Disseminate** information to the correct groups in the correct sequence.

C   **Casualties:** Number, type, and condition.
H   **Hazards:** Types, severity, impacts, and status.
A   **Access:** Management control points, safe routes in, and reception centers.
L   **Location:** Specific grid reference or prominent feature of the event.
E   **Emergency Services:** What support is required.
T   **Type:** Nature and type of crisis incident.
S   **Start Logging:** Start collating information from the beginning of the event.

Specific-to-event reports should then be compiled and distributed when circumstances permit. Verbal briefings should deliver the critical and time-sensitive materials that must be shared within the company and supporting groups; these briefings are then supported by written reports that capture documented information for use and reference.

Serious Incident Reporting

While there is significant value in developing tailored data calls to reflect the wide range of postulated risks a company might face, there is also mileage in having a catch-all incident data call which meets the generic needs of those risks which might not have been anticipated; or span multiple areas. Companies should develop a standardized *serious incident report* (SIR) to document and manage information flow on serious events that occur within a project or region. The report should be completed and released during and following each serious incident, either to capture multiple risk natures or to reflect a gap in company reporting templates. Companies may wish to have staged reports to capture the details of a fluid event requiring initial, interim, and closure reports. All reports must be completed correctly and in sufficient detail, as they may be used for audit or investigation purposes. The company or its subcontracted vendors might have preferences regarding formatting as well as the distribution list—these should be in alignment with the *communications plan* (see Chapter 1). An agreement should be reached between the company and external parties to ensure that reports capture all necessary details and are sent only to agreed recipients. Serious incidents might include hostile incidents resulting in injury, death, or major project problems; severe injury or death from natural causes or accidents; serious industrial accidents or evacuations; serious legal or reputational situations; and the loss of a critical of high-value asset. The following provides a suggested format for a SIR.

Serious Incident Report Incident Management Data Call

Company Information

Company Name:		Incident Date:	
Project Name:		Report No.:	
Project Country:		Report Code:	
Project Location:		Project Code:	
Restriction Level:		Distribution Code:	

Reporting Authority

Appointment	Name	Telephone	E-Mail

Information Data Call

Ref	Report Factor	Report Facts
1	Project name:	
2	Project location:	
3	Personnel involved:	
4	Injuries (nature and names):	
5	Fatalities (names):	
6	General description of incident:	
7	When did it occur?	
8	Is the event ongoing, or complete?	
9	What risks remain?	
10	What assistance is required?	
11	What assistance has been called on?	
12	Local government involvement:	
13	Military or embassy involvement:	
14	What local crisis management actions have been taken? What policies have been implemented? *What are you doing?*	
15	Photos and map references of the incident:	
16	Damage to facilities or assets:	
17	What assistance is required:	
18	Other information:	

It is useful to catalog and distribute measures that have been tried and have either failed or succeeded during a crisis situation in order to avoid duplication and demonstrate efforts being taken to a wider audience, as well as illustrate the degree of focus being paid toward resolving an issue. It also provides a fail-safe to ensure that no options are accidently overlooked. A common failing found within response measures is for the crisis management team, either local or corporate, to not mention failed efforts, but rather to focus on successful approaches. This can create further questions and not illustrate the efforts and routes being pursued to resolve an issue. A full reporting of successes and failures is important during a crisis situation—as well as for any postincident investigations. A simple format should be used to track all efforts attempted, such as the example provided here:

Problem	Approach	Success/Failure	Explain Result	Led By	When Tried
▪					
▪					
▪					
▪					

Incident Management Plan Risk Assessment Reports

While typically a function of the crisis response team (CRT), an IMP risk assessment report can in some instances be useful for the incident response team (IRT) to indicate how a crisis event may impact the company from a grassroots perspective, as well as any recommendations on how both the IRT and CRT should counter or mitigate these risks. This will feed immediate concerns and information from the source of the event in order to supplement the data response materials forwarded during the initial stages of a crisis. A basic IMP risk assessment of how the event may affect the company can prove useful to support risk mitigation at all levels in the early stages of an emergency.

The IMP risk assessment should not be confused with the responsibilities of the crisis response team and specialist responders, who should conduct more comprehensive risk assessments and evaluations during and following the crisis. The IMP risk assessment is a tool designed to provide an immediate and local perspective of the problems and impacts likely to occur that might fall outside of normal reporting formats within the IMP. The following provides an example of a simple IMP risk assessment report:

IMP Risk Assessment Report Incident Management Data Call

Company Information

Company Name:		Incident Date:	
Project Name:		Report No.:	*Initial/Interim/Final*
Project Country:		Report Code:	
Project Location:		Project Code:	
Restriction Level:		Distribution Code:	

Reporting Authority

Appointment	Name	Telephone	E-Mail

Information Data Call

Ref	Report Factor	Report Facts
1	**Immediate Concerns**	

1 Immediate Concerns

- Is there an immediate risk to personnel?
- Is there an immediate risk to the company's reputation?
- What risks are presented to resources or facilities?
- Is there a risk to third parties?
- How long before any of these risks occur? How much time is there?

2 Situation

- What is the cause or motive of the risk event?
- Is it likely to get worse?
- Are other (different) threats likely to occur?
- What happened, where, and when?
- What effects are likely (best, likely, and worst case)?

3 Complicating Factors

- What legal implications are there?
- What media interest has been shown?
- What environmental factors will hamper the resolution of the problem?

4 Recommendations

- What should be done by the IRT?
- What should be done by the CRT?
- What assistance is required?

Sample Crisis Information Capture Reports

The following section provides examples of some *crisis information capture reports*. The list and report contents offered are not designed to be exhaustive or all-inclusive, but to illustrate how information capture and dissemination, as well as response guidelines, can work to complement each other when a company and its employees deal with an emergency situation. Companies should seek to align the questions posed in such reports to their response guidelines, as well as to their unique corporate interests and the particular operating environment in which a business activity or project may be taking place. Questions should be designed to meet three basic needs:

1. Increase organizational understanding.
2. Enable effective management decision making.
3. Provide documented evidence.

The first information capture box is designed so that the issuer captures administrative details such as which region, country, and project the report came from, what restrictions might apply in terms of information sharing, when the incident happened, and any administrative codes or numbers that might be attached to the report. A reference column has been included at the left-hand side of each chart to guide managers through questions they should be asking. A blank column is at the right-hand side so that information is succinctly captured with questions and answers on one document. The structure of reports should be simple, consistent, and cognizant of the range of capabilities and experience within the company, in terms of both those providing information and those interpreting the reports.

Vehicle-Borne IED Incident Management Data Call

Company Information

Company Name:		**Incident Date:**	
Project Name:		**Report No.:**	
Project Country:		**Report Code:**	
Project Location:		**Project Code:**	
Restriction Level:		**Distribution Code:**	

Reporting Authority

Appointment	Name	Telephone	E-Mail

Information Data Call

Ref	Report Factor	Report Facts
1	Where did it happen?	
2	What type of vehicle was involved?	
3	Are there any follow-on threats?	
4	When did it happen?	
5	Number of casualties:	
6	Severity of injuries (refer to the Casualty Report):	
7	Names of casualties (if known):	
8	Where have casualties been taken?	
9	What (if any) company property has been damaged?	
10	Affiliation of assailant if known:	
11	What is the status of hostile persons?	
12	What liaison has occurred with other security agencies? Have emergency responders arrived?	
13	What impact is there on current security measures? Provide details:	
14	What immediate security measures are being taken? Has the area been secured? Has a quick response force (QRF) been mobilized?	
15	What activities are being undertaken by external security agencies?	
16	Has an incident control point (ICP) been established? What is the safe route in:	
17	Have all personnel been accounted for? Provide details of missing personnel:	
18	Has the area been cordoned off? Is it secured?	
19	What assistance is required?	
20	Other remarks or information:	

Casualty or Injury Incident Management Data Call

Company Information

Company Name:		**Incident Date:**	
Project Name:		**Report No.:**	
Project Country:		**Report Code:**	
Project Location:		**Project Code:**	
Restriction Level:		**Distribution Code:**	

Reporting Authority

Appointment	Name	Telephone	E-Mail

Information Data Call

Ref	Report Factor	Report Facts
1	Name of the casualty:	
2	Nationality of the casualty:	
3	When did the incident occur?	
4	Where did the incident occur?	
5	**Casualty Details**	
	▪ What is the nature of the injury?	
	▪ What is the severity of the injury?	
	▪ What level of consciousness does the casualty have?	
	▪ Is the casualty in pain?	
	▪ What is the age of casualty?	
	▪ What gender is the casualty?	
	▪ What religion is the casualty?	
	▪ Physical robustness of casualty:	
	▪ Are there previous medical conditions?	
	▪ Is the casualty on medication? List:	
	▪ What medications have been given? List:	
	▪ What medical assistance has been rendered? Provide details:	
	▪ What medical assistance is required?	
	▪ What level of medical assistance is in place?	

(continued)

(*continued*)

6   Was the injury due to hostile actions or an accident?

7   Were others involved, and who are they?

8   Who is in charge of the situation?

9   Where is the casualty now?

10   By what means was the casualty evacuated?

11   Does the casualty need to be moved again?

12   What external help is required?

13   Were weapons or sensitive equipment lost or damaged during the incident?

14   If so, were attempts made to retrieve the weapons or equipment?

15   What is management doing now?

16   What other assistance is required?

17   Other remarks or information:

Missing Persons Incident Management Data Call

Company Information

Company Name:		**Incident Date:**	
Project Name:		**Report No.:**	
Project Country:		**Report Code:**	
Project Location:		**Project Code:**	
Restriction Level:		**Distribution Code:**	

Reporting Authority

Appointment	Name	Telephone	E-Mail

Information Data Call

Ref	Report Factor	Report Facts
1	What is/are the name(s) of the missing person(s)?	
2	What are their titles?	
3	What are their nationalities?	
4	Where do they work?	
5	Are they vulnerable or high-profile?	
6	Whom do they report to?	
7	When was the last contact made?	
8	Where were they last known to be?	
9	Were they with anyone, and if so who?	
10	How long have they been missing?	
11	Do they have a known history of failing to keep contact?	
12	Have they expressed that they feel like someone is following them, or that threats have been made against them?	
13	Are they depressed, undergoing investigation, facing arrest, or in any other form of trouble?	
14	Are there any known or perceived threats against them, or the group to which they belong?	

(continued)

(continued)

15 What actions have been taken to locate them?
- Police
- Hospitals
- Family and friends
- Other

16 Are there external agencies that might be able
to support locating them? Has the embassy
been informed?

17 What is management doing now?

18 What assistance is required?

19 Other remarks or information:

Road Traffic Accident Incident Management Data Call

Company Information

Company Name:		Incident Date:	
Project Name:		Report No.:	
Project Country:		Report Code:	
Project Location:		Project Code:	
Restriction Level:		Distribution Code:	

Reporting Authority

Appointment	Name	Telephone	E-Mail

Information Data Call

Ref	Report Factor	Report Facts
1	What date and time did the incident occur?	
2	What is the name of the driver?	
3	What are the names of the passengers?	
4	Does the driver have a license to operate the vehicle?	
5	Should the person have been driving?	
6	Where did the incident occur?	
7	How did it occur?	
8	Were there injuries or fatalities?	
9	Was any of the local population involved? Provide details:	
10	Were any animals involved? Provide details:	
11	Was the incident due to negligent driving? Provide details:	
12	Was it caused by hostile forces? Provide details:	
13	Is the vehicle still serviceable?	
14	Were the police present? Is there a police report?	
15	What are the local laws regarding leaving the scene of an accident, or compensation and liability?	

(continued)

(continued)

16 Has any member of the company been arrested
    or detained? if so, who and where are they?

17 What punishments are connected to the
    accident, especially if fatalities have occurred?

18 Have any other groups been notified: embassy,
    legal, or others?

19 What assistance is required?

20 Other information:

Driver: Accident Report Form

Directions

- Keep copies of this form with the vehicle.
- Fill out the report as soon as possible after the incident.
- Be sure to list names, locations, dates, and times.
- Provide as many facts as you can.

Report Identification Number:	Company/Project/Date/Time/Name
Report To:	

1   Date:

2   Location:

3   Description of what happened:

4   Who was involved?
    - Name and nature of injury:
    - Name and nature of injury:
    - Name and nature of injury:
    - Name and nature of injury:

5   What did you do?

6   Where exactly did the accident occur?

7   How did the accident occur?

8   Describe weather conditions:

9   Describe the road conditions:

10 Direction your car was going:

11 What speed were you traveling at?

12 What type of vehicle were you driving?

13 Do you have a license to operate the vehicle?

14 Had you consumed any alcohol?

(continued)

(continued)

15 What direction was the other vehicle going?

16 On which side of the center line were you?

17 Did you give a warning signal? If so, what type?

18 Did the other party give a warning signal?

19 Were your vehicle's lights on?

20 Were the other vehicle's lights on?

21 At what time did you first see danger?

22 Estimate speed you were then traveling:

23 Estimate speed other vehicle was traveling:

24 At the time of collision, estimate your speed:

25 Estimate other vehicle's speed at the time of collision:

26 If an intersection accident, which vehicle reached intersection first?

27 For what purpose was company vehicle being used?

28 Were the police notified of this accident?

29 List names of investigating officers?

30 Do you have a copy of the report?

31 Was any property damaged? If so, what:

32 Were any animals injured or killed? If so, what:

33 Have the police charged you? If so, with what:

34 What is the license plate number of the vehicle you were driving?

35 Any other information:

Accident Schematic: Draw a Diagram of the Accident Location with Distances:

(continued)

(*continued*)

Driver's Signature:

Date:

Appointment (Title):

Printed Name:

E-Mail:

Phone Number:

Location:

Manager Name, E-Mail,
and Phone Number:

Manager's Signature:

Date:

Appointment (Title):

Printed Name:

E-Mail:

Phone Number:

Location:

Reporting To:

Manager's Assessment:

Facility Physical Security Breach Incident Management Data Call

Company Information

Company Name:		**Incident Date:**	
Project Name:		**Report No.:**	
Project Country:		**Report Code:**	
Project Location:		**Project Code:**	
Restriction Level:		**Distribution Code:**	

Reporting Authority

Appointment	Name	Telephone	E-Mail

Information Data Call

Ref	Report Factor	Report Facts
1	Date and time when the breach occurred:	
2	In what location/site did the breach occur?	
3	At what specific point did the breach occur (gate, fence, perimeter)?	
4	How did the breach occur?	
5	Who reported the breach?	
6	How many persons are involved in the breach?	
7	How many vehicles are involved in the breach?	
8	What is the nature of the intruders (age, race, gender, clothing, equipment)?	
9	Are the intruders armed? If so, with what?	
10	Did hostilities occur? Are they considered dangerous?	
11	Is the intent or objective of the intruders known (criminals, demonstrators, activists, terrorists)?	
12	What, if anything, was stolen or sabotaged?	
13	Who was on guard duty?	*(continued)*

(continued)

14   Are there casualties? If so, who are they?
       Provide details:

15   Has the area been secured since
       the breach occurred?

16   Are all employees and clients
       accounted for? Provide details of
       missing persons:

17   What security enhancement
       measures were taken immediately
       following the incident?

18   Do any policies and procedures
       require change?

19   Has the area been swept for
       intruders/devices?

20   Are security personnel conducting
       checks/sweeps?

21   Are physical repairs to security
       structures required?

22   What response plans need to be
       implemented? What is management
       doing now?

23   Have government or law
       enforcement been notified?
       What responses have they made?

24   What are the key risks to personnel,
       facilities, materials, and resources?

25   Has an incident control point (ICP)
       been established? What is the safe
       route in?

26   What assistance is required?

27   Other information:

Kidnapping and Ransom Incident Management Data Call

Company Information

Company Name:		**Incident Date:**	
Project Name:		**Report No.:**	
Project Country:		**Report Code:**	
Project Location:		**Project Code:**	
Restriction Level:		**Distribution Code:**	

Reporting Authority

Appointment	Name	Telephone	E-Mail

Information Data Call

Ref	Report Factor	Report Facts
1	How many people were kidnapped?	
2	Name(s) of victim(s); do they have any medical conditions that might place them at additional risk?	
3	Appointments or titles:	
4	Are they employees or subcontractors?	
5	Are next of kin details available? Do any of the victims have medical conditions?	
6	When did it happen?	
7	Where did it happen?	
8	Where were the victims last seen?	
9	What were the victims doing at the time of the kidnapping? Who were they meeting?	
10	Have threats been made previously against the victims? If so, what were they?	
11	Have any government or law enforcement agencies been involved?	
12	Was the kidnapping witnessed? If so, by whom? Has a statement been taken?	
13	Describe the event if witnessed:	

(continued)

(continued)

14   Describe the number, race, gender, dress, age, and vehicles of the kidnappers, if they are known:

15   Were violence and/or weapons used? Describe what happened:

16   Was anyone injured? If so, describe injuries:

17   Have any demands been made? If so, describe these in detail:

18   What is management doing now?

19   What assistance is required?

20   Other information:

Media Management Incident Management Data Call

Company Information

Company Name:		**Incident Date:**	
Project Name:		**Report No.:**	
Project Country:		**Report Code:**	
Project Location:		**Project Code:**	
Restriction Level:		**Distribution Code:**	

Reporting Authority

Appointment	Name	Telephone	E-Mail

Information Data Call

Ref	Report Factor	Report Facts
1	What happened?	
2	Who was involved?	
3	Where did the event occur?	
4	When did the event occur?	
5	Which media organizations were on scene?	
6	What information do they have?	
7	Has anyone spoken to the press? If so, who?	
8	What are the names, organization details, and contact details of the media asking questions?	
9	Did they film the event?	
10	Did they have access to the event location itself?	
11	Are they still on-site?	
12	What are they doing?	
13	What is the attitude of the press?	
14	What questions have they asked?	
15	What is management doing now?	
16	What assistance is required?	
17	Other information:	

Detention or Arrest Incident Management Data Call

Company Information

Company Name:		**Incident Date:**	
Project Name:		**Report No.:**	
Project Country:		**Report Code:**	
Project Location:		**Project Code:**	
Restriction Level:		**Distribution Code:**	

Reporting Authority

Appointment	Name	Telephone	E-Mail

Information Data Call

Ref	Report Factor	Report Facts
1	Name of detainee:	
2	Nationality of detainee:	
3	Age, gender, health, medications required:	
4	Details of crime: ▪ Severity ▪ Impacts on external persons ▪ Possible sentence ▪ Aggrieved party details ▪ Other	
5	Detainee's supervisor (name, number, e-mail, location):	
6	Arresting authority:	
7	Location of detainee:	
8	Location of arrest:	
9	Date and time of arrest:	
10	What injuries, if any, were suffered during arrest?	
11	Risks faced by detainee:	
12	External support agencies:	
13	Arrest report to following organizations: ▪ Embassy ▪ Military ▪ Police ▪ Other	

(*continued*)

(continued)

14   Legal issues:

- Court date, time, and location.
- Is bail available?
- Access to detainee by legal counsel.
- Can items be taken to the detainee?
- Can compensation be made?

15   Has the detainee's family been informed?

16   What assistance is required?

17   Other information:

Hostage Situation Incident Management Data Call

Company Information

Company Name:		Incident Date:	
Project Name:		Report No.:	
Project Country:		Report Code:	
Project Location:		Project Code:	
Restriction Level:		Distribution Code:	

Reporting Authority

Appointment	Name	Telephone	E-Mail

Information Data Call

Ref	Report Factor	Report Facts
1	What is/are the name(s) of the hostage(s)? Were they targeted specifically or indiscriminately?	
2	Do the hostages have any medical conditions that might place them at greater risk?	
3	Who is holding them hostage? Is there a relationship? Does the individual or group have a history of undertaking hostage situations? If so, what were the outcomes?	
4	What are the motives or agendas of the individual or group? What is the mental state of the perpetrator(s)?	
5	When were they taken hostage?	
6	Where were they taken hostage?	
7	Were there any witnesses? If so, provide statement:	
8	Is the reason for the hostage situation known? Are there any demands?	
9	When was the initial contact made with the perpetrator, and who was contacted?	
10	Have law enforcement, military, embassy, or other agencies been alerted? Are they on scene? How effective are local law enforcement and other agencies in dealing with hostage situations?	

(continued)

(continued)

11   What is the mental health of the
       perpetrator?

12   Is the perpetrator armed? If so, with what?

13   Are other personnel at risk? Has the area
       been cleared and cordoned? Is it secure?

14   Have the hostages' families been
       informed?

15   Has an ICP been established? What is the
       safe route in?

16   Are there floor plans of the facility? If so,
       where are they?

17   What is management doing now?

18   What assistance is required?

19   Other information:

Suspect Call Incident Management Data Call

Company Information

Company Name:		**Incident Date:**	
Project Name:		**Report No.:**	
Project Country:		**Report Code:**	
Project Location:		**Project Code:**	
Restriction Level:		**Distribution Code:**	

Reporting Authority

Appointment	Name	Telephone	E-Mail

Information Data Call

Ref	Report Factor	Report Facts
1	Time of call:	
2	Person taking the call:	
3	Content of call:	
4	What demands were made, and what threats were posed?	
5	Age, gender, accent, race, characteristics of caller:	
6	Number registered on phone:	
7	Is this the first such call, or have there been others? If others, when?	
8	Does the call sound genuine, or does it sound like a prank call?	
9	Did the person identify himself or herself or the group?	
10	Were there any background noises? Can the call be recorded?	
11	Have the police been informed? If so, have they responded?	
12	What is management doing now?	
13	What assistance is required?	
14	Other information:	

Civil Unrest Incident Management Data Call

Company Information

Company Name:		**Incident Date:**	
Project Name:		**Report No.:**	
Project Country:		**Report Code:**	
Project Location:		**Project Code:**	
Restriction Level:		**Distribution Code:**	

Reporting Authority

Appointment	Name	Telephone	E-Mail

Information Data Call

Ref	Report Factor	Report Facts
1	What is the source of the unrest? Is it widespread or localized? What is the temperament of the crowd?	
2	Is company property or are employees in present danger?	
3	Is the company facility secure? Will the facility provide protection during the civil unrest situation?	
4	Who is being targeted? Are the threats general or specific?	
5	Should the evacuation plan be implemented? What immediate and near-term measures have been taken?	
6	Has contact been made with the military/government agencies? Have they been asked for advice?	
7	What are the implications for future company business in the area?	
8	What security enhancements have been undertaken? What alert state is in force?	
9	Have supporting military deployed assets?	
10	Have arrangements been made to either store or destroy sensitive company equipment and documents?	
11	Have all personnel been accounted for?	
12	What are the names of missing personnel, if any? Where are they, and what risk are they subject to?	
13	Has an ICP been established? What is the safe route in?	
14	What is management doing now?	
15	What assistance is required?	
16	Other information:	

Unexploded Ordnance or Suspect Package Incident Management Data Call

Company Information

Company Name:		Incident Date:	
Project Name:		Report No.:	
Project Country:		Report Code:	
Project Location:		Project Code:	
Restriction Level:		Distribution Code:	

Reporting Authority

Appointment	Name	Telephone	E-Mail

Information Data Call

Ref	Report Factor	Report Facts
1	What was the date and time that the materials were found?	
2	Were the materials moved or touched? If so, by whom and when?	
3	Has a possible owner been looked for?	
4	Location of the materials (as specific as possible):	
5	Type of materials found (description, size, color, packaging, wires seen, markings):	
6	Name and telephone number of the finder:	
7	Have personnel been evacuated from the hazard area?	
8	Have all personnel been accounted for?	
9	Where has the incident control point been established? What is the safe route in?	
10	Have any devices detonated? If so, what injuries and damages have occurred?	
11	Have any calls been received indicating the nature of the device? Have individuals or groups claimed responsibility?	
12	Have safe havens been cleared to ensure that no secondary devices are present?	
13	Have police, bomb disposal, or other groups been alerted? Have they responded?	
14	Has the area undergone the six Cs?	
15	What is management doing now?	
16	What assistance is required?	
17	Other information:	

Suspect Letter Incident Management Data Call

Company Information

Company Name:		**Incident Date:**	
Project Name:		**Report No.:**	
Project Country:		**Report Code:**	
Project Location:		**Project Code:**	
Restriction Level:		**Distribution Code:**	

Reporting Authority

Appointment	Name	Telephone	E-Mail

Information Data Call

Ref	Report Factor	Report Facts
1	What was the date and time when the suspect letter was found?	
2	Were the materials moved or touched? If so, by whom and when?	
3	How large is the letter?	
4	Location of the letter now (as specific as possible):	
5	Type of materials found (description, size, color, packaging, wires seen, odors, grease marks, postal markings):	
6	Name of the finder:	
7	Have personnel been evacuated from the hazard area?	
8	Have all personnel been accounted for?	
9	Where has the incident control point been established? What is the safe route in?	
10	Have any devices detonated? If so, what injuries and damages have occurred?	
11	Have any calls been received indicating the nature of the device? Have any individuals or groups claimed responsibility?	
12	Have police, bomb disposal, or other groups been alerted? Have they responded?	
13	Has the area undergone the six Cs?	
14	What is management doing now?	
15	What assistance is required?	
16	Other information:	

Destruction Plan Incident Management Data Call

Company Information

Company Name:		**Incident Date:**	
Project Name:		**Report No.:**	
Project Country:		**Report Code:**	
Project Location:		**Project Code:**	
Restriction Level:		**Distribution Code:**	

Reporting Authority

Appointment	Name	Telephone	E-Mail

Information Data Call

Ref	Report Factor	Report Facts
1	Why has the destruction plan been implemented?	
2	Has the destruction plan been carried out? If so, give date and time of completion:	
3	What materials have been saved or transferred (see Destruction Report)?	
4	What materials have been destroyed (provide Destruction Report)?	
5	What materials could not be destroyed, and what impact does this have (provide Destruction Report)?	
6	What assistance is required?	
7	Other information:	

Repatriation Incident Management Data Call

Company Information

Company Name:		**Incident Date:**	
Project Name:		**Report No.:**	
Project Country:		**Report Code:**	
Project Location:		**Project Code:**	
Restriction Level:		**Distribution Code:**	

Reporting Authority

Appointment	Name	Telephone	E-Mail

Information Data Call

Ref	Report Factor	Report Facts
1	Name and Social Security number of the deceased:	
2	What was the cause of death?	
3	What were the date, time, and location of the death?	
4	Where is the deceased now?	
5	Are there suitable facilities for storing the body until transport is available?	
6	When will a full incident report be available?	
7	Are there risks posed to other persons?	
8	Have any government agencies been informed? If so, who and when?	
9	Does the family know?	
10	Does the media know?	
11	Have all personnel effects been inventoried?	
12	Are all documents available and ready?	
13	Has the religious denomination and any special requirements been identified?	
14	Has a mortuary been identified? Provide details:	
15	What assistance is required?	
16	Other information:	

Information Security Breach Incident Management Data Call

Company Information

Company Name:		Incident Date:	
Project Name:		Report No.:	
Project Country:		Report Code:	
Project Location:		Project Code:	
Restriction Level:		Distribution Code:	

Reporting Authority

Appointment	Name	Telephone	E-Mail

Information Data Call

Ref	Report Factor	Report Facts
1	When did the information security breach occur?	
2	Where did it occur?	
3	What information has been compromised?	
4	Has information been stolen?	
5	Who was responsible for the information?	
6	Is the identity of the person or group in possession of the information known?	
7	What immediate impacts will the loss or breach have?	
8	What interim and long-term impacts will the loss or breach have?	
9	What actions have been taken to retrieve the information?	
10	What actions have been taken to prevent further loss?	
11	What actions have been taken to mitigate the risks?	
12	Have the authorities been alerted?	
13	What assistance is required?	
14	Other information:	

Domestic Terrorism or Special-Interest Groups Incident Management Data Call

Company Information

Company Name:		**Incident Date:**	
Project Name:		**Report No.:**	
Project Country:		**Report Code:**	
Project Location:		**Project Code:**	
Restriction Level:		**Distribution Code:**	

Reporting Authority

Appointment	Name	Telephone	E-Mail

Information Data Call

Ref	Report Factor	Report Facts
1	When did the incident occur?	
2	Where did it occur?	
3	Which group is involved, and how many are there?	
4	What activities are they undertaking? ▪ Espionage/surveillance ▪ Occupancy or sit-ins ▪ Harm to personnel ▪ Threats and intimidation ▪ Pranks and general harassment ▪ Property or material damage ▪ Demonstrations ▪ Other	
5	What are their agenda and objectives? Are they violent or peaceful?	
6	Are the media present? If so, which ones?	
7	Is the group breaking any laws?	
8	What impacts is the situation having on employees?	
9	What impacts is it having on operations?	
10	Are the work site, area, and facility secure? What security alert state is in force?	
11	Have any materials or information been stolen or removed from the site?	

(continued)

(continued)

12 Can facility or site security contain
    the situation?

13 Have local law enforcement been
    informed? Have they deployed?

14 Has an ICP been established? What is
    the safe route in?

15 What is management doing now?

16 What assistance is required?

17 Other information:

Complaints Incident Management Data Call

Company Information

Company Name:		**Incident Date:**	
Project Name:		**Report No.:**	
Project Country:		**Report Code:**	
Project Location:		**Project Code:**	
Restriction Level:		**Distribution Code:**	

Reporting Authority

Appointment	Name	Telephone	E-Mail

Information Data Call

Ref	Report Factor	Report Facts
1	Who is making the complaint?	
2	What is the nature of the complaint?	
3	Does the complaint have grounds?	
4	Is there physical evidence to support the complaint?	
5	Does the complaint warrant police involvement?	

6	What immediate impacts will the complaint have on personnel or the company?
	
	  ▪ Physical
	  ▪ Operational
	  ▪ Liability
	  ▪ Reputational
	  ▪ Relationships	

7	What immediate impacts will the complaint have on operations?	
8	Has the issue occurred before?	
9	Who is the subject of the complaint?	
10	Are there risks to the company? If so, what are they?	
11	Has an investigation been conducted? If so, when will the report be ready?	
12	What immediate actions are being taken by local management?	
13	What assistance is required?	
14	Other information:	

Mugging or Robbery Incident Management Data Call

Company Information

Company Name:		**Incident Date:**	
Project Name:		**Report No.:**	
Project Country:		**Report Code:**	
Project Location:		**Project Code:**	
Restriction Level:		**Distribution Code:**	

Reporting Authority

Appointment	Name	Telephone	E-Mail

Information Data Call

Ref	Report Factor	Report Facts
1	When did the robbery happen?	
2	Where did it happen?	
3	Who was the victim?	
4	Has the person been injured? What is the victim's emotional and physical status?	
5	Where is the victim now?	
6	Was the robbery violent or nonviolent?	
7	What was stolen, and what value is attributed to it?	
8	Have the local authorities been informed? If so, did they respond?	
9	Was any information or material stolen that could place personnel at risk?	
10	Was any information or material stolen that could place the company at risk?	
11	What actions have been taken by local managers?	
12	What risks are presented to other employees?	
13	What support is required?	
14	Other information:	

Pending Detention and Exit Denial Incident Management Data Call

Company Information

Company Name:		Incident Date:	
Project Name:		Report No.:	
Project Country:		Report Code:	
Project Location:		Project Code:	
Restriction Level:		Distribution Code:	

Reporting Authority

Appointment	Name	Telephone	E-Mail

Information Data Call

Ref	Report Factor	Report Facts
1	Name of the potential detainee:	
2	Nationality of the potential detainee:	
3	Age, gender, health, medications required:	
4	Details of crime or problem: ▪ Severity ▪ Impacts on external persons ▪ Possible sentences ▪ Other	
5	Potential detainee's supervisor (name, number, e-mail, location):	
6	Potential arresting authority:	
7	Location of potential detainee:	
8	History or background of the problem:	
9	What solutions are there to the problem?	
10	Has local legal support been engaged?	
11	What are the risks faced by potential detainee?	
12	Have external support agencies been notified (embassy, legal)?	
13	Has the family been informed?	

(*continued*)

(continued)

14 Are there risks presented to the group or
   others? Provide details:

15 Should personnel be relocated? If so, when
   and to where?

16 What is management doing now?

17 What support is required?

18 Other information:

Loss of Sensitive or High-Value Materials Incident Management Data Call

Company Information

Company Name:		**Incident Date:**	
Project Name:		**Report No.:**	
Project Country:		**Report Code:**	
Project Location:		**Project Code:**	
Restriction Level:		**Distribution Code:**	

Reporting Authority

Appointment	Name	Telephone	E-Mail

Information Data Call

Ref	Report Factor	Report Facts
1	What was lost or stolen? What type of value is placed on the item?	
2	What serial numbers or accounting identifiers belong to the item?	
3	How many items or what quantity of materials were lost or stolen?	
4	When was the material lost or stolen?	
5	How was the material lost and where? <ul><li>Espionage</li><li>Loss</li><li>Theft</li><li>Damage</li><li>Destruction</li></ul>	
6	Who was responsible for the material when it was lost or stolen?	
7	What impacts will the loss have in legal or government licensing terms?	
8	What physical risk impacts does the loss have to personnel?	
9	What risk impacts does the loss have to project operations?	
10	What impacts does the loss have to the company's reputation?	

(continued)

(continued)

11   What actions have been made to recover
      the items? What is management doing now
      for recovery?

12   Have local authorities been informed? Are
      they supporting the recovery efforts?

13   What actions are being taken now by
      management?

14   What support is required?

15   Other information:

Indirect or Direct Fire Attacks Incident Management Data Call

Company Information

Company Name:		**Incident Date:**	
Project Name:		**Report No.:**	
Project Country:		**Report Code:**	
Project Location:		**Project Code:**	
Restriction Level:		**Distribution Code:**	

Reporting Authority

Appointment	Name	Telephone	E-Mail

Information Data Call

Ref	Report Factor	Report Facts
1	When did the attack occur?	
2	Have any employee or contractor injuries occurred? Provide details:	
3	Has any damage to facilities occurred? List damage and effects:	
4	How many rounds landed outside of the site or facility?	
5	How many rounds landed within the site or facility?	
6	Has the attack stopped, or is it ongoing?	
7	Are other risks present other than indirect fire (IDF)?	
8	Has the location been secured from a complex attack? What security alert state is in force?	
9	Have all staff been accounted for? List missing persons:	
10	Has a UXO sweep been conducted if the attack is over? Is there a UXO threat?	
11	Have local authorities or support agencies been notified? Have they responded?	
12	What actions are being taken now?	
13	Has an ICP been established? What is the safe route in?	
14	What assistance is required?	
15	Other information:	

Workplace Violence Incident Management Data Call

Company Information

Company Name:		**Incident Date:**	
Project Name:		**Report No.:**	
Project Country:		**Report Code:**	
Project Location:		**Project Code:**	
Restriction Level:		**Distribution Code:**	

Reporting Authority

Appointment	Name	Telephone	E-Mail

Information Data Call

Ref	Report Factor	Report Facts
1	When did the event occur? Is it ongoing?	
2	Where did it occur?	
3	Who was subject to the workplace violence? Give name and details:	
4	Who was the aggressor? Give name, details, and relationship:	
5	Was the aggressor an employee, contractor, client, relation, or other?	
6	What was the nature of the event (physical, verbal)?	
7	Has anyone been injured? Provide details:	
8	Is the victim safe and removed from the aggressor?	
9	Is the aggressor armed? Provide details:	
10	What is the mental and emotional state of the aggressor?	
11	Is there a history associated with this event? Provide details:	
12	Has local security responded, and is the problem under control?	
13	Have local law enforcement been informed? Have they responded, and are they on-site?	
14	What actions are managers undertaking now?	
15	What assistance is required?	
16	Other information:	

Threats, Coercion, or Intimidation Incident Management Data Call

Company Information

Company Name:		**Incident Date:**	
Project Name:		**Report No.:**	
Project Country:		**Report Code:**	
Project Location:		**Project Code:**	
Restriction Level:		**Distribution Code:**	

Reporting Authority

Appointment	Name	Telephone	E-Mail

Information Data Call

Ref	Report Factor	Report Facts
1	When did the threats occur?	
2	Where did they occur?	
3	How were threats made: phone, e-mail, letter, in person?	
4	Who has been threatened? Give names and details:	
5	Is the aggressor known? Is the aggressor an individual or a group? Provide details:	
6	Is there a relationship between the aggressor and victim?	
7	What demands are being made? What is the agenda of the aggressor? Is it considered a real threat?	
8	Is there a history or background to this event? Provide details:	
9	Is the victim safe from physical harm?	
10	Have local authorities been informed? Have they responded?	
11	Are risks presented to other individuals?	
12	What actions is management taking now?	
13	What support is required?	
14	Other information:	

Chemical, Biological, or Radiological Threats Incident Management Data Call

Company Information

Company Name:		Incident Date:	
Project Name:		Report No.:	
Project Country:		Report Code:	
Project Location:		Project Code:	
Restriction Level:		Distribution Code:	

Reporting Authority

Appointment	Name	Telephone	E-Mail

Information Data Call

Ref	Report Factor	Report Facts
1	When did the event happen?	
2	Where did the event happen?	
3	What physical or other warning/indicator signs were/are present? ▪ Animals ▪ People ▪ Smells ▪ Mists and fogs ▪ Alerts ▪ Sensors	
4	What do you believe the cause to be? ▪ Chemical ▪ Biological ▪ Radiological	
5	What effects are there on employees and other staff? Provide details:	
6	Have personnel moved indoors and sealed off vents and doors?	
7	Are personnel on high ground?	
8	Are personnel upwind or downwind?	

(continued)

(continued)

9　Are all personnel accounted for? Provide details of missing personnel:

10　What effects are there on employees and other staff? Provide details:

11　What actions is management taking?

12　Has an ICP been established? What is the safe route in?

13　What support is required?

14　Other information?

Small Arms Fire Incident Management Data Call

Company Information

Company Name:		Incident Date:	
Project Name:		Report No.:	
Project Country:		Report Code:	
Project Location:		Project Code:	
Restriction Level:		Distribution Code:	

Reporting Authority

Appointment	Name	Telephone	E-Mail

Information Data Call

Ref	Report Factor	Report Facts
1	When did the small arms fire (SAF) event occur?	
2	Where did it occur?	
3	Is the type of gunfire identifiable?	
4	Is the SAF still occurring?	
5	Have there been any injuries?	
6	Has there been any damage to structures, facilities, or materials? Provide details:	
7	Is the area secure from complex attack? What alert state is in force?	
8	What other risks might be presented by a SAF attack (explosive, toxic, industrial)?	
9	Are personnel in bunkers or behind solid walls?	
10	Are all personnel accounted for? Provide details of missing persons:	
11	Have local police or other authorities been informed? Are they responding?	
12	Do personnel need to evacuate the site? If so, when and where?	
13	What actions is management taking now?	
14	Has an ICP been established? What is the safe route in?	
15	What assistance is required?	
16	Other information:	

Complex Attack Incident Management Data Call

Company Information

Company Name:		**Incident Date:**	
Project Name:		**Report No.:**	
Project Country:		**Report Code:**	
Project Location:		**Project Code:**	
Restriction Level:		**Distribution Code:**	

Reporting Authority

Appointment	Name	Telephone	E-Mail

Information Data Call

Ref	Report Factor	Report Facts
1	When did the attack occur?	
2	Where did the attack occur?	
3	Is the attack ongoing or complete?	
4	How large was the aggressor group?	
5	Is the identity of the aggressor group known? Provide details:	
6	What was the nature of the aggressor group? ▪ Criminal ▪ Mob/riot ▪ Insurgent/terrorist	
7	Were they armed? Provide details:	
8	What were their agenda and objectives? Did they succeed?	
9	Were there any injuries? Provide details:	
10	Has anyone been kidnapped? Provide details:	
11	Have any equipment, structures, or materials been damaged? Provide details:	
12	Are the facility and personnel secure or still at risk? What alert state is in force?	
13	Has the area been cleared of intruders and possible UXOs/IEDs?	

(continued)

(continued)

14   Does the site need to be evacuated? If so,
      to where?

15   Have local authorities been alerted? Have
      they responded?

16   What actions are managers taking now?

17   Has an ICP been established? What is the
      safe route in?

18   What support is required?

19   Other information:

Explosive Attack or Sabotage Incident Management Data Call

Company Information

Company Name:		**Incident Date:**	
Project Name:		**Report No.:**	
Project Country:		**Report Code:**	
Project Location:		**Project Code:**	
Restriction Level:		**Distribution Code:**	

Reporting Authority

Appointment	Name	Telephone	E-Mail

Information Data Call

Ref	Report Factor	Report Facts
1	When did the attack occur?	
2	Where did the attack occur?	
3	Were there any injuries? Provide details:	
4	What structures, materials, or machinery were damaged? Provide details:	
5	What outstanding explosive threats are there? Provide details:	
6	What secondary threats have resulted from any explosions? Provide details:	
7	Has the area been swept for additional threats and is now secure?	
8	Have support agencies been notified? Have they responded?	
9	What actions is management taking now? What alert state is in force?	
10	What support is required?	
11	Other information:	

Family Liaison Incident Management Data Call

Company Information

Company Name:		**Incident Date:**	
Project Name:		**Report No.:**	
Project Country:		**Report Code:**	
Project Location:		**Project Code:**	
Restriction Level:		**Distribution Code:**	

Reporting Authority

Appointment	Name	Telephone	E-Mail

Information Data Call

Ref	Report Factor	Report Facts
1	Name and details of the employee:	
2	What is the situation and background of the incident?	
3	Who from the family has been in touch? Provide details and contact numbers:	
4	What are they requesting?	
5	How are they responding to the situation: upset, aggressive, angry, panicking?	
6	What support can be offered locally?	
7	Is there media involvement? Provide details:	
8	Are there legal or liability implications? Provide details:	
9	What is management doing now?	
10	What support is required?	
11	Other information:	

Computer-Related Incidents Incident Management Data Call

Company Information

Company Name:		**Incident Date:**	
Project Name:		**Report No.:**	
Project Country:		**Report Code:**	
Project Location:		**Project Code:**	
Restriction Level:		**Distribution Code:**	

Reporting Authority

Appointment	Name	Telephone	E-Mail

Information Data Call

Ref	Report Factor	Report Facts
1	When did the incident happen?	
2	Where did it happen?	
3	Which systems were affected?	
4	Has information been:	
	▪ Lost?	
	▪ Stolen?	
	▪ Corrupted?	
5	What are the impacts?	
6	Have IT resources been mobilized to resolve the issue?	
7	Has a law been broken?	
8	Is the cause of the problem known?	
9	Have the police or federal agencies been notified?	
10	What support is required?	
11	Other information:	

Disciplinary Issues Incident Management Data Call

Company Information

Company Name:		**Incident Date:**	
Project Name:		**Report No.:**	
Project Country:		**Report Code:**	
Project Location:		**Project Code:**	
Restriction Level:		**Distribution Code:**	

Reporting Authority

Appointment	Name	Telephone	E-Mail

Information Data Call

Ref	Report Factor	Report Facts
1	When did the disciplinary issue happen?	
2	Where did it happen?	
3	What was the nature of the disciplinary issue?	
4	What was the severity of the issue?	
5	Have any laws been broken?	
6	Are external groups involved?	
7	What risks are associated with the event?	
8	What actions are managers taking now?	
9	Do the police need to be involved?	
10	What punishments are associated with the issue?	
	• Verbal warning	
	• Written warning	
	• Counseling	
	• Dismissal	
	• Arrest and detention	
11	What support is required?	
12	Other information:	

Office, Facility, or Hotel Fires Incident Management Data Call

Company Information

Company Name:		Incident Date:	
Project Name:		Report No.:	
Project Country:		Report Code:	
Project Location:		Project Code:	
Restriction Level:		Distribution Code:	

Reporting Authority

Appointment	Name	Telephone	E-Mail

Information Data Call

Ref	Report Factor	Report Facts
1	When did the fire happen, or is it ongoing?	
2	Where did it happen?	
3	What is the nature of the fire? ■ Electric ■ Fuel ■ Chemical ■ Other	
4	What is the scope of the fire (how large)?	
5	Are there secondary hazards? ■ Combustible ■ Toxic ■ Explosive ■ Other	
6	Have all personnel been accounted for? List missing persons and locations:	
7	Are any personnel trapped? List names and locations:	
8	Are there casualties? List names and injuries:	
9	Are surrounding facilities at risk?	
10	Has the area been cordoned off?	
11	Has an ICP been established? What is the safe route in?	

(*continued*)

(continued)

12   Have emergency services been notified?
     Have they responded?

13   Are there any other threats posed to
     personnel?

14   Are there critical materials or information
     items that need to be rescued? Provide
     details for locating them:

15   What is management doing now?

16   What assistance is required?

17   Other information:

Espionage Incident Management Data Call

Company Information

Company Name:		**Incident Date:**	
Project Name:		**Report No.:**	
Project Country:		**Report Code:**	
Project Location:		**Project Code:**	
Restriction Level:		**Distribution Code:**	

Reporting Authority

Appointment	Name	Telephone	E-Mail

Information Data Call

Ref	Report Factor	Report Facts
1	When did the espionage incident happen?	
2	Where did it happen?	
3	What happened, and what level of severity is associated with the event? Provide details:	
4	Who, if anyone, was involved from the company?	
5	What external parties were involved?	
6	What was the nature of the event: verbal, physical, IT?	
7	What immediate risk implications does this have for the company? Provide details:	
8	What long-term implications does this have for the company? Provide details:	
9	Have measures been taken to reduce the effects of the event? Provide details:	
10	Have local authorities been informed? Have they responded?	
11	What are managers doing now?	
12	What assistance is required?	
13	Other information:	

Site Occupation Incident Management Data Call

Company Information

Company Name:		**Incident Date:**	
Project Name:		**Report No.:**	
Project Country:		**Report Code:**	
Project Location:		**Project Code:**	
Restriction Level:		**Distribution Code:**	

Reporting Authority

Appointment	Name	Telephone	E-Mail

Information Data Call

Ref	Report Factor	Report Facts
1	When did the site occupation happen? Is it still on going?	
2	Where did it happen?	
3	How many people are involved?	
4	Who are they and what is the agenda of the group? Provide details:	
5	Are they nonviolent or aggressive?	
6	Have they injured or threatened employees? Provide details:	
7	Have they damaged facilities or materials? Provide details:	
8	Have they gained access to sensitive areas? Provide details:	
9	Can local security manage the situation?	
10	Have local law enforcement authorities been informed? Have they responded?	
11	How is this affecting employees and operations? Provide details:	
12	Has the area been swept for harmful substances and materials?	
13	Is the media present? Provide details:	
14	What are managers doing now?	
15	What assistance is required?	
16	Other information:	

Demonstrations Incident Management Data Call

Company Information

Company Name:		**Incident Date:**	
Project Name:		**Report No.:**	
Project Country:		**Report Code:**	
Project Location:		**Project Code:**	
Restriction Level:		**Distribution Code:**	

Reporting Authority

Appointment	Name	Telephone	E-Mail

Information Data Call

Ref	Report Factor	Report Facts
1	When did it occur? Is it ongoing?	
2	What is the nature of the demonstration? ▪ Antigovernment ▪ Anti-West ▪ Peace ▪ Labor dispute ▪ Other	
3	What is the temperament of the crowd? ▪ Peaceful ▪ Aggressive ▪ Violent	
4	What is the focus of the demonstration? ▪ Other group or party ▪ General focus ▪ Company or employees	
5	What are the agenda and objectives of the demonstration?	
6	What risks are presented to personnel?	
7	What risks are presented to facilities?	
8	What risks are presented to materials?	
9	What life span is expected for the demonstration? ▪ Hours ▪ Days ▪ Longer	

(continued)

(continued)

10 What risks are presented to personnel?

11 What risks are presented to facilities?

12 Are personnel accounted for? List missing persons and locations:

13 Is the facility secure?

14 Have other travelers been alerted to stay away?

15 Have local authorities been informed? Have they responded, and in what manner?

16 What is management doing now?

17 Is a site evacuation required (and safe)?

18 What assistance is required?

19 Other information:

Blackouts and Power Loss Incident Management Data Call

Company Information

Company Name:		**Incident Date:**	
Project Name:		**Report No.:**	
Project Country:		**Report Code:**	
Project Location:		**Project Code:**	
Restriction Level:		**Distribution Code:**	

Reporting Authority

Appointment	Name	Telephone	E-Mail

Information Data Call

Ref	Report Factor	Report Facts
1	When did the power loss occur?	
2	What area is involved?	
3	What risk implications does it have for personnel? Provide details:	
4	What risk implications does it have for facilities? Provide details:	
5	What risk implications does it have for materials? Provide details:	
6	Is an emergency generator available?	
7	Is this a common problem?	
8	What actions are being taken by management?	
9	What support is required?	
10	When do you expect power to return?	
11	Other information:	

Floods or Tidal Waves Incident Management Data Call

Company Information

Company Name:		**Incident Date:**	
Project Name:		**Report No.:**	
Project Country:		**Report Code:**	
Project Location:		**Project Code:**	
Restriction Level:		**Distribution Code:**	

Reporting Authority

Appointment	Name	Telephone	E-Mail

Information Data Call

Ref	Report Factor	Report Facts
1	When did the flood or tidal wave occur?	
2	What area is involved?	
3	Are all personnel accounted for? Provide details of missing persons and locations:	
4	Are there any injuries? Provide details:	
5	Is there any damage to facilities or materials? Provide details:	
6	Are personnel in a safe area? Where are they?	
7	Do any employees have serious medical conditions that present a risk?	
8	What other hazards are associated with the event? Provide details:	
9	Is there sufficient water and food for personnel?	
10	Has the location been marked for emergency responders? If so, how and where?	
11	What are managers doing now?	
12	What support is required?	
13	Other information:	

Earthquakes Incident Management Data Call

Company Information

Company Name:		**Incident Date:**	
Project Name:		**Report No.:**	
Project Country:		**Report Code:**	
Project Location:		**Project Code:**	
Restriction Level:		**Distribution Code:**	

Reporting Authority

Appointment	Name	Telephone	E-Mail

Information Data Call

Ref	Report Factor	Report Facts
1	When did the earthquake occur?	
2	What area was affected? What was the severity of the earthquake?	
3	Are there any injuries? Provide details:	
4	Were any facilities damaged? Provide details:	
5	Are there any secondary hazards? ▪ Fires ▪ Floods ▪ Electrical ▪ Toxic ▪ Gas	
6	Are all personnel accounted for? Provide details of missing persons:	
7	Are personnel in a safe location? Provide details:	
8	Are any persons trapped in collapsed buildings? Provide names and locations:	
9	Have emergency responders been alerted to any issues? Have they responded?	
10	What is management doing now?	
11	What assistance is required?	
12	Other information:	

Pandemics Incident Management Data Call

Company Information

Company Name:		Incident Date:	
Project Name:		Report No.:	
Project Country:		Report Code:	
Project Location:		Project Code:	
Restriction Level:		Distribution Code:	

Reporting Authority

Appointment	Name	Telephone	E-Mail

Information Data Call

Ref	Report Factor	Report Facts
1	When did the pandemic occur?	
2	What area is affected?	
3	What is the nature of the pandemic? Provide details:	
4	How was the pandemic identified? Provide details:	
5	Are project staff within an affected area?	
6	Are any employees ill or infected?	
7	What instructions have local authorities provided?	
8	Is an evacuation possible and safe?	
9	Are medicines available to counter the threat?	
10	Are sufficient resources (water and food) available to remain in the location?	
11	Should the local workforce be sent home? Is it safe and appropriate to do so?	
12	Have local authorities been informed? Are they responding?	
13	Are local authorities capable of managing the pandemic?	
14	Have other agencies responded? Provide details:	
15	What are managers doing now?	
16	What resources and assistance are required?	
17	Other information:	

Hurricanes and Tornadoes Incident Management Data Call

Company Information

Company Name:		**Incident Date:**	
Project Name:		**Report No.:**	
Project Country:		**Report Code:**	
Project Location:		**Project Code:**	
Restriction Level:		**Distribution Code:**	

Reporting Authority

Appointment	Name	Telephone	E-Mail

Information Data Call

Ref	Report Factor	Report Facts
1	When is the storm expected, or when did the storm occur?	
2	What area is affected?	
3	How severe is the storm? ▪ High severity ▪ Medium severity ▪ Low severity	
4	Are there any injuries? Provide details:	
5	Are all personnel accounted for? Provide details of missing personnel:	
6	Are personnel in a safe location? Provide details:	
7	Are there any secondary hazards? ▪ Fire ▪ Flood ▪ Electrical ▪ Toxic ▪ Other	
8	Have emergency responders been alerted? Have they responded?	
9	Is it safe to evacuate the area ahead of the storm? Provide route and destination:	
10	What is management doing now?	
11	What assistance is required?	
12	Other information:	

Volcanic Eruptions Incident Management Data Call

Company Information

Company Name:		**Incident Date:**	
Project Name:		**Report No.:**	
Project Country:		**Report Code:**	
Project Location:		**Project Code:**	
Restriction Level:		**Distribution Code:**	

Reporting Authority

Appointment	Name	Telephone	E-Mail

Information Data Call

Ref	Report Factor	Report Facts
1	When did the volcanic eruption occur? Is it still on going?	
2	What area is affected?	
3	Are there any injuries? Provide names and details:	
4	Have all personnel been accounted for? Provide names and details of missing personnel:	
5	What is the severity of the volcanic eruption?	
6	Is it necessary to evacuate the area? Provide route and destination:	
7	What symptoms are there with the eruption? ▪ Ashfall ▪ Mudflows ▪ Aftershocks ▪ Lava flows ▪ Toxic fumes ▪ Forest fires ▪ Other	
8	What other areas might be affected?	
9	Have travelers been alerted to avoid the area?	

(continued)

(continued)

10   Have emergency services been alerted?
Have they responded?

11   Has the local government issued instructions?
What are they?

12   Is there any critical equipment or information
that must be evacuated? Provide details:

13   What is management doing now?

14   What support is required?

15   Other information:

Sandstorms Incident Management Data Call

Company Information

Company Name:		**Incident Date:**	
Project Name:		**Report No.:**	
Project Country:		**Report Code:**	
Project Location:		**Project Code:**	
Restriction Level:		**Distribution Code:**	

Reporting Authority

Appointment	Name	Telephone	E-Mail

Information Data Call

Ref	Report Factor	Report Facts
1	When did the sandstorm occur? Is it still on going?	
2	What area is affected? Which direction is the sandstorm headed?	
3	What is the severity of the sandstorm?	
4	How long is it expected to last?	
5	Have all personnel been accounted for? Provide details and locations of missing personnel:	
6	Are there any injuries? Provide details:	
7	Have facilities been closed down and vents closed?	
8	What are managers doing now?	
9	What support or resources are required?	
10	Other information:	

Landslides Incident Management Data Call

Company Information

Company Name:		**Incident Date:**	
Project Name:		**Report No.:**	
Project Country:		**Report Code:**	
Project Location:		**Project Code:**	
Restriction Level:		**Distribution Code:**	

Reporting Authority

Appointment	Name	Telephone	E-Mail

Information Data Call

Ref	Report Factor	Report Facts
1	When did the landslide occur? Is it still ongoing?	
2	What area is affected? How severe is the landslide?	
3	Are there any injuries? Provide names and details:	
4	Are there any structural damages? Provide details and extent:	
5	Have all personnel been accounted for? Provide details of missing personnel:	
6	Has the area been evacuated?	
7	Have travelers been alerted to stay away from the area?	
8	Have emergency services been alerted? Have they responded?	
9	Are additional hazards present? ▪ Flooding ▪ Fires ▪ Gas leaks ▪ Electrical ▪ Structural ▪ Other	
10	What is management doing now?	
11	What support is required?	
12	Other information:	

Forest Fires or Brush Fires Incident Management Data Call

Company Information

Company Name:		**Incident Date:**	
Project Name:		**Report No.:**	
Project Country:		**Report Code:**	
Project Location:		**Project Code:**	
Restriction Level:		**Distribution Code:**	

Reporting Authority

Appointment	Name	Telephone	E-Mail

Information Data Call

Ref	Report Factor	Report Facts
1	When did the fire occur? Is it still ongoing?	
2	What area is affected?	
3	How severe is the fire?	
4	What direction is it traveling?	
5	Are there any injuries? Provide names and details:	
6	Is there any damage to facilities or materials and assets? Provide details:	
7	Has the immediate area been evacuated?	
8	Have downwind areas been evacuated?	
9	Have all personnel been accounted for? Provide details of missing personnel:	
10	Have facilities been wet down to reduce fire hazards? Have facilities been closed down?	
11	Are there other hazards that could result? ▪ Explosive ▪ Toxic ▪ Other	
12	Is there critical equipment or information that needs to be rescued? Provide details and location:	

(continued)

(continued)

13   Have emergency services been alerted?
Have they responded?

14   Has local government issued instructions?
What are they?

15   What is management doing now?

16   What assistance is required?

17   Other information:

Summary

When companies consider which questions to present in such crisis management information capture sheets, they should consider the lowest and highest levels of crisis response or management user. Questions should be designed to prompt the local managers to seek critical information, as well as to then provide condensed and focused information which can be transmitted throughout the organization, as well as to external supporting groups. The reports can be used in conjunction with the crisis management guidelines in order to both practically respond to a situation, as well as concurrently provide critical information. Where possible, companies should try to minimize response sheets to avoid repetition, amalgamating any that have the same questions. Conversely, managers should not confuse matters by attempting to place several major topics onto a single report sheet and thus dilute critical information and run the risk of undermining the value of the report, or confusing the user.

Users should seek to use concise verbiage when reporting information, while providing sufficient depth and explanation so that those removed from the emergency event can gain a thorough understanding of what is occurring, its implications, and what actions are being taken by incident managers. This will assist the organization in better understanding the situation, as well as reducing time and effort taken by corporate or country management who might seek further clarifications and information from those often hard pressed in practically dealing with a situation. Some form of instruction or training can be useful in order to ensure that the right level of information is provided and the correct focus is applied. Language barriers and varying written language capabilities will present a challenge at times. Companies can also use such reports as an evidence chain following an event, although a balance between managers or users attempting to offer quick and immediate information, as opposed to worrying over the content, accuracy, and delivery of information should be struck. As with any policy or guideline, flexibility is key, and such information capture formats should be amenable to adaptation and augmentation where required.

Acknowledgments

Pamela Blyth: I would like to thank my mother whose tact and diplomacy, combined with her ability to bring calm to any form of crisis situation, would make her an ideal envoy to the United Nations. While working within Iraq running oil and gas programs, my mother deployed to the United States within eight hours of notification when my wife slipped down a flight of stairs while six months pregnant, and for every birth she automatically deploys to help take care of our brood. If anyone needs to understand how a *Special Response Team* should work, she has written the manual.

The Wiley Team: I would like to thank the John Wiley & Sons publishing team—a superb group who have provided invaluable advice and guidance for both my first book *Security and Risk Management: Protecting People and Sites Worldwide*, as well as this second effort. Their patience, detailed reviews and impressive experience in turning a first rough first draft into a polished final edition has been greatly appreciated. My personal thanks to Sheck Cho (Senior Editor), who makes space within his hectic schedule every time I visit New York to meet with me and give me the benefit of drawing upon his impressive wealth of experience and knowledge—I thoroughly enjoy our lunches and consider Sheck a friend. My thanks also to Natalie and Helen, who with great patience have walked me through the multiple steps of editing with good humor and impressive energy.

Robert Molina: A good friend, Robert Molina's experience as the Director for Global Security Verizon, and now as the Global Security Manager for LyondellBasell was instrumental in shaping much of the content of this book. Despite a hectic globetrotting lifestyle he kindly took the time to review the book on several red-eye flights and offered some priceless observations and recommendations. Robert has an impressive wealth of experience in managing crisis events across most, if not all, of the risk types listed within this book. His insights, recommendations, and contributions have been invaluable and greatly appreciated.

Glenn McLea: My sincere thanks to Glenn McLea (Corporate Security Director for Parsons Corporation) who has been an invaluable sounding board and the source of much appreciated advice and guidance since I departed from the Royal Marines. Glenn has reviewed all of my books as a second set of professional eyes, and has contributed both to the validation of the content, as well as to ensuring I didn't miss anything too important. Glenn has brought a wealth of experience, knowledge, and professional expertise to support the creation of this work, as well as *Risk and*

Security Management: Protecting People and Sites Worldwide. Glenn is a close friend, mentor, and inexhaustible source of knowledge and support.

Ray Baysden: I would like to offer my appreciation for the pragmatic and detailed advice and recommendations made by Ray Baysden, a retired U.S. State Department senior manager with a wide array of experience in security and crises contingency operations abroad. Ray's understanding of both the commercial space, as well as government and international organization crisis management practices, brought real value to the structure, concepts, and delivery of the materials within this book. Ray provided some unique insights into the complexity and nuances of Enterprise Resilience—offering valuable observations (based on an impressive array of real life experiences) on how to make the materials sensible, usable and effective. Ray is a good friend and a source of great advice.

Timothy Bowen: My thanks to Tim Bowen, Security Director for BearingPoint, who kindly provided a detailed review of this book and offered excellent observations from the corporate officer and end user's perspective. Managing complex programs within remote and often challenged environments, Tim has a personal understanding of the value of good crisis management systems and procedures and experience in designing business continuity management plans which support the effective resolution and management of emergencies—meeting corporate, business, and safety needs. Tim has an impressive amount of experience in dealing with crisis events globally and his insights, perspective, and recommendations were invaluable during the editing of the book.

Paul Harris: I would also like to thank Inspector Paul Harris of the Metropolitan Police who brought his wealth of experience and knowledge in enterprise resilience and crisis management to ensure that the content of this book was aligned with government practices and standards, as well as the commercial business implications which drive the requirement for a solid Business Continuity Management Plan. Working as part of the London Olympics Security Committee, Paul offered some invaluable insights into areas which could be better explained, as well as some significant input in terms of additional content and structuring. Paul continues to be a good friend and a source of insightful ideas and concepts.

Index

Printed and bound by CPI Group (UK) Ltd, Croydon, CR0 4YY

17/04/2025

14658864-0001